Dark Lanterns

Dark Lanterns

SECRET POLITICAL SOCIETIES, CONSPIRACIES, AND TREASON TRIALS IN THE CIVIL WAR

FRANK L. KLEMENT

LOUISIANA STATE UNIVERSITY PRESS

BATON ROUGE AND LONDON

COPYRIGHT © 1984 BY LOUISIANA STATE UNIVERSITY PRESS
ALL RIGHTS RESERVED
MANUFACTURED IN THE UNITED STATES OF AMERICA
DESIGNER: BARBARA WERDEN
TYPEFACE: LINOTRON TIMES ROMAN
TYPESETTER: G & S TYPESETTERS, INC.

LIBRARY OF CONGRESS CATALOGING IN PUBLICATION DATA

Klement, Frank L.
Dark lanterns.

Bibliography: p.
Includes index.
1. United States—Politics and government—Civil War,
1861–1865.   2. United States—History—Civil War, 1861–
1865—Underground movements.   3. United States—History—
Civil War, 1861–1865—Societies, etc.   4. Secret societies
—United States—History—19th century.   5. Trials
(Treason)—United States.   I. Title.
E458.8.K673   1984   973.7   84-834
ISBN 0-8071-1174-0

CONTENTS

ILLUSTRATIONS

PREFATORY REMARKS

THE TERMS *dark lanterns* or *dark lantern societies* were popular during the 1850s and 1860s. They were frequently applied to such political secret societies as the Knights of the Golden Circle and the Union Leagues.

In a way, this study is but an extension of my interest in Civil War Copperheadism, that is, Democratic opposition to the Lincoln administration.

In many ways, the contentions that result from my study of the secret political societies, the supposed conspiracies, and the Indianapolis and Cincinnati treason trials run counter to the orthodox or accepted interpretations. Since revisionists have the responsibility of proving their contentions, this work is heavily footnoted so that readers will realize why certain statements were made or interpretations advanced.

While dramatic events on the military front or in Washington drew most of the headlines and spotlights, the backstage occurrences were an important part of the war. Military victories preserved the Union; home-front events affected civil rights. The question of civil rights emerges in nearly every one of the eight chapters.

ACKNOWLEDGMENTS

A HISTORIAN'S indebtedness goes beyond the sources used and librarians, curators, and archivists who lent a willing hand. It includes those whose ideas may have been borrowed and whose writings furnished the setting for this specialized study. It also includes those who provided funds and the incentive to spend more than ten years researching the subject, transforming the stacks of notes into chapters, and trying to make the whole greater than the sum of its parts.

Two fellowships provided subsidy for some of the research. The Marquette University Graduate Research Committee granted a summer fellowship that enabled me to spend the summer of 1972 in Washington, D.C., completing the extraction of information from the resources of the National Archives and the Library of Congress. A summer fellowship, granted by the Huntington Library, enabled me to spend June and July of 1974 in an ideal setting for scholars and gave me the chance to use materials unavailable elsewhere. In addition, a Leverhulme Research Fellowship enabled me to spend the 1975–1976 academic year as a visiting professor at the University of Sussex, England, giving me the opportunity to revise and rewrite several chapters again.

During the past ten years I have had the part-time services of six graduate students who served the Department of History at Marquette University as research assistants. They checked my footnotes, sought to provide first names for initials, perused the *Official Records of the Union and Confederate Armies* and newspapers for specific information, and chased down bibliographical data. The roll call of competent helpers included Emily Pfizenmaier, Patricia Hosey, Richard Fogarty, Dennis Mueller, John Langellier, Thomas Kreif, and Helen Wanken.

I also want to thank Thomas B. Alexander for reading the manuscript and calling attention to lapses from proper syntax, as well as pointing out misspelled words and typographical errors.

Once more I am indebted to my wife, Laurel, in so many ways. She typed the first manuscript as well as the revised drafts. "La reconnaissance," Jean Baptiste Massieu once wrote to a friend, "est la mémoire du coeur." I would like to adopt Massieu's words as my own.

Dark Lanterns

INTRODUCTION

DURING THE agonizing days of the American Civil War four secret political societies, often known as dark lantern societies, became household words throughout the North. One, the Union League, was a patriotic political organization, intent upon buttressing northern morale and giving support to the war program of the Lincoln administration. The other three—the Knights of the Golden Circle, the Order of American Knights, and the Sons of Liberty— have passed into history as Copperhead societies, umbrellas for antiwar Democrats and bases for treasonable activities.

Secret societies, whether fraternal or political, were widespread throughout the North during the 1850s. Two of the better-known fraternal orders, the Freemasons and the Odd Fellows, had a long history, reaching back into the previous century and further. The Know-Nothings, the popular name of a secret political party that existed from 1852 to about 1860, grew out of the lodge meetings of the Order of the Sons of America in Pennsylvania and the Order of the Star Spangled Banner in New York. During the presidential campaign of 1860, the Wide Awakes, Republican activists who met secretly and paraded openly, counteracted the work of a variety of Democratic associations that held secret sessions and worked for the election of local, state, and national candidates. In fact, secret political activity seemed commonplace on the eve of the Civil War and the dark lantern aspect attracted rather than repelled potential members.

Each of the four prominent dark lantern societies had a historical base, and the founding of each can be pinpointed as to time and place. The first of the four, the Golden Circle, had its beginnings in Cincinnati a few years before the war, but it was largely confined to paper until its founder became a southerner in 1861 and revised its original objectives. Even then it remained more fantasy than fact. The second of the four, the Union League, had multiple roots, the most discernible traced to Illinois in 1862. The third, the Order of American Knights, based in St. Louis, passed through several stages before its founder sought membership outside of Missouri in 1863. The order gained national headlines when a political-minded colonel composed his "startling revelations" in midyear, 1864. The fourth, the Sons of Liberty, also endured an evasive existence until Indiana Governor Oliver P. Morton's man Friday

I

published his exposé on June 28, 1864. The order received extensive publicity during the Indianapolis treason trials of late 1864 and early 1865.

While the Golden Circle had a strange history all its own, Democrats who promoted the Order of American Knights and the Sons of Liberty during 1863 and 1864 claimed that the societies were legitimate agencies, intended to protect their civil rights, win elections, and counter the effective work of the Union League. Union Leaguers, on the other hand, insisted that their patriotic organization needed to be vitalized and expanded to counteract the work of the Knights of the Golden Circle, the Order of American Knights, and the Sons of Liberty, decried and described as tainted with treason and nefarious in design. The contentions and countercontentions, intertwined with rumors and suppositions, wove a maze of contradictions that obscured the facts and confused the unwary.

The facts about each of the three so-called Copperhead secret societies (the K.G.C., O.A.K., and S.L.) were embroidered with many rumors and much hearsay, some incidental, most contrived. "Some rumors occur spontaneously," two noted sociologists wrote recently; "some are carefully constructed by propagandists and other manipulators."[1] Both statements certainly were true of the myriad of rumors and suppositions that beclouded the issues during the apprehensive and wearisome days of the American Civil War. Centuries ago Virgil recognized that hearsay possessed magical wings: "Rumor! What evil can surpass her speed? In moments she grows mighty, and achieves strength and dominion as she swiftly flies." And Shakespeare, commenting upon the same social phenomenon in *King Henry VI*, wrote:

> Rumor is a pipe
> Blown by surmises, jealousies, conjectures,
> And of so easy and so plain a stop
> That the blunt monster with uncounted heads,
> The still-discordant wavering multitude
> Can play upon it.

The Civil War provided a nearly perfect setting for rumor and propaganda. It was a long war, and a cover of apprehension and fear blanketed the country. Political rivalries reached a new level of intensity, heightening hatreds and distrust. Leaders of the rival political parties, especially in the upper Midwest, cloaked themselves in dogmatism and intolerance, viewing their rivals with jaundiced eyes. Such antiwar Democrats as Clement L. Vallandigham of Ohio, Lambdin P. Milligan of Indiana, and Wilbur F. Storey of Illi-

---

1. Ralph L. Rosnow and Gary Alan Fine, *Rumor and Gossip: The Social Psychology of Hearsay* (New York, 1976), 5.

nois, certainly were one-minded in their views on emancipation, centralization of power in Washington, and the use of military commissions to try
civilians. Such straitlaced Republicans as Governor Morton of Indiana, editor
William F. Comly of the Dayton *Daily Journal*, and Major Henry L. Burnett
were just as dogmatic and adamant, brooking no opposition to governmental
policy and waging a war of proscription against all who refused to swim with
the current.

Patriotism and nationalism, generated by the party in power, bred an intolerance that cried out for vengeance. Self-styled patriots, especially those of
the Republican persuasion, tended to view Democrats like Vallandigham and
Milligan as traitors, friends of Jeff Davis, and anathema to their cause. "If
there be any of the rebel tribe [Democrats desirous of peace or critical of the
Lincoln administration] in Huntington County," a respected Republican
stated, "it is the duty of loyal citizens to destroy them as they would rattle-
snakes." One prominent Republican, known for his radical views, argued that
Democratic dissenters had only two rights, "the right to be hanged and the
right to be damned." Editor Comly tied a string of epithets to every Democratic congressman who failed to support all Lincoln administration measures: "A TRAITOR, A MONSTER; A DISGRACE TO HIS ANCESTRY, A SHAME TO
POSTERITY, A FOUL STAIN UPON HIS BIRTH." [2] Once, after Vallandigham had
given a procompromise, propeace speech, he was denounced as "a traitor" by
scores of Republicans and characterized as "a secession toad" and "a hyena."
One influential party member even suggested that they hang Vallandigham
"first and apologize afterward." [3]

A Republican-sponsored "loyalty crusade" put Democrats at a disadvantage and fastened the term *Copperhead* upon critics of policies of the Lincoln
administration. The crusade for conformism, with the party in power serving
as both judge and jury, led to intimidation and abuse of thousands of Democrats. Wilbur Storey, editor of the critical Chicago *Times*, was felled several
times by "unknown assailants" who detested his editorial policy.[4] Mobs
wrecked or burned more than two dozen Democratic-owned printing plants as
a means of intimidating the editors. Mobs, sometimes led by soldiers on

2. Huntington (Ind.) *Herald*, October 9, 1861 (The statement was attributed to Isaac De-
Long, father of the editor of the Republican-oriented *Herald*); William G. "Parson" Brownlow,
quoted in the Cleveland *Leader*, October 31, 1862; Dayton *Daily Journal*, June 16, 1861.

3. Chillicothe *Advertiser*, n.d., and Cincinnati *Commercial*, n.d., both quoted in the Dayton
Daily Empire, February 7, 1863; Edwin D. Morgan to Elihu B. Washburne, January 31, 1863, in
Elihu B. Washburne Papers, Library of Congress.

4. Justin E. Walsh, *To Print the News and Raise Hell: A Biography of Wilbur F. Storey*
(Chapel Hill, 1968). George Winston Smith, "Generative Forces of Union Propaganda: A Study
in Civil War Pressure Groups" (Ph.D. dissertation, University of Wisconsin, 1940) explores the
relationship between loyalty and political propaganda.

3

furlough, broke up Democratic party rallies, insisting upon conformity as they understood it. Respected Republicans sometimes promised Democratic editors the noose, or tar-and-feather parties, or a ride out of town on a rail. The intimidation sometimes even followed Republican election victories. One who was intimidated reported: "The Abolish had an illumination here last night. Such a time! I never want to see the like again. The *negroes and whites together* visited the houses of prominent Democrats—hissed, groaned, and throwed stones thro the windows. They broke all the large windows in Dr. Wallace's Drug Store, and many others. . . . Their conduct would have shamed devils out of hell." [5]

The insistence upon conformity extended to the churches. Henry Clay Dean, an Iowan who had mixed religion and politics successfully before the war, lost his license as a Methodist preacher because he talked of compromise and criticized various measures of the Lincoln administration. Federal marshals arrested several Democratic clergymen who gave sermons on the theme "Blessed are the peacemakers." After the war was over, one patriotic Methodist bishop bragged, "Our ministers were true to the national cause; no one would have been tolerated if he had shown any sympathy for Democratic preachments." [6]

Timid and faint-hearted Democrats bowed to the pressure for conformity, either restricting what they said in public or reshaping their rationale. Bolder spirits and the more dogmatic resisted the pressure and justified their own views, becoming more defiant in the process. They intensified their partisanship and demonstrated their essential conservatism by resisting the changes the war imposed upon the country.[7] They insisted that they were loyal to the Union and the Constitution and had the right to criticize the Lincoln administration, even in the midst of a fratricidal war. Partisan Democrats rationalized their position defiantly: "Let whatever may come, the Democracy will abide by their time-honored principles, by the Constitution and the Union. We will neither surrender our rights nor forsake them. We will maintain our constitutional liberty at all hazards and, as a necessary step toward that end, we will defend the Union in like manner. We are for the Constitution as it is, and the Union as it was." [8]

There was fear in some Democratic circles that bipartisan support of Presi-

5. Charles M. Gould to Samuel S. Cox, October 15, 1863, in Samuel S. Cox Papers (microfilm), Hayes Memorial Library, Fremont, Ohio.
6. Rev. P. S. Bennett, *History of Methodism in Wisconsin* (Cincinnati, 1890), 207.
7. I have treated Democratic critics of the Lincoln administration as conservatives and dissenters in a book entitled *The Copperheads in the Middle West* (Chicago, 1960).
8. Wisconsin State Democratic Platform (the so-called Ryan Address), September 3, 1862, in George H. Paul Papers, State Historical Society of Wisconsin Library, Madison.

dent Lincoln's measures and the war might lead to the disintegration of their party and a military dictatorship. Party loyalty, as well as racist views, prompted some Democrats to denounce emancipation. They saw the flood of arbitrary arrests as a threat to civil rights. Some western sectionalists, like Milligan and Vallandigham, feared that the war would lead them to become serfs of "the lords of the looms," the masters of capital and "revived Whiggery"—making "Western people paupers and slaves forever." [9] Some of the more bigoted Democrats, who saw Lincoln as incompetency personified, were even anxious to seek votes in the field of war weariness and to fan the flames of racism. "It is a pity," one angry Democrat wrote, "that there is not a more tormenting hell than kept by Beelzebub" for Lincoln and his "abolition fiends." [10]

Nor did Democrats stand passively by when Republicans spewed forth cries like "traitor," "Copperhead," or "friend of Jeff Davis." They were as adept at applying epithets to Republicans, inventing such terms as "Blowsnakes," "Jacobins," and "Miscegenatists." When Republicans promised nonconformists that they would pay a price, threatening their lives or property, bolder spirits promised tit for tat. One suggested that Democrats follow the law of retaliation, delivering "*instant, summary and ample reprisals upon the persons and property* of those who, by language or conduct, incited such outrages." One such bolder spirit, threatened by Republicans, recommended the law of retaliation to his subscribers. "Matches are cheap," he wrote. "If fanatics and fools seek mob law and anarchy, by all means let them have it. Burn down and destroy theirs as they have or may destroy yours. By dark or by daylight—by fire or by powder—feed those who may injure you the dish they prepare. . . . For every dime of your property destroyed by political opponents, destroy a dollar's worth in return. Stores, houses, barns, offices, and churches burn." [11]

The war of words bred distrust and apprehension. Some Democrats talked or thought of secret political societies or mutual protection societies as the means to protect their rights. Republicans devised and developed the Union League to carry out their objectives—win elections, bolster Union morale, give blanket support to the government, and gain converts to their cause. A few Democrats, dismayed at the success of the Union League, tried to form secret political societies of their own; the Order of American Knights and the

9. Samuel Medary, in (Columbus, Ohio) *Crisis*, January 28, 1863.
10. John W. Kees to Cox, April 12, 1862, in Cox Papers.
11. Clement L. Vallandigham to "Messrs. Hubbard," February 17, 1864, published in Dayton *Daily Empire*, March 1, 1864; Marcus Mills "Brick" Pomeroy, in LaCrosse *Weekly Democrat*, October 10, 1864.

Sons of Liberty thus came into being. Fearing that their rights might be compromised and free elections might disappear, they saw secret political societies as a means to protect themselves and their rights and to help elect Democrats to office.

Consensus history, inadvertently of course, justifies that which has happened; the coming of the Civil War, World War I, and World War II are simple examples. Consensus history presents majority views as the true views and colors the roles of dissenters in black or gray because nationalism shapes the minds of men and guides the hands of historians. At times, even though they may be largely insubstantial or imaginary, the suppositions and apprehensions of the majority are presented as facts or as correct interpretations. The political propaganda of the majority party, used effectively, sometimes gains respectability and a place in history; myths and legends thus become a part of accepted history. This was true of portions of the nationalistic interpretation of the Copperheads, the Knights of the Golden Circle, the Order of American Knights, the Sons of Liberty, and the Indianapolis and Cincinnati treason trials. Nationalism, it seems, blesses the marriage of myth and history.

During recent decades, revisionists have challenged the contentions of earlier historians who believed the Civil War to be ordained, inevitable, and irrepressible. They have been challenged in turn by those who would revise the revisionists. Radical Republicans were defrocked by historians of the 1930s and 1940s, only to be reanointed by historians of the 1950s and 1960s. Some writers have reevaluated Civil War generals, tarnishing some of the halos polished by earlier nationalist historians. Every idea or action of President Lincoln and the members of his cabinet and Congress has been put under a historical microscope. Even the Copperheads have gained a measure of rehabilitation, being presented as conservatives or misguided partisans rather than as traitors whose blood was yellow, minds blank, and hearts black. Only accounts dealing with the secret political societies and the Indianapolis and Camp Douglas conspiracies remain as they were constructed more than a hundred years ago. The dark lantern societies, like the Knights of the Golden Circle, Order of American Knights, and Sons of Liberty are still misrepresented by Civil War historians, for myths and legends make it difficult to separate fancy from fact.

CHAPTER I

George Bickley and the Knights of the Golden Circle

THE STORY of the Knights of the Golden Circle as it developed during the Civil War evolved out of a few facts, considerable conjecture, and a generous measure of fiction. Word of Golden Circle activity dated back to the prewar years and revolved around George Bickley, an enigmatic character who resided in or near Cincinnati during the 1850s. Little is known of his pre-Cincinnati days, except that he was a Virginian born in Louisa County and a onetime resident of Tazewell County in the southwestern corner of the state.[1]

When George Washington Leigh Bickley arrived in Cincinnati in 1851, he brought with him a glib tongue, a generous supply of gall, and a manu-script entitled "History of the Settlement and Indian Wars of Tazewell County." He quickly won a measure of success and acceptance. Claiming to hold a medical certificate from the University of London, class of 1842 —a barefaced lie—Bickley secured an appointment as lecturer at the Eclectic Medical Institute. Then he found a publisher for his manuscript about Tazewell County.[2] He married a well-to-do widow (Mrs. William Dodson), tapped her resources for his various schemes, and achieved a semblance of respectability.

1. Only one Bickley is listed in the earliest census and tax records of Virginia. John Bickley, evidently the grandfather, is listed as a poll tax payer and owner of twelve slaves in Augusta B. Fothergill and John Mark Naugle (comps.), *Virginia Tax Payers, 1782–89: Other Than Those Published in the United States Census Bureau* (1940), 10. John Bickley's name does not appear in the 1810 and 1820 tax lists and census records, but those of two sons, Humphrey and Joseph Bickley, appear in both. See Netti Schreiner-Yantis (transcriber and comp.), *A Supplement to the 1810 Census for Virginia: Tax List of the Counties for Which the Census Is Missing* (Privately printed, 1971), A7.

2. Cincinnati *Weekly Nonpareil*, April 17, 1852, in a news story gives his full name as George Washington Leigh Bickley. In time Bickley substituted Lamb for Leigh. He claimed to have studied under the famous Dr. John Elliotson, who supposedly signed the diploma. University of London authorities failed to find Bickley's name anywhere in the school records. Furthermore, Dr. Elliotson resigned from the faculty in 1838. See Ollinger Crenshaw, "The Knights of the Golden Circle: the Career of George Bickley," *American Historical Review*, XLVII (1941), 24 n. According to a later Tazewell County historian, Bickley spent only seven weeks "gathering data" and writing his book, *History of the Settlement and Indian Wars of Tazewell County, Virginia* (Cincinnati, 1852), which was replete with "mistakes." See William C. Pendleton, *History of Tazewell County and Southwestern Virginia* (Richmond, 1920), 235.

In the years that followed, however, nearly everything he touched turned to dross. He joined a Know-Nothing lodge shortly before it was torn asunder by internal dissension. He tried to organize a Cincinnati branch of the Continental Union, but the effort fizzled.[3] He founded a new literary magazine, the *West American Review*, but it lasted less than six months. Next he tried to establish a conservative newspaper as "an antidote" to Horace Greeley's New York *Tribune*, but the project died aborning. While living on his wife's farm in Scioto County, he edited the (Portsmouth) *Ohio Pennant* for a spell and tried his hand at land speculation, but the panic of 1857 affected his land venture adversely. Then, surreptitiously, he tried to transfer his wife's property to his own name, but his brother-in-law (a respected Cincinnati banker) intervened in the nick of time. Disgusted with Bickley's brashness and his penchant for lies and deceit, his wife gave him the gate.[4]

Returning to Cincinnati from Scioto County, Bickley caught on with a company organized to promote inventions, handle patent cases, and publish a weekly called the *Scientific Artisan*, where he lasted less than two months as editor. A fellow worker later characterized him as "an ignorant pretender, as restless and scheming as he was shallow, very vain of his person, exceedingly fond of military display, and constantly engaged either in devices to borrow money and crazy schemes of speculation, or in debaucheries less creditable even than his swindling."[5]

After his dismissal as editor of the *Scientific Artisan*, Bickley developed two other schemes. One dealt with the organization of a drill team, equipped with a variety of uniforms, to travel all over the world and put on exhibitions featuring "intricate maneuvers."[6] The second included the creation of the Knights of the Golden Circle as an agency to carve out an empire for himself and his followers somewhere in Mexico. This second fantasy rescued Bickley from oblivion and gave him a niche in history.

Bickley's filibustering fantasy was born of the expansionist spirit of the

3. Imbued with the spirit of Manifest Destiny, George Lippard of Philadelphia had established the Continental Union in the 1840s. The Cincinnati *Weekly Nonpareil*, June 17, 1852, credited Bickley with inaugurating a lodge named "Brotherhood of Union, Wayne Circle No. 192, Continent of America, No. 37, State of Ohio."

4. Eli Kinney [the brother-in-law] and David Cady, statement, February 7, 1864, in Reports on the Order of American Knights, Records of the Office of the Judge Advocate General, National Archives.

5. Quoted in Cincinnati *Daily Gazette*, August 6, 1863. During the 1850s, Bickley's name appears in only three Cincinnati city directories. The 1855 directory lists him as a printer and boarder. The entry in the 1858 directory reads: "Bickley, G. W. L., eclectic physician, boards 297 W. 5th Street." The entry in the 1859 directory says "Bickley, George W., editor *Scientific Artisan*, bds Gibson House."

6. Cincinnati *Daily Gazette*, August 6, 1863; Charles Cist, *Sketches and Statistics of Cincinnati in 1859* (Cincinnati, 1859), 358–59.

1850s, perhaps prompted by Narciso Lopez's excursions to Cuba and William Walker's successful expedition into Nicaragua. Bickley envisioned the Golden Circle as an agency to "go forth and plant new colonies, build up new markets, and expand the area of Anglo-Americanism," perhaps colonizing and finally annexing "northern Mexico to the Dominion of the United States as in the case of Texas." Of course, his own pockets would be filled with membership fees in the process.[7] Bickley's anti-Catholicism, revealed in his flirtation with Know-Nothingism, made him view Mexico as "a papal fief"; his filibustering scheme would strike a blow against Catholicism and popery as well as helping to superimpose the "superior Anglo-American civilization" upon the "inferior" Spanish-Americans. "We are," Bickley stated in the degree booklet he had composed, "only the tools in God's hands to regenerate Spanish-America."[8]

Bickley not only prescribed the ritual, oaths, and passwords but also provided for one-, five-, and ten-dollar memberships, depending upon the degree desired by the applicant. He devised a great seal with the words UNION and POWER in bold letters and made himself head of the order, signing documents as "President General of the American Legion, K.G.C." The dreamer evidently hoped to accumulate fame and fortune by becoming "the grey-eyed man of Destiny."[9]

While trying to formalize his fantasy (he later claimed to have established two chapters of the Golden Circle, one in Cincinnati and the other in Scioto County), Bickley tried to maintain his solvency by begging for funds and favors from his wife, who was staying with a daughter in Memphis. Having already been fleeced too often, however, Mrs. Bickley turned her back upon the wolf in sheep's clothing. She refused to forgive him for his past transgressions, and she refused to give him a cent. He returned to Cincinnati empty-handed and unrepentent.[10]

Fearful of being recognized by creditors who were hounding him, Bickley turned to high comedy. He donned false whiskers and registered at the Spencer House as General Baez. A creditor saw through the disguise and began badgering him, demanding immediate and full satisfaction. Cornered, Bick-

7. George Bickley, "Statement of Facts," August 8, 1863, in George Bickley Papers, Reports on the Order of American Knights; Cincinnati *Commercial*, February 9, 1861; Cincinnati *Daily Gazette*, August 6, 1863.

8. [George Bickley], *K.G.C.* (degree booklet, n.d., in Bickley Papers), 2. Bickley's anti-Catholicism is also revealed in his exclusion of "all worshippers of the Pope" from membership in the Wayne Circle of the Continental Union.

9. Cincinnati *Daily Gazette*, August 6, 1863. The degree booklet and the great seal, with the date 1858 in the stamp, are in the Bickley Papers.

10. Eli Kinney and David Cady, statement, February 7, 1864, in Reports on the Order of American Knights; Cincinnati *Daily Gazette*, August 6, 1863.

ley promised to pay what he owed next morning. Not wishing to end his Cincinnati sojourn in jail, he packed his carpetbag and left town on the midnight train, taking his packet of K.G.C. materials and a shabby reputation with him. [11]

Bickley visited several eastern cities before making Washington, D.C., his temporary headquarters. He received some publicity for himself, his colonizing scheme, and the Golden Circle in some New York and Baltimore newspapers. In addition to handing out blurbs to unsuspecting editors, he also distributed a few copies of a sixty-three page booklet entitled *Rules, Regulations, and Principles of the Knights of the Golden Circle*. The booklet promised that the Golden Circle "would fight the battles of the South on Mexican soil." [12]

The publicity accorded Bickley's vague and grandiose scheme caused some concern in diplomatic circles, Republican newspapers, and antislavery quarters. It was even suggested by one Republican editor that the filibustering fantasy had the "implied approval if not direct sanction" of President James Buchanan. [13]

Pleased with the publicity, Bickley drifted southward in March, 1860, occasionally speaking about his project and the need for funds and recruits. In New Orleans he found a handful of followers and even the editorial endorsement of several newspapers. [14] His false claims about supportive funds in banks, Benito Juarez's blessings, and the widespread existence of the Golden Circle brought in a few members. "The Knights of the Golden Circle," a New Orleans editor speculated, "expect to be off in the course of a few weeks. The Government will not molest them, as they will arm themselves outside the jurisdiction of the United States." [15]

While Bickley was on a trip into Alabama, the roof caved in. Several New Orleans recruits checked his story about supportive funds in local banks, decided he was both liar and imposter, read him out of the Golden Circle, and exposed him in the press. [16] Bickley tried to salvage his project and reputation by calling "a national convention" to meet in Raleigh, North Carolina, in early May, 1860. The so-called convention evolved into a fiasco and some southern editors recognized that Bickley was little more than a pretender and braggadocio. "Conservative and law-abiding citizens," one discerning editor wrote,

11. Cincinnati *Daily Gazette*, August 6, 1863.
12. The booklet had a September 12, 1859, publication date and was printed by Benjamin Urmer, 248 Canal Street, New York. Bickley's scheme, concerned with "some port in Mexico," received mention in the New York *Daily Tribune*, January 7, 1860.
13. Cleveland *Leader*, January 20, 1861; Dayton *Daily Empire*, March 31, 1861, quoting an unnamed Baltimore newspaper.
14. New Orleans *Courier*, March 6, 1860, wished Bickley "God speed" and termed the project "a noble cause."
15. New Orleans *Courier*, March 31, 1861.
16. Card, appearing in the New Orleans *True Delta*, April 3, 1861; Bickley's response (via a card), New Orleans *Courier*, April 5, 1861.

"would do well to keep clear of this secret organization. The South has troubles enough already, without secretly arming to invade the States of a distracted sister Republic. . . . Let the laws and treaty obligations be observed." [17]

Undaunted by the setbacks, Bickley boldly suggested that all southerners who held slaves contribute five dollars apiece to his project to annex and colonize Mexico; the romancer even claimed that he had $498,000 "already secured." Then, in "an address" planted in some southern newspapers, Bickley invited every member and those wishing to belong to "the military department" of the Golden Circle "to repair" to a camp "near Fort Ewen, on the south bank of the Rio Nueces . . . in Encinal county, Texas, by the fifteenth of September, 1860." [18]

Although he was more interested in the presidential election than in his filibustering scheme, the self-styled head of the Golden Circle nevertheless turned his steps toward Texas in late July, supposedly to organize the rendezvous on the banks of the Nueces River. There was more interest in his enterprise in Texas than he had found in the other southern states, and Bickley organized several chapters of his secret society here and there. [19] Yet the planned rendezvous evaporated, failing for lack of followers and funds, as well as through the incompetency of the promoter.

Recognizing belatedly that Texans, too, were more interested in secession and the election of 1860 than in a vague filibustering scheme, Bickley tried to transform the Golden Circle into a military organization capable of guaranteeing southern rights and repelling Yankee invaders. On his way to Montgomery, the provisional capital of the newly organized Confederacy, Bickley stopped over in Galveston, where he posed as the brother of "General Bickley, head of the K.G.C." Prevaricating again, he claimed to have had much to do with "the working of secession in Western Texas." [20] Earlier he had designated Knoxville, Tennessee, where a nephew lived, as the new headquarters of the Golden Circle; so he now turned his steps northward from Montgom-

17. Mobile *Daily Mercury*, April 6, 1861 (newspaper clipping in Bickley Papers); Raleigh (N.C.) *Semi-weekly Standard*, May 12, 1861.

18. Cleveland *Leader*, July 26, 1861; "An Open Letter to the Knights of the Golden Circle," signed "Geo. Bickley, K.G.C., President of the American Legion, Richmond, Va., July 17, 1860," published in Richmond *Whig* (clipping, n.d., in Bickley Papers).

19. James Pike, *The Scout and Ranger: Being the Personal Adventures of Corporal Pike of the Fourth Ohio Cavalry* (Cincinnati, 1865), 123–30; Jimmie Hicks (ed.), "Some Letters Concerning the Knights of the Golden Circle in Texas, 1860–1861," *Southwestern Historical Quarterly*, LXV (1961), 80–86; *Diary of Salmon P. Chase, July 21, 1861, to October 12, 1862 (Annual Report of the American Historical Association, 1902)* (2 vols.; Washington, D.C., 1903), II, 70.

20. Edward C. Wharton (editor of the Galveston *News*) to "Dear Sir," April 9, 1861, published in *The War of the Rebellion: A Compilation of the Official Records of the Union and Confederate Armies* (128 vols.; Washington, D.C., 1880–1901), Ser. 1, Vol. I, 625, hereinafter cited as *OR*.

ery, taking his great seal, a pocket of newspaper clippings, a deflated ego, and his daydreams with him.[21]

While Bickley was futilely seeking to make his dreams come true in the South, the North was becoming interested in the Knights of the Golden Circle. Rumors spread that some members of James Buchanan's cabinet belonged to a southern-based secret society and that this organization intended to seize the nation's capital and prevent Lincoln's inauguration.[22]

The widespread rumors prompted congressmen to urge an investigation, and the House of Representatives set up a select committee to inquire if "any secret organization, hostile to the government of the United States" existed in the District of Columbia and if any government officials were members. The select committee, headed by a member of Lincoln's party, promptly brought forth a report. "The Committee are unanimously of the opinion," the document stated, "that the evidence produced before them does not prove the existence of a secret organization, here or elsewhere, . . . that has for its object, upon its responsibility, an attack upon the Capitol, or any public property here, or an interruption of any of the functions of the Government."[23]

Northerners, however, had more faith in their fears than in a congressional committee report. Rumors about subversive societies and secret plots continued to circulate, with the Golden Circle getting the most attention. Horace Greeley and his New York *Tribune* contributed to the rumors by publishing a story that a group of secessionists, belonging to "the inner temple of the Knights of the Golden Circle" intended to burn New York City, Philadelphia, and Boston to the ground.[24]

In May and June, 1861, rumors about Golden Circle activity shifted from New York and Washington to Kentucky and adjacent states. Some of the suppositions stated that members of the K.G.C. were trying to get Kentucky to secede and join the Confederacy. George D. Prentice, the competent and influential editor of the Louisville *Daily Journal*, charged that a subversive society was trying to plunge Kentucky into a civil war, promote secession, and destroy the state's "neutrality." A Unionist, campaigning for a congressional seat against a States' Righter, charged that his opponent had received the endorsement of "General Bickley" and the Golden Circle.[25]

21. "An Open Letter to the Knights of the Golden Circle," July 17, 1860.

22. Dayton *Daily Journal*, January 17, 1861; [?] to Joseph Holt, January 5, 1861, in Joseph Holt Papers, Library of Congress.

23. *Congressional Globe*, 36th Cong., 2nd Sess., Pt. 1, pp. 571–72, 913; *House Reports*, 36th Cong., 2nd Sess., No. 79, pp. 5, 145. The select committee was headed by William A. Howard of Michigan.

24. New York *Daily Tribune*, May 4, 1861. The *Tribune* quoted from an anonymous letter, supposedly headed "Louisville, Ky., April 30, 1861."

25. Louisville *Daily Journal*, May 22, 1861; [?] to "Editor of the Louisville *Journal*," June 6, 1861, published in Louisville *Daily Journal*, June 8, 1861.

Bickley, evidently pleased with the free publicity that he and his order were receiving, fanned the flames with an "open letter" that reached the desks of several editors. Bickley's letter claimed that the Golden Circle had eight thousand members in Kentucky and that the Confederate flag was destined to fly over the state capitol. Brash as ever, he also issued a circular entitled *Volunteers Wanted*, stating he wished to organize "a Voltigeur Corps of Kentuckians" and suggesting that interested individuals forward a five-dollar membership fee his way.[26]

Two Kentucky Unionists, anxious for information about Bickley and the Golden Circle, sent him the five-dollar membership fees and received a packet of information in return. Both used the material received in the mail and a variety of suppositions to publish exposés. Dr. Anthony A. Urban's filled three columns of fine print in the Louisville *Journal*.[27] Joseph W. Pomfrey, a resident of Covington, Kentucky, wrote a lengthy exposé, which was published in Cincinnati under the title *A True Disclosure and Exposition of the Knights of the Golden Circle, Including the Secret Signs, Grips, and Charges, of the Third Degree as Practiced by the Order.*[28]

The Louisville *Daily Democrat* described how to join the order:

A gentleman desiring to be a K.G.C., and to organize a castle, will address a note to the President of the Legion, K.G.C. (Gen. George Bickley), at Knoxville, Tennessee, enclosing evidence of his standing and character, when the form of an obligation will be sent to him, which he will fill out and acknowledge before a magistrate, or notary public, and return, and enclose with it the sum of five dollars, whereupon the following castle works and papers will at once be forwarded: 7 First Degree Books and 7 Keys, 7 Second Degree Books and 7 Keys, 2 copies of "Instructions," 1 Roll Book, 1 Set Receipts, 20 copies "K.G.C. Address," 1 copy "Rules and Regulations." And such other papers as are needed.

"Almost any imbecile," the paper concluded, could join the K.G.C. if he had five dollars to throw away.[29]

---

26. Louisville *Daily Courier*, May 20, 1861; Dayton *Daily Journal*, June 10, 1861. The Circular, *Volunteers Wanted*, dated June 29, 1861, was published in the Louisville *Daily Journal*, July 18, 1861.

27. Louisville *Daily Journal*, July 18, 1861; Major John M. Wright to Brig. Gen. Nathaniel C. McLean, August 16, 1863, in Reports on the Order of American Knights. Dr. Anthony A. Urban's name appears only in six Louisville city directories between 1855 and 1869, each time with a different address. He is listed as a pharmacist once and as a physician five times.

28. A note on the cover says that the booklet was "printed for the author." Later evidence and events will discredit Pomfrey as a draft dodger, forger, liar, and proponent of fraudulent claims against the U.S. government. Five packets that deal with Pomfrey's claims are in the Records of the Adjutant General's Office, Records of the Office of the Judge Advocate General.

29. Louisville *Daily Democrat*, September 2, 1861.

Nevertheless, the popularity of Pomfrey's pamphlet prompted James M. Hiatt, an Indianapolis newspaperman and patriot, to compose his own exposé, adding a new dimension to the Golden Circle story. He blamed the order for the growth of secession in the South, the annexation of Texas, the Mexican War, and efforts to impose a proslavery constitution upon Kansas. "The Knights of the Golden Circle," Hiatt averred, "were secessionists proper and their history is the history of secession." [30]

The three exposés had a wide circulation in Ohio and made Bickley's name well known. Hiatt's account, especially, sold like hotcakes. "We understand," a reliable observer noted, "that large orders for it have been received by the publisher from all parts of the country." [31] The fact that Bickley had once lived in Cincinnati made Ohioans especially interested in any stories or rumors about the Golden Circle. Several Republican editors, interested in linking local Democrats to Bickley's order, devised a new form of political propaganda. The editor of the Bucyrus *Journal*, for example, contended that Golden Circle members were numerous in several Democratic strongholds and that "at least three lodges" flourished in his county, "teaching nothing but the rankest treason." [32]

The rumors spread from Ohio, making the Knights of the Golden Circle known from Maine to California. Editors east and west not only published portions of the exposés but added editorial comments. A Boston-published exposé, borrowing heavily from the others, competed for attention in New England. [33] An entirely new play, titled *Knights of the Golden Circle*, opened at the New Bowery Theatre in New York City on July 20, 1861. Patriots in California who feared that General Albert Sidney Johnston, a southerner in command of the Department of the Pacific, might be involved in a conspiracy, raised the Golden Circle bugaboo. Reports circulated that some sixteen to eighteen thousand Californians belonged to the Knights of the Golden Circle and that traitorous plots were in process. The so-called Johnston Conspiracy was based more upon fears than facts. [34]

30. [James M. Hiatt], *An Authentic Exposition of the K.G.C., Knights of the Golden Cricle; or, A History of Secession from 1834 to 1861* (Indianapolis, 1861), 77. The booklet was printed by C. O. Perrine, publisher. Some historians (*e.g.*, James D. Horan) have mistakenly listed C. O. Perrine as the author rather than the publisher since Hiatt hid behind anonymity.

31. Indianapolis *Daily State Sentinel*, July 8, 1861.

32. Bucyrus (Ohio) *Weekly Journal*, September 27, 1861; Dayton *Daily Journal*, August 22, 1861; John A. Carter to John Sherman, August 15, 1861, in John Sherman Papers, Library of Congress.

33. *K.G.C.: A Full Exposure of the Southern Traitors; The Knights of the Golden Circle. Their Startling Schemes Frustrated. From Original Documents Never Before Published. (Five Cent Monthly)* (Boston, 1861).

34. Robert C. Rogers *et al.* to Simon Cameron, August 18, 1861, in *OR*, Ser. 1, Vol. L, 589–91. The myth that Golden Circle activists presented a problem in California was developed

War psychosis, plus the popularity of suppositions about the Golden Circle, tempted some Marion County Republicans in Ohio to concoct "revelations" to discredit leading Democrats and affect the election returns. They made Thomas H. Hodder, editor of the (Marion) *Democratic Mirror*, their especial target. Hodder had alienated many with his carping editorials, which railed against President Lincoln, the Republican party, and the war. Hodder claimed, for example, that Republicans, by opposing compromise, deserved most of the blame for bringing on the war. Indignant Republicans retaliated with threats to burn down his shop, tar and feather him, and even hang him from some tree branch. Democratic friends of Hodder's, believing him to be a victim of organized bigotry, developed a rather informal mutual protection society. It had no officers and no ritual. Its members, however, agreed upon "a signal of distress" when either they or the offices of the *Democratic Mirror* were threatened by a mob. Naturally, all members of the ill-organized mutual protection society were Democrats.[35]

As political tensions mounted and election day (October 8, 1861) approached, some local Republicans, including the son of the editor of the Marion *Republican*, forged documents that linked Hodder and his mutual protection society to the Knights of the Golden Circle. The bogus "second oath" read: "And I further promise and swear in the presence of Almighty God, and the members of the Golden Circle, that I will not rest or sleep until Abraham Lincoln, now president, shall be removed out of the Presidential chair, and I will wade in blood up to my knees, as soon as Jefferson Davis sees proper to march with his army to take the city of Washington and the White House, to do the same." The coterie of Republicans who framed Hodder offered other supposed evidence which they claimed to have seized in a raid upon "a K.G.C. castle": an affidavit of an imagined spy, a list of Democrats belonging to the secret subversive society, several letters, and the confessions of a young Democrat whom they had plied with corn whiskey. Although the strange "second oath" should have been enough to stamp the whole thing a humbug, a partisan federal marshal arrested editor Hodder, Dr. John M. Christian, leader of the Marion County Democracy, and Frederick Court, the country bumpkin who had been plied with liquor. The exposé, based on the forged

---

in Elijah R. Kennedy, *The Contest for California in 1861* (Boston, 1912) and Charles M. Dustin, "The Knights of the Golden Circle," *Pacific Monthly*, XXVI (1911), 152–65. Kennedy set the number of Golden Circle members in California in 1860 at eighteen thousand. Dustin says that a hundred thousand Californians belonged to the subversive organizations, the Knights of the Golden Circle and the Knights of the Columbian Star. The "Johnston Conspiracy," as well as the accounts written by Kennedy and Dustin, are discredited in Benjamin F. Gilbert, "California and the Civil War," *California Historical Society Quarterly*, XL (1961), 160–85. Also see Benjamin F. Gilbert, "The Mythical Johnston Conspiracy," *ibid.*, XXVII (1949), 165–73.

35. *History of Marion County, Ohio* (Chicago, 1883), 448–49.

documents and some suppositions, made headlines in Ohio newspapers on the eve of the election. The headlines in the (Columbus) *Ohio State Journal*, official organ of the Republican party, read: "Important Arrest! A 'Castle' of the Knights of the G.C. Assaulted by the U.S. Marshal!! The Records Seized! A Commander Taken!" [36]

Democrats, of course, denied the Golden Circle allegations, contending they were the concoction of dishonest men intent upon influencing the election returns. The editor of the Democratic-oriented (Columbus) *Ohio Statesman* charged that "the show" had been staged by a politically minded marshal to discredit the opposition party. Furthermore, the same editor added, the bogus "second oath" had come off the same press as the Marion *Republican*. [37]

A trial, held in the district court in Cleveland, cleared the air and brought to light the fact that the federal marshal and the son of the editor of the Marion *Republican* had "managed the show"—composing the "second oath," forging other documents, and framing Hodder and Christian. Furthermore, there was not a shred of evidence to link Hodder's loosely organized mutual protection society to the Knights. [38]

Grand jury investigations in Crawford and Franklin counties also discredited preelection Republican claims that the Golden Circle was active in Democratic strongholds. The Crawford County grand jury interrogated twenty-five witnesses, including the editor of the Bucyrus *Journal*, who had repeatedly claimed that a secret prosouthern society existed in the area. The repentent editor admitted under oath that he had no evidence to support his K.G.C. contentions. [39] The Franklin County grand jury also heard a procession of witnesses, including two editors who had circulated Golden Circle rumors to discredit the Democracy. When the editor of the *Ohio State Journal* was pressed to explain the contradiction between his preelection K.G.C. claims and his admission to the grand jury that he had no evidence to offer, he gave a simple explanation. As an editor, he was free to make accusations and print rumors; as a witness, he was under oath to tell the truth. The Republican editor of the (Columbus) *Capital City Fact* also had a humiliating experience.

36. (Columbus) *Ohio Statesman*, October 15, 1861; *History of Marion County, Ohio*, 448–49. The oath, along with other documents, was published in the (Columbus) *Ohio State Journal*, October 8, 1861, as well as in a large number of other Republican newspapers.

37. *Ohio Statesman*, October 15, 1861,

38. *Ibid.*, October 16–19, 1861; (Columbus) *Crisis*, October 24, 1861; Cleveland *Leader*, October 18, 1861. The Cincinnati *Daily Enquirer*, October 19, 1861, featured an article entitled "Exposure of a Villainous Political Trick."

39. Grand jury report, published in *Ohio Statesman*, December 22, 1861. The report ended with the statement: "We are forced to the conclusion that the Knights of the Golden Circle exist in this county in imagination alone."

After admitting to the grand jury that he had no evidence for the K.G.C. tales he had publicized in his newspaper, he made a public retraction of his charges in order to evade a libel and slander suit, which had been initiated against him by editors Samuel Medary of the *Crisis* and Matthias Martin of the *Ohio Statesman*, both accused of belonging to the K.G.C.[40]

Except for the election results, Democrats gloried in the turn of events. Use of the K.G.C. bogeyman, one editor contended, disgraced the Republicans who had devised the "electioneering trick"; they now stood naked and exposed.[41] Samuel Medary, who had been maligned the most, told the readers of his noted newspaper that Republicans had been guilty of "disgraceful deviltry" by devising "a diabolical electioneering scheme" and creating "a roorback of huge dimensions." "We believe," he added, "that this secret organization [the K.G.C.] . . . has no existence in reality, and it was furthermore our honest conviction that the whole affair was concocted by a few dishonest politicians to influence well-meaning men to vote against the Democratic party nominees."[42]

Another sheaf of Golden Circle suppositions were harvested in Michigan, where rumormongers parlayed former president Franklin Pierce's visit into a spy scare. Pierce took a trip to Detroit to visit Robert McClelland, who had served in his cabinet, and to Saginaw to visit a niece. Vague K.G.C. rumors gave the editor of the Detroit *Tribune* an excuse to suggest that Pierce's visit was associated with a "foul conspiracy." He ended an editorial conjecture with an irreverent slur: "Our opinion is [that] Franklin Pierce is a prowling traitor spy."[43]

Indignant because Republicans had maligned a man whom he respected, Dr. Guy S. Hopkins decided he would "trick" and embarrass those who devised and circulated Golden Circle or conspiracy rumors. He composed a hoax letter, filled with extravagant accounts of a "secret league" and assertions that Pierce was "an agent" of that "extensive organization." He expected the Republican editors of the Detroit *Tribune* and Detroit *Leader* to accept the letter as genuine, publish a "gigantic exposé," and eat humble pie when they found they had been taken in. "My fartherest expectation," he con-

40. *Ohio Statesman*, December 22, 1861; Cincinnati *Daily Enquirer*, October 30, 31, 1861, June 12, 1862.
41. Mansfield (Ohio) *Shield and Banner*, November 14, 1861, paraphrased in the Detroit *Free Press*, November 20, 1861.
42. *Crisis*, November 7, 28, 1861. Ohio's contributions to the building of the K.G.C. bogeyman are detailed in Frank L. Klement, "Ohio and the Knights of the Golden Circle: The Evolution of a Civil War Myth," *Cincinnati Historical Society Bulletin*, XXXII (1974), 7–27.
43. Detroit *Tribune*, September 25, 1861.

fessed at a later date, "was that it would be sent to one of the treason-shrieking newspapers and, when exploded, would produce lots of 'fun.'"[44]

Dr. Hopkins' plan to entrap Republican editors who circulated K.G.C. tales backfired. Federal marshals seized Hopkins and two of his friends and carted them off to Fort Lafayette. While they were imprisoned and denied the chance to explain their intentions publicly, Republican newspapers published the hoax letter, circulated Golden Circle rumors, slandered former president Pierce, and enjoyed the discomfiture of Democrats. Inadvertently, Dr. Hopkins had helped build bigger bubbles rather than pricking them. It was, all in all, a strange turn of events.[45]

Illinois and Indiana furnished most of the Golden Circle rumors in 1862. Each of the states had a governor interested in a bogeyman and each of the governors had an aide who was imaginative and aggressive. Furthermore, in each state, the Democrats were regaining political ground lost in earlier years.

Joseph K. C. Forrest, a confidant of Governor Richard Yates and the Springfield correspondent for the Chicago *Tribune*, concocted most of the Golden Circle rumors that circulated in Illinois in 1862. Forrest's first set of "revelations," made early in the year, was intended to discredit the Illinois state constitutional convention meeting in Springfield. The convention, controlled by vindictive and shortsighted Democrats, practiced high-handed partisanship—halving the four-year term of the Republican governor, redrawing congressional district lines, investigating Governor Yates's distribution of state money, shearing him of his military authority, and seeking to manufacture political propaganda. Correspondent Forrest tried to discredit the constitutional convention by linking its members to the Golden Circle. "It has been rumored for some days," Forrest wrote for publication in the Chicago *Daily Tribune*, "that there were Knights of the Golden Circle and members of mutual protection societies in the convention. . . . The number of K.G.C.'s has been placed so high, as to come within a few votes of a majority of the convention." The *Tribune*'s editor added embroidery of his own: "There are men in that convention who would not hesitate to involve our people in anarchy—who wait only the favorable moment to seize the military power of the state, and to turn the arms of Illinois upon the flag of our common country."[46]

44. Guy S. Hopkins to William H. Seward, December 29, 1861, in Guy S. Hopkins Papers, Civil War Political Prisoners' Records, State Department Files, National Archives. The hoax letter, written in pencil and dated October 5, 1861, was addressed to "R.M.C." [Robert McClelland]. It is also in the Hopkins Papers.

45. *OR*, Ser. 2, Vol. II, 1244–47. Frank L. Klement, "Franklin Pierce and the Treason Charges of 1861–1862," *Historian*, XXIII (1961), 436–48, and "The Hopkins Hoax and Golden Circle Rumors in Michigan, 1861–1862," *Michigan History*, LXVII (1963), 1–14, explore various aspects of this strange story.

46. Chicago *Daily Tribune*, February 11, 1862.

The Democratic delegates, who were playing a brazen political game, re-acted angrily to the smear practiced by Forrest and the *Tribune*. They denied the K.G.C. charges publicly and appointed a special committee to investigate Forrest's contentions. When called before the committee, Forrest admitted shamefacedly that he had no evidence to substantiate his charges. Governor Yates and U.S. marshal David L. Phillips also admitted they had no tangible evidence and apologized for calling members of the convention "disloyal." Having chased every available rumor down a dead-end street, the special com-mittee—half of the members of which were Republicans—presented a report labeling all K.G.C. rumors false and asking that Forrest be censured for invent-ing allegations, circulating falsehoods, and giving dignity to gossip.[47]

Golden Circle rumors, dormant for several months, resurfaced when the newly drafted constitution came up for its ratification test in June. Forrest, leading the Republican assault against the brazenly partisan document, stated that all "the traitorous Knights of the Golden Circle" endorsed it, and the Chi-cago *Tribune* used the old cliché that the proposed constitution was "con-ceived in sin and brought forth in iniquity," that it was the handiwork of "se-cession mouthing politicians, many of them Knights of the Golden Circle." Even Governor Yates, angry that the new constitution halved his term even though he was legally elected for four years, argued that a vote against the document was a vote against the Knights of the Golden Circle. After the shod-dily partisan constitution failed to be ratified, Republican editors thanked "the patriotic citizens" for scorning the "Copperhead Constitution" and repudiat-ing "the Knights."[48]

Illinois residents had a brief respite from Golden Circle rumors while For-rest worked at a desk in Washington, D.C., but he returned late in July to seek a position as aide on Governor Yates's staff. Forrest promised "to repay the favor [of a job] with interest," pointing out that his ties with the Chicago *Trib-une* could help the governor and his party.[49] Yates needed help badly, for a Democratic resurgence was in progress. The credibility of the Lincoln admin-istration had slipped badly. The economic recession that had engulfed the Midwest in 1861 and early 1862 had not yet given way to war prosperity, and the populace reacted strongly against the wave of arbitrary arrests in Illinois and several other Midwestern states.

Forrest, now on Yates's payroll, made an effort to stem the Democratic tide

47. *Journal of the Constitutional Convention of the State of Illinois, Convened at Springfield on January 7, 1862* (Springfield, 1862), 941–42.

48. Chicago *Daily Tribune*, May 8, June 2, 5, 9, 11, 14, 16, 21, 1862; Lacon (Ill.) *Gazette*, June 25, 1862.

49. Joseph K. C. Forrest to "Dear Governor" [Yates], July 30, 1862, in Governor Richard Yates Papers, Illinois State Historical Library, Springfield.

by composing a report/exposé about the Knights of the Golden Circle to be used as political propaganda. The Chicago *Tribune*, for which Forrest continued to serve as Springfield correspondent, published "the revelations" in its issue of August 26, 1862. Forrest's incredible account relied heavily upon letters (several of them anonymous) that had reached the governor's desk, four affidavits (each signed with an *X* by an illiterate), and a report by a Republican serving as a government spy. Forrest's fertile imagination filled in the gaps. In summary, the exposé claimed that many castles of the Golden Circle existed in Illinois, that prominent Democrats belonged to the subversive society, and that Knights actively discouraged volunteering, encouraged desertion, and sowed the seeds of discontent.[50]

Almost all Republican newspapers in the state published Forrest's report in whole or in part, although it was little more than a shameless electioneering document. The Carbondale *Times* added an editorial comment that the Golden Circle had at least thirty thousand members in southern Illinois. Even many out-of-state papers summarized Forrest's story, sometimes adding suppositions of their own. "It is thought in Washington and Springfield," the editor of the New York *Evening Post* asserted, "that there are in Illinois not less than seven hundred treasonable societies based upon some modification of the plan upon which the Knights of the Golden Circle build."[51]

Illinois Democrats challenged Forrest and his "fantasies." The Golden Circle bogeyman, one stated, was devised to affect the fall elections, discredit prominent Democrats, and justify the arbitrary arrests already made. Time would prove, several said, that Forrest was a liar and that his exposé heaped one falsehood upon another. The prominent Democrats whom Forrest linked to the Golden Circle expressed indignation and categorically denied membership in any such society. "I have never at any time belonged to any secret organization," one wrote resentfully, "and I have all my life opposed secret organizations, believing them to be fundamentally and radically wrong in a republican government."[52] Neither the denials nor indignation, however, stopped the propagation and spread of the Golden Circle rumors in Illinois.

50. Chicago *Daily Tribune*, August 26, 1862. Two dozen letters, in the Yates Papers, provided Forrest with quotations which he incorporated into his composition. The four questionable affidavits are with David L. Phillips' report to Secretary of War Edwin M. Stanton, September 4, 1862, in the Lafayette C. Baker–Levi C. Turner Papers, Adjutant General's Records. Albert P. Davis' [the government detective] "Report," n.d., is in the John P. Clemenson Papers, Civil War Political Prisoners' Records. Forrest's role in devising Golden Circle rumors and reports is discussed in greater detail in Frank L. Klement, "Copperhead Secret Societies in Illinois During the Civil War," *Journal of the Illinois State Historical Society*, XLVIII (1955), 152–80.

51. Carbondale *Times*, n.d., quoted in (Springfield) *Illinois State Journal*, August 30, 1862; New York *Evening Post*, n.d., quoted in the (Springfield) *Illinois State Register*, August 30, 1862.

52. Samuel S. Marshall (seeking a U.S. Senate seat), quoted in the *Illinois State Journal*, September 12, 1862; James C. Allen (seeking a congressional seat), quoted in the *Illinois State*

The situation in Indiana in many ways paralleled that in Illinois. Governor Oliver P. Morton, like his Illinois counterpart, had been elected to a four-year term in 1860 and resented the Democratic resurgence. Neither governor wanted to face a hostile legislature in January of 1863. One of Morton's aides, Colonel Henry B. Carrington, served as the chief architect in building the K.G.C. air castles in Indiana.

When Governor Morton appointed him to speed up the recruitment and organization of Indiana troops in mid-year of 1862, Colonel Carrington could look back upon a checkered career in law, newspaper work, and politics. He came to Indianapolis to a desk and a duty, bringing with him the belief that abolitionism was a worthy crusade, that the Republican party was divinely ordained, and that Democrats who criticized the president or opposed the war were traitors and fools.[53]

When Carrington came to Indiana he found Golden Circle rumors already widespread. Hiatt's exposé, published earlier in Indianapolis, had had a wide readership. In addition, Berry R. Sulgrove, editor of the Indianapolis *Daily Journal* and a confidant of the governor, had given publicity to every old rumor and invented some new ones.[54] Judge James Hughes, a convert to republicanism, had written a letter (after being closeted with Governor Morton) which stated that a subversive society, "understood to be hostile to the payment of direct taxes to support the war" was "rapidly spreading throughout the State."[55] Then there was a grand jury report, written by a Republican activist, John Hanna, who was a close personal friend of the governor. After the grand jury had brought forth forty-seven indictments—not a single one for treason or subversive activity—Hanna added an *obiter dictum*, which claimed that a "traitorous secret order" was widespread in Indiana, with "some fifteen thousand estimated members" belonging to "castles and lodges."[56]

It did not take Colonel Carrington long to build upon the K.G.C. foundation he had inherited. Before the year's end he composed a long report for

---

Register, August 28, 1862; William R. Morrison to "Dear Sir," August 15, 1862, copy in William R. Morrison Papers, Illinois State Historical Library; William J. Allen to Maj. Gen. George B. McClellan, September 6, 1862, in the Baker-Turner Papers.

53. No satisfactory study of Carrington exists. Charles B. Galbreath, "Henry Beebee Carrington," *Dictionary of American Biography*, III, 521, is sketchy.

54. Indianapolis *Daily Journal*, December 30, 1861, March 28, 1862; Indianapolis *Daily State Sentinel*, January 3, 11, April 7, 1862.

55. Judge James Hughes to Oliver P. Morton, June 16, 1862, published in Indianapolis *Daily Journal*, June 19, 1862. Speculation existed that Hughes wrote the letter in a bid to keep his judgeship and that Morton wanted the letter to read at the approaching Republican state convention.

56. "Report of the United States Grand Jury, in District Court of the United States, for the District of Indiana, May Term, 1862," in "United States District Court Order Book, May 21, 1860, to November 24, 1863," in Federal Records Center, Chicago. I used this grand jury report when it was still in the Federal Building, Indianapolis. For a critical evaluation of the grand jury report, see Kenneth M. Stampp, *Indiana Politics During the Civil War* (Indianapolis, 1949), 151.

Washington on subversion in Indiana. "A secret order," he wrote to Secretary of War Edwin M. Stanton, "exists in this vicinity to incite desertion of soldiers with their arms, to resist the arrest of deserters, to stop enlistments, to disorganize the army, to prevent further drafting—in short, a direct avowal to stop this war." This subversive order, Carrington added in his lengthy document, possessed "oaths and signs and watchwords" and its rapid spread explained the alarming desertion rate. Instead of blaming war weariness, disillusionment with the war, and his own inefficiency for the lack of recruits, Carrington pointed his finger at the K.G.C.[57]

Other states offered bits and pieces. The editor of the Cincinnati *Daily Times* claimed that he had evidence that a castle of the Golden Circle existed in his city and that members had been solicited at Democratic meetings. James J. Faran, Democratic editor of the Cincinnati *Daily Enquirer*, repudiated these claims and concluded, "The whole thing shows that the K.G.C. took no root here and that the attempt to make the public believe that such a lodge existed in the city is one of the most vicious and detestable impositions that the war has produced." In Washington, Senator Benjamin F. Wade publicly stated that evidence showed that William L. Yancey, "prince of secessionists" and prewar U.S. Senator from Alabama, had initiated General George B. McClellan into the Golden Circle "18 mo. or 2 years ago at Cincinnati." In Kentucky, an ardent Unionist composed another exposé of the Golden Circle and had it published as a thin booklet. The anonymous author borrowed heavily from Dr. Urban's exposé, which had been published a year earlier in the Louisville *Daily Journal*, and added a few embellishments of his own. He wrote, for example, that newspapers like the Detroit *Free Press*, Chicago *Times*, Milwaukee *News*, and Cincinnati *Daily Enquirer* functioned as auxiliaries of the order.[58]

Circulated by ardent Unionists trying to organize a patriotic league, the booklet had a restricted reading audience. A copy of it fell into the hands of an Iowa soldier campaigning in Kentucky, and he incorporated much of its contents in a long, long letter that he wrote to a friend, Jesse Clement, the editor of the Dubuque *Times*. The editor offered the letter, which filled three columns of fine print, to his readers as evidence that his scattershot charges of

57. Carrington's role in developing Golden Circle rumors for Governor Morton are treated in greater detail in Frank L. Klement, "Carrington and the Golden Circle Legend in Indiana during the Civil War," *Indiana Magazine of History*, LXI (1965), 31–52.

58. Cincinnati *Daily Times*, April 3, 5, 1862; Cincinnati *Daily Enquirer*, April 6, 8, 1862; Jacob R. Rister to Benjamin F. Wade, March 30, 1862, in Benjamin F. Wade Papers, Library of Congress; *Congressional Globe*, 37th Cong., 2nd Sess., 1736; *K.G.C.: An Authentic Exposition of the Origins, Objects, and Secret Work of the Organization Known as the Knights of the Golden Circle* (Louisville, Ky., 1862). The booklet was credited to "the United States National Union Club."

Golden Circle activity in Iowa had substance. Clement received help from outsiders in promoting the idea that traitors and Knights were numerous in Iowa. The Chicago *Tribune* called Dubuque "a sinkhole of treason" and claimed there was a chapter of the K.G.C. active in the city. Even Horace Greeley and his New York *Tribune* got into the act. "It is known here," Greeley's paper stated, "that a secret organization exists in Dubuque, Iowa, to resist the collection of taxes." [59]

Illinois and Indiana provided most of the reports and rumors of Golden Circle activity in 1863 as they had the previous year. Both states had strong-minded Republican governors feuding with Democratic-controlled state legislatures, and in both there was a widespread reaction to Lincoln's emancipation measures and federal conscription. Some Democratic newspapers that had given the war qualified support in 1861 and 1862 turned on Lincoln like mad dogs after he issued his proclamation of emancipation. War weariness and antiwar sentiment nurtured a peace crusade that appalled Governors Yates and Morton. Bolder Democratic spirits, interpreting the election returns of late 1862 as a repudiation of the Lincoln administration, became more daring and more vicious in their attacks upon the president and the Republican governors who supported the war. Small wonder that Governors Yates and Morton believed their states to be teetering on the brink of a volcano.

Friends advised Governor Yates of Illinois that he would be in trouble when the state legislature convened in early January. Tactless Democrats bragged that Yates's wings would be clipped, and Republicans feared the Copperhead-dominated legislature would pass "rash and vicious legislation." "Draw now the sword for battle," one Republican advised Governor Yates, "and throw away the scabbard." [60]

Governor Yates and his loyal aide, Joseph Forrest, sought ways to discredit the mischief-minded and impudently partisan state legislature. They solicited letters from army officers and circulated the soldiers' views as the true views. Forrest, experienced in manufacturing treason tales, raised the Golden Circle bugaboo again. He turned over to the Republican press a letter which supposed that "three hundred secret lodges of traitors" existed in Illinois, spewing treason and planning "an uprising." He concocted a report that a "delegation of peacemakers," representing the legislature and the Golden Circle, had departed for Richmond to negotiate an armistice, arrange for the "abdica-

---

59. Dubuque *Weekly Times*, April 17, 1862; Chicago *Daily Tribune*, April 8, 1862; New York *Daily Tribune*, May 7, 1862. The story of Golden Circle rumors in Iowa is more extensively detailed in Frank L. Klement, "Rumors of Golden Circle Activity in Iowa During the Civil War Years," *Annals of Iowa*, XXVII (1965), 523–36.

60. David L. Phillips to Lyman Trumbull, December 24, 1862, in Lyman Trumbull Papers, Library of Congress; William S. Pope to Yates, November 7, 1862, in Yates Papers.

tion" of President Lincoln, and pledge constitutional amendments favorable to the rebels of the South. Governor Yates's imaginative aide added that the K.G.C.'s activities were widespread, a "Grand Council" having been established in the nation's capital to encourage forcible resistance to the draft and aid in the establishment of a "Northwestern confederacy." [61]

Democrats ridiculed Forrest's farfetched allegations. Charles H. Lanphier, editor of the *Illinois State Register*, led the attack upon Yates's aide and his treason tales. Lanphier called Forrest "a deliberate, studied, and infamous LIAR" and "a foul-mouth calumniator." Acrimony dripping from his pen, Lanphier added, "He has made the study of the habits and customs of the K.G.C. his specialty, and is *au fait* with the genuine specimen as Aggassiz [*sic*] with antediluvian birds and fishes." [62]

Forrest's absence from Illinois during June and July, 1863, gave state residents a two-month respite from additional K.G.C. stories, but he returned in August to offer further revelations in an effort to influence the fall elections. Soon after his return he reported that seventy-one castles of the Golden Circle were organized in Illinois, and Republican newspapers promptly published his allegations. A week later he stated that the Knights were responsible for the peace-and-compromise resolutions that had been adopted by the state Democratic convention. He blamed the Fulton County "disorders" on the Golden Circle, ignoring the fact that an "unduly alarmed" federal marshal had brought on the incident through his arrogance and rudeness. He reported that members of the K.G.C. were planning a massacre of Union Leaguers, "on the order of the St. Bartholomew massacre in France." He also circulated a report that William C. Quantrill, the notorious Missouri bushwhacker, had attended the state Democratic convention. Occasionally, as letters, anonymous or otherwise, reached Governor Yates's desk, Forrest released them to a select group of Republican editors as evidence to support his montage of allegations. [63]

Editor Lanphier of the *Illinois State Register* acted as spokesman for the Democracy. He denied and denounced Forrest's allegations as fast as he made them—a nigh hopeless task, for the charges came as "thick as the leaves of Vallambrosa [*sic*]." He characterized the charges as "lying accounts" designed to affect the elections. He suggested that the state would be rid of "K.G.C. scares, exposés, and silly statements" if Governor Yates and his aide, "an extraordinary liar," left the state for good. Nobody in the county,

61. Uri Manly to Yates, March 7, 1863, in Yates Papers; Chicago *Journal*, May 3, 1863. Forrest relayed this story to such papers as the (St. Louis) *Missouri Democrat* and the Chicago *Daily Tribune*; it was published in both.

62. *Illinois State Register*, May 14, 16, 1863.

63. Chicago *Daily Tribune*, August 16, 1863; *Illinois State Journal*, August 20, September 8, 1863; *Illinois State Register*, August 23, 1863.

Lanphier added, could match Forrest's ability "to invent misrepresentations" and manufacture political lies.[64]

Unlike Yates, who left this chore to Forrest, Governor Morton took a large hand in dispensing Golden Circle tales in Indiana. The situation was so critical that he dared not leave it to others. The Copperhead-dominated state legislature in Indiana was even more brazen than that in Illinois. Injudicious and immoderate Democratic legislators, overstepping the bounds of propriety, tried to usurp executive authority, gerrymander the state, and embarrass the governor. Morton countered by refurbishing the K.G.C. scarecrow he had planted in the political fields the year before. He denounced the Golden Circle in a speech at a Union gathering in Indianapolis on January 14, accusing the Democratic party of supporting the subversive society's scheme to establish a "Northwest Confederacy." Soon after, he repeated the same charges at Shelbyville and other Republican rallies. The Indianapolis *Daily Journal* published Morton's contentions and they made the rounds of the Republican press.[65]

Members of Morton's inner circle, all of whom had a vested interest in turning back the rising Democratic tide, took up the good fight. Berry Sulgrove of the Indianapolis *Journal* pitched in with a two-column story about the Knights of the Golden Circle, mixing suppositions and misrepresentations in equal proportions.[66] William R. Holloway, Morton's brother-in-law and personal secretary, arranged for the publication of a brief K.G.C. exposé and then sponsored its distribution to Republican clubs and Union League offices.[67] Colonel Henry B. Carrington, for whom Morton had the War Department establish the District of Indiana (headquartered at Indianapolis), contributed a dozen different stories. In the months that followed, he again became the chief propagator of Golden Circle contentions.

Carrington renewed his war against the Golden Circle with a lengthy special report to President Lincoln and Secretary of War Stanton. The five-page document dwelt upon the dangers that subversive societies posed in the state. Firmness and force, Carrington stated (perhaps anticipating the governor's rather dictatorial tactics), would be needed to stamp out treason on the home front. He ended his strange report with a Republican article of faith: God allowed "trial by war" to test the nation, and the fruits of emancipation were noble and manifold.[68]

64. *Illinois State Register*, August 5, 15, 16, 1863.
65. Indianapolis *Daily Journal*, January 15, 25, February 13, 1863.
66. *Ibid.*, January 19, 1863.
67. Both the K.G.C. exposé/booklet and instructional booklets on how to organize Union Leagues were published for Holloway by Asher and Company, Indianapolis. Both are among the items in the Henry K. English Papers, Indiana Division, Indiana State Library, Indianapolis.
68. Henry B. Carrington to President Lincoln, January 14, 1863, in Robert Todd Lincoln Papers, Library of Congress.

Sometimes Carrington used the Golden Circle ploy to excuse his errors of judgment. Once, for example, he sent two sergeants outside of his jurisdiction, which was limited to Indiana, to arrest four soldiers, supposedly deserters. The sergeants sought their quarry in Illinois, but just as they made their arrests in Marshall, Clark County, they were themselves arrested. A Democratic sheriff, resenting the "invasion from Indiana," charged Carrington's two sergeants with kidnapping. A Democratic judge, Charles H. Constable, ruled in favor of his friend the sheriff and against the sergeants, setting bail at five hundred dollars and ordering them to appear before a Democratic-dominated grand jury on a charge of kidnapping Illinois citizens.[69]

Blaming the Knights of the Golden Circle for his dilemma, Carrington took steps to rescue his imprisoned sergeants. First he sent a telegram to Governor Yates that the four deserters were being harbored by the Clark County lodge of the Golden Circle. Next he secured the permission of his military superior, General Horatio Wright, and Governor Morton to commandeer a special train and take a force of 250 to rescue the sergeants, seize the "four deserters," and arrest Judge Constable. He carried out his mission with the finesse of Falstaff. Again he blamed the Golden Circle as a way of covering up his errors of judgment and his senseless measures.[70]

In the days that followed, Carrington raised the Golden Circle issue frequently. When antidraft riots appeared probable, he blamed the Knights. When deserters evaded authorities in the backcountry, he supposed that the Golden Circle was aiding the fugitives. In fact, he saw K.G.C. shadows in Democratic closets, partially because he equated all Democratic activity with treason.[71]

In mid-March, Carrington composed a lengthy report for his governor and President Lincoln. The document, borrowing heavily from Dr. Hiatt's earlier exposé, traced the origin of the Knights of the Golden Circle and explained the order's supposed signs, passwords, degrees, and objectives. "The fact is," Carrington wrote with an air of certainty, "that the *order has grown faster than the party leaders wished and has assumed a shape and bitterness that may not be controlled if it breaks forth, even by them.*" He closed his recital of

69. [Appleton's] *Annual Cyclopedia and Register of Important Events of the Year 1863* (New York, 1864), 472–73.

70. Carrington to Yates, telegram, March 10, 1863, in Yates Papers. Carrington ignores many of the facts and presents a very biased account in a twenty-four page manuscript, "The Constable Case," n.d., in the Henry B. Carrington Papers, Archives Division, Indiana State Library, Indianapolis. Judge Samuel H. Treat of the Southern District of Illinois reprimanded Carrington and intervened to get Judge Constable released.

71. Indianapolis *Daily Journal*, February 26, March 27, April 6, 1863; Carrington to Brig. Gen. Lorenzo Thomas, February 2, 1863, in Carrington Papers.

supposed facts and real fears with a paragraph endorsing the need for firmness on the home front and victories on the military front.[72]

The strange document may have been a justification of Governor Morton's prorogation of the Democrat-controlled and uncooperative state legislature and Colonel Carrington's series of arbitrary acts—censoring the mails, forbidding citizens to have arms, suppressing a newspaper, and denying Democrats the right to criticize. Anyway, Governor Morton took a trip to Washington, D.C., in April, 1863, and handed a copy of Carrington's memorandum to Lincoln, perhaps adding his own concern about the Golden Circle and the state of affairs in Indiana.[73]

After Morton returned to Indianapolis, he called a meeting of state officials to consider the challenge of subversion and the Golden Circle in the Hoosier State. The governor also expressed his concern publicly in speeches. A subversive society, he said, was widespread, powerful, and traitorous. The laws must be enforced and the order suppressed![74]

In early July, while Governor Morton was still busy campaigning against subversion and Democratic perfidy, Hoosiers were shocked by the invasion of Morgan's raiders. Confederate General John H. Morgan's mounted infantry, numbering about 2500 men, crossed the Ohio River on July 8 and headed for Corydon. When it became evident that the rebel raiders were heading for Ohio rather than Indianapolis, Colonel Carrington's superior, General Milo S. Hascall, ordered him to take a trainload of troops and intercept the invaders at the border. Carrington, in a drunken stupor at the time, failed to carry out the orders, and Morgan and his men crossed into Ohio. Carrington's superior, consequently, arrested him for "drunkenness and inefficiency" and removed him from command of the District of Indiana.[75]

Governor Morton intervened. He had the general who had arrested Carrington assigned elsewhere. And Carrington rather promptly regained command of the District of Indiana. His friends covered up for him.[76] Berry Sulgrove contended in his paper that Morgan had escaped because the Knights of the Golden Circle had aided the rebel raiders by providing food, horses, infor-

---

72. Carrington, "Memorandum of Condition of Public Affairs in Indiana, to be Submitted to the President and the Honorable Secretary of War," March 19, 1863, in Robert Todd Lincoln Papers. This document is included in *OR*, Ser. 2, Vol. II, 363–67.

73. Morton to Carrington, telegram, April 4, 1863, in Carrington Papers.

74. Indianapolis *Daily Journal*, April 20, 21, 1863.

75. Milo S. Hascall, "Report" (MS, September 25, 1865, in Archives Division, Indiana State Library). In the report, Hascall was reviewing his Indiana assignment.

76. William H. H. Terrell, a member of the Indianapolis "junta," doctored Hascall's manuscript before it was published in *Report of the Adjutant General of the State of Indiana* (8 vols.; Indianapolis, 1865–69), I, 276–77. The doctored document made no mention of Carrington's drunkenness, removal, or imprisonment.

mation, and encouragement—thus giving birth to another K.G.C. myth. Carrington promptly adopted the story as his own, using it (rather than his drunkenness and inefficiency) to explain why Morgan had escaped capture by Indiana troops. The story improved in the retelling; one added dimension was the supposition that Morgan's invasion was to correspond with a K.G.C.-sponsored uprising intended to lead to the establishment of a separate northwestern confederacy.[77]

A second July, 1863, event seemed to add substance to the Carrington-Morton contentions about the Golden Circle. It was the sudden appearance of George Bickley upon Indiana soil and his subsequent arrest and imprisonment.

After Bickley had made headlines in Kentucky and Tennessee during 1861, supposedly establishing K.G.C. headquarters in Knoxville, he slipped into obscurity. In September, 1861, he visited Richmond, begged for a colonelcy, and promised to raise a regiment of Kentucky cavalry for the Confederate army. Richmond authorities turned a deaf ear. Sometime later, he tried to convince Virginia's governor that he was raising a battalion of light dragoons and needed money and supplies. Again he received no encouragement or aid. On his way back to Knoxville he stopped over in Bristol, Tennessee, for a few days. There he penned a strange statement, compounded of braggodocio, self-deceit, and nonsense: "I have built up practical secession and inaugurated the greatest war of modern times." Then, early in 1863, Bickley received orders to report for "assignment to duty" as a surgeon to General Braxton Bragg's army, recuperating after the costly battle of Murfreesboro (Stones River).[78]

Bickley evidently served in Bragg's army for several months, for on June 10, 1863, he signed a voucher for pay from January 28 to June 9 as "surgeon, 29th N.C. Rgt." Evidently, however, he deserted and returned to the Shelbyville sector where he had earlier been living with a backwoods belle who had borne him a child. In a letter dated June 22, 1863, while he was supposedly serving as a surgeon in Bragg's army, he stated that he was "in the society of his family." [79]

While Bickley was at home, the Union lines pushed southward. He soon

77. Indianapolis *Daily Journal*, July 15, 22, 25, 1863; Henry B. Carrington, "The Morgan Raid Through Indiana, 1863" (MS, n.d., in Carrington Papers). James D. Horan, *Confederate Agent: A Discovery in History* (New York, 1954), 7–34, repeats the myth and embroiders upon it.

78. George Bickley to "Hon. Secretary of War, Confederate States," September 3, 1861, in Bickley Papers; Bickley to John Letcher, February 3, 1862, in Records of the Adjutant General's Office; Bickley, "Statement," September 14, 1862, Bristol, Tenn., and "Special Orders No. 23," January 28, 1863, Office of the Adjutant and Inspector Generals," both in Bickley Papers.

79. Voucher, signed by Bickley on June 10, 1863, in Records of the Adjutant General's Office; Bickley to J. A. Blakemore, June 22, 1863, mentioned in Blakemore to Bickley, June 27, 1863 (Shelbyville), in Bickley Papers.

found himself within Union lines and near the headquarters of Brigadier General Richard V. Johnson in Tullahoma. On July 6, rather brazenly, Bickley and his "family" presented themselves at Johnson's headquarters. He asked for a pass in his own name and gave the name of Eli Kinney of Cincinnati, his wife's brother, as a "reference." [80]

Raking their collective memory, officers at Johnson's headquarters associated Bickley's name with some of the Golden Circle exposés. One asked Bickley if he were the head of the Knights of the Golden Circle. Bickley denied any connection with the order but added that his "Uncle George" had been its founder. [81] General Johnson reported his suspicions to his superior, who promptly sent several telegrams to Cincinnati to check Bickley's references and claims. When Bickley returned two days later to pick up the pass promised him, General Johnson ordered the shifty-eyed applicant to proceed directly to Major General Ambrose E. Burnside, headquartered in Cincinnati and commanding the Department of the Ohio. Johnson also instructed a detective to trail the threesome and arrest them if they deviated from the prescribed route. [82]

Instead of reporting to General Burnside as directed, Bickley headed toward central Indiana. The detective trailing Bickley arrested him in Albany and confiscated his papers and trunks. Bickley again denied that he was connected to the Golden Circle in any way, again saying his Uncle George was the founder. The contents of the confiscated trunk proved Bickley a shameless liar as well as a pretender and a bigamist. His companion's trunk contained nothing save clothing, but a female detective found "the star and seal of the Order and some valuable papers hidden within the clothes she was wearing." [83]

The detective accompanied the Bickleys to Louisville, where they were placed in a military prison. Bickley's bubble had burst. Half a dozen Cincinnati citizens identified the prisoner as the man who had tried to found the Golden Circle in Cincinnati during the 1850s. One even characterized Bickley as "a very accomplished, uncommonly plausible and utterly untrustworthy individual." Eli Kinney, Bickley's onetime brother-in-law, wrote a most uncomplimentary statement. [84]

When the miscellaneous contents of Bickley's trunk were inventoried, they must have proved disappointing to officials interested in linking Bickley and the Golden Circle to Democrats. There was not a copy of a single letter to or

80. Major William M. Wiles, report for Maj. Gen. William S. Rosecrans, July 20, 1863, in Reports on the Order of American Knights.

81. Major John H. Wright to Wiles, August 1, 1863, *ibid.*

82. Wiles, "Statement," August 20, 1863, *ibid.*

83. Marcellus Mundy to Capt. A. C. Sample, report July 18, 1863, *ibid.*

84. Larz Anderson to "General [McLean]," report, February 6, 1864, Eli Kinney and David Cady, statement, n.d., both *ibid.*

from any Confederate official or northern Democrat. There was not a shred of evidence that a single castle of the Knights of the Golden Circle had been installed anywhere, north or south. In a sense, the contents of Bickley's trunk proved him a dreamer and a pretender.[85]

Federal officials evidently decided against a civil or military trial for Bickley, lest the proceedings and testimony discredit the K.G.C. exposés and rumors still circulating in the public press. So army officials kept Bickley in solitary confinement in Louisville, denying him visitors and counsel. His arrest, however, made headlines and seemed to validate contentions that the Golden Circle was more than a myth.[86]

While a prisoner, Bickley composed a four-page statement as a vindication. He insisted that the prewar organization he had founded possessed honorable goals of which every "red-blooded American" and expansionist might be proud. "As to the Bogus organization in the Northwestern States," he insisted, "I am as ignorant as a man in China—I have not been north since such a thing was known there and I have had nothing to do with it in any way, either directly or indirectly."[87]

Early in August, 1863, authorities secretly and expeditiously transferred Bickley to the state prison in Columbus. He wrote long letters successively to Secretary of State William H. Seward, General Jere T. Boyle, General William S. Rosecrans, Secretary of War Edwin M. Stanton, and Governor David Tod of Ohio.[88] After failing to get a hearing, he wrote a plaintive petition to President Lincoln, bidding for sympathy:

> I am now in a cell seven by three and a half feet, which contains besides myself, a bed, a stool, and water and urinal buckets. . . . In this living tomb, days, weeks, and long months pass, and I know nothing of what is taking place in my country. I hear the sound of no human voice save the whispering of the convicts, fellons [sic], and murderers who surround me. I am not allowed to write to my family or friends, to converse with anyone save as an officer may speak to me. In a word, sir, I am buried alive.[89]

85. "List of Items Found in the Possession of G. W. L. Bickley," July 17, 1863, *ibid.* The contents included several of Bickley's addresses and pronouncements as "President of the American Legion, K.G.C.," a pamphlet containing the rules and regulations of the K.G.C., a packet of letters, newspaper clippings, a song entitled "Land of My Birth" (evidently composed by Bickley), three packages of powder (later analyzed as opium, rhubarb, and gum gambage), and miscellaneous material.

86. Indianapolis *Daily Journal*, July 20, 21, 1863; Cincinnati *Daily Gazette*, August 6, 1863.

87. Bickley, "Statement of Facts," August 8, 1863, in Bickley Papers.

88. Each of the letters was lengthy, several covering four pages of fine script. Information incorporated was contradictory at times. Bickley's letter to Seward, dated August 14, 1863, is in the Baker-Turner Papers.

89. Bickley to Lincoln, December 18, 1863, in Bickley Papers.

30

Bickley received no reply from his president, but pursuant to instructions from the Secretary of War early in 1864, federal officials transferred him from Columbus to Fort Lafayette, in New York City. The prisoner continued his letter-writing campaign, albeit without any success. One of his letters, filling fourteen pages of legal-size foolscap, reached Lincoln's desk. Bickley promised that, if freed, he would "instruct" Golden Circle members "to support" the president and the administration—even helping to effect his reelection. "I feel that the time has arrived," he stated as if he still lived in a dream world, "that the *President can use me* and ought, therefore, to know me." [90] Federal officials let Bickley languish in his dungeonlike cell in Fort Lafayette for a year. On March 14, 1865, the War Department transferred him to Fort Warren, in Boston Harbor. There he awaited the end of the war and dreamt of what might have been.

Bickley's capture and incarceration, in mid-July of 1863, practically coincided with the change of the tide of the war. Gettysburg and Vicksburg, of course, helped immeasurably, as did the Union wedge splitting Tennessee. The peace crusade ebbed and Republicanism regained respectability. The Union Leagues, energized by political propaganda about the Golden Circle, prepared for the October and November elections.

Golden Circle suppositions as political propaganda surfaced here and there. Ohio, one of the political battlegrounds because of Vallandigham's gubernatorial candidacy, had more than its fair share. Some editors developed the theme that the state was "on the verge of civil war" because of the "deep and desperate schemes" promoted by the Knights of the Golden Circle. "The secret, sworn, and armed bands of the K.G.C.'s," the editor of the Cleveland *Leader* stated, "may present a living breastwork of defense to any itinerant traitor that may venture within our border." One of the most imaginative and most popular stories was that the Golden Circle had formulated a plot to take over the polls on election day, October 13, and elect Democrats, including Vallandigham, to office. The subversive society, according to this rumor, which was published in nearly every Republican newspaper in Ohio, planned to bring in fifty thousand voter-members from Kentucky and Illinois as the means to effect the daring scheme. [91] Apparently, the greater the rumor's implausibility, the greater its popularity.

Occasional Golden Circle stories appeared in the press during the early months of 1864, especially as political propaganda before the early April

90. Bickley to Lincoln, July 10, 1864, in John Nicolay–John Hay Papers, Illinois State Historical Library.

91. Cleveland *Leader*, September 17, 1863; *Ohio State Journal*, August 27, 1863; Cincinnati *Daily Commercial*, August 26, 1863. The *Commercial*'s headline read: "Copperhead Villainy! Sound the alarm."

elections.[92] After midyear, 1864, however, Golden Circle reports and rumors gave way to stories concerned with two other supposedly secret societies, the Order of American Knights and the Sons of Liberty. Those who composed the exposés of these two groups incorporated the supposition that Golden Circle members had just changed their cloaks, not their traitorous objectives.

Golden Circle rumors continued to appear in the newspapers, although infrequently. Joseph K. C. Forrest, preparing a circular to energize Union Leaguers, raised the same old bugaboo. The K.G.C., he stated in his circular, had made plans to "steal the fall elections" in Illinois.[93] Some Ohio Republicans devised a more fanciful tale: General George B. McClellan, the Democratic presidential nominee, had visited General Lee's headquarters to assure him he was an ally, fighting the battles of the South "on the free soil" of the North.[94] Some Pennsylvanians saw the ghostly hand of the Golden Circle behind the disaffection so widespread in Columbia County and fabricated a story about Knights defying the government and building a fortress in the mountains.[95] Even California contributed some K.G.C. tidbits on the eve of the 1864 elections.[96] Those in the forefront of the propaganda campaign, however, circulated reports and exposés concerning the Order of American Knights and the Sons of Liberty and viewed tellers of Golden Circle tales as out of date.

Democratic editors denied the K.G.C. rumors as they had from the very beginning. "The readers of Republican newspapers," wrote one,

> if the fact was not specifically announced, are well advised as to the approach of a ward, township, a city, or state election. Just on the eve of one of these events, the Administration or Abolition prints are filled, brimful, with all sorts of charges about "Knights of the Golden Circle," ready for treason, strategems [sic] and spoils, and all that stuff. Since the inauguration of the dominant political party in power, these charges have been rung against the Democracy in every conceivable shape, upon the eve of every election, no matter how insignificant its character.

The same editor, a Hoosier, also spoke sharply of Governor Morton and the constant barrage of Golden Circle rumors emanating from Indianapolis:

92. Indianapolis *Daily Journal*, April 1, 1864; Quincy (Ill.) *Whig*, May 6, 1864, quoted in the *Illinois State Register*, May 8, 1864.

93. Flyer, dated October 31, 1864, in Elihu B. Washburne Papers, Library of Congress.

94. Cincinnati *Daily Times*, October 20, 1864; Theodore C. Pease and James G. Randall (eds.), *Diary of Orville Hickman Browning* (2 vols.; Springfield, 1927–29), I, 537–38.

95. John G. Freeze, *History of Columbia County* (Philadelphia, 1890), 218; James M. Battle, *History of Columbia and Montour Counties* (Philadelphia, 1879), 192.

96. Gustav Brown to Capt. A. Jones Jackson, report, October 16, 1864, Capt. Robert Robinson to Brig. Gen. John S. Mason, November 1, 1864, both in *OR*, Ser. 1, Vol. L, 1018–19, 1037.

"After a diligent search of three years, he [Morton] has failed to produce any evidence to sustain his charges of the disloyalty of the Democratic party. The K.G.C., as far as the Democratic party is concerned, exists only in his imagination."[97]

After Lincoln won reelection in November, 1864, rumors of Golden Circle activity disappeared. The assassination of the president, however, brought forth one last round of K.G.C. rumors. The assassination plot, some supposed, was engineered by members of that nefarious society. A government agent visited George Bickley in his cell in Fort Warren to ask if the order, in one way or another, was involved in the death of the president.[98]

Rumors about the Golden Circle during the war years were really "much ado about nothing." Although Bickley was a true historical character, he did not possess the qualities to make his dreams come true. The exposés concocted and circulated so extensively in the upper Midwest consisted mostly of rumors, conjecture, and fancy. The Golden Circle was a bogeyman devised for political gain.

97. Indianapolis *Daily State Sentinel*, April 5, May 3, 1864.
98. James R. Gilmore to Holt, April 22, 1865, in Holt Papers; Maj. Harvey A. Allen, notations and enclosures, May 18, 1865, in Bickley Papers.

CHAPTER II

The Union Leagues: Patriotic Secret Societies

THE UNION LEAGUES that emerged during the war evolved out of social and political needs, nurtured by patriotism. Those established in the states of the upper Midwest were more partisan and less social and spontaneous than the Union Leagues that arose in Boston, Philadelphia, and New York. All, however, played an important role in supporting the war, underwriting northern morale, and contributing to the reelection of Lincoln in 1864.

A tidal wave of patriotism engulfed the North as word of the surrender of Fort Sumter shocked the nation. Flags flew on every hand "till the whole Northern heavens seemed a perfect aurora borealis of stars and stripes." Count Adam Gurowski, manning an observation post in the nation's capital, noted the public reaction and wrote in his diary: "I am not deceived in my faith in the North; the excitement, the wrath is terrible. Now the people is fusion, as bronze." [1]

Time—aided considerably by

Union military defeats, the devastating depression that afflicted the upper Midwest, and resurgent partisanship —tempered the emotions. As the wave of patriotism ebbed, some Republican leaders took steps to enlist public opinion in support of the war and the Lincoln administration. In Pekin, Illinois, several local leaders established a Union League club as a means to shape public opinion. The idea later swept over the upper Midwest like a prairie fire, and such clubs became a vibrant political force that left its stamp upon both the Civil War and Reconstruction.

Although the Union League was not fully formalized until midyear, 1862, its nebulous roots went back to the Wide Awakes of 1860 and the Union Clubs that sprang up in the border states early in 1861. The Wide Awakes, Republican party activists who helped to elect Lincoln to the presidency, existed in almost every northern state in 1860. They traced their beginnings to Hartford, Connecticut, where in March of 1860, local Republican activists provided an escort for Cassius M. Clay, a controversial Kentuckian scheduled to

1. (Chicago) *Prairie Farmer*, June 6, 1861; Adam Gurowski, *Diary . . . from March 4, 1861, to November 2, 1862* (Boston, 1862), 23.

speak at a party rally. Soon they formalized their activity, choosing the name Wide Awakes and devising an initiation ritual and some secret passwords. In the parades, each member carried a lighted oil lamp atop a four-foot stick, which could easily be converted into a weapon against rowdies bent upon disrupting a procession or party rally. The idea, well publicized in the Republican press, caught on, and Wide Awake clubs were organized by the thousands from Maine to Missouri. They lent color and excitement to the election campaign of 1860. On election day Wide Awakes policed the polls, challenging all persons not known to be voters. After Lincoln's election they sponsored jollifications and victory parades. Some twenty thousand with lighted torches marched down Broadway, making the famous New York street "a sea of flames its entire length." The Hartford Wide Awakes, who had started it all, marched in the parade carrying a large banner that read, "How the Original Jacobs Have Grown!" [2] The clubs disbanded after the election, but the experiment and experience served as a seedbed for the Union Leagues that developed two years later.

The Union League that arose in Illinois in 1862 also drew ideas and inspiration from the Union Clubs that had developed in the border states, especially Missouri, Kentucky, and Tennessee. Unconditional Union men in Missouri and Kentucky turned toward secret associations to counter the work of secessionists. In Missouri, for example, patriots in St. Louis organized a Union Club to nullify the efforts of Governor Claiborne Jackson to take the state into the Confederacy. Prominent citizens, including Francis Preston Blair, Jr., helped to organize a semisecret association that stressed the need to arm, organize, and control local militia companies. In various communities outside of St. Louis, Unionists readied themselves to oppose secessionists with "knives, hatchets, shotguns, or anything they can get their hands on." [3] Functioning as committees of correspondence, the Union Clubs in Missouri created a loose statewide organization for which the St. Louis club acted as mother hen. [4]

In Kentucky, John M. Delph, the newly elected mayor of Louisville, and George D. Prentice, former Yankee and able editor of the Louisville *Daily Journal*, joined hands to organize the state's first Union Club in January of 1861. It was to be a secret club "to make steadfast Union men known to each

2. Freeport (N.Y.) *Wide Awake*, November 3, 7, 1860, cited in Clement M. Silvestro, "None but Patriots: The Union Leagues in Civil War and Reconstruction" (Ph.D. dissertation, University of Wisconsin, 1959), 14. The origin of the Wide Awakes in Connecticut is treated in John D. DeWitt, *Lincoln in Hartford* (Hartford, 1962), 2–3.

3. John P. Lancaster to James O. Broadhead, July 3, 1861, in James O. Broadhead Papers, Missouri Historical Society, St. Louis.

4. (St. Louis) *Missouri Democrat*, September 6, 1861.

other, and accessible to each other in case of trouble."[5] The Louisville Union Club sent out agents to organize like associations in every congressional district. The approach of the August elections served as an incentive to join, but Prentice played another ace. He published Dr. Anthony A. Urban's exposé of the Knights of the Golden Circle in his newspaper to spur the agents and organizers of Union Clubs to action.[6] Although some of the local clubs were loosely organized and little more than haphazard mutual protection societies, others were active and most effective, guided by zealous patriots who promoted weekly meetings, evolved a ritual and initiation ceremonies, and adopted signs of recognition, passwords, and identification badges. The use of the Golden Circle bogeyman to spur Union Club expansion and activity proved so effective that the state organization later published its own exposé.[7]

The Union Club movement, successful and extensive in Kentucky, spread to Maryland and Tennessee as well as some sectors of Indiana and southern Ohio. Baltimore patriots took the lead in Maryland, organizing a Union Club in September, 1861, "to oppose the secret machinations of the enemies of our government, upon the same principle of the Union Clubs of Kentucky."[8] A number of such clubs also sprang up in some of the border counties, especially in Indiana and the Cincinnati area where antiwar sentiment was popular. Hoosier patriots, in midyear of 1861, made an effort to establish a statewide federation of Union Clubs, "organized on a military basis" with signs, a ritual, and a cryptographic alphabet, but the movement died aborning.[9]

The Union Club movement also spread from Kentucky into eastern Tennessee, where antisecessionist sentiment flourished. But after the start of the war, Confederate troops overran the area, forcing some of the Union Club leaders to flee for their lives. One such club official, who made his way as a fugitive to Tazewell County, Illinois, provided a positive and tangible link between the Union Clubs of eastern Tennessee and the Union League organized in Pekin on June 25, 1862.

Patriots of Pekin, a city known for its distilling industry before the war, had every reason to be concerned with the turn of events by midyear, 1862.

5. Robert M. Kelly, "The Secret Union Organization in Kentucky in 1861," in *Sketches of War History, 1861–1865: Papers Prepared for the Military Order of the Loyal Legion of the United States, 1888–1889* (Cincinnati, 1890), 3.

6. Louisville *Daily Journal*, July 18, 1861.

7. United States National Union Club, *K.G.C.: An Authentic Exposition of the Origins, Objects, and Secret Work of the Organization Known as the Knights of the Golden Circle* (Louisville, 1862). The booklet, interestingly, came off the same press that printed Prentice's Louisville *Journal*.

8. *Proceedings of the National Convention, Union League of America, Held at Cleveland, May 20 and 21, 1863, with Reports, Etc., Etc.* (Washington, D.C., 1863), 10, 20–21.

9. Items entitled "Charter," "Cryptographic Alphabet," and "Private Instructions" are in the William H. English Papers, Indiana Historical Society Library.

The farm depression of 1861–1862 and the loss of the southern market had brought hardship to residents of Pekin and Tazewell County, for much of the whiskey had formerly been shipped down the river to parched southern throats. As farm prices tumbled and financial and commercial firms experienced hard times, disaffection spread, undermining prowar sentiment and the Republican hold upon county offices. Democratic critics grew bolder and more blatant, the more vulgar abusing Republicans or uttering sentiments that bordered on treason. Furthermore, Democratic successes in the April, 1862, elections worried Republicans seeking ways to revive their party and prepare ground for the fall political wars.

George H. Harlow, a prominent Pekin Republican, envisioned a secret patriotic league, similar to the one that had functioned in eastern Tennessee, as the means to check the Democratic tide and rally his party's members to support Lincoln and the war. Harlow, a onetime Whig, had come to Pekin from northern New York State in 1854. Starting his Pekin career as a partner in a store, he turned to buying and selling grain, becoming a successful and wealthy commission merchant. He became active in organizing the Republican party in Pekin, and his business office also became county headquarters for distributing party literature.[10]

As Democrats became more defiant and overbearing, Harlow and some friends talked of organizing a home guard as well as some kind of secret association of unconditional Union men. On June 25, 1862, Harlow and ten others, including two Pekin residents who had once belonged to a Union Club in eastern Tennessee, met to effect a local organization. Briefed by his friends from Tennessee, Harlow described the organization and activity of the Union Clubs of eastern Tennessee and suggested a patriotic dark lantern society along the same lines. He made a fervent presentation. Speaking of fidelity to flag and country and of patriots "who hated treason," he repeated again and again such phrases as "our dear old flag" and "liberty and Union." Harlow urged "that some steps be taken whereby true Union men could be known and depended upon in an emergency" through an organization which might be a "powerful instrument in the hands of true Union men in sustaining and encouraging the [Lincoln] administration in its efforts to put down treason and traitors; to maintain the laws; and to keep inviolate the principles of the constitution and the Declaration of Independence."[11]

---

10. *Proceedings of the State Grand Council of the U.L.A. of Illinois, at Its Second Annual Session, Held at Springfield, Wednesday, September 2nd, A.D. 1863* . . . (Springfield, 1863), 1.

11. *Ibid.*, 9, 12; George H. Harlow Record Book (as Grand State Secretary of the Union League of Illinois, 1862–1865) (microfilm copy in State Historical Society of Wisconsin Library, Madison). Harlow's original record book is in the possession of the Union League Club of Chicago.

Harlow and his ten associates then declared themselves to be members of the Union League, the name they selected for their new secret patriotic society. While candles flickered upon an improvised altar, one of the former Tennesseans administered the same oath taken by those who had joined the Union Clubs in eastern Tennessee. The new dark lantern members adopted a hastily drawn set of bylaws, borrowed portions of their ritual from the Masonic order, contrived some passwords and signs of recognition, and devised an elaborate initiation procedure. Hoping to extend their society to neighboring communities, the Pekin-based secret society named one of its members "a traveling agent."

The traveling agent, the Reverend John W. M. Vernon, infused with the spirit and energy of the apostles of old, found converts for the cause. In July he succeeded in establishing a council in nearby Peoria with the assistance of Enoch Emery, editor of the city's Republican newspaper. Emery's endorsement opened other doors. Converts, mostly Republicans, established a council in Springfield on August 4, 1862. In the weeks that followed, perhaps because the fall elections intensified political interest, councils were also established in Bloomington, Kingston, Decatur, and La Salle.

Joseph Medill, editor of the influential Chicago *Tribune*, envisioned the Union League as an auxiliary of the Republican party and helped initiate a chapter in Chicago. For some time, prominent Chicago Republicans had wondered how to corral the votes of the independent voter, and a secret patriotic society seemed like an excellent political stratagem. Proposing patriotic clubs "like in Kentucky," one wrote, "I think we can get in a multitude of loyal Democrats." [12] Medill's participation in the movement practically ensured its success by giving the new secret society respectability.

As the Union League added new lodges and new converts, the Pekin council set up a state convention for September 25, 1862, in Bloomington. The organizers were pleased with the turnout, for twenty-five delegates representing twelve councils participated. Furthermore, the delegates were "enthusiastic" and confident that their work would aid the country in its struggle for "life and liberty." Medill, widely respected in Republican circles, represented the Chicago council. The delegates predicted that the order would spread and play a role in the fall elections. Mark Bangs of the Lacon council (Marshall County) offered the opinion that the new dark lantern society would contribute to a resurgence of Republicanism and the demise of the Democracy.

The delegates set to work in a hurry. They drafted a constitution for the state council, revised the ritual and "unwritten work," and standardized the signs, grips, and passwords. Then they elected Bangs, a state circuit judge,

12. Grant Goodrich to Elihu B. Washburne, May 29, 1862, in Elihu B. Washburne Papers, Library of Congress. Goodrich proposed organizing patriotic clubs "like in Kentucky."

grand president and Harlow, still the key figure in the organization, secretary. Medill accepted the chairmanship of the executive committee. Before adjourning, the newly organized Illinois Grand Council set its next meeting date "the second Wednesday of January [1863]." [13]

But the optimism so prevalent at the Bloomington meeting of the Union League soon evaporated. Public reaction to the many arbitrary arrests made in Illinois during the "August roundup" and to Lincoln's preliminary emancipation proclamation of September 22 played into Democratic hands. So did the defeat of General John Pope's army at Second Bull Run. Some translated the economic grievances of the 1861–1862 depression into anti-Lincoln sentiment. Enlistments lagged and patriotism retreated in the face of revived partisanship. Democrats gleefully predicted that their party would win the November elections and capture control of the next state legislature.

Republicans fought back. They brought out the Golden Circle skeleton from the closet and made the Chicago *Tribune*'s exposé of August 26 a political document. [14] Harlow, functioning as executive secretary of the Union League, intensified his efforts to establish new councils in Illinois. He succeeded in organizing some here and there, arguing the need to counter the work of the Golden Circle. "Union societies in opposition to the K.G.C. are being formed in Egypt [a term applied to the southernmost counties in Illinois]," the Republican newspaper in Springfield reported; "one was organized in Williamson County. The object is to sustain the Administration and the war." [15]

Harlow also urged that efforts be made to extend the Union League beyond Illinois' borders, especially into the neighboring states. In October, Medill, in behalf of the executive committee, authorized John Wilson (onetime land agent for the Illinois Central Railroad Company and a man with many contacts) "to organize councils in any part of the United States." While on a tour of duty in Washington, D.C., Wilson persuaded some midwesterners stationed there to form a chapter. The Washington council, which, Wilson later claimed, was established on October 27, 1862, had a rather tenuous existence in its first year. [16]

Despite Harlow's exertions, the movement failed to make much headway. After the fall elections it languished for several months. Many prominent Republicans viewed the Union League unfavorably. Some, like Gustav Koerner (a prominent Forty-eighter and later a governor of Illinois), regarded all secret

13. *Proceedings of the State Grand Council . . . of Illinois*, 10–11.

14. Chicago *Daily Tribune*, August 26, 1862; Carbondale *Times*, n.d., quoted in the (Springfield) *Illinois State Journal*, September 10, 1862.

15. *Illinois State Journal*, August 28, 1862.

16. *Proceedings of the State Grand Council . . . of Illinois*, 10–12.

societies skeptically. "But although much urged," Koerner later wrote, "I did not join the League, either then or afterwards, as I had a decided antipathy against all secret political . . . societies or lodges." [17]

Harlow's apprehensions about the fall elections proved to be most realistic. He lost his bid to retain the clerkship of the circuit court for a second two-year term; in fact, Democrats swept all of the offices of Tazewell County. Furthermore, Democrats won most of the congressional seats and captured full control of the state legislature, setting up a confrontation with the Republican governor, Richard Yates.

Yates expressed alarm as Democratic braggarts promised to hogtie him and shear his powers. Always apprehensive, he had earlier asked for authority to declare martial law. [18] Now he shivered in his boots as he sparred with the legislature, which convened early in January, 1863. Yates's aide, Joseph K. C. Forrest, tried to discredit the trouble-making legislators by insinuating that some of them belonged to the Knights of the Golden Circle and that their goal was "revolutionary action." [19]

As Yates and the Copperhead-controlled legislature feuded, the Illinois version of the Union League met in its second state conference, this time in Springfield, on January 14, 1863. Aroused by the insults and intimidation the state legislature was visiting upon the governor and chastened by the election returns of the previous November, the Republican delegates to the state council sought ways to check the Democratic tide and the peace movement.

The situation was discouraging, however. The Union League, active before the fall election, had withered on the vine in the six weeks that followed. Only ten delegates representing seven Illinois counties showed up at the state council meeting of January 14. Neither Joseph Medill nor Enoch Emery, perhaps the two most prominent members, attended. Furthermore, John Wilson, whom the executive committee had authorized to establish councils outside of Illinois, defected and organized his own patriotic secret society, a rival for members and attention.

Harlow, still the guiding spirit of the Illinois-based organization, made a Herculean effort to rally support for the league. He talked emotionally of the need for the Union League, and he assured the handful attending that all it needed to make it "a complete success" was "the encouragement and co-operation of Union men." [20] Before adjourning, the State Grand Council au-

17. Gustav Koerner, *Memoirs of Gustav Koerner, 1809–1898* (2 vols.; Cedar Rapids, Iowa, 1909), II, 433.

18. Richard Yates to Edwin M. Stanton, telegram, August 7, 1862, in Lafayette C. Baker–Levi C. Turner Papers, Records of the Adjutant General's Office, Records of the Office of the Judge Advocate General, National Archives.

19. *Missouri Democrat*, January 7, 1863; Chicago *Daily Tribune*, January 6, 7, 1863.

20. *Proceedings of the State Grand Council . . . of Illinois*, 12.

thorized Harlow and Professor Daniel Wilkins (also a member of the executive committee) to call upon Governor Yates and ask for his aid and advice.

In a "long and very interesting interview," Harlow and Wilkins described the league's aims, the possibilities, and the "discouraging prospects." Yates, politically astute, envisioned a revitalized Union League as an instrument to undermine the Democratic-dominated legislature, reactivate the Republican party, and counter the peace movement. He therefore gave the league his blessing and urged that it be extended to "every town and county in the State." Furthermore, he promised to give the struggling organization his "hearty cooperation and assistance." [21]

Yates was as good as his word. He put the support of his office and his party behind the league, and with Yates's endorsement goading them, members of the executive committee met in Peoria six days later, on January 20. Buoyed by Harlow's renewed enthusiasm, both Medill and Emery were there. They promised to use the columns of their newspapers to promote and support the league. The attendant members plotted "a vigorous campaign" for members and appointed agents to crisscross the state and locate "true Union men" who would organize local councils. The committee authorized the agents to administer the Union League oath to local Republican leaders, and Harlow, as executive secretary, promised to send out charters in the name of the State Grand Council. Medill also endorsed the suggestion that the league spread to the nearby states, especially Iowa, Wisconsin, Michigan, Indiana, and Ohio. [22]

Harlow's work as executive secretary evolved into a full-time job, for the viciously partisan actions of the Democratic-controlled state legislature proved to be a powerful stimulant, and the league spread rapidly. Encouraging news came from every corner of the state. After an old friend of President Lincoln took over the leadership, the Springfield council grew in size and importance. A member reported in February that "the League numbers already some four hundred of our most loyal and best citizens." A Republican living in northern Illinois gloated, "Union Leagues are springing up like the Wide a Wak Companys [*sic*] did at the last election. We are getting cut and dried for the Knights [of the Golden Circle] & we intend to give them both ends of the poker if they don't behave themselves." [23]

The spread of the Union League also spurred a revival of the Republican party, the two working hand in hand. Republicans, functioning through the Union Leagues in their local communities, passed resolutions supporting the Union, lauded the heroics of the soldiery, and denounced "treason" on the

---

21. *Ibid.*
22. *Ibid.*
23. P. P. Enos to Lyman Trumbull, February 6, 1863, in Lyman Trumbull Papers, Library of Congress; Charles C. Royce to Washburne, February 23, 1863, in Washburne Papers.

home front. Patriotic fervor prompted one Union Leaguer to write, "Traitors are being informed that this *Government must* and shall be preserved." [24]

The phenomenal growth of the Union League in Illinois, added to a desire to keep their stepchild in hand, prompted Medill and Harlow to suggest a regional conference of the order. Medill, with the aid of Harlow and Emery, drafted and signed a circular asking the state's councils of the Union League to select delegates to a regional conference to meet in Chicago on March 25, along with representatives from Wisconsin, Ohio, Michigan, Iowa, the District of Columbia, and "perhaps other states." The purpose, the circular said, was to form "a national organization." [25] Harlow and Medill may also have been influenced by the fact that some patriotic leagues in eastern cities were considering organizing nationally. They did not want a society which they had founded and nurtured to fall into the hands of others.

THE UNION LEAGUES that had developed in Philadelphia, New York, and Boston had no organic link to the organization founded in Illinois and spreading over the upper Midwest. There was more spontaneity and less calculation, less partisanship and more social emphasis. Each of the Union Leagues that sprouted in Philadelphia, New York, and Boston developed in its own way.

As early as 1859, an organization called the Union League existed in New York City. It was composed essentially of conservatives, including some Democrats, who deplored sectionalism and abolitionism and claimed an especial reverence for the Constitution and the Union. Its president, James Monroe, openly endorsed the Constitutional Union party ticket in 1860. In fact, Monroe asked "fellow citizens" to organize "under the flag and swell the ranks of the Union League" and to vote for "the Constitution and the Union." Such action, and "the help of God," he said, would "preserve the Temple of Liberty." [26]

Because he hitched his wagon to a losing horse in the presidential sweepstakes in 1860, Monroe saw his New York–based Union League disintegrate and die. The northern reaction to the Fort Sumter affair also helped, for those who preached compromise and moderation in the months that followed received naught but scorn. Before the year ended Monroe's organization was dead and buried, almost unmourned. [27]

The same name but with a new supporting cast came into prominence in

24. H. G. McPike to Trumbull, February 23, 1863, in Trumbull Papers.

25. *Proceedings of the State Grand Council . . . of Illinois*, 13.

26. [Union League], *Preamble, Constitution, and Rules and Regulations of the Union League* (New York, 1859), and [Union League], *Address of the National Executive Committee of the Union League to the Citizens of the United States. . . .* (New York, 1860), 13–15, both quoted in Guy J. Gibson, "Lincoln's League: The Union League Movement During the Civil War" (Ph.D. dissertation, University of Illinois, 1957), 2–6.

27. Gibson, "Lincoln's League," 2–7.

New York and Philadelphia little more than a year later. These organizations owed their origin directly to several men who dominated the United States Sanitary Commission, a volunteer association dedicated to supplementing the work of the U.S. Medical Bureau. Prominent members of the commission in Philadelphia and New York became the founders of the Union Leagues in their respective cities.

Wolcott Gibbs, a New Yorker and a member of the executive committee of the U.S. Sanitary Commission, conceived the idea of "a patriotic club" to foster "sentiments of nationality" as against "state particularity" in mid-year, 1862. He advanced the idea to follow committee members while they were all returning via train to their homes in Philadelphia and New York. After Gibbs and several colleagues had disembarked in Philadelphia, the Reverend Henry W. Bellows and George Templeton Strong continued discussing Gibbs's idea until the train reached New York. "It was then and there resolved," Bellows wrote later, "to make the idea a fact." [28]

The Philadelphians, however, acted first. George H. Boker and Judge John Innes Clark Hare, meeting one day in mid-November, talked of withdrawing from "social relations with disloyal men" and forming a club of their own. Boker, moved to action, went to the offices of the *North American*, a Republican newspaper, to discuss the idea with Morton McMichael, the editor. Together they compiled a list of prospective members, all unconditional supporters of the war. They next sounded out several of the prospects and received a favorable response. Benjamin Gerhard offered his home as a meeting place. A dozen attended the organizational meeting of November 15 at Gerhard's home. Judge Hare, one of the guiding spirits, led the discussion and emphasized the need to support the Lincoln administration and the war. One who attended later stated the objective of the club: "It was to be a center of sentiment for Union men." [29]

The second meeting took place at Boker's house on November 22. At several successive meetings the would-be members proposed articles of association, and the organization gradually evolved from a social club to a patriotic one. In drafting the statement of organization, affiliation with the Republican administration was deleted and stress put upon the general goal of supporting the war and the Union, thus attracting individuals who might not have joined a more partisan association. [30]

28. Henry W. Bellows, *Historical Sketch of the Union League Club of New York: Its Origin, Organization, and Work, 1863–1879* (New York, 1879), 11, 19–20; Allan Nevins and Milton H. Thomas (eds.), *The Diary of George Templeton Strong: The Civil War* (4 vols.; New York, 1952), III, 307.

29. George H. Boker, quoted in Gibson, "Lincoln's League," 41.

30. Maxwell Whiteman, *Gentlemen in Crisis: The First Century of the Union League of Philadelphia, 1862–1962* (Philadelphia, 1975), relates the founding of the Philadelphia Union League in detailed and scholarly fashion.

By the time of the eighth meeting, the name had changed from Union Club to Union League. The membership elected William T. Meredith as president and Boker as secretary. The new patriotic organization sponsored weekly public meetings at which prominent speakers discussed "national topics." It created a "board of publication" to raise funds and publish patriotic tracts for distribution "throughout the country." It generated nationalism and insisted that "loyalty to country" was a proper qualification of candidates for public office. It attracted the city's intellectuals and soon gained a national reputation for its activities, especially the mass meetings and the flood of pamphlets. Boker composed a circular emphasizing the organization's patriotic objectives. "It does not seek to influence elections," he stated, "farther than to prevent offices falling into the hands of disloyal or notoriously incapable men." [31] Thanks to the energy and enthusiasm of Boker, the Philadelphia league established chapters in other nearby cities and soon considered promoting a national organization under its own aegis.

The Philadelphia story had a sequel in New York City. Henry Bellows, already national president of the U.S. Sanitary Commission, became the central figure in the establishment of the Union League of New York. Like its Philadelphia counterpart, the New York organization passed through several stages. It started out as the "National Club," seeking to fuse social prestige and patriotic sentiment, but gradually evolved into the Union League. "Absolute and unqualified loyalty" to the federal government and "unwavering support" of the war became the conditions of membership. "The urgency of the present great national crisis, and the revolutionary schemes which some unprincipled men are plotting to accomplish," a central statement read, "make it the immediate duty of all loyal citizens to organize themselves [so] as to give the most efficient support to the national cause." [32]

In formalizing their patriotic club, the New Yorkers borrowed the organizational pattern and articles of association of their Philadelphia brethren. Besides Bellows and George Templeton Strong, sixty-four others signed up as charter members, including such notables as William Cullen Bryant, Francis Lieber, and Franklin H. Delano. The organization rented the "hideous but spacious" Henry Parish house on Union Square for $6,000 a year as headquarters, named Robert B. Minturn, a merchant prince, president, and set up a series of dinners as well as public meetings. It sponsored a gigantic public

31. Boker circular letter (put out early in 1863), quoted in Gibson, "Lincoln's League," 41. Also see Union Club of Philadelphia, *Proceedings of a Meeting of the Union Club of Philadelphia, Held at the League House, December 27, 1870* (Philadelphia, 1871), 23, 25–26.

32. Union League Club of New York, *Report of Executive Committee, Constitution, By-laws, and Poll of Members, January, 1864* (New York, 1864), 5, quoted in Gibson, "Lincoln's League," 62.

rally on March 14, 1863, at the Cooper Institute, with former senator Andrew Johnson of Tennessee as principal speaker. An enthusiastic crowd repeatedly cheered as Johnson turned on his best oratory, reported in an uncomplimentary fashion by the sniveling correspondent of the London *Times*, who challenged the comments in Republican newspapers as "unionist utterances." [33]

The founding fathers of the Union League of New York had trouble deciding whether they should openly endorse emancipation and denounce states' rights. In the end they watered down the pledge of loyalty, disappointing some of the zealous patriots. One complained that the action opened membership even to notorious Copperheads: "Fernando Wood could sign its [revised] test of membership." [34]

By the time the Union League of New York opened its clubhouse on May 12, it had a membership list of 350. At its first "open house" George Bancroft, already a famous historian, and Henry Bellows gave short speeches. George Templeton Strong, in attendance at the affair, gloried in its success. This was proof that New York's aristocracy endorsed the war; the league in effect informed England and France that "the intelligent, cultivated, [and] gentlemanly caste" in the North supported the war. [35]

Some of the more imaginative New York members talked of establishing "an affiliated organization . . . throughout the country." Several contacted Union League members of Philadelphia about a joint venture to develop a countrywide "League of loyal citizens." The idea, however, found small favor with the general membership, and so the leaders turned toward devising a coalition of the three clubs in the cities of New York, Philadelphia, and Boston to consider "establishing some common basis of action." [36] If measures could be taken to unite the Union League clubs into one gigantic confederation, the prestigious New York club did not want to be caught on the outside looking in.

In many ways, the Union Club of Boston followed the same path as the New York and Philadelphia organizations. The Boston-based club also started out as a socially oriented one, whose members happened to support the war and the Lincoln administration. Several members of the pretentious Somerset Club, upset over the lukewarm patriotism of many compatriots, founded "an establishment" as "a rallying point for the gentlemen of intelligence, public spirit, and social prominence who believed that the Union could be preserved

33. (London) *Times*, March 31, 1863.

34. Nevins and Thomas (eds.), *Diary of Strong*, III, 302. Fernando Wood had previously served three terms as a Democratic mayor and had been elected to Congress in 1862. He was a well-known opponent of the war in 1863.

35. *Ibid.*, III, 321–22.

36. Bellows, *Historical Sketch*, 44, 57–77.

by the announced policy of President Lincoln." Membership would be limited to "clubable men, who not only thought and felt alike upon the great questions of the day, but who would find it pleasant to meet socially and converse upon these questions." As in New York, the roots of the Boston club fed upon eastern snobbery. "We want a place," one of the founders said, "where gentlemen may pass an evening without hearing copperhead talk." [37]

Samuel Gray Ward, sole representative of Baring-Brothers & Company in the United States, took the lead in founding the Boston club. He was a close personal friend of Ralph Waldo Emerson, both being charter members of a discussion-and-dining group, the Saturday Club. After some preliminary discussion sessions, which took place in his business office, Ward arranged "a more formal meeting" at his home on February 4, 1863. John Murray Forbes, a wealthy Boston merchant and entrepreneur, and Amos Lawrence, one of the "lords of the looms," lent prestige to the gathering by their presence. Those assembled agreed upon the appointment of "an organizing committee of fifteen." [38]

The organizing committee listed several articles of faith for the proposed club, limiting membership to those who possessed "an unqualified loyalty to the Constitution and the Union" and "unwavering support of the Federal Government in efforts for the suppression of the Rebellion." The committee invited selected citizens, including Charles Sumner, to attend a meeting to hear a report on "organizing a Club in this city, and to take action thereon." [39]

At its organizational meeting of February 27, 1863, the club formalized its objectives and bylaws, elected Edward Everett president, and rented the spacious Abbott Lawrence residence overlooking Boston Common as its headquarters. By mid-March, membership passed the four hundred mark.

John Murray Forbes directed the club toward support of policies advocated by Radical Republicans, at times scuffing the scruples of the more conservative members. Forbes urged both of the state's U.S. senators, Charles Sumner and Henry Wilson, to join the organization and lend it their prestige. "The other clubs here are haunts of hunkerism," Forbes wrote to Sumner; "this one we hope to make useful and pleasant too. . . . The Governor [John A. Andrew] is with us, and most of the good and true." [40] Forbes, a close personal friend of Governor Andrew, not only kept the state's chief executive informed of the club's activities but even solicited his aid in building up the membership.

37. Samuel L. Thorndike, *The Past Members of the Union Club of Boston and a Brief Sketch of the History of the Club, July, 1893* (Boston, 1893), 607.

38. *Ibid.*, 605–609.

39. Printed circular [of the Union Club of Boston], dated February 28, 1863, and addressed to Charles Sumner, in Charles Sumner Papers, Widener Library, Harvard University, Cambridge, Mass.

40. John Murray Forbes to Charles Sumner, March 4, 1863, *ibid.*

On April 9, 1863, the Boston Union Club sponsored an immense public rally in Boston. Many of "the leading men of the state" attended. Edward Everett, one of the country's best-known orators, gave a stirring patriotic speech, urging all northerners to prove their loyalty by giving full support to the Lincoln administration and the war.[41]

THE UNION LEAGUE that was spreading from Illinois into neighboring states in 1863 had little in common with the socially oriented eastern clubs developing in Philadelphia, New York, and Boston. In the upper Midwest the league was developing as the strong right arm of the Republican party; in the eastern cities the league was more a by-product of patriotism and less an auxiliary of the party. Republican governors in the upper Midwest actively supported the league, sometimes playing the main role in its organization or expansion. In Illinois, the Union League did not begin to flourish until Governor Yates gave it his blessing and full support in January, 1863. In Indiana the league was actually organized from the top down, directly out of the governor's office.

Governor Oliver P. Morton, using a one-hundred-dollar "gift" from a banker friend, sent telegrams to three "loyal men from each county" (invariably Republicans) asking them to meet in Indianapolis on January 8, 1863, in an "emergency" and secret session. At that secret session, Morton regaled the assembled Republicans with tales of subversion and Golden Circle activity. He expressed the fear that the Copperhead-dominated state legislature "would attempt to wrest the Government from the constituted authorities & revolutionize." He also related rumors about a plot to seize the Indianapolis arsenal as the first step of a conspiracy to take the Northwest out of the Union.[42]

After making his impassioned plea, Morton instructed the "delegates" to return home and counter Copperhead duplicity by forming "secret societies" and organizing for political gain at the grass-roots level. Members of Morton's junto provided assistance. Colonel Henry B. Carrington, the governor's right-hand military man, composed some treason tales about the Knights of the Golden Circle to provide incentive for the organizers and to give the new Republican secret society a raison d'être. William R. Holloway, the governor's brother-in-law and personal secretary, provided the local organizers with an exposé/booklet about the K.G.C. and a set of instructions on how to organize local and county chapters of the new patriotic society. Berry R. Sulgrove

41. Boston *Daily Traveler*, April 10, 1863, cited in Silvestro, "None but Patriots," 60. Gibson, "Lincoln's League," devotes twenty-six pages (78–103) to the story of the Union Club of Boston.
42. Calvin Fletcher Diary, January 2, 5, 11, 1863 (MS in Calvin Fletcher Papers, Indiana Historical Society Library). Fletcher, a millionaire, was both friend and confidant of Governor Morton.

of the Indianapolis *Journal* published a two-column story about the Golden Circle as political propaganda.[43]

The governor's efforts promptly bore fruit. The "Lincoln Leagues"— which later accepted the name Union Leagues—emerged almost overnight. Within weeks they existed in every county, and by midyear Indiana boasted more than a hundred councils and more than twenty thousand members.

In Michigan, Governor Austin Blair encouraged the organization of Union League councils in cities and counties. The early organizers secured charters from George Harlow, executive secretary of the Illinois Grand Council and promoter of a regional association. Early in 1863, however, councils in Michigan formed their own state organization. State pride prompted sixty councils to surrender the charters received from Harlow and substitute those provided by the state officers in Michigan.[44]

Iowa's first Union Club was organized at a nonpartisan "Union meeting" held in Keokuk late in February, 1863. Moderate Republicans, supported by some "War Democrats," suggested that old party lines were obsolete and unwanted until the Union was "saved and the Rebellion only a thing of the past."[45] Fearing that a bipartisan movement might dissolve their party, however, Republican spokesmen like Frank W. Palmer, editor of the *Iowa State Register*, persuaded the party's hierarchy to establish a series of Republican-sponsored Union Clubs and to make them a secret and militant arm of the party. Harold M. Hoxie, a federal marshal who doubled as a member of the state's Republican central committee, provided a stimulant in the form of tales about Golden Circle activity in Iowa. Hoxie received an assist from Dubuque Republicans, who argued that a Union League was needed to counteract the K.G.C. and "an organized conspiracy . . . to revolutionize the government."[46]

Working behind the scenes, Republican leaders established Union Clubs in a dozen counties and on March 20 fused them into a Union League at Ottumwa.[47] The new league made an effort to support the "patriotic" (that is,

---

43. *Ibid.*, January 2, 1863; Henry B. Carrington to Abraham Lincoln, January 14, 1863, in Robert Todd Lincoln Papers, Library of Congress; William R. Holloway, instructions on how to organize and K.G.C. exposé/pamphlet, in Henry K. English Papers, Indiana Division, Indiana State Library; Indianapolis *Daily Journal*, January 19, 1863. This account relied upon Carrington's composition.

44. Gibson, "Lincoln's League," 287. Gibson devotes considerable space to the Michigan scene.

45. Keokuk (Iowa) *Gate City*, March 5, 1863, quoted in Olynthus B. Clark, *The Politics of Iowa During the Civil War and Reconstruction* (Iowa City, 1911), 179.

46. Harold M. Hoxie to Stanton, September 18, 1862, in Baker-Turner Papers; Dubuque *Herald*, March 11, 1863, denied the allegations, stating, "These men have no knowledge of such an organization [the K.G.C.], for there is none. They are making this the pretext for their organization simply that they may be allowed to proceed without interference."

47. (Des Moines) *Iowa State Register*, February 18, March 25, 1863.

Republican) ticket in the April election and claimed some credit for the favorable results. "Our *Union* organization is perfect," one of the sponsors wrote to Governor Samuel J. Kirkwood, "and we have good reason to be proud of our first effort." [48]

Governor Kirkwood lent a hand to the practice of beating the bushes in search of Golden Circle members and encouraging the spread of the Union League as a patriotic countermeasure. [49] On June 16, the day before the Republican state convention met in Des Moines, those active in the Union League held "a secret conclave" and organized a "Grand Council for the State of Iowa." They listened to patriotic speeches, adopted resolutions stressing the importance of loyalty, and named delegates to a national convention, rumored to be meeting in Washington, D.C., on July 4. [50]

MEMBERS OF THE Union League, whether in Iowa or Illinois, found themselves in competition with another patriotic organization, known as the S.B., or Spartan Band. This struggling semimilitary organization was the brainchild of John Wilson, who had been a colonizer for the Illinois Union League, and John Trimble, Jr., another Chicagoan. When the Union League seemed to disintegrate after the November elections of 1862, as evidenced by the poor attendance at the Illinois State council meeting of January 2, 1863, Wilson became convinced that the Union League movement had no future. He and Trimble promptly stepped into the breach, charting a more militant society on paper. They patterned their new secret patriotic order after the German Bunds, which had undermined Napoleon's hold upon Prussia by reviving German nationalism and regenerating a spirit of patriotic pride.

John Trimble, Jr., Wilson's partner in the establishment of the S.B., had a reputation for shifting his enthusiasms to suit the fad of the hour. He was an ex-pedagogue, an ex-abolitionist, and an ex-minister (Episcopalian). He was also a Mason, a Republican, and a restless soul seeking a new crusade. The S.B. provided a new opportunity, and the post of General Secretary, a new responsibility. Joseph Medill gave his stamp of approval, allowing the S.B. circulars and pamphlets to be printed by the *Tribune* company. [51] The endorsement seemed to be a plus for the fledgling society seeking respectability.

Wilson and Trimble drafted a constitution, compiled some bylaws, and

48. George W. O'Brien to "Dear Governor [Kirkwood]," April 7, 1863, in Samuel J. Kirkwood Papers, State Department of History and Archives, Historical Library, Des Moines, Iowa.

49. Samuel J. Kirkwood, "To the People of Iowa," a proclamation dated March 23, 1863, published in *The War of the Rebellion: A Compilation of the Official Records of the Union and Confederate Armies* (128 vols.; Washington, D.C. 1880–1901), Ser. 3, Vol. III, 82–93.

50. *Iowa State Register*, June 23, 24, 1863.

51. George Winston Smith, "Generative Forces of Union Propaganda: A Study in Civil War Pressure Groups" (Ph.D. dissertation, University of Wisconsin, 1940), 256.

composed a thirty-two-page booklet, supposedly "to educate the people . . . in the principles of patriotism." Article I of the lengthy constitution listed five specific objectives:

1. To preserve, through all coming time, the unity of the United States from disintegration and decay.
2. To secure to posterity our birthright of freedom, speech, and action.
3. To afford to people of other lands an asylum, a refuge from tyranny, oppression, and political wrongs.
4. To perpetuate the memory of the founders of this great Republic and of their worthy and immortal successors.
5. To teach by covenants, emblems, and solemn ceremonies, the harmony, strength and beauty of National unity.

The bylaws provided for five classes of members, from privates to generals, and based the organization on the military. Each township would have a company of twenty-five or more. Four or more companies would make up a regiment, the county-level grouping. In each congressional district, there would be a brigade, comprising four or more regiments. Each state would make up a division, which would of course be under the command of "the Honorable John Wilson, Commander-in Chief." [52]

Wilson and Trimble prepared a pamphlet that listed Joseph Warren, George Washington, Thomas Jefferson, Daniel Webster, and Henry Clay as "patrons" of the order; each was regarded as a patriot and nationalist. It restricted membership to free white males who were "persons of effective, sober, and good character and habits." It emphasized the "fraternal brotherhood" angle, and expressed the hope that members would buy emblems, jewelry, and "paraphernalia" to provide income—along with the membership fees—for the coffers of the S.B. [53]

In February the S.B. launched an aggressive drive for memberships, placing advertisements in Republican newspapers of the upper Midwest. [54] The membership campaign made slow headway. Nevertheless, Trimble and Wilson found "patriots" willing to serve as "major generals" in Iowa, Wisconsin, Michigan, and New York. Wilson became head of the Illinois division as well as commander-in-chief of the national organization. The cofounders also set up a twenty-five-member "Board of Control," composed entirely of Chicago residents. On paper, the S.B. seemed to be half hope and expectation, half reality.

52. *Constitution of the S.B.* (Chicago, 1863), 3, 5, 18, 22, in General Courts Martial Records, Records of the Office of the Judge Advocate General.
53. *"S.B.": Guide to Enlistment* (Chicago, 1863), *passim*, in General Courts Martial Records.
54. Advertisement, in Iowa City *Republican*, February 18, 1863.

The Spartan Band secured few new members, however, for it was denounced by Democratic spokesmen and undermined by Republicans involved in organizing and promoting the Union League. "It don't require Lord Rosse's telescope," one Democratic editor wrote, "to see the 'nigger in the woodpile,' and we trust no Democrat, no truly loyal citizen, will suffer himself to be honied or humbugged into the embraces of this fresh-blown charmer." He thought it was Know-Nothingism "resurrected" and "Black Republicanism taking another dodge." Some Democrats envisioned the S.B. as a militant and military organization, as a potential threat to their rights and liberties—perchance the advance guard of a military dictatorship.[55]

A few Democrats, anxious to discredit the S.B., pretended an interest in organizing a company or regiment in order to obtain "secrets" and information from the Chicago headquarters. They then turned the materials, including the secret oaths and passwords, over to Democratic editors to publish exposés. Such exposés, appearing in half a dozen Democratic newspapers, hindered the effectiveness of the S.B. membership campaign.[56]

Republicans involved in Union League leadership also tried to discredit the Spartan Band. John L. Scripps, the Republican postmaster of Chicago and onetime owner of the Chicago *Tribune*, characterized the group as a "bogus affair," primarily intended to be "a money making enterprise." Governor Yates, endorser of the Union League, refused to endorse the S.B., evidently viewing it as a rival rather than an ally. Although Wilson pretended that the S.B. had 25,000 members, the number who paid membership fees perhaps did not exceed 250.[57]

While the S.B. struggled for existence, the Union League flourished, largely because the Republican hierarchy promoted it assiduously. Harlow was recruiting and enrolling new members and sending out charters to new councils, but he became concerned about rumors that the Philadelphia league planned to set up a national organization and that the Washington-based Union League was planning to sponsor a national gathering in the nation's capital on July 4. Harlow and company countered by calling for a regional conference in Chicago on March 25 as the first step toward sponsoring a national conference of their own. In a way, it was a game of jockeying for power and prestige.

55. R. H. Sylvester, in (Iowa City) *State Press*, February 21, 1863; Charles H. Lanphier, in (Springfield) *Illinois State Register*, March 4, 1863.
56. *Illinois State Register*, March 4, 1863; Dubuque *Herald*, March 11, 1863; (Canton, Ill.) *Fulton County Ledger*, March 16, 1863.
57. John L. Scripps to John C. Begley, March 18, 1863, in John L. Scripps Papers, Yates, comments written on Thomas Giddis to Yates, February 27, 1863, and John D. Bartlett, Jr., *et al.* to Yates, February 17, 1863, both in Governor Richard Yates Papers, all in Illinois State Historical Library, Springfield. The 250 figure is a calculated guess. Unless membership lists are found, any estimate is sheer conjecture.

The March 25 regional conference in Harlow's own backyard proved quite successful. Illinois' 404 councils with 27,330 members were represented in Chicago by 80 delegates. In addition, delegates reported from Ohio, Indiana, Michigan, Wisconsin, and Iowa. After beating the Union League drums and berating the Knights of the Golden Circle and other purveyors of treason, the assembled delegates, with Harlow running the show, issued a call for a national convention to meet in Cleveland on May 20, six weeks before the assemblage scheduled by the Washington council. The resolution invited all "councils and kindred associations" to send representatives, asserting that the time had come to combine "all loyal organizations . . . into one strong, effective, and harmonious association of unconditional Union men." Such a conference "would harmonize the conflict of jurisdiction." The delegates elected sixteen representatives to attend the proposed Cleveland convention, including Dr. Edward A. Guilbert, major general of the Iowa Spartan Band. Evidently the S.B. was considered one of the "kindred associations." Then, in a bid for a compromise, the delegates appointed a committee to confer "with the Washington organization" and urge its members to send representatives to Cleveland and help to establish "a National G.C. [Grand Council] of the U.L.A." [58]

In one sense, the Union League of which Harlow was the guiding genius had outmaneuvered the Washingtonians. On the other hand, the Union League of Washington was already functioning as "a national council" and held several aces. After being "formally instituted" by John Wilson, representing the State Grand Council of Illinois, the league had gone off on its own. James M. Edmunds, an old friend of Lincoln and a popular Illinois Republican, accepted the headship of the stepchild and led it towards maturity. President Lincoln, sensing that the Union League could become an effective political force, urged Edmunds to build new bridges. Edmunds worked hand in glove with Lincoln in selecting the twelve members of the national council, which the Washington-based Union League sponsored. President Lincoln evidently wanted the league as an ally and astutely took steps to prevent it from becoming an agency of the Radical Republicans or his political enemies. [59] In time, Edmunds' organization, functioning as "a national council," began issuing charters to leagues being organized in neighboring states. Since councils in Connecticut, Rhode Island, Maryland, and Delaware looked to Washington as the parent organization, Edmunds' league was a national council in fact as well as in name. It was sensible for Edmunds to argue that the national council should be located in Washington, for every state was represented there by federal appointees and agents as well as congressmen.

58. *Proceedings of the State Grand Council . . . of Illinois*, 13–16.
59. William O. Stoddard, Jr. (ed.), *Lincoln's Third Secretary: The Memoirs of William O. Stoddard* (New York, 1955), 100–105.

It was not difficult for Harlow's and Edmunds' organizations to effect a backstage compromise. James C. Conkling, head of the influential Union League council in Springfield, was a personal friend of both Edmunds and President Lincoln. So was Joseph Medill, the most influential member of the Chicago council. Cooperation and fusion of the two groups seemed logical in order to keep the ambitions of Philadelphia leaguers in bounds and to prevent the Radical Republicans from gaining control of the national organization. The backstage agreement ensured the participation of the Washington-based Union League in the Cleveland convention. James M. Edmunds would preside and Washington would become home base of the national council. Harlow's league surrendered, but to friends.

The Cleveland convention of May 20 met in an aura of mixed hopes and expectations. John W. Forney, confidant of President Lincoln as well as owner of the Philadelphia *Press* and editor of the Washington *Chronicle*, made his presence known. Postmaster General Montgomery Blair, one of the so-called conservatives in Lincoln's cabinet, came to give the major address. Radical Republicans of Cleveland, fearing that moderates would dominate the convention, sponsored a mass meeting the evening before and brought in U.S. Senator John Sherman as the speaker. Secretary of the Treasury Salmon P. Chase, his presidential ambition getting out of hand, had a number of loyal lieutenants at the meetings. And Edwin M. Stanton, the energetic secretary of war with radical leanings, sent a special spy to get a firsthand report on the convention.[60]

Delegates to the convention met behind closed doors, took oaths of secrecy, and received a password to get into future sessions. After electing Edmunds as presiding officer, the delegates turned to the thorny problems at hand. Should the S.B., represented by several delegates, be merged with the new national organization without surrendering its identity? In the end, the convention deemed it inexpedient "to connect a military organization" with the Union League of America. John Wilson, self-styled commander-in-chief of the Spartan Band, then withdrew his credentials and left for home, somewhat chagrined, to watch his brainchild die a lingering death.

An emotional speech by Senator James H. Lane of Kansas caused some consternation among the conservatives. All in all, however, the basic decisions pleased the conservative element—and perhaps President Lincoln as well. The delegates, according to the terms of the backstage agreement, elected Edmunds grand president of the Union League of America, selected one of Lincoln's personal secretaries, William O. Stoddard, as corresponding secretary, and des-

60. Cleveland *Leader*, May 20, 1863; *Missouri Democrat*, May 25, 1863; Rufus Spaulding *et al.* to John Sherman, May 12, 1863, in John Sherman Papers, J. M. Stone to Salmon P. Chase, May 29, 1863, in Salmon P. Chase Papers, Stanton to David P. Brown, May 25, 1863, in "Letterbooks," Edwin M. Stanton Papers, all in Library of Congress.

ignated Washington as national headquarters. They devised a compromise ritual and a common constitution, which provided for nine national officers and an executive committee of twenty-four. Joseph Medill was named one of the twenty-four. Since all nine national officers were Washington-based, as were seven of the twenty-four members of the executive committee, Grand President Edmunds and his coterie won operational control of the newly created Union League of America. Yet, since state councils possessed autonomy, the U.L.A. was little more than a common umbrella.[61]

In the weeks that followed, the national organization made an effort to extend the Union League of America to the remaining states while state councils conducted aggressive campaigns to install new chapters in every county and hamlet. In Illinois, for example, the number of councils increased to 1,068, with a membership in excess of 125,000 by September, 1863.[62] The leaders of the Philadelphia and New York leagues, however, remained reluctant to surrender their dreams of leadership and admit they had been outmaneuvered by Edmunds and the Washingtonians.

Local and state councils geared themselves to influence the results of the October and November elections. "All young men about to become voters," one Union League directive read, "should be brought within the influence of the organization, before their opinions become fixed in the wrong direction." There was further advice: "All returned soldiers should be immediately sought out and cordially invited within your councils."[63]

Local councils of the Union League established reading rooms, providing Republican newspapers and pamphlets published by the Union Leagues of Philadelphia, New York, and Boston. The Philadelphia league's extensive publication program had broadcast tracts throughout the country, and the New England Loyal Publication Society, sponsored by the Boston Union League, also turned out scores of patriotic pamphlets. The Loyal Publication Society established by the Union League of New York spent nearly $30,000 during the three years of its existence, publishing 900,000 copies of ninety different pamphlets. It distributed its patriotic tracts to 649 Union League councils, 474 ladies' associations, 744 editors, 26,160 private individuals, and countless soldiers in the field.[64] Titles of the pamphlets varied from *The Causes of the War* and *Emancipation Is Peace* to *No Party Now, but All for One Country*.

61. *Proceedings of the National Convention*, 1–9, 12–15. Gibson, "Lincoln's League," devotes a full chapter (pp. 104–20) to the Cleveland convention. Ironically, Edmunds took the same title, "Grand President," that Harlow had as head of the Illinois state council.

62. *Proceedings of the State Grand Council . . . of Illinois*, 16.

63. *Proceedings of the State Grand Council of the U.L.A. of Michigan at Its Special Meeting Held in Detroit . . . March 2, 1864* (n.p., n.d.), 13.

64. Frank Freidel, "The Loyal Publication Society: A Pro-Union Propaganda Agency," *Mississippi Valley Historical Review*, XXVI (1939), 359–76.

The latter, written by Francis Lieber, stated that joining the Union League was a duty and a way to show respect for the flag.[65]

Union League members in Ohio made it their special project to defeat Clement L. Vallandigham, the Democratic gubernatorial candidate then in exile in Canada. Vallandigham, critic of President Lincoln and ardent advocate of peace and compromise measures, had been arrested by General Ambrose E. Burnside, tried by a military commission, and exiled to the Confederacy. In some Ohio cities Union League volunteers canvassed every household in every ward and township to defeat Vallandigham and elect John Brough, the Union party candidate.[66]

In order to stimulate Union League activity, Republican governors in such states as Indiana, Illinois, and Iowa raised the Golden Circle bugaboo again. Joseph K. C. Forrest spread the story in Illinois that the Knights of the Golden Circle were planning to massacre Union Leaguers, that the subversive society had brought on the disorders in Fulton County, and that seventy-one castles existed in the state.[67] In Indiana, Governor Morton continued to denounce the Golden Circle publicly while his righthand military man, Colonel Carrington, covered up his errors of judgment by crying "Wolf!" too.[68] Ohio Union Leaguers circulated a tall tale about supposed plans of the K.G.C. in Ohio to import fifty thousand fellow members from neighboring states to win the governorship for Vallandigham.[69]

Democrats not only denied all Golden Circle allegations but complained that the Union League was blatantly partisan, a mere mask to hide "the deformed head of Republicanism." They applied a variety of epithets to the League: "Jacobin Clubs," "Uncle Lincoln's Asses," "Black Knights of Abraham," "Republican K.G.C. Organization," and "dis-Union Leagues."[70] The Democratic editor of the *Illinois State Register* wrote derisively, "It is reported that the loyal leagues are issuing a new badge, it being a *negro's* head in India rubber, with this appropriate motto in silver letters: 'The constitution be damned!' " An Iowa Democrat, excelling in the art of vilification, wrote: "It is the same old saw, new set. Snakes crawl out of their skins annually, but

65. [Francis Lieber], *No Party Now, but All for One Country* (New York, 1863), 8.
66. Canvass books, in Cuyahoga County Records, Western Reserve Historical Society, Cleveland, Ohio.
67. Chicago *Daily Tribune*, August 16, 1863; *Illinois State Journal*, August 20, September 8, 1863; *Illinois State Register*, August 23, 1863.
68. Indianapolis *Daily Journal*, April 20, 21, July 15, 22, 25, 1863; Henry B. Carrington, "The Morgan Raid Through Indiana, 1863" (MS, n.d., in Henry B. Carrington Papers, Archives Division, Indiana State Library).
69. Cincinnati *Daily Commercial*, August 26, 1863; Cleveland *Leader*, September 17, 1863; (Columbus) *Ohio State Journal*, August 27, 1863.
70. *Fulton County Ledger*, August 11, 1863; *Illinois State Register*, February 3, August 28, 1863; Indianapolis *Daily State Sentinel*, April 6, 1863; Detroit *Free Press*, January 20, 1864.

55

in our enlightened country, the anti-democratic vertebrae crawl into a new epidermis about quadriennially on the average. . . . Of course, to every man who has an idea above an oyster, the Union League humbug, which is manipulated by disunionists, is perfectly transparent, and will be shunned, as a whitened sepulchre or political brothel." [71]

Not only did Democrats claim that the Union League was partisan, but they resented the flood of pamphlets that covered the countryside. "You can hardly go into a public office or a store," a New York Democrat complained, "but you will see such documents on tables, counters, and even *posted* as handbills." Several New York Democrats, headed by Samuel F. B. Morse, made an effort to counteract the Union League's propaganda campaign by organizing an agency of their own, naming it Society for the Diffusion of Political Knowledge. [72]

As the rumblings of discontent grew louder in June of 1863, Governors Yates of Illinois and Morton of Indiana took steps toward organizing the Union Leaguers into "independent [military] companies," an idea that made Democrats uneasy. Such military companies, Yates reasoned, might serve as "home guards" or "loyal legions" and sustain the state and national governments if antidraft rioting became widespread or subversive plots produced a rebellion. Governor Morton even provided arms from the state armory for Union Leagues that organized military "legions." Carrington seconded his governor. "I am not in favor of secret societies, and have never even joined the Union League," Morton's military commander wrote, "but your companies of the Legion are essentially the development of Washington's own plans, and may become the safeguard of liberty." [73]

As election day approached, the tide began to turn against the Democrats. The Union League contributed mightily, as did Union victories at Gettysburg and Vicksburg and war prosperity, which visited the upper Midwest, serving as "the lance of Achilles, healing by its touch the wounds of war and desolation." [74] Republicans won the crucial gubernatorial contests, defeating Vallandigham in Ohio and George W. Woodward in Pennsylvania.

71. Charles H. Lanphier, in *Illinois State Register*, August 4, 1863; LeGrand Byington, editor, in (Iowa City) *State Press*, April 18, 1863.

72. O. W. Smith to Samuel F. B. Morse, May 28, 1863, in Samuel F. B. Morse Papers, Library of Congress; Morse to Sidney Breese, February 4, 1863, in Sidney Breese Papers, Illinois State Historical Library. One of the pamphlets published by Morse's society, *Results of Emancipation* (New York, 1863), revealed Morse's antiblack prejudice.

73. Yates's endorsement on A. B. Cherry to Yates, June 30, 1863, George W. Harlow to Yates, July 6, 1863, A. G. Meacham to Harlow, July 2, 1863, all in Yates Papers; Carrington to "Gentlemen [Legion of Johnson County, Indiana]," October 3, 1863, in "Letterbook," Carrington Papers.

74. William H. Russell, in (London) *Times*, March 17, 1863; Cincinnati *Daily Gazette*, November 9, 1863.

Union Leaguers took a good measure of credit for the election results. "A great political battle has been fought," George Harlow said, "and victory has perched on the banner of those fighting for liberty and Union." Leading lights of the Union League of Pennsylvania also believed that their society had contributed mightily. "We worked hard, the Union League, very hard," one of the bigwigs wrote, "and we felt we deserved success, and when it came we did enjoy it. We have swept the city, with its great patronage—carried the [state] Legislature and triumphed throughout." The Union League of Philadelphia celebrated the election results by electing President Lincoln and his cabinet, save Postmaster General Montgomery Blair, to membership in their patriotic organization.[75]

While members were still celebrating the victories scored in the October and November elections, delegates gathered in Washington, D.C., for the second national convention of the Union League of America. George Harlow typified some of the midwesterners who made a special trip to the capital city for the three-day convention. Most of the delegates, however, were congressmen or Washington-based bureaucrats. Talk in the cloakrooms revolved around such subjects as "the Missouri situation," reconstruction, and Salmon P. Chase's presidential ambitions.

Grand President James M. Edmunds gaveled the congress to order late on the morning of December 9, 1863. More than 175 delegates claimed to represent 4,554 councils with approximately 716,950 members. The roll call of states proved that the Union League of America was a loosely organized federation of state councils, jealous of their prerogatives and power. It was evident that much organizational work remained to be done. The grand president had just issued a state charter to Delaware. Maine had only five councils and approximately three hundred members. Green Adams, sixth auditor of the Treasury Department, claimed to represent the Union League of Kentucky; yet he reported that, as far as he knew, the state had "no regular Union organization." Missouri had only five councils but claimed 22,800 members—undoubtedly raising many eyebrows. On the other hand, several states had an active, extensive, and well-structured organization. Illinois, thanks chiefly to the work of Harlow, led the way with 1,088 councils and 140,000 members. New York State delegates reported 306 councils and 92,000 members while Pennsylvania claimed 263 and 80,000. William E. Chandler, a member of the legislature of New Hampshire, boasted that every town in his state had an organized and active council. A Rhode Island delegate claimed that the league

75. George H. Harlow, quoted in *Illinois State Register*, January 26, 1864; Horace Binney, Jr., to Henry W. Bellows, October 17, 1863, in Henry W. Bellows Papers, Massachusetts Historical Society, Boston; (Columbus) *Daily Ohio State Journal*, November 6, 1863.

membership in his state totaled one-third of the eligible voters, making it a potent political force.[76]

After delegates were accredited and state reports completed, the grand president read the recommendations of the executive committee. One recommendation asked state councils to keep in contact with the national officers. Organizational problems existed, Edmunds complained, and "subordinate councils" had not been sending reports to Washington. The national council was operating on a bare-bones budget, with but a pittance ($509.07) in the treasury. Edmunds ended his report by advocating the two controversial suggestions of the executive committee that the U.L.A. draft and publicize "a declaration of principles" and that the league take the lead in establishing "a new political party" (the Union National party).[77]

Some straitlaced Republican delegates gasped at the thought of deserting an established party and sharing patronage with former Democrats. These delegates wanted more partisanship, not less. They wanted to discuss the so-called basic issues. Missouri radicals wanted emancipation extended and Brigadier General John M. Schofield removed from command of the Department of the West. Some of the activists wanted Edward Bates and Montgomery Blair eased out of President Lincoln's cabinet. A few even wanted the Union League to back Salmon P. Chase's bid for the presidency.

Radical members made the most noise during the early deliberations. They tabled that part of the executive committee's report "as relates to [a separate] party" and a declaration of principles. They set up a special committee to call on Lincoln and demand the recall of General Schofield. They also struck the gong for Chase; U.S. Senator James H. Lane and Governor Thomas Carney, both Kansans, gave speeches interpreted as "an eloquent and bitter indictment of the Administration in general and the President in particular."[78]

The radicals overplayed their hand. The vituperative attack upon Lincoln backfired. William O. Stoddard, the aide to President Lincoln who doubled as corresponding secretary of the U.L.A., started the reaction with a blistering attack upon delegates who criticized the administration. He angrily insisted that delegates were blaming President Lincoln "for deeds he had never done." He even accused one of the malcontents of being "a direct agent of Jeff Davis, Robert E. Lee, Satan, Slavery, and the Confederate Rebellion."[79]

No one replied to Stoddard. Meanwhile, Lincoln placated the Missouri

76. *Proceedings of the Annual Meeting of the Grand National Council, Union League of America, Held at Washington, December 9, 10, 11, 1863* (Washington, D.C., 1863), 8–10.
77. *Ibid.*, 11–12.
78. *Ibid.*, 12–13.
79. William O. Stoddard, "The Story of a Nomination," *North American Review*, CXXXVIII (March, 1884), 268.

delegates by agreeing to remove Schofield. The convention then proceeded smoothly. Its pro-Lincoln tone was evident in a resolution "cordially endorsing the Administration and the President," which passed by a wide margin—with only nine negative votes. The delegates wound down their business in a hurry. They approved a motion to levy a tax of ten cents per member to cover the cost of printing political tracts for the presidential election of 1864. They also set the next meeting date—the day before the scheduled meeting of the Union National Convention. (Democrats would refer to it as the Republican National Convention.) The Union League evidently hoped to influence the choice of the presidential nominee.

Lincoln's friends, in and out of the Union League, set to work immediately to assure the president's reelection, some working to make the organization a vehicle for his renomination. James Conkling, the Illinois congressman who headed the Springfield council, worked hard to keep the Illinois league in Lincoln's hip pocket.[80] Isaac N. Arnold, another Illinois congressman, gave a rousing endorsement of Lincoln at a meeting of the Washington, D.C., council. "Lincoln," he bluntly asserted, "should be allowed to complete the work he had so well begun." Joseph Medill, central figure in the Chicago council, had earlier waxed hot and cold, but even he recognized that Lincoln had regained much of the prestige he had lost earlier in the year. "As between Mr. Lincoln and Mr. Chase," the editor of the Chicago *Tribune* stated, "the chances appear to be at least ten to one in favor of the former in the country." John W. Forney, one of the vice-presidents of the Union League, praised Lincoln in the columns of the Washington *Chronicle* as "a good man" who possessed "those rare qualities that God occasionally takes from angels and gives to creatures." [81]

Many Union League councils openly endorsed Lincoln's candidacy, undermining the hopes of Chase first, John C. Frémont later. The Nashville, Tennessee, council, made up almost exclusively of federal appointees and army officers, passed resolutions endorsing Lincoln's reelection with Andrew Johnson as vice-president.[82] The Union League of New Hampshire, meeting in Concord in early January, endorsed Lincoln's renomination with a flourish, and the following day the Republican State Convention, meeting in the same building in the same city, ratified the league's action.[83] The week after, the influential Union League of Philadelphia, perhaps at Forney's prompting, rec-

80. Printed circular, dated December, 1863, Illinois Council No. 25, Union League of America, in Robert Todd Lincoln Papers.

81. New York *Herald*, December 24, 1863; Chicago *Daily Tribune*, December 31, 1863; Forney, quoted and criticized in the (Madison) *Wisconsin Patriot*, January 18, 1864.

82. Chicago *Daily Tribune*, January 7, 1864.

83. *Minutes and Proceedings of the New Hampshire Union League of America, January 4 and 5, 1864* (Concord, 1864), 8–9, cited in Silvestro, "None but Patriots," 190.

ommended Lincoln's reelection. Even Senator Lane, who had so frequently criticized the president, came to his assistance at a critical hour, keeping the Union League of his state out of the hands of the grasping Chase men.[84] Edward Bates, Lincoln's attorney general, viewed the efforts of Chase's allies to use the Union League to bolster "a losing cause" as the "brazen impudence of a few revolutionary radicals to betray the Union Leagues and steal their strength which is really great and dead against the radicals."[85] Outplayed in the political arena, Chase publicly asked that his name be dropped from the list of contenders, evidently fully realizing that the influential and extensive Union League of America was in the hands of Lincoln's friends.

The collapse of the Chase boom prompted some of Lincoln's Republican critics to turn to Frémont as their hope. Missouri Germans, who controlled the Union League in their state, took the lead in advocating Frémont's candidacy. They were helped along by the disorganized support of some abolitionists and scattered dissidents. Frémont's friends tried to postpone the meeting of the national convention for a month or two, hoping that his stock might rise and Lincoln's fall in the interim.[86] When that tactic failed, they issued a call for a convention to meet in Cleveland on May 31 "for consultation and concert of action in respect to the approaching presidential election."[87]

The Cleveland conference, meeting shortly before the Union National Convention was scheduled to open in Baltimore, nominated Frémont, added John Cochrane as his running mate, and drafted "a radical platform." Frémont accepted the nomination conditionally, saying he would withdraw if someone other than Lincoln were nominated at Baltimore.[88]

Joseph Medill, solidly in Lincoln's camp in early 1864, expressed disgust that a number of Union Leaguers had participated in the Cleveland convention, calling it a blunder "too absurd for comment."[89] Medill and other supporters of Lincoln's candidacy looked forward to the gathering of Union League of America delegates on the eve of the Union National Convention. Interestingly, two-thirds of the delegates to the former would sit as delegates to the latter the next day.

A handful of anti-Lincoln men, mostly radicals from Missouri and Kansas,

---

84. A. C. Jackson to Washburne, February 10, 1864, in Washburne Papers.

85. Howard K. Beale (ed.), *The Diary of Edward Bates, 1859–1866 (Annual Reports of the American Historical Association,* 1930, IV) (Washington, D.C., 1933), 347.

86. Alexander Randall to Elisha W. Keyes, May 20, 1863, in Elisha W. Keyes Papers, State Historical Society of Wisconsin Library, Madison.

87. (Madison) *Wisconsin State Journal,* May 10, 1864.

88. Chicago *Daily Tribune,* June 7–9, 1864. William F. Zornow, *Lincoln and the Party Divided* (Norman, Okla., 1954) treats the Republican half of the election campaign of 1864 in scholarly fashion.

89. Chicago *Daily Tribune,* June 3, 7–9, 1864.

made a nuisance of themselves during the early deliberations of the Union League convention. But Grand President Edmunds kept the situation in hand. Lane, who had earlier earned a reputation for his radicalism, put Lincoln's critics at a disadvantage by an eloquent pro-Lincoln speech. He spoke of the president's "long-suffering, patience, faithful toil, [and] utter unselfishness." If the Union League failed to endorse Lincoln and the National Union Convention failed to nominate him, it "would sunder the Union, make permanent the Confederacy, reshackle the slaves, dishonor the dead, and disgrace the living." [90]

With the oratory done, the convention set about its business. It adopted a resolution endorsing Lincoln's reelection. It asked for a constitutional amendment abolishing slavery and for the distribution of confiscated lands to soldiers and former slaves. It adopted a resolution thanking the soldiers and sailors for their "heroic service." One statement read, "All who bear arms for their country are entitled to protection of the national government without distinction of color or nationality." Before adjourning, the convention named a thirty-three-member delegation to call upon President Lincoln and inform him of the Union League's endorsement and support. [91]

The next day, June 7, the National Union Convention also met in the Front Street Theater. The delegates, many of whom had participated in the previous day's proceedings, had little more to do than endorse the Union League's action. John W. Forney stated that the convention really had no choice to make, that the choice had already been made. The gathering seemed all "unanimity and enthusiasm." [92] The delegates incorporated the Union League resolutions of the previous day into the party platform. And they named Lincoln as their presidential candidate with Andrew Johnson as his running mate.

When the Union League's delegation met with Lincoln on June 12, he accepted their best wishes and the set of resolutions pledging fealty to him. After thanking them for their favor and the Union League's support he added the oft-quoted aphorism that "it was not best to swap horses when crossing streams." [93]

Several days later, the Union National Party Committee met in Washington. Henry J. Raymond, chairman of the committee (and editor of the New York *Times*) presided. Senator Lane, a member of both the committee and the

90. Stoddard (ed.), *Lincoln's Third Secretary*, 214.

91. *Proceedings of the Union League of America, June 6, 1864* (Washington, D.C., 1864), 6–7.

92. John W. Forney, quoted in Philadelphia *Press*, June 10, 1864; Stoddard, *Lincoln's Third Secretary*, 214.

93. Abraham Lincoln, "Reply to Delegation from the National Union League, June 9, 1864," in Roy P. Basler (ed.), *The Collected Works of Abraham Lincoln* (9 vols.; New Brunswick, N.J., 1953), VII, 383–84; New York *Daily Tribune*, June 10, 1864.

Union League, suggested fusing the work of the two in behalf of Lincoln's election. His resolution "authorized and requested [the chairman of the Union National Party Committee] to correspond with the president of the National League [*i.e.*, the Union League of America] in regards to the Presidential campaign." [94] Thus the Republican party, acting through Raymond's committee, formally joined hands with the Union League of America, both dedicated to the reelection of Lincoln.

In the weeks that followed, Grand President Edmunds and the Union League put their shoulders to the wheel. State councils established more local councils and league membership climbed skyward. Local councils opened more reading rooms and distributed campaign propaganda. "We have established a good reading room, well furnished," one local leaguer reported to a state official, "and it is filled most of the time." [95] Union League councils distributed political pamphlets and patriotic tracts furnished by the Union Congressional Committee, the Loyal Publication Society, the New England Loyal Publication Society, and the Philadelphia Union League.

Despite the good work of the Union Leagues, Lincoln's chances of reelection seemed to ebb in August. Republican leaders took steps to heal the party schism, persuading Frémont to withdraw as a presidential candidate, in return for which Lincoln dropped Montgomery Blair from his cabinet.

Soon the skies brightened. Midwestern farmers, thanks partly to army purchases, began enjoying "a prosperity so enormous as to challenge belief." [96] Generals Philip Sheridan, by winning three separate battles in the Shenandoah Valley, and William T. Sherman, by capturing Atlanta, gave the lie to the shopworn Copperhead contention that the war was a failure. And the Union Leagues, generating nationalism while circulating political tracts, waged war upon Democrats generally and George B. McClellan as a presidential candidate particularly.

The October elections in Indiana, Ohio, and Pennsylvania indicated a trend that brought smiles to Republican faces. Party workers and league members, spurred on by the scent of victory, worked harder. The November election returns put Lincoln in the White House for another term, increased the Republican majority in Congress, and gave the Republican party control of every state legislature and governor's mansion north of the Ohio River and the Mason-Dixon Line.

The Union League deserved a major share of the credit for the resounding

94. Henry J. Raymond, report of the meeting of the National Union Party Committee in Washington, June 10, 1864, in (Washington, D.C.) *National Intelligencer*, June 14, 1864.

95. George H. Otis to Lucius Fairchild, September 10, 1864, in Lucius Fairchild Papers, State Historical Society of Wisconsin.

96. (London) *Times*, September 24, 1864.

Republican triumph. "The Union League was a very powerful engine in the canvass," Edmunds chortled, "and in the opinion of its members, was the organization of all others which brought about this glorious result." [97] The League had truly become a powerful political organism, serving effectively as the strong right arm of the Republican party. Having helped to secure the re-election of Lincoln and a victory for his party, the Union League was ready to turn to the important issue of reconstruction.

97. James M. Edmunds to Lincoln, November 1, 2, 1864, in Robert Todd Lincoln Papers; *Resolutions Adopted by the National Union League of America at Its Annual Session Held in Washington City, D.C., December 14 and 15, 1864, and Directed to Be Laid Before the President* (Washington, D.C., 1864), 5.

CHAPTER III

Phineas C. Wright, the Order of American Knights, and the Sanderson Exposé

THE COMPLEX and rather bizarre story of the Order of American Knights, which has gone into the annals of Civil War history as a secret subversive society, centered around two inconspicuous men. The first, Phineas C. Wright, an enigmatic entrepreneur who futilely sought honors and recognition, built a molehill. The other, John P. Sanderson, a second-rate politician who became a third-rate army officer, transformed Wright's molehill into a mountain via his revelations.

Wright, once a resident of upper New York State, moved to New Orleans in 1850 and lived on the fringe of obscurity while trying to establish himself as a lawyer. He moved the location of his law office nearly every year, an indication of his insecurity and lack of success.[1] Both drifter and

dreamer, he had trouble harnessing his considerable ability and establishing himself as a reputable citizen. A later acquaintance characterized Wright as "a most imprudent and visionary man." Another stated, "He was one of the greatest romancers I have ever known, and when he was talking he scarcely knew whether what he was saying was true or false."[2]

During his ten-year stay in New Orleans, Wright read or heard about

1. Cohen's *New Orleans and Lafayette Directory . . . 1850* (New Orleans, 1850), 174, lists "P. C. Wright, Counsellor at Law, 77 Common." His name does not appear in the 1851 directory. Cohen's *New Orleans Directory . . . 1852* (New Orleans, 1852), 244, lists Wright as attorney-at-law with his office at "87 Gravier," while Cohen's 1853 directory

indicates Wright's office at "d. 169 Royal." The next year's directory lists his office at "59 St. Charles." Cohen's 1855 directory, p. 246, lists "P. Wright, Att.-at-Law" but gives no address. Cohen's *New Orleans and Southern Directory . . . 1856* (New Orleans, 1856), 269, contains the entry "P. C. Wright, att.-at-law, Metairie Ridge." Mygatt & Company's *New Orleans Directory . . . 1857* (New Orleans, 1857), 302, lists "P. C. Wright, Atty., Bayou Ridge, Bayou St. John." Gardner & Wharton's *New Orleans Directory . . . 1858* (New Orleans, 1858), 328, has the same listing. Gardner's New Orleans directories for 1859 and 1860 do not list Wright.

2. James A. McMaster, testimony before the Cincinnati Military Commission, March 25, 1865, in *House Executive Documents*, 39th Cong., 2nd Sess., 519.

the filibustering activities of Narciso Lopez and William Walker, and he evidently dreamed of some project that might bring him fame and fortune. This fantasy helped to bring the Order of American Knights into being, "consumated [*sic*] in the winter of 1856–57" and intended to combat egocentric sectionalism, "repress the spirit of partisanship," and preach conservative political doctrine, including "the great principles which are at the foundation of all well ordered government, as we have been taught these principles by our forefathers." [3]

Wright's means and objectives were vague, varied, and ephemeral. There was an ill-defined Central American colonial scheme. In some undefined way the American Knights were expected to promote fraternalism and fellowship, after the style of the Freemasons and Odd Fellows. There would be a massive effort to educate the people at large in matters relating to government, with states' rights glorified as a cardinal principle. The "proper principles" would be imposed upon the public "through schools, academies, colleges, the press, and public lectures." [4]

Wright did not originally regard the Order of American Knights as a secret society. "The masses," wrote the man who thought his pen was a wand, "were to be instructed in the lessons of the 'vestibule' and when found worthy were to be instructed in a sign or pass-word, which were to be the only 'secrets' to be preserved." Wright added, "In the higher grades of the order, especially beyond the 'First Degree,' few were to be admitted and those should be men of tried and acknowledged worth, cultivated and enlightened intellect, and ardent patriotism." [5] Since Wright evidently believed he had the essential qualities in abundance, he preempted the headship of the order for himself, taking the title supreme grand commander.

Wright's Order of American Knights, still no more than a proposed organization, remained in limbo when its forty-year-old founder left New Orleans in the spring of 1857 and headed for the St. Louis area. He spent the remainder of that year and all of the next trying to establish himself, first in Missouri and then in Iowa and Illinois. The bitter fruits of the panic of 1857 destroyed opportunities and ruined his hopes. He finally decided to settle in St. Louis, returning to New Orleans in the fall of 1860 to move his wife and his packet of O.A.K. memorabilia to the largest city on the upper Mississippi. [6]

3. Phineas C. Wright, statement while incarcerated in Fort Lafayette, March 1, 1865, in Lafayette C. Baker–Levi C. Turner Papers, Records of the Adjutant General's Office, Records of the Office of the Judge Advocate General, National Archives.

4. Wright, statement while a prisoner in Fort Warren, April 27, 1865, in Joseph Holt Papers, Library of Congress.

5. Wright, statement, March 1, 1865, in Baker-Turner Papers.

6. No St. Louis city directories of the 1855–1865 era list Wright's name. In his statement of March 1, 1865, he wrote: "In the summer of 1860 I settled in St. Louis to reside there perma-

Wright's indifferent success in business and law nullified his efforts to exert influence in Democratic circles in St. Louis. Nevertheless, after President Lincoln issued his preliminary proclamation of emancipation, Wright composed several political tracts and urged Democrats to rally to the cause. "This corrupt administration," he wrote to a prominent Illinois Democrat, "is resolved to total annihilation of the government designed and supported by the constitution—to build upon its remains a strong, irresponsible, central despotism." [7]

Wright's intense opposition to Lincoln's policies prompted federal authorities in St. Louis to accuse him of secessionist sympathies. They instructed him to take a loyalty oath and he grudgingly complied. Galled by the practices of federal authorities, especially the military commanders, Wright tried to revive the defunct Order of American Knights and alter its original objectives. He envisioned the refurbished O.A.K. as an agency that might defend civil rights, counteract the work of the nascent Union League, advance the peace crusade, and bestir conservatives to political action. Since he feared that Democrats might have to resort to force to keep their civil rights, he talked of establishing a military arm of the American Knights, which would function as a branch of the state militia, "under the sanction of state laws and authority." [8]

On February 22, 1863, Phineas C. Wright waved his wand and transformed a handful of Democratic acquaintances into a "temple" of the Order of American Knights. He installed Charles L. Hunt, a journeyman lawyer who doubled as the Belgian consul in St. Louis, as the grand commander of the Missouri branch of the American Knights and Charles E. Dunn, a field superintendent for the Gas Light Company, as deputy grand commander. No evidence indicates that either Wright or Hunt established other "temples" within Missouri, and the St. Louis "temple" remained an infirm and ineffective one. [9] No reputable St. Louis Democrat joined the American Knights and the party hierarchy never gave the struggling order its blessing.

After having some copies of "a declaration of principles" printed, Wright

---

nently. In the fall of that year, four days after the election [of Lincoln], I went to New Orleans to spend the winter in maturing some important business which had long since been entrusted. I remained until February, 1861 when I returned home to St. Louis."

7. Wright to John Dean Caton, November 1, 1862, in John Dean Caton Papers, Library of Congress.

8. List of individuals who took the loyalty oath on January 24, 1863, in St. Louis, in Union Provost Marshals' File of One-Name Papers *re* Citizens, Records of the Office of the Judge Advocate General. National Archives; Wright, statement, April 27, 1865, in Holt Papers; Wright, statement, March 1, 1865, in Baker-Turner Papers.

9. Wright, statement, March 1, 1865, in Baker-Turner Papers. Kennedy's *St. Louis Directory, 1859* (St. Louis, 1859) lists W. T. Mali as the Belgian consul, but the *St. Louis Directory, 1860* (St. Louis, 1860) lists Hunt as holding the post. The same directory lists Dunn as "supt public lamps."

took an extended trip into Illinois to sell his strange bill of goods to Democrats in that state. He spoke of the need of Democrats to organize as a secret society in order to counter the work of the Union League, "defend itself and its rights at the polls," and win elections. He offered the Order of American Knights as a vehicle to achieve such objectives.[10]

Matters looked "decidedly ugly" during the spring of 1863. Some citizens seemed to be "almost frenzied in opposition to the war," and Republican governors in some states clamped down hard on dissidents.[11] Governor Richard Yates of Illinois was arming some councils of the Union League and encouraging members to organize "loyal companies." General Ambrose E. Burnside's summary treatment of Clement L. Vallandigham and his suppression of the Chicago *Times* seemed to be a threat to the civil rights of all Democrats. If freedom of speech and press were denied Democrats, one editor stated, the right to vote was a farce.[12] Some believed that even the right to vote was threatened.

In spite of widespread Democratic disaffection, Wright had trouble convincing party leaders that the Order of American Knights offered the means to redress their grievances. In the first place, Wright was an unknown, without standing in the Democratic party. In the second place, Wright's tendency to substitute verbosity for logic made the wary distrust him.[13] In the third place, influential Democratic newspapers like the Chicago *Times* and the *Illinois State Register* had instructed the party faithful to work in the light of day and avoid dark lantern societies, political or otherwise.[14]

Nevertheless, the man from Missouri instituted councils or temples of the Order of American Knights in several Illinois counties and cities. After preaching Democratic doctrine to a gathering in Jerseyville (Jersey County), Wright proposed banding them into a chapter. This was done with a minimum of procedure and a maximum of vagueness, so that the members did not know whether they had joined a Democratic association or a temple of the American Knights. Wright also met with Democrats in several other counties, trying to inveigle them into joining his order by extending the privilege to everybody who wanted it and dispensing with any obligation the new members did not like.[15]

10. Wright, statement, March 1, 1865, in Baker-Turner Papers.
11. William R. Morrison to "Dear Gov. [Richard Yates]," March 31, 1863, in William R. Morrison Papers, Illinois State Historical Library.
12. Detroit *Free Press*, June 5, 1863.
13. McMaster, testimony before the Cincinnati Commission, March 25, 1865, *House Executive Documents*, 39th Cong., 2nd Sess., 519.
14. Chicago *Times*, March 6, 1863; (Springfield) *Illinois State Register*, February 24, 1863.
15. Wright, statement, March 1, 1865, in Baker-Turner Papers; McMaster, testimony before the Cincinnati Commission, March 25, 1865, in *House Executive Documents*, 39th Cong., 2nd Sess., 519.

Wright scored a coup in Springfield while he was functioning as an observer at the Democratic state convention of June 17, 1863. He talked to some Democrats interested in "an auxiliary organization" that might serve as a mutual protection society, a guarantor of civil rights, and an electioneering agency on the order of the Wide Awakes of 1860. After the convention adjourned, Wright and a handful of delegates met in a side room. With a minimum of hocus-pocus, he put the assembled "clear through" all three degrees, and each became head of the order in his respective county. Amos Green, who had been arbitrarily arrested the previous August and elected to the state legislature while in prison, received the title grand commander. S. Corning Judd, an old acquaintance of President Lincoln, accepted a position on the state council. Later, Judd listed the O.A.K. objectives as he understood them: to "place selves in antagonism to the so-called Loyal Leagues," "to protect and assert our own rights under the Constitution and laws," and to develop "an auxiliary of [the] Democratic party." [16]

Wright's organization, as far as Illinois was concerned, functioned ineffectively, if at all. It was plagued by disinclination and a lack of trust in its founder. Furthermore, Charles H. Lanphier of the *Illinois State Register* and Wilbur F. Storey of the Chicago *Times*, the state's two most important Democratic editors and party spokesmen, shunned the new dark lantern society.

Late in the summer of 1863, Phineas C. Wright took a trip to New York City to seek a new job. While there he tried to persuade James A. McMaster, editor and proprietor of the *Freeman's Journal*, to give his support to the Order of American Knights. McMaster had spent six months as a federal prisoner because of his vicious criticism of President Lincoln; so Wright evidently thought that the dauntless editor might be the logical one to head the society in New York State. Wright had tried to pave the way for his interview by asking an old acquaintance to recommend the O.A.K. founder "as a worthy and honest gentleman." But the ploy backfired, for the acquaintance told McMaster that Wright was an impractical, irksome, and moody man. [17]

When Wright called at McMaster's office, the editor of the *Freeman's Journal* received him with misgivings. Wright began inauspiciously by telling two lies—that he was a "missionary" of the Order of American Knights rather than its purported head and that the organization was widespread and flourishing in the upper Midwest. Wright pulled "voluminous papers" out of his carpetbag as he rambled on about the objectives, structure, and expansion of the

16. Wright, statement, March 1, 1865, in Baker-Turner Papers; S. Corning Judd, statement before the Cincinnati Commission, April 1, 1865, in *House Executive Documents*, 39th Cong., 2nd Sess., 542.

17. McMaster, testimony before the Cincinnati Commission, March 25, 1865, in *House Executive Documents*, 39th Cong., 2nd Sess., 519.

American Knights. He asked McMaster to head the order in New York, saying it was not really necessary "to read the lessons or pledges—that they were understood" by dedicated Democrats. Without McMaster's formal approval or disapproval, Wright "inducted" the editor "through all the degrees." Occasionally, during the strange performance, McMaster objected to certain passages or propositions, and each time Wright promised to make changes or strike out sentences. Before the strange game ended, Wright had authorized McMaster, as head of the order in New York State, to extend exemptions to any worthy member, bypass any obligation, and let each applicant take what he liked and "let the rest go." [18]

On his way back to St. Louis, Wright stopped off in Indianapolis and met Harrison H. Dodd, who had earlier suggested that Democrats organize a mutual protection society. An embittered partisan, Dodd believed he had been persecuted for his political faith. He listened to Wright, seemed to sympathize with the O.A.K. idea and objectives, and evidently accepted the mantle of membership. The two went over to the editorial offices of the Indianapolis *State Sentinel* to feel out Joseph J. Bingham, who doubled as executive secretary of the Democratic State Central Committee.

With Dodd as his second, Wright concocted a fancy tale for Bingham, claiming that, while serving as counsel in the celebrated Gaines case, he had discovered a secret patriotic society dating back to Revolutionary War days. General Edmund P. Gaines, Wright claimed, had belonged to that organization, as had Washington, Madison, Jefferson, and "Light-Horse Harry" Lee. The society had supported the war, invigorated politics, and established "the present form of government." Democrats interested in preserving the government in the form devised by the "founding fathers" and negating the influence of the "Jacobins" should revive that old patriotic Revolutionary War society. In fact, Wright added, he had already done just that, founding the Order of American Knights and establishing temples in Missouri, Illinois, New York, and even Central America. Wright insisted that the O.A.K. was a going and growing concern, on the threshold of greatness. He urged the recalcitrant and questioning Bingham to join the order and lend his support to the worthy project. Bingham, however, bluntly stated his opposition to secret political societies of every variety, as he had the previous year in the pages of his newspaper. He asserted that he had never seen any good come from them. [19]

Bingham and his fellow Democrats had every reason to be concerned with

---

18. *Ibid.*, 520–21.

19. Joseph J. Bingham, testimony before the Indianapolis Military Commission, October 24, 1864, in General Courts Martial Records, Records of the Office of the Judge Advocate General; Indianapolis *Daily State Sentinel*, June 24, 1863. No evidence has been found to substantiate Wright's claim of involvement in the Gaines case.

the state of affairs in Indiana. Local chapters of the Lincoln League, or Union League, were organizing militia companies, designated "loyal legions." Military commanders of the District of Indiana were violating civil rights. After proroguing the state legislature on a technicality, Governor Morton was running a taut ship. There was some concern, still unwarranted, that free elections might come to an end. In such a situation, it is indeed suprising that more Democrats did not turn toward a secret party auxiliary as a mutual protection society and a redeemer of civil rights.[20]

After the rebuff in Bingham's office, Dodd and Wright hunted up several other prominent Indianapolis Democrats. They received some shoulder-shrugging, several promises, and repeated expressions of apprehension. Dodd and Wright then took a trip to Terre Haute to visit with several Democrats and promote the institution of a state council of the Order of American Knights. There, on August 27, 1863, Wright set up an Indiana branch of the O.A.K., dispensing with the formal ritual. Delana R. Eckles of Greencastle was chosen to head the state council with Dodd as second in command. Eckles' scruples soon after prompted him to set aside the title grand commander, and a month later, at a reorganization meeting on September 24, Dodd donned the mantle. David T. Yeakel of Lafayette took over as Dodd's deputy, and William M. Harrison of Indianapolis as grand secretary. The controversial Dr. William A. Bowles of French Lick and the outspoken John G. Davis of Rockville also seem to have lent their names to the American Knights.[21]

Actually, Wright's excursion into Illinois, Indiana, and New York bore little fruit. McMaster, supposedly head of the O.A.K. in New York State, let matters drift. Dodd held a reorganization meeting of the state council in Indianapolis and even enticed Bingham to join the secret society in November, 1863. Bingham later reported on a state council meeting of the O.A.K. that he attended at Democratic party headquarters. Dodd presided and William M. Harrison served as secretary. Only a dozen were present, including Lambdin P. Milligan, John G. Davis, Joseph Ristine, David T. Yeakel, William A. Bowles, George A. Corless, John C. Athon, Nicholas Vandergriff, and Rich-

20. Kenneth M. Stampp, *Indiana Politics During the Civil War* (Indianapolis, 1949), 158–85, deals with the situation in 1863 in the Hoosier State. Emma Lou Thornbrough, *Indiana in the Civil War Era, 1850–1880*, History of Indiana, III (Indianapolis, 1965), also treats Indiana politics of 1863 in scholarly fashion.

21. William M. Harrison, testimony, in Benn Pitman (ed.), *The Trials for Treason at Indianapolis, Disclosing the Plans for Establishing a North-western Confederacy: Being the Official Record of the Trials Before the Military Commission Convened by Special Orders No. 129, Headquarters, District of Indiana* (Cincinnati, 1865), 80–82, 89; Bingham, testimony before the Indianapolis Commission, October 24, 1864, in General Courts Martial Records.

ard Cushman. All took the "short form," that is, no ritual, ceremonies, or hocus-pocus. Dodd appointed several committees, assigning Bingham to the Committee on Literature to consider whether the O.A.K. should start its own newspaper. Later in the day, Bingham's committee gave a negative report on the proposition, citing lack of funds. The meeting lasted from ten o'clock in the morning until late afternoon, with periodic recesses. Four months after joining the O.A.K., Bingham dropped out.[22]

The O.A.K. was even more tenuous in Illinois. Only a handful of hopefuls attended a once-postponed meeting of the state council in Chicago. Amos Green, as state commander, presided and made a speech. That attendance was so meager and disheartening that the state council never met again.[23] The Illinois branch tended to drift into oblivion.

Early in December, 1863, Wright's O.A.K. met in "national convention" in Chicago. McMaster, planning a trip to Windsor, Canada, to visit Clement L. Vallandigham, stopped over in Chicago to take part in the proceedings and to verify some of Wright's contentions. He was surprised to see Wright in the chair, presiding "as the head of the whole concern." Indignant because he believed that Wright had deceived him on several counts and disillusioned because so few Democratic worthies were present, McMaster denounced the affair as "a humbug." Taken aback, Wright defended himself as best he could and, bluffing again, urged McMaster to take a tour of several Illinois counties and prove to himself that O.A.K. members were numerous. After several speeches and considerable disagreement, the members wound down the ineffective session. Should the "supreme council" meet again? Several suggested convening in New York City on February 22, 1864, to coincide with a meeting already scheduled there by peace-minded Democrats seeking a means to check the movement to nominate George B. McClellan as the party's presidential candidate.[24]

To check out Wright's claims that the order was "potent" in nearby cities and counties, McMaster made a visit to several of the cities. He came back convinced that the order was a myth and Wright a "humbugger." Then McMaster proceeded to Windsor to visit Vallandigham, still an exile in Canada. Talk turned to the Order of American Knights as a vehicle for peace-minded Democrats. McMaster, always free with advice, told Vallandigham to have nothing to do with the organization—"in its present form." It was, McMaster

22. Bingham, testimony before the Indianapolis Commission, October 24, 1864, in General Courts Martial Records.
23. William G. Ewing and Judd, testimony before the Cincinnati Commission, March 5, April 1, 1865, both in *House Executive Documents*, 39th Cong., 2nd Sess., 311–18, 541–42.
24. McMaster, testimony before the Cincinnati Commission, March 25, 1865, *ibid.*, 520–25.

said, a "transparent" and "palpable humbug." Until Vallandigham returned
to "the States" and knew with whom he was dealing, the New Yorker added,
it would be best for him to "keep out of such things." [25]

McMaster's charge on the convention floor that Wright was a pretender and
the order little more than an illusion undermined Wright's efforts to keep the
O.A.K. alive. If the organization was not already a corpse, there was little life
left in it. Aware that the O.A.K. needed a nudge to counter McMaster's demeaning contentions, Wright composed a document entitled "Occasional Address of Supreme Commander," had copies printed in St. Louis, and circulated a few to friends.

In many ways a strange document, the circular stated a devotion to states'
rights and Jeffersonian principles, expressed an abhorrence of President Lincoln's "unconstitutional acts," and decried the spread of "Black Republicanism." It listed and discussed four objectives: (1) to educate members to be
loyal and down-the-line Democrats, with a leaning toward states' rights,
(2) to counteract the designs and work of such secret societies as the Union
Leagues, the Knights of the Golden Circle, and the Know-Nothings, (3) to
promote friendship and fellowship among the members, and (4) to provide a
place of refuge in Central America for the multitudes being made destitute
and homeless by the war. Finally, it asked all "Brothers" to arm themselves
and prepare for the "eventual crisis" when the "Administration" would purge
the polls and establish "a military dictatorship." The self-styled supreme
commander did not put his own name to the lengthy document, instead devising the pseudonym P. Caius Urbanus. [26]

Early in January, 1864, Wright returned to New York City to seek a job in
the offices of the New York *Daily News.* He met Benjamin Wood, congressman and co-owner of the *News* "for the first time" and secured a position in
the circulation department. Evidently, Wright was able to convince the Wood
brothers that he had considerable influence in western Democratic circles and
could "extend the circulation of the paper and advance its interests." [27]

Wright began his chores at the *News* on January 18, 1864, by composing a
circular letter asking prominent Democrats to use their "kind offices & influence to extend the circulation of the *News.*" Wright suggested that the *News*
could become "a medium of the interchange of sentiment & opinions of the

25. *Ibid.*
26. P. Caius Urbanus [Phineas C. Wright], "Occasional Address of Supreme Commander"
(printed circular, December 8, 1863, in John P. Sanderson Papers, Ohio Historical Society, Columbus). The document also appeared in *The War of the Rebellion: A Compilation of the Official
Records of the Union and Confederate Armies* (128 vols.; Washington, D.C., 1880–1901), Ser.
2, Vol. VII, 282–86, hereinafter cited as *OR.*
27. Wright, statement, March 1, 1865, in Baker-Turner Papers.

friends of peace." [28] The circular letter referred to the *News* as "our especial organ"—a phrase which historians have interpreted in a number of ways. [29] The circular letter, printed on the same presses that produced the *News*, was sent to prominent Democrats and leading party newspapers.

The *News* also published Wright's "Occasional Address of the Supreme Commander." This action alienated McMaster again, and served as the excuse for another quarrel. McMaster, supposedly still a member of the Supreme Council of the Order of American Knights, reprimanded the supreme commander for publishing a document not "authorized" by the body. Wright replied with another lie that he did not know why or how the document had appeared in the columns of the *News*. [30]

The Order of American Knights, dying because of inept leadership, emitted its last gasp on February 22, 1864. On that day a handful of propeace Democrats, seeking to check the McClellan boom, met in New York City. Several had previously belonged, some only nominally, to the American Knights. They had little to offer in the way of nurturing the peace movement or checkmating McClellan's candidacy. Eventually the discussion turned to the desirability of organizing or endorsing a dark lantern political society. Some argued that such an agency could neutralize the work of the Union Leagues, protect the rights of Democratic dissenters, and elect propeace candidates. The strange powwow proved an exercise in futility. McMaster endorsed a society without oaths, rituals, and degrees—one that would require only "a pledge of honor"—and proposed to call the new organization either "States' Rights Association" or "Sons of Liberty." Still incensed at Wright, he insisted that the Order of American Knights deserved dissolution and death. Wright, who was not even invited to this conference of antiwar Democrats, could neither defend nor advocate his society. A few thought that a secret society, with a ritual and an element of mystery, could serve the Democratic party as an auxiliary organization, but the delegates could agree upon neither the form nor substance the society should take. In the end, the members present named Amos Green to head a committee to draft a declaration of

28. Circular letter (printed), dated January 18, 1864, in General Courts Martial Records. This item was confiscated in the raid on Daniel W. Voorhees' office in Indianapolis in August, 1864.

29. George Fort Milton, *Abraham Lincoln and the Fifth Column* (New York, 1942), views the phrase as proof that Wright had made the New York *Daily News* the "especial organ" of the Order of American Knights. It is more sensible to view the phrase as proof that Wood and Wright hoped to enhance the circulation of the *News* by making it the "especial organ" of the peace movement, then gathering momentum, especially in the upper Midwest.

30. McMaster, testimony before the Cincinnati Commission, March 25, 1865, in *House Executive Documents*, 39th Cong., 2nd Sess., 523–25.

principles and Dr. Thomas C. Massey, who had spoken most firmly in favor of a Democratic secret society, to give shape to such an organization. Massey's committee, plagued by disagreement, "made no headway," failed to bring in a report, and left the subject in limbo. Most of the delegates, however, agreed to shuck the Order of American Knights, adopt the Sons of Liberty as the could-be organization, and invite Clement Vallandigham, still in Ontario, to be the head of the secret association.[31] It was evident, when all was said and done, that the assembled delegates had repudiated Wright and his pretensions. The Order of American Knights was dead, dead, dead.

Wright, meanwhile, tended to his duties in the office of the New York *Daily News*. He was confronted by two realistic responsibilities; one was to bring his wife, who had remained behind in St. Louis, to New York, and the second was to further the circulation of the *Daily News* in the upper Midwest. In April, 1864, Wright made an attempt to carry out his plans. After renting suitable quarters in New York City, Wright instructed his wife to pack her personal belongings, meet him in Detroit, and plan to accompany him back east. He would visit Democrats in several Michigan cities, give some speeches, and secure new agents and subscribers for the *Daily News*.[32]

After arriving in Detroit, Wright crossed over to Windsor to visit Vallandigham at the Hirons House. Perhaps he intended to interview the exile for the *Daily News*, but he later testified that he never got to see Vallandigham.[33] After returning to Detroit, while awaiting the arrival of his wife, Wright took a trip on the Detroit & Milwaukee Railroad. He stopped at every "important place" on or near the line, seeking new agents and subscribers. Then, while he was staying at the Rathbun House in Grand Rapids, Wright was arrested upon the orders of Major General Samuel P. Heintzelman, commanding the Department of the Ohio, headquartered in Cincinnati. His captors conducted him to Fort Lafayette without fanfare, and he remained a prisoner until the war was over.[34]

THE MAN WHO built Wright's O.A.K. molehill into a mountain also had a checkered career. After dabbling in law, newspaper work, Know-Nothingism,

---

31. Amos Green, McMaster, and Clement L. Vallandigham, testimony before the Cincinnati Commission, February 3, March 25, 29, 1865, all *ibid.*, 503–509, 519–21, 523–25. It is interesting to note that both McMaster and Green testified that the Order of American Knights was "abolished."

32. Wright, statement, March 1, 1865, in Baker-Turner Papers.

33. *Ibid.*

34. Samuel P. Heintzelman Journal, April 28, 1864, in Samuel P. Heintzelman Papers, Library of Congress; Heintzelman to Lt. Col. Paul von Radowitz, instructions, April 25, 1864, in Union Provost Marshals' File of One-Name Papers *re* Citizens. Wright's own account of his arrest and incarceration is in John A. Marshall, *American Bastile: A History of the Illegal Arrests and Imprisonment of American Citizens During the Late Civil War* (Philadelphia, 1878), 218–35.

and politics in Pennsylvania, John P. Sanderson joined the newly organized Republican party, hanging onto Simon Cameron's coattails. When Cameron was named secretary of war in President Lincoln's cabinet, Sanderson became a chief clerk in the War Department. Later Cameron used his influence to secure a colonelcy in the U.S. army for his confidant and clerk.

Colonel Sanderson's superiors shuffled him from one unimportant, behind-the-lines assignment to another. West Pointers, who held most of the field commands, preferred other academy graduates as staff officers and feared to entrust a field assignment to one who held his rank because of political pull.

While Sanderson was seeking a more challenging assignment in Ohio, Republican friends introduced him to the proprietors of the Louisville *Journal*, which needed a new editor. The proprietors promptly offered Sanderson the position. While debating whether to sheath a colonel's sword and pick up an editor's quill, Sanderson met Major General William S. Rosecrans. "Old Rosy," in command of the Army of the Cumberland, offered the politically minded colonel a position on his staff. Colonel Sanderson accepted, just at the time Rosecrans' army was being readied for an invasion of northern Georgia.

Disaster struck Rosecrans' army at Chickamauga. Confederate troops, under General James Longstreet, broke through the Union right and drove two corps off the field—General George Thomas, unaware at first of the reverse on the right, stood fast and saved the army from a complete disaster. Rosecrans and his newly named aide, swept along in the retreating current, made their way to Chattanooga, arriving there ahead of most of the retreating troops. Sanderson not only helped to console the disconsolate Rosecrans, but wrote most of the official report on the disastrous encounter.

When Major General U.S. Grant deposed Rosecrans and put Thomas in his stead, the discredited general went to Newport Barracks to await a new assignment. Sanderson tagged along.[35]

While spending long hours at Newport Barracks across the river from Cincinnati, the two read the city's Republican newspapers. The Cincinnati *Gazette* and the Cincinnati *Commercial* were then waging a war of words against Democrats generally and Vallandigham's gubernatorial candidacy in particular. Both newspapers gave much publicity to the Knights of the Golden Circle, especially to rumors that the Knights were engaged in a plot to import fifty thousand member-voters from neighboring states to put the exile into the executive mansion.[36]

In time General Rosecrans received orders to report to St. Louis to assume command of the Department of the Missouri. Rosecrans invited Sanderson to

35. John P. Sanderson Journal, January 2, February 13, 1864, in Sanderson Papers.
36. The story first appeared in the Cincinnati *Daily Commercial*, August 26, 1863, but the editors warmed up the rumors each week until the October 13 election.

accompany him and serve as provost marshal general of the department. Charles A. Dana, an assistant to Secretary of War Edwin M. Stanton, disapproved of the appointment of Colonel Sanderson to such a responsible position. Dana believed that Sanderson was guilty of cowardice at Chickamauga and that he was unqualified and thoroughly incompetent, holding a colonelcy only because he had been Cameron's protégé. Dana, therefore, tried to void or delay the appointment of Sanderson as provost marshal general of the Department of the Missouri.

Eventually, the military committee of Congress approved Sanderson's appointment and he packed his bags and headed for St. Louis, his pride sorely wounded. Rosecrans and Sanderson had learned of Dana's opposition through friends, and Sanderson confided his contempt for Dana to his journal, calling him "an infamous libeler . . . no more than the meanest of all knaves and scoundrels, the man of all work that is dirty & stinks in the nostrils of honest men—CHARLES A. DANA." [37]

By the time Sanderson set up the headquarters of the provost marshal general of the Department of the Missouri at the Lindell Hotel in St. Louis, the Order of American Knights had been dissolved in fact if not officially. [38] Phineas C. Wright was holding down a desk in an office of the New York *Daily News*. Peace Democrats, who had met in New York on February 22, had thrown the order overboard. The Illinois "state council" had ceased to function. And in Wright's home state of Missouri, the state council was inactive. Wright's O.A.K. project was a fantasy.

Sanderson, caught up in a world of reality, tried to transform the chaos which he inherited into order. Plundering and smuggling were widely practiced, and conditions within the Department were "pitiable." [39] Meanwhile, factionalism was splitting the Republican party. Unionists, divided into radical and conservative factions, seemed to hate each other more than they hated the secessionists and Democrats. [40] Clearly, Sanderson had a most difficult assignment. Success would prove him a worthy officer and erase the stigma attached to his name in Washington.

Some prominent Unionists urged General Rosecrans and his provost marshal general to reintroduce the "policy of assessments," in which wealthy "might-be secessionists" were held responsible for damage to the property of

37. Sanderson Journal, March 25, 1864.

38. (St. Louis) *Missouri Republican*, March 5, 1864.

39. Sanderson Journal, March 10, 1864.

40. Brig. Gen. Clinton B. Fisk to "General [Rosecrans]," June 25, 1864, in Letters Received, 1861–1867, Department of the Missouri, U.S. Army Commands, National Archives; Francis P. Blair, *The Jacobins of Missouri and Maryland, Speech of Hon. F. P. Blair of Missouri, Delivered in the House of Representatives, February 27, 1864*, (n.p., n.d.), 1–2, 11.

those who supported the war and the Lincoln administration.[41] Republican
leaders also urged Rosecrans to dissolve the "Paw Paw companies" organized
in some Democratic sectors of the state as enrolled militia. Republicans
tended to view the Paw Paws as prosouthern or disloyal organizations.[42] Reports that notorious bushwackers like William C. Quantrill and "Bloody Bill"
Anderson were preparing to resume their raids alarmed Unionists everywhere. The rumor that Confederate General Sterling Price, headquartered in
Texas, was planning to invade Missouri in the spring added to Rosecrans'
concerns and apprehension. Evidently the Rosecrans-Sanderson duo had
jumped from the frying pan into the fire.

Beset by complaints, rumors, and distrust on every hand, Colonel Sanderson did not know which way to turn. Inept and inexperienced as an administrator and blinded by his own political prejudices, he took drastic and extraordinary action. He ordered clergymen to take oaths of allegiance, closed
grog shops at will, and made wholesale arrests, often based upon rumor and
partisanship.[43] Naturally, he alienated most Democrats. Sanderson's tendency
to view all critics as "men of disloyal sentiments" and his efforts to recruit
blacks for the U.S. service roiled the Democratic beehive and complicated an
already messy situation.

A procession of persons visited Sanderson's quarters in the Lindell Hotel.
Some asked for favors, others offered advice, and most registered complaints.
The assortment included beggars, rumormongers, storytellers, rascals, ac-
cusers, and accused. The new provost marshal general seemed especially interested in all rumors or reports about the Knights of the Golden Circle, the
Paw Paws, the Corps de Belgique, and the Order of American Knights. He
found the rumors plentiful and the evidence scanty and contradictory.

Sanderson also perused the files left behind by his predecessor. Three items
especially intrigued him. One was a confiscated letter (seized in the mail)
written by a prominent St. Louis Democrat to a friend suggesting that the
latter meet him in Windsor for a get-together with other peace-at-any-price
Democrats. The second letter, written by a prominent Unionist, stated that

41. (St. Louis) *Missouri Democrat*, July 12, 14, 19, 1864. W. Wayne Smith, "An Experiment in Counter-insurgency: The Assessment of Confederate Sympathizers in Missouri," *Journal of Southern History*, XXXV (1969), 361–80, discusses conditions objectively and eruditely.

42. Peter Graff to "Commanding General [Rosecrans]," February 14, 1864, Holt County
Unionists, petition, February 23, 1864, both in Letters Received, 1861–1867, Department of the
Missouri, U.S. Army Commands. Howard V. Canon, "The Missouri Paw Paw Militia of 1863–
1864," *Missouri Historical Review*, LXII (1968), 431–48, cuts through myth and propaganda to
present the Paw Paw story as solid and scholarly history.

43. Sanderson Journal, March 16, 1864; "A Friend" to General Rosecrans, March 11, 1864,
and [?] "To RoseKrenz," n.d., both in Letters Received, 1861–1867, Department of the Missouri, U.S. Army Commands.

"secret organizations" had been formed "in every vicinity" and that an "uprising" was in the wind. The third item, the most puzzling of the lot, bore the title "Occasional Address of the Supreme Commander" and was signed "P. Caius Urbanus, Supreme Commander"—an apparent pseudonym. It expressed an "abhorrence" of President Lincoln's "unconstitutional acts, denounced emancipation policy, and glorified states' rights." The salutation "Brothers" occurred frequently in the text, as if he were addressing fellow-members of a dark lantern society. It possessed a tone of defiance, suggesting that all "Brothers" arm themselves for the day when Lincoln tried to establish a military despotism. "We will with our swords, if need be," a closing call-to-action stated, "sweep away these clouds and welcome the splendor which shall glow in its old-time brilliancy upon the arms of our several States, redeemed from the thraldom [sic] of an irresponsible 'despotism.' " [44]

Sanderson also heard reports that Thomas C. Reynolds, who claimed the governorship of Missouri although he was in exile in Texas, had printed circulars urging southern sympathizers to form "Confederate Associations." [45] Were these associations linked to the Knights of the Golden Circle about which Sanderson had heard so much while on duty in Ohio and at Newport Barracks?

While seeking evidence concerning subversive activity, Sanderson came across a brazen renegade named G. Byron Jones, alias James C. Johnston. Jones, who had earlier engaged in some guerrilla activity, returned to Missouri in 1863 to seek recruits for the Confederate army. Exposed by Unionists, he fled to Nebraska, where he was arrested. Brought back to Missouri, he was lodged in the jail in St. Joseph. Desirous of his freedom and aware that Republicans wanted the Paw Paws disbanded, Jones concocted an exposé and had it planted in the St. Joseph *Tribune*. Jones claimed that the Paw Paws had been secretly sworn into the Confederate service, had pledged to surrender their arms to a Confederate recruiting officer, belonged to the Knights of the Golden Circle, befriended bushwacker Quantrill, and constantly communicated with Confederate commander Sterling Price. [46]

Two St. Joseph lawyers, both Republicans who believed the worst about the Paw Paws, visited Jones at the city jail. The fast-talking renegade implied that he had much more to tell and claimed he was eager to expose "the most

44. Christian Kribben to Robert M. Renick, August 16, 1863, in Sanderson Papers; Daniel Bates to Rosecrans, February 28, 1864, in Letters Received, 1861–1867, Department of the Missouri, U.S. Army Commands; Urbanus [Wright], "Occasional Address of Supreme Commander."

45. Thomas C. Reynolds to T. A. Lubbock, August 29, 1863, Reynolds to James A. Seddon, January 31, 1864, both in Thomas C. Reynolds Papers, Library of Congress.

46. G. Byron Jones to John P. Sanderson, March 5, 1864, in Union Provost Marshals' File of One-Name Papers *re* Citizens.

consumate [*sic*] scheme of rascality ever conceived in the minds of men." The fellow was an unmitigated liar.[47] Nevertheless, the two lawyers, taken in by his story, persuaded Sanderson to transfer Jones to a St. Louis prison and interview him. Sanderson, soon thereafter, interviewed and interrogated G. Byron Jones and wrote a summary of his statements for the record.[48]

On the day that Sanderson interrogated Jones he had two other unusual callers. Both claimed they had once been rebel officers (captured, then paroled) and both offered vague information about the Knights of the Golden Circle, the Corps de Belgique, and the Order of American Knights, using the terms interchangeably. Both claimed to have once belonged to secret rebel organizations, claimed they could gain access to Missouri lodges, and sought appointment as government detectives. Sanderson, rationalizing that it took a thief to catch a thief, put both on his payroll as detectives. One of the new agents took the name William Jones; the other passed himself off as William Stinson.[49]

Sanderson soon added more detectives to his staff, running the number to twelve. The detectives combed St. Louis and Missouri for evidence of subversive activity, and attended Democratic rallies and ward meetings. Several inveigled their way into local meetings of the "Democratic Associations," dominated by activists trying to breathe new life and spirit into a divided party. They picked up some rumors but no tangible evidence of subversion.

Two of Sanderson's sleuths made the acquaintance of Charles L. Hunt, a loquacious fellow who called himself a "Peace Democrat" and who spoke disrespectfully of President Lincoln at every opportunity. Hunt had mixed law, land speculation, farming, and politics—none successfully—while serving as Belgian consul in St. Louis. He told one of the detectives that Vallandigham, then in exile in Canada, would return home in early July, probably while the Democratic national convention was in session in Chicago. Hunt also talked freely about the Order of American Knights, its objectives, internal organization, and its future. He even pretended there were 8,000 members in St. Louis and 23,000 in Missouri. He claimed to hold the title of grand commander in Missouri and said he intended to meet with other leaders from other states in a meeting in Detroit.[50]

47. James V. Lewis and J. W. Harris, affidavits, both dated February 8, 1864, in the Sanderson Papers, prove that Jones was a thoroughly unworthy individual.

48. G. Byron Jones, statement, reduced to writing by Col. Sanderson, n.d., in Sanderson Papers. Jones's statement also appeared in *OR*, Ser. 2, Vol. VIII, 239–40.

49. Sanderson Journal, March 9, 1864; Sanderson to Rosecrans, report, June 12, 1864, in Reports on the Order of American Knights, Records of the Office of the Judge Advocate General.

50. William Jones to "Dear Sir" [Sanderson], report, n.d., "Statement of William Taylor," n.d., both in Sanderson Papers. The *St. Louis Directory, 1860* lists "Charles L. Hunt, 33 Chestnut" as both lawyer and Belgian consul.

Sanderson's agents, most trespassing outside of the Department of the Missouri, collected a stack of rumors and a lot of miscellany as they scoured the upper Midwest: members of the Knights of the Golden Circle were numerous in Missouri; Confederate General Price had established the Corps de Belgique; the Order of American Knights had sworn "not to take up arms against the Confederacy" but to resist the draft and to establish a "Northwest Confederacy." [51]

Some of the information, collected by Sanderson's agents, struck closer to home. Hunt, the self-named head of the O.A.K. in Missouri, claimed that Charles E. Dunn, an embittered Democrat who earned a living as superintendent of the public lamps, was his deputy grand commander. Dunn had been active in Fillmore's campaign for the presidency in 1856, had backed the Bell-Everett ticket in 1860, and advocated peace and compromise during the war. E. H. A. Habicht, the twenty-one-year-old printer who had set the type for the "Occasional Address of the Supreme Commander," was known for his antipathy toward abolition and the Lincoln administration. He had frequently made indiscreet remarks, calling Union soldiers "hireling warriors," and Lincoln "vile deceiver," "tyrant," "knave and buffoon," "idiot," and "traitor." P. Caius Urbanus, it turned out, was the pen name of Phineas C. Wright, the national head of the O.A.K, and he had left for a job in New York City. [52]

As Sanderson's search for evidence of a subversive society developed, his detectives fanned out seeking needles in haystacks in Louisville, Chicago, Detroit, Dayton, Cincinnati, Indianapolis, and even New York City. [53] Detectives representing Colonel Sanderson and others hired by governors and by department and district commanders, stepped on each other's toes, seeking information that did not exist and usually reporting rumors and suppositions rather than facts. At times ludicrous incidents occurred. In Indianapolis, for example, one of Sanderson's detectives initiated one of Governor Morton's into a "secret society" that did not exist. Morton's detective, in turn, initiated another of Sanderson's into the same fictitious society. [54]

51. William Stinson to Sanderson, report, May 14, 1864, William Jones to Sanderson, report, n.d., both *ibid.*

52. Charles E. Dunn to C. R. Johnston, July 17, 1864, [?] to Capt. Tullen (U.S. police), May 29, 1864, E. H. A. Habicht, statement, June 6, 1864, all in Union Provost Marshals' File on One-Name Papers *re* Citizens; "Statement of William Taylor." Three different St. Louis city directories listed Charles E. Dunn as "supt public lamps."

53. "Abstracts of Expenditures, Contingent Fund, Department of the Missouri," in Vouchers, Secret Service Payments, Auditors' Records, Treasury Department, National Archives; "Scouts, Guides, Spies, and Detectives, Two or More, 1861–1866," in Provost Marshal General's Office, National Archives.

54. Edward J. Hoffman [one of Sanderson's agents], report, May 25, 1864, Sanderson Papers.

Several of Sanderson's agents and "witnesses" were genuinely competent, while others were rascals and liars. One, Byron H. Robb, was a convicted perjurer and "a damnable villain"; yet his "revelations" about a steamboat-burning conspiracy were circulated in the press and evidently accepted at face value by Sanderson.[55] Mary Ann Pitman (alias Mary Hays) became one of Sanderson's "key witnesses," and her revelations formed the basis for official reports. Caught smuggling, she told tall tales to impress Sanderson and gain her freedom. She claimed that she had held a commission as Lieutenant Rawley in Company F of the Twelfth Tennessee Infantry of the Confederate army under General Nathan Bedford Forrest. Later, she claimed, she had helped to raise Company I of the Twenty-second Tennessee, commanding the company in the Battle of Shiloh. Her litany of lies included claims that she and General Forrest had attended a meeting of the Order of American Knights in Tennessee, had seen a list of members, and had noticed that the name of George B. McClellan was there. She also claimed that Jefferson Davis belonged to the O.A.K. and that General Sterling Price headed the southern branch and Clement L. Vallandigham the northern half.[56]

In addition to collecting evidence from informers, reliable or otherwise, and his corps of detectives, Colonel Sanderson clipped stories and rumors from newspapers and exchanged information and suppositions with General Samuel P. Heintzelman, commanding the Department of the Ohio, and with the governors of Illinois and Indiana. Rumors of conspiracies and subversive society activity continued to make the rounds, sometimes improving in the retelling. Since 1864 was an election year, certain politicians had a vested interest in exposés and revelations that possessed propaganda value. Rumors made the rounds that subversive societies planned to free Confederates being held in northern prison compounds, burn government property in St. Louis and Cincinnati, assassinate Republican governors, and establish a northwestern confederacy.[57]

55. Byron H. Robb, report, August 10, 1863, in Citizens' File, 1861–1865, War Department Records, National Archives; Byron H. Robb to James A. Garfield, January 9, 1864, in James A. Garfield Papers, Library of Congress; endorsement on letter, Robb to "Colonel [Sanderson]," August 26, 1863, in Union Provost Marshals' File of One-Name Papers *re* Citizens.

56. "Examination of Mary Ann Pitman," May 24, 1864, Mary Ann Pitman, statement, December 3, 1864, both in Union Provost Marshals' File of One-Name Papers *re* Citizens. Sanderson's interrogation of Pitman is in *OR*, Ser. 2, Vol. VII, 345–55. None of her claims were borne out by either Confederate or Tennessee records.

57. Quincy (Ill.) *Whig*, May 6, 1864; Indianapolis *Daily Journal*, April 30, 1864; Herbert M. Hoxie, in *OR*, Ser. 3, Vol. III, 68–69; Calvin Fletcher Diary, March 31, 1864 (MS in Calvin Fletcher Papers, Indiana Historical Society Library); Brig. Gen. John T. Copeland to Maj. O. D. Green, May 1, 1864, Robert Drake to Capt. Scott, December 14, 1864, both in Letters Received, 1861–1867, Department of the Missouri, U.S. Army Commands.

As the stack of evidence, substantive and questionable, accumulated on Sanderson's desk, he was beset by particular problems. His bid for a brigadier generalship, endorsed by General Rosecrans, struck a snag in Washington. Dana and Stanton still questioned his competency, and the charge of cowardice at Chickamauga refused to go away. A second problem with the War Department developed when Secretary Stanton refused to pay the bill for Sanderson's dozen detectives, most of whom were operating outside of the Department of the Missouri. Sanderson's contingency funds had long since been spent. Then too, conditions within Sanderson's department had deteriorated, reflecting unfavorably upon him and his office. There were rumors that guerrilla leaders were getting ready for their summertime raids and that General Price's offensive into Missouri would soon be on the way.

Sanderson, evidently, saw an exposé of the Order of American Knights as the means to gain his brigadier's star, refurbish a tarnished reputation, and influence the November elections. His detectives had provided some tangible evidence about the order's objectives and its leading lights in Missouri, and they had reported reams of rumors. Unfortunately, as far as Sanderson was concerned, his two most competent detectives, Edward F. Hoffman and James M. Forrester, had found no substantial evidence about subversive activity of the O.A.K. or confirmation of any conspiracies.[58]

To justify his generalizations about the American Knights and a northwestern conspiracy, Sanderson ordered Charles L. Hunt, Charles E. Dunn, E. H. A. Habicht, Dr. John Shore, and Dr. James A. Barret arrested. All five were Democrats, all were critical of the Lincoln administration, and all favored peace and compromise. Dr. Barret had a serious indiscretion to his credit, having allowed his brother-in-law, a Confederate recruiting agent, to stay overnight at his house.

The men were confined in the Gratiot Street Prison. Sanderson interrogated them individually, promising each his freedom if he would confess to involvement in O.A.K. activity and implicate bigger game.[59] Each of the five denied implication in any conspiracy. Hunt, supposed head of the O.A.K. in Missouri, claimed he had dropped his membership three weeks earlier. As Belgian consul, he appealed to President Lincoln for his release and the return of papers seized. Dr. Barret wrote a letter protesting his innocence to General U. S. Grant, an old friend, and asking him to intercede in his behalf.

58. See their lengthy reports in the Sanderson Papers or in *OR*, Ser. 2, Vol. VII, 254–56, 258–79, 301–304, 307–10, 722–24, 726–27, 731–33, 739–41.
59. Sanderson, "Special Orders, No. 139," May 27, 1864, "Special Orders, No. 150," June 8, 1864, H. L. McConnell, statement, n.d., all in Charles L. Hunt Papers, Citizens' File, 1861–1865, War Department Records; Habicht, statement, June 6, 1864, in Union Provost Marshals' File of One-Name Papers *re* Citizens.

Although much of his evidence was contradictory and questionable, Sanderson began to compose his first report on secret societies and "the plot to overthrow the government." Before he was midway into the report, he asked General Rosecrans for permission to convey it personally to Washington. He could find out while there what forces were delaying his bid for the brigadier generalship. A War Department ruling forbade officers to travel to Washington on routine business, however, and Rosecrans, anticipating a refusal from the White House, wrote to Governor Yates and Congressman James A. Garfield, asking them to intercede with the president. Rosecrans evidently hoped that pressure from Garfield and Yates would convince the president that Sanderson had important revelations. Furthermore, such tactics would circumvent Secretary of War Stanton, Rosecrans' and Sanderson's nemesis.[60]

Lincoln, however, remained unimpressed, evidently having little faith in the promised revelations and not wishing to be a party to the violation of a War Department order. Rosecrans then tried another tack. He sent portions of Sanderson's exposé and selections from the supporting documents to the governors of Missouri and Pennsylvania. He begged the governors to use their influence with President Lincoln. Governor Andrew G. Curtin and Congressman Garfield, who had served on Rosecrans' staff earlier in the war, visited the White House and read portions of the material Sanderson had sent them. The President still seemed unimpressed, evidently giving priority to the War Department ruling.

Thinking the groundwork well laid, Rosecrans then sent a telegram to Lincoln, saying he had "detailed information" about "a plot to overthrow the Government" and asking for an order to forward documents to Washington "by a staff officer [Sanderson]." Rosecrans arranged for other support for his stratagem. Both Governor Yates and Judge David Davis, a confidant of the president, sent telegrams supporting Rosecrans' request, saying that "the information" possessed "national importance."[61]

Lincoln was too smart to become a pawn in the Sanderson-Rosecrans game. He recognized that Rosecrans was trying to circumvent the War Department, perhaps even trying to bring the president into conflict with his Secretary of War. Nor did he give much credence to revelations previously made. Too much bunkum had already been passed off on an unsuspecting public. Evading what he thought might be entrapment, Lincoln sent a wire to Rosecrans:

---

60. Rosecrans to Garfield, June 4, 1864, Garfield Papers; Rosecrans' statement to reporter, published in Washington (D.C.) *Evening Star*, November 2, 1889.
61. Rosecrans to Abraham Lincoln, telegram, June 2, 1864, in Robert Todd Lincoln Papers, Library of Congress; Rosecrans to John Nicolay, November 5, 1889, in John Nicolay–John Hay Papers, Illinois State Historical Library.

"When your communication shall be ready, send it by Express. There will be no danger of its miscarriage." [62]

Rosecrans parried Lincoln's request by telegraphing back that the information was too important and "too grave" to entrust to "the Express." Governor Yates, at Sanderson's urging, seconded Rosecrans' reluctance and asked the president to summon the commander of the Department of Missouri or his provost marshal general to Washington "immediately." Lincoln remained unconvinced. "If it is a matter of such overwhelming importance," he told John Hay, his personal secretary, "I don't think Sanderson is the proper person to whom to entrust it." Still wary, Lincoln added, "I am inclined to think that the object of the General is to force me into a conflict with the Secretary of War and to make me overrule him on this matter." Adroit and cautious, Lincoln resolved the problem by sending John Hay to interview both Rosecrans and Sanderson and bring the "extraordinary evidence" back to Washington. [63]

While Lincoln's trusted emissary was on his way to St. Louis, Sanderson spent long hours sifting his growing stack of evidence and composing the exposé, which took the form of a report addressed to General Rosecrans. It evolved into a long document, twenty-two pages of legal-size foolscap, detailing the history of the Order of American Knights and a supposed plot "to overthrow the government." It was a scissor-and-paste job, a montage of a few facts, many suppositions, and some outright lies.

Although Sanderson knew or should have known, for example, that Phineas C. Wright was the author of the "Occasional Address of Supreme Commander," he credited the document to Clement L. Vallandigham, still in exile in Canada but planning to return to Ohio. Although no substantial evidence supported the contention, Sanderson stated that the Order of American Knights had been conceived at the headquarters of Confederate General Sterling Price and that the subversive dark lantern society was really "another form" of the Knights of the Golden Circle. He credited the O.A.K. with a single, sinister objective, "the overthrow of the Federal Government, and the creation of a Northwestern Confederacy." The report claimed that "the general commanders of the different states" had met in New York City on February 22 to plan "an uprising" and to coordinate their treasonable activities. It predicted that Vallandigham's return to the United States would coincide with the meeting of the Democratic national convention in Chicago—a meeting then scheduled

---

62. Lincoln to Rosecrans, telegram, June 7, 1864, in Letters Received, 1861–1867, Department of the Missouri, U.S. Army Commands.

63. Rosecrans to Lincoln, telegram, June 8, 1864, in Robert Todd Lincoln Papers; Lincoln, quoted in Tyler Dennett (ed.), *Lincoln and the Civil War in the Diaries and Letters of John Hay* (New York, 1939), 187–88; Lincoln, "Order to John Hay," June 10, 1864, Lincoln to Rosecrans, instructions, June 10, 1864, both in Robert Todd Lincoln Papers.

for July 4 but postponed to late August. "While he is there," Sanderson's collection of suppositions stated, "he is to make a speech, proclaiming open resistance to national authorities—in a word, he is to inaugurate a rebellion in the free states." [64]

Letting his imagination run wild, Sanderson incorporated a variety of other suppositions into the exposé. He estimated that the O.A.K. had half a million members in the upper Midwest, with 140,000 in Illinois, over 100,000 in Indiana, and 80,000 in Ohio. "Members of the Southern section of it, which is under the control of General Price," the report stated, "can meet and confer with members of the Northern section under the control of Vallandigham with perfect impunity." Sanderson's incredible document claimed that the American Knights' password was Nu-oh-lac, "being the word Calhoun spelled backwards." The sign of recognition, which Sanderson presented with a straight face, bordered on the absurd: "The street sign of recognition is given by placing the hand of the left arm on the right breast and raising the right to an angle of 45 degrees, with the shoulders on a line with them. The grip is a full grasp of the hand, with the index finger so extended as to rest on the wrist of the person addressed. The toe of the person desiring to be recognized is also placed at the hollow of the foot of the other." Sanderson concluded the report with an assumption for which he had only hearsay and rumor as evidence: "This order is in truth the great lever used by the rebel government for its military operations." [65]

John Hay arrived in St. Louis about the same time as a telegram sent to Rosecrans by Secretary of War Stanton at the president's request. This uncoded message—a measure of Lincoln's and Stanton's lack of faith in Sanderson—ordered the release of Charles L. Hunt if he were still being held prisoner and asked that "the papers and archives of the Belgian consulate" be returned.[66] Evidently Sanderson had failed to notify Washington that he had arrested Hunt, Charles E. Dunn, and Dr. James A. Barret as a means to give credibility to his tale about the O.A.K. and the "plot to overthrow the government."

After an unsavory dinner at the Lindell Hotel, General Rosecrans conducted John Hay up to his room, closed the door, lit a cigar, and recited the O.A.K. apprehensions and suppositions in great detail. Later Sanderson came and added footnotes to Rosecrans' recital, stressing the role and reliability of

64. Sanderson to Rosecrans, report, June 12, 1864, in Reports on the Order of American Knights. This report, the first of three composed by Sanderson, is published in *OR*, Ser. 2, Vol. VII, 228–39.

65. *Ibid.*

66. Edwin M. Stanton to Rosecrans, telegram, June 13, 1864, in *OR*, Ser. 1, Vol. XXXIV, Pt. 4, p. 337.

Mary Ann Pitman, though, if he did not realize that she was a congenital liar, he was naïve and addlebrained. In time, Hay accompanied Sanderson to his office. He sat restlessly while Sanderson read at length from his report or selections from the hundred documents he had accumulated as evidence. Hay then returned to Rosecrans' room and the two talked long into the night. Hay promised that he would lay the matter before the president. Because his instructions were rather vague, Hay did not ask for a copy of Sanderson's twenty-two page exposé or of "any of the papers in the case." [67] Nor did Sanderson hand a copy of his report to Hay and ask him to present it to the president. This meant that Hay would have to give Lincoln a verbal report, along with his impressions.

Hay was inclined to place some faith in Sanderson's revelations, but he saw an ulterior motive in Rosecrans' actions and tactics. He believed that Rosecrans wanted to "thwart and humiliate" Stanton and that Sanderson was trying to "impress" Lincoln, evidently to rehabilitate a tarnished reputation and secure the coveted promotion. Hay also believed that Rosecrans had overplayed his hand, and that one purpose of the O.A.K. report was to get the War Department to pay the exorbitant expenses for Sanderson's corps of detectives. Earlier the Secretary of War had denied Rosecrans' request for a contingency grant to them. [68]

Hay returned to Washington to report on his extraordinary mission. "The President," he confided to his diary, "seemed not well pleased that Rosecrans had not sent all the papers by me, reiterating his want of confidence in Sanderson, declining to be made a party to a quarrel between Stanton and Rosecrans, and stating in reply to Rosecrans' suggestion of the importance of the greatest secrecy, that a secret which had already been confided to Yates, Morton, Brough, Bramlette, and their respective circle of officers could scarcely be worth keeping now." Not only did Lincoln question Sanderson's motives and veracity, but he also believed the Order of American Knights "a mere political organization, with about as much malice and as much puerility as the Knights of the Golden Circle." He promised, nevertheless, to write to Rosecrans "at an early day." [69]

In the days that followed, Rosecrans and Sanderson realized they had painted themselves into a corner. Their reputations receded in Washington,

67. John Hay, quoted in Dennett (ed.), *Lincoln and the Civil War in the Diaries and Letters of John Hay*, 189–91.

68. *Ibid.*; Col. James A. Hardie (War Department) to Rosecrans, June 13, 1864, in Letters Received, 1861–1867, Department of the Missouri, U.S. Army Commands; Rosecrans to Lincoln, June 14, 1864, in Robert Todd Lincoln Papers.

69. Lincoln and Hay, quoted in Dennett (ed.), *Lincoln and the Civil War in the Diaries and Letters of John Hay*, 192–93.

for their O.A.K. contentions had failed to convince Lincoln, Stanton, or Grant. In fact, Grant asked Stanton to intercede in behalf of Dr. James A. Barret, a friend of long standing. Stanton subsequently instructed Rosecrans to release the St. Louis physician, slapping Sanderson's dirty hands again.[70]

Repudiated in Washington, Sanderson and Rosecrans changed their tactics, turning to newspaper friends and political allies to get their revelations before the people. Sanderson revised and rewrote his exposé, giving it the appealing title "Conspiracy to Establish a Northwestern Confederacy."[71] He assured friends that the document contained some startling "revelations."

The exposé claimed that American Knights were as numerous as the leaves on the trees. The order was centered in the upper Midwest, members being most numerous in Illinois, Indiana, and Ohio. Sanderson incorporated selections from Wright's "Occasional Address of Supreme Commander" and again credited its authorship to Vallandigham. He also included sections from the reports of some of his detectives, as well as the contentions of Mary Ann Pitman and Byron H. Robb. He claimed that the true objective of the American Knights was to inaugurate a revolution and to establish in the upper Midwest a separate confederacy aligned with the Confederate States of America. He linked the O.A.K. to the Democratic party, even asserting that the "McClellan Minutemen," organizing in New York to promote his presidential aspirations, belonged to the American Knights. In promoting the establishment of a northwestern confederacy, the exposé averred, the O.A.K. had proved itself an agent of southern traitors; General Price headed the southern branch of the traitorous organization, with Vallandigham as his agent and servant.[72]

The editor of the *Missouri Democrat*, a radical Republican newspaper despite its name, published Sanderson's exposé in its entirety and added his endorsement. As an important Republican whose friendship Sanderson had cultivated, he even published some of the "evidence," which seemed to give credibility to the report.[73]

Other Republican editors, recognizing the propaganda value of Sanderson's political potpourri in the developing presidential contest, not only published the document but wrote editorials to squelch the skeptical. The Chicago

70. U.S. Grant to Stanton, telegram, June 25, 1864, in *OR*, Ser. 2, Vol. VII, 411; Sanderson, "Special Orders, No. 184," in Union Provost Marshals' File of One-Name Papers *re* Citizens.
71. Sanderson, "Conspiracy to Establish a Northwestern Confederacy" (MS, [July 28, 1864], Sanderson Papers). There is no copy of it in the National Archives, nor does it appear in the *Official Records*. It was first published in the *Missouri Democrat*, and then in countless other newspapers. This document drew heavily from Sanderson's reports of June 12 and July 22, published in *OR*, Ser. 2, Vol. VII, 228–34, 314–17.
72. Sanderson, "Conspiracy to Establish a Northwestern Confederacy."
73. *Missouri Democrat*, July 28, 1864.

Tribune, *Illinois State Journal*, and the Cincinnati *Gazette* helped to popularize and publicize the "startling revelations." Even the New York *Tribune* published Sanderson's exposé in full and gloried in the discomfiture of the Democrats. The *Tribune* not only found Vallandigham, who had returned to Ohio two weeks earlier, and the American Knights guilty of "treason" and perfidy but asserted that the 200,000 "McClellan Minutemen" of New York were also involved in the conspiracy. Even some of the Confederate newspapers, grasping at straws, reprinted portions of the O.A.K. revelations appearing in the northern Republican newspapers.[74]

Sanderson also turned to his political friends to give his exposé widespread publicity. He sent a copy of "Conspiracy to establish a Northwestern Confederacy" to Governor Curtin of Pennsylvania, and he urged Governor Yates to use the "startling revelations" to good effect: stir the Union Leagues to action, discredit the Democracy, and influence voters in the fall elections.[75]

Midwestern Democrats, of course, denounced and discredited the concocted exposé. The Democratic-minded editor of the *Missouri Republican* ridiculed the whole affair in an editorial, "Chops and Tomato Sauce." "The getter-upper of these 'startling revelations,' " the editor wrote, "has done his work in an exceedingly bungling style, full of contradictions and inconsistencies." It was, added the editorial writer, a collection of fabrications devised to pander to "men's love of mystery." More than humbuggery was at stake, however, for men had been arbitrarily arrested with "all channels of denial closed to them."[76]

The Democratic editor of the New York *World* dismissed Sanderson's revelations as "a huge canard," and an indignant editorial writer on the staff of the New York *Journal of Commerce* wrote a vicious critique and stinging rebuke:

> Some stupid or wily agent, of the radicals out West, had discovered a mare's nest, and sent on recently a long rigmarole about a Northwest conspiracy. The agent of the press in St. Louis, who was victimized by this scamp, deserves sharp censure. A greater lot of trash and falsehood was never concocted for the telegraph wires. It is one of the old "Lincoln dodges" to affect the Chicago [Democratic National] Convention

---

74. Cincinnati *Daily Gazette*, July 30, 1864; Chicago *Daily Tribune*, July 31, 1864; (Springfield) *Illinois State Journal*, July 30, August 1, 1864; New York *Daily Tribune*, July 29, 1864; Richmond *Daily Dispatch*, August 26, 1864. The *Dispatch* based its account upon the revelations published in the Chicago *Daily Tribune*.

75. The editor of the *Missouri Democrat* had received a letter (dated July 28, 1864, and written by L. Newland) that urged the use of revelations for political gain and he passed the letter on to Sanderson. The expositor, in turn, forwarded the letter to Governor Yates and added an endorsement. The letter is in the Governor Richard Yates Papers, Illinois State Historical Library.

76. *Missouri Republican*, July 29, 1864.

and elevate the falling stock of the administration party; but is so weak an invention as not even to command contempt this hot weather. . . . Will someone ascertain the name of the incorrigible stupid who sent this long story over the wires.[77]

Wilbur F. Storey, editor of the Chicago *Times*, who was mentioned in the exposé as one of the O.A.K. leaders, stated that he had "never belonged to *any* secret organization." In fact, he added, until the time of the St. Louis revelations, he had "never heard" of any scheme or "movement or purpose in any quarter for the erection of a Northwestern Confederacy." Henry N. Walker of the Detroit *Free Press* added his words of disbelief, deriding the "Epicurean morsel" discovered by "an obscure Provost Marshal" in St. Louis. "Doubtless the idea of such a scheme," Walker wrote, "originated in the brain of some apprehensive, conscience-stricken 'loyal leaguer' who, cognizant of the profligacy and desperation of an administration tottering in its fall, thus gives it the benefit of an impromptu conspiracy." The indignant and perceptive editor added: "Like the shrewd Alcibiades who cut off the tail of his canine companion in order to give the people something else than himself to talk about, the Administration has hatched an alarming plot at St. Louis, to further dismember the Union, by separating the Northwest from the North, and it gives items to show there is something to this plot. The whole is got up to divert public attention from the misdeeds of the party in power." Showing disdain for Sanderson's exposé, editor Walker asked an interesting question: "Is the appetite of the miscegens and shoddy-ites so depraved that it constantly requires to be fed on humbugs, sensational dispatches, and falsehoods?"[78]

No Democratic editor exhibited more indignation than Charles H. Lanphier of the *Illinois State Register*. He wrote long, lively, and angry rebuttals, contending that Republicans had cried "Wolf!" so often that nobody believed the "sensations" or "scares" anymore. "The plots," Lanphier wrote, "have taken a thousand shapes; they have been designed to resist enrollment and the draft, to systemize desertion, to discourage enlistments, to cut railroads and thus prevent reinforcements from being forwarded, to kidnap and abduct Lincoln, and to organize troops for rebels in the border states; and the latest and most absurd is a 'plot for the establishment of a northwestern confederacy.'" Lanphier referred to the so-called discoveries as "mare's nests" and "washer woman conspiracies." And he wondered if Sanderson's exposé had been de-

---

77. New York *World*, August 2, 1864; New York *Journal of Commerce* (clipping, n.d., in Sanderson Papers).

78. Chicago *Times*, July 30, 1864; Detroit *Free Press*, August 22, 2, 1864.

vised and publicized as an excuse to establish martial law in the upper Midwest, so that the Lincoln administration could control the 1864 elections.[79]

Democratic denials and rebuttals stopped neither the circulation nor the popularization of Sanderson's O.A.K. revelations. His story later served as the foundation for Joseph Holt's report on secret societies prepared shortly before the November election.[80] Sanderson's exposé also served as the basis for myths that entered the stream of history after the war.

Democrats guessed that Sanderson's tall tales about the American Knights were devised largely as propaganda to discredit the Democracy and influence election results. None of them, evidently, realized that the ambitious colonel stationed in St. Louis had personal reasons for composing the exposé, that he wanted to rehabilitate a tarnished reputation, cover his failures as an administrator, and gain a brigadier general's star. Nor did Democrats know the irony of it all—that Sanderson's exposé was prepared after the Order of American Knights was a corpse.

Sanderson's O.A.K. exposé did help to win the 1864 elections, and Rosecrans gloried in the fact that it had "aided everywhere the triumph of the Union cause." Sanderson, however, did not live to see it, nor did he live long enough to refurbish his reputation and gain the brigadier generalship he coveted. After a month-long illness, he died in St. Louis on October 14, 1864.[81] Sanderson's Civil War career—checkered and scarred at best—would have been buried in dusty archives had he not concocted an exposé that maligned Vallandigham, put the national spotlight upon a dark lantern society named the Order of American Knights, and created a subversive-society legend with nine lives.

79. *Illinois State Register*, August 4, 1864.
80. Holt's report is the topic of Chapter V.
81. Rosecrans to Garfield, December 30, 1864, in Garfield Papers; *Missouri Democrat*, October 15, 1864.

CHAPTER IV

H. H. Dodd, the Sons of Liberty, and the Carrington Exposé

THE STORY of the Sons of Liberty is much like that of the Order of American Knights. Both were dark lantern societies with political objectives. Both were intended to be auxiliaries of the Democratic party and antidotes to the effective and successful Union League. Both had a principal founder, little success, and a limited membership; both fell victim to exposés prepared for political gain. The chief characters may have been different, but the main themes and the central plot remained much the same.

The story of the Sons of Liberty, in a large measure, revolved around the name of H. H. Dodd, a Hoosier who preferred his initials and never signed his full Christian name. Whereas George Bickley of the Golden Circle and Phineas C. Wright of the American Knights emerged from obscurity to gain notoriety, Dodd represented middle-class America and respectability before he became entangled in a web of his own making, the Sons of Liberty.

Harrison Horton Dodd could point to an ancestor, the progenitor of the famous Dodd family, whose name appeared in Connecticut records as early as 1647. His maternal grandfather had fought in the American Revolution and, during the later years of his life, lived in Jefferson County, New York. His father, a respected resident of Brownville, New York, had built and commanded the second American steamboat on Lake Ontario, sailing that inland sea "the greater part of thirty years." Young H. H. and an older brother had attended the common schools of Brownville before the father moved his brood to Toledo, Ohio, then a community of twenty souls. H. H. attended Gambia College for a term before entering upon a commercial career. At the age of twenty-three he married Anna Marie Bradford, one of the three pretty and respected daughters of "the Cooperstown Bradfords." Family tradition, verified by genealogical records, traces the Bradfords of Cooperstown to William Bradford, second governor of Plymouth Colony.[1]

H. H. Dodd made a small splash

1. The reminiscences of Julia Donley Dodd, who married H. H. Dodd's grandson,

in Toledo during the prewar years. He served as treasurer of a local organization of "Forwarders, Commission Men and Dealers" during the 1850s and belonged to the Masons and the Toledo Musical Association for several years.[2] He joined the Whigs "with a rush," and when that party disintegrated, he became an ardent Know-Nothinger. He sought the mayoralty as a Know-Nothinger in 1855, damning the "pauper Irish and Dutch democrats," whom he regarded as a threat to the American dream. Collecting only a hatful of votes, he expediently sloughed his interest in nativism and transferred his enthusiasm to the rising Republican party.

When brother John became state auditor of Indiana in 1856, H. H. Dodd moved from Toledo to Indianapolis and exchanged his Republican hat for a Democratic one. With political contacts and printing contracts available, the two brothers organized H. H. Dodd & Company, establishing themselves in a highly competitive field.[3] Playing the role of opportunist, H. H. appeared at Democratic party caucuses and city and county rallies and conventions. He claimed to revere Thomas Jefferson and Andrew Jackson as worthy political prophets.

The patriotic tide that engulfed the North after Fort Sumter affected Democrats as well as Republicans. H. H. Dodd, caught up in the excitement of the hour, advertised for recruits for the "Marion Dragoons," evidently hoping for a captaincy or a colonelcy.[4] The company failed to materialize; so Dodd returned to his office to attend to business matters, including plans to publish a city directory.[5]

In the weeks that followed, the patriotic tide ebbed and many Democrats became disillusioned with the war. As the fall elections approached, some Democrats became outright critics of the Lincoln administration and treason charges were hurled at them. A campaign of intimidation developed. Rowdies, fanning the flame of patriotism, vented their wrath upon the Terre Haute *Journal*, edited by an unrepentant Democrat. "Everything in the office and composing room, including presses, etc.," an observer noted, "were hurled into the street in the wildest destruction." The pressure for conformity extended in every direction. Calvin Fletcher, banker and friend of the governor,

fill eleven pages in a family journal now in the possession of her daughter, Mrs. John Gaffin, 371 E. Division Street, Fond du Lac, Wisconsin. H. H. Dodd's ancestry is traced in Allison Dodd and Joseph F. Folson, *Genealogy and History of the Daniel Dodd Family in America* (Bloomfield, N.J., 1940), I, 49, 88, 159.

2. Clark Waggoner, *History of Toledo and Lucas County* (New York, 1888), 474, 482.

3. The Indianapolis *Daily Journal*, January 31, 1864, gives sketchy information regarding Dodd's prewar years. He became, for a time, the "head and fount" of the Sons of Malta in Indianapolis.

4. John H. Holliday, *Indianapolis and the Civil War* (Indianapolis, 1911), 561.

5. Indianapolis *Daily State Sentinel*, December 13, 1863.

complained that the government had "given contracts to Secessionists and Jews" like "John Elder, [the] 2 Dodds, [and] John Talbert."[6]

Dodd had an early brush with forces encouraging conformism. On August 31, 1861, he attended the Marion County Democratic Convention in Indianapolis, called to endorse a slate of officers and approve a series of resolutions. Named one of the marshals, he also sought his party's nomination for county clerk, but it was an honor that escaped him. While the final speaker was excoriating Republicans for their sins, some self-styled patriots rushed the platform and threatened to pistol-whip the speaker for daring to criticize President Lincoln. Dodd, a six-footer whose blue eyes flashed fire, rebuked the ruffians and helped to restore order and reconvene the meeting. His courage, coupled with tact, gained respect even from his political enemies. Later in the evening, the same ruffians, after visiting the grog shops, formed a vigilante committee and "hunted up" leading Democrats to force them to take an oath of loyalty or suffer the consequences. Interestingly, these bullies did not visit Dodd's home although they intimidated others, including Joseph J. Bingham, editor of the Democratic-oriented Indianapolis *State Sentinel*.[7]

Instead of rebuking such practices, it seemed as if Governor Oliver P. Morton and editor Berry R. Sulgrove of the Republican-minded Indianapolis *Journal* approved them. Sulgrove even termed the action of the mob "a first rate joke," intensifying the indignation of such Democrats as Bingham and Dodd.[8]

In the months that followed, H. H. Dodd climbed the political ladder slowly, sometimes slipping along the way. He gained recognition as a zealous, hardworking, and reliable member of the party. Personable and characterized as a "very kind hearted fellow," he widened his circle of acquaintances by speaking at dozens of local Democratic rallies, usually ward or township meetings.[9] He learned to call upon the spirit of Jefferson or Jackson for guidance or inspiration and to condemn "the extremists"—the abolitionists of the North and the secessionists of the South. He convinced himself, while trying to convince others, that Republicanism was a political heresy and that civil rights were endangered. Dodd's ability to please a partisan audience made them overlook the fact that his past was a blend of inconsistency and changing enthusiasms, with a strong strain of opportunism and imprudence.

6. Terre Haute *Express*, October 22, 1861, quoted *ibid.*, October 23, 1861; Calvin Fletcher Diary, December 21, 1861, (MS in Calvin Fletcher Papers, Indiana Historical Society Library, Indianapolis).

7. Indianapolis *Daily State Sentinel*, September 2, 1861; Indianapolis *Daily Journal*, September 2, 1861.

8. Indianapolis *Daily Journal*, September 1, 1861.

9. Cincinnati *Daily Enquirer* (n.d.), quoted in Indianapolis *Daily Journal*, November 4, 1864. At a later date, a colleague characterized Dodd as "a very hot-headed and injudicious man," whose "plans and projects would be in inverse ratio to his means to carry them into effect."

While his printing firm was getting out the 1862 Indianapolis city directory, H. H. Dodd continued to work in the political vineyards. He served as chief marshal at the Democratic State Convention, which met in Indianapolis on January 2, 1862. He also spoke at occasional county meetings or party rallies, gaining a reputation as an effective speaker.[10]

While patrolling the polls in his precinct during the October 14 (1862) elections, Dodd witnessed the so-called Elder incident. John R. Elder, publisher of the Indianapolis *State Sentinel* and venerable Democrat, had offered his services as a poll watcher to challenge unregistered voters bent on voting for opposition candidates. He challenged several soldiers who insisted upon voting even though their names did not appear on the poll lists. When the election judges upheld Elder's protest, one of the soldiers started an argument with the challenger and accused him of prorebel sympathies. Some twenty soldiers, all insisting upon voting illegally, then attacked Elder and made him flee for his life.[11] This incident seems to have made an indelible impression upon Dodd, evolving into a fear that civil rights might be lost and free elections disappear in Indiana.

Governor Morton failed to denounce the soldiers involved in the Elder incident, and Colonel Henry B. Carrington, commander of the same soldiers, failed to discipline or reprimand them. Editor Sulgrove of the Indianapolis *Journal* failed to rebuke the soldiers for taking things into their own hands and even implied that dissenters had no rights. Democrats, of course, were dismayed and concerned. Should they organize a mutual protection society to insure their rights and maintain free elections?

The October elections buoyed Democratic hopes and stunned the Republicans. Democrats elected their slate of state officers by a majority of more than nine thousand votes, won seven of the eleven congressional contests, and secured a tenuous control of both houses of the state legislature. Luckily for the Republicans, Governor Morton's seat was not contested, for he had been elected to a four-year term in 1860. It was evident to all that Governor Morton would face a hostile state legislature during the early months of 1863.

Dodd, like Democrats generally, gloried in the election returns, regarding them as a repudiation of Republican policies. He spoke at several party jollifications, including one in Hendricks County where four thousand Democrats enjoyed a sumptuous barbecue and an array of speakers who roasted the Republicans. Heartened, Dodd appeared more often in the Democratic marketplace. He served on the finance committee at the December meeting of the Marion County Democratic Club.[12] The following month Indianapolis Demo-

10. Indianapolis *Daily State Sentinel*, January 9, July 18, 1862.
11. *Ibid.*, October 15, 1862.
12. *Ibid.*, November 1, December 13, 1862.

crats elected him president of their citywide association, proof that many of his colleagues regarded him as a reliable and deserving fellow.

In his acceptance speech, Dodd stated his fears that the federal union, as Jefferson knew it, was "gone forever—a thing of the past." Its place, Dodd said, had been taken by a consolidated government that had a tendency toward despotism. Republicans ought to give up their isms for the sake of unity and the country's welfare. He commented that the Republican claims of a conspiracy to take the Northwest out of the Union were pure propaganda, but he insisted that the West would never become the slave and servant of New England. Nor did he believe Republican talk about the Knights of the Golden Circle. He quipped that he did not want to hurt the sale of the Golden Circle booklet published by a rival printing plant.[13] But Dodd foresaw the birth of such an organization if Democrats were pressed too much:

> There might be an order, however, not for any treasonable purposes, but to keep the powers that be within their constitutional limits, a true and devoted Union order . . . and if some men wished to find out its objects and aims further than this, they have only to do as they have done before, place arms in the hands of their sons and send them to the polls in company with hired ruffians to intimidate and overawe peaceful citizens in the exercise of their constitutional right. Let them try this again, and they might find out what the secret order meant.[14]

H. H. Dodd was not the only Hoosier who thought that his rights were being eroded and his constitutional guarantees threatened. Even Bingham, the rather conservative editor of the Indianapolis *State Sentinel*, implied that Democrats might have to organize mutual protection societies. Bingham had wondered aloud, "Is it not time that the people should openly organize for their own protection?"[15]

The early months of 1863 tested the mettle and convictions of Democrats and Republicans alike. Indiana was an excellent testing ground. There was widespread reaction to Lincoln's proclamation of emancipation in some quarters, and a genuine belief that it was unconstitutional and unwise. The debate over federal conscription heightened tensions and partyism. Republican members of the state legislature bolted to break a quorum and bring the session to an end in order to nullify Democratic efforts to usurp some of Governor Morton's powers. The impasse between Morton and the so-called Copperhead

---

13. C. C. Perrine & Company, a firm in competition with H. H. Dodd & Company, had published James M. Hiatt's *An Authentic Exposition of the K.G.C., Knights of the Golden Circle; or, A History of Secession from 1834 to 1861* (Indianapolis, 1861).

14. Indianapolis *Daily State Sentinel*, January 28, 1863.

15. *Ibid.*, January 16, 1863.

legislature led to the collapse of constitutional power in Indiana and in the end the governor ran the show in a rather arbitrary fashion.[16]

Morton's sins paled, however, when compared to those of Colonel Carrington and Brigadier General Milo S. Hascall. Carrington, commanding the military District of Indiana, issued a series of edicts that alarmed Democrats: he censored the mail and the telegraph, established a network of spies, arrested a state circuit judge, and sought summary powers. Once Carrington defied Chief Justice Samuel E. Perkins of the state supreme court, invading his chambers and tearing up a writ the judge had issued. Hascall, characterized as "a village lawyer whom the misfortune of his country converted into a brigadier-general," also used his authority in a distressing fashion.[17] When his commander, General Ambrose E. Burnside, issued "General Orders, No. 38," April 27, 1863, announcing that "the habit of declaring sympathies for the enemy [would] be no longer tolerated," Hascall responded with "General Order No. 9." This extension and interpretation of Burnside's order declared that all newspaper reports or speeches endeavoring "to bring the war policy of the Government into dispute" would bring arrest and trial by military courts.[18]

Democrats denounced such infringement of freedom of speech and of the press. Some defied Hascall. The editor of the Plymouth *Democrat* called Hascall "a donkey." Hascall ordered the indiscreet editor arrested, taken to Cincinnati, and arraigned before a military court. For good measure, Hascall suppressed the Columbia City *News* and the South Bend *Forum*.

To Governor Morton's credit, he opposed the appointment of Hascall, was critical of his "General Order No. 9" and his conduct, and agitated for his removal. He succeeded in June of 1863, when Indiana and Michigan were combined into a single military district under General Orlando B. Willcox. Willcox, too, served at Morton's pleasure and was eventually replaced by Carrington, back for another stint with Morton.

In addition to the threat from the military, furloughed soldiers or self-styled patriots exerted pressure upon dissenters. In March, 1863, for example, a group of Union soldiers (most of them paroled prisoners taken at Murfrees-

16. Kenneth M. Stampp, *Indiana Politics During the Civil War* (Indianapolis, 1949), 158–85, deals with the situation in a chapter entitled "The Collapse of Constitutional Government." The same ground is covered, albeit more sympathetically, in Lorna Lutes Sylvester, "Oliver P. Morton and Hoosier Politics During the Civil War" (Ph.D. dissertation, Indiana University, 1968), 157–203. Chapter V, "Disunion at Home" (pp. 180–224) in Emma Lou Thornbrough, *Indiana in the Civil War Era, 1850–1880*, History of Indiana, III (Indianapolis, 1965), exemplifies excellent scholarship.

17. (London) *Times*, June 4, 1863.

18. *The War of the Rebellion: A Compilation of the Official Records of the Union and Confederate Armies* (128 vols.; Washington, D.C.; 1880–1901), Ser. 2, Vol. V, 485; Indianapolis *Daily State Sentinel*, April 27, 1863.

boro) stopped in Richmond to destroy the offices of the *Jeffersonian*. Then too, Indiana Democrats were concerned about General Burnside's suppression of the Chicago *Times* and the summary treatment accorded Clement L. Vallandigham. They recognized that the brash general's action was a threat to their rights as well as Vallandigham's. "For when his right goes down," stated one Democratic editor who had no special love for Vallandigham, "there goes down with it my right, and yours, and every man's." [19]

Democrats were also concerned about Governor Morton's campaign to discredit all who refused to join hands with Republicans by labeling them traitors, Copperheads, or secessionists. Morton claimed that the Knights of the Golden Circle were active in Democratic strongholds, and he implied that Republicans had a monopoly on patriotism. Reports circulated that Morton was organizing the Lincoln Leagues and that Colonel Carrington was arming some chapters that possessed military auxiliaries. Democrats feared that these Loyal Legions might be used by Morton to control the elections, quash civil rights, and sustain the governor's one-man rule.

Blatant partisanship, practiced by both sides, engendered bitterness, hatreds, and distrust. It reached a new intensity in the spring of 1863 and was cultivated with ferocity, especially in Indiana. Republicans thought it unpatriotic for Democrats to seek votes in the field of war weariness and public apprehension about military conscription. They reacted with anger and Democrats repaid them in kind.

Encouraged by the election results of the previous fall, Democrats looked forward to the April elections and sought to rally their disorganized forces. Dodd again entered the political lists, scheduling half a dozen speaking engagements. He spoke at a Democratic rally at Vortland on March 12, 1863, and at the First Ward Democratic meeting in Indianapolis six days later. Then he took a trip to Danville to address a mass meeting of the Democracy of Hendricks County. The trip proved to be a harrowing experience. The train took him only as far as Cartersville, where he had to hire a carriage to complete the trip to Danville. Rowdies, aided by some soldiers on furlough, harassed the Indianapolis Democrat, mixing verbal abuse with threats of violence. His experiences in Danville were also most unpleasant. In the first place, Republican-minded officials had denied Democrats the use of the county courthouse where the meeting had originally been scheduled; so local party members had rescheduled the meeting out-of-doors. Then, while the rally was in session, armed Union Leaguers drilled nearby. Ruffians, at the fringe of the crowd, interrupted speakers, shouted obscenities, and occasionally fired revolvers in the air. While Dodd was speaking, some of the rowdies

19. Detroit *Free Press*, May 26, June 7, 1863.

rushed the platform, mixing curses and insults. After order was restored and the session ended, Dodd began the homeward trek. He was threatened again en route to Cartersville, and then while he was awaiting the arrival of his train at the depot, a mob of "soldiers and Union League members" seized Dodd. They threatened him, jostled him, and called him a traitor. Some suggested tarring and feathering him; the more savage suggested he be strung up in the nearest tree. The arrival of the train, the influence of some moderates, and "the intervention of Providence" led to Dodd's release and departure for home.[20] He arrived in Indianapolis visibly shaken by his harrowing experiences and perhaps more than ever convinced that civil rights and free elections might disappear unless Democrats organized themselves to protect their lives and their liberties.

The sufferance of Indianapolis Democrats was sorely tested during the April elections when there was a series of unsavory incidents, including some acts of violence. Soldiers stationed near Indianapolis, especially those at Camp Morton, voted at nearby polling places in defiance of laws and proper procedures. The frequency of intimidation at the polling places caused some of the more timid and wary Democrats to stay home rather than face abuse in public. When Republicans refused Democrats representation on the election boards, the entire slate of Democratic nominees for city office withdrew in protest, implying that free and fair elections no longer existed in the state's largest city.[21] Dodd and his fellow Democrats seemed to believe that only abuse and defeat would greet them at the polls.

Events seemed to go from bad to worse. The defeat of Union forces under "Fighting Joe" Hooker at Chancellorsville convinced some of the war-weary and faint-hearted that the South could not be conquered by force of arms. Dodd, who had vacillated on the question of war-or-compromise, now became an out-and-out peace man. Reports of military misrule in Kentucky, rumors about the use of black troops, and General Hascall's officious military edicts made Democratic blood boil.

As General Hascall tested the tolerance of his critics, the Indiana Democracy assembled in Indianapolis on May 20 for a state convention. Perhaps twenty thousand of the party faithful attended, many crowding around the half dozen speakers' platforms, the size of each group being directly proportional to the orator's reputation and oratorical ability. The largest assemblage crowded around the main platform where Daniel W. Voorhees, "the Tall Sycamore of the Wabash," and Thomas A. Hendricks, "the Shelbyville Oracle," held forth.

Informed that General Hascall had mobilized some army units nearby and

20. Indianapolis *Daily State Sentinel*, March 30, 1863.
21. *Ibid.*, May 2, 3, 1863, Indianapolis *Daily Journal*, May 2, 1863.

believing that the brash general intended to overawe the Democracy, Voorhees made a bid for martyrdom. He blistered the Lincoln administration, criticized the treatment accorded Vallandigham, and in a crescendo of eloquence, lauded civil liberties as the bulwark against despotism.

While Voorhees orated, a disturbance took place at one of the outlying stands, where soldiers rushed the platform and stopped a speech by Samuel R. Hanill of Sullivan County, a stronghold of Copperheadism. Numerous fights between soldiers and Democrats followed and a score of the latter were arrested—some for defying the soldiery, some for uttering "disloyal sentiments," and some for carrying concealed weapons. Soon after, while Hendricks was addressing the crowd at the main stand, soldiers on the fringe of the crowd formed ranks for action. With fixed bayonets, they advanced and asked the speaker to cease his "treasonable utterances." Just when bloodshed seemed inevitable some officers and several squads of cavalry arrived and ordered the trouble-making soldiers away. Hendricks ended his speech abruptly, the assembled hurriedly approved a set of resolutions, and the chairman adjourned the meeting as rowdyism became more and more prevalent.[22]

Later, as the Cincinnati and Bellefontaine trains pulled out of the station loaded with Democrats, several imprudent passengers fired their pistols in the air as a goodbye gesture. Military authorities used the indiscretions as an excuse to stop the trains, search the passengers, and confiscate the weapons. Republicans, with tongue in cheek, later dubbed the incident "the Battle of Pogue's Run."[23]

H. H. Dodd considered the events of May 20 another affront to Democrats, another instance when constitutional rights were violated. He took the lead, at least in Indianapolis, in urging Democrats to consider a secret political society that might serve as a mutual protection agency, a guarantor of civil rights and free elections, and a counterweight to the Lincoln, or Union, Leagues. He received no support from members of the party hierarchy. Joseph Bingham of the *State Sentinel* had adamantly put himself on record against such dark lantern societies.[24] Then Dodd's desire to establish a Democratic organization on the order of the Union League received a setback from another quarter. Soon after he assumed his command in June, 1863, General Willcox issued a decree outlawing such organizations regardless of party. The general took his action without consulting Governor Morton, creator of the Lincoln League in

22. Indianapolis *Daily State Sentinel*, May 21, 22, 1863.
23. Milo S. Hascall, "Report" (MS, September 25, 1865, in Archives Division, Indiana State Library, Indianapolis); Indianapolis *Daily Journal*, May 21, 1863; Indianapolis *Daily State Sentinel*, May 21, 27, 1863. Military headquarters reported that forty-five weapons were taken from Democrats aboard the train. The editor of the Indianapolis *Journal*, exaggerating as always, claimed that between fifteen hundred and two thousand pistols were confiscated.
24. Indianapolis *Daily State Sentinel*, June 24, 1863.

Indiana, much to Morton's displeasure.[25] The governor soon succeeded in replacing the new commander.

Dodd, evidently, shelved his hopes for a secret Democratic society for the time being and returned to cultivating his political fields. He gave a Fourth of July oration at a party picnic in Lawrence Township. There he traced the coming of the war, trying to convince his audience that fanaticism was ruling the day. Abolition, Dodd said, was but a vicious form of it. He spoke out for peace, compromise, and reunion. He did not favor a dishonorable peace, he said, but one that was just and reasonable and would lead to reunion. And he counseled obedience to the law, even to the widely detested conscription act.[26]

The following month Dodd met Phineas C. Wright, still trying to spread the gospel of the Order of American Knights. Wright found a believer in Dodd, for the Indiana Democrat had convinced himself that Governor Morton might purge the voting rolls and that civil rights might be erased. Dodd eventually accepted the headship of the Indiana branch of the O.A.K., but he had little luck in making the organization a vibrant force in the state.[27]

While involved with Wright's dark lantern society, Dodd continued to promote the Democratic party. He was the featured speaker, for example, at a Morocco gathering of Democrats of Newton County on August 20. Then, in early September, he took a trip to Rensselaer to address a Democratic rally nearly 2,500 strong. He handled the Lincoln administration critically, directing most of his fire at the use of federal troops to control the elections of Kentucky. He also expressed the fear that bayonets might be used to keep Democrats from voting in Indiana and other key states of the upper Midwest. The ballot box, Dodd declared dogmatically and dramatically, was the last hope of the people, and when and if they are denied voting rights, it is time to resist. Dodd was but reciting sentiments expressed by other Democrats, thinking that such outspoken views might discourage any inclination to purge the rolls. The editor of the Sullivan *Democrat*, for example, had expressed the same sentiments in an editorial: "No Burnside or bayonets shall stand between the people of Indiana and the expression of their will. They must vote their sentiments, even if they have to clear a path to the polls with their swords. Liberty is worth fighting for or it is worth nothing." [28]

25. Willcox's proclamation, dated June 30, 1863, is published in William H. H. Terrell, *Report of the Adjutant General of Indiana* (8 vols.; Indianapolis, 1869), I, "Appendix," 278.

26. Indianapolis *Daily State Sentinel*, July 6, 1863.

27. William M. Harrison, testimony, in Benn Pitman (ed.), *The Trials for Treason at Indianapolis, Disclosing the Plans for Establishing a North-western Confederacy: Being the Official Record of the Trials Before the Military Commission Convened by Special Orders No. 129, Headquarters, District of Indiana* (Cincinnati, 1865), 89.

28. Indianapolis *Daily State Sentinel*, August 20, September 15, 1863; Sullivan (Ind.) *Democrat*, August 27, 1863.

A Methodist minister who heard Dodd speak at Rensselaer interpreted his remarks as treasonable and lodged a complaint with the provost marshal of the district, even asking for the arrest of the "traitor." The provost marshal, without a warrant and without authority, took Dodd into custody. Indignant Democrats talked of recrimination or a rescue, and a crowd began to assemble at one of the grog shops. Saner heads prevailed; some sensible and concerned Republicans convinced the provost marshal that he should give Dodd his freedom as a means to forestall mob action. After his release, Dodd cooperated with local authorities by sending word to his would-be rescuers that he had been set free. In this instance, at least, Dodd deserved credit for cooperating with leading citizens of Rensselaer to prevent a riot.[29]

The unsavory incident more than ever convinced Dodd that a mutual protection society was not only desirable but absolutely necessary if Democrats were to preserve their rights and liberties. Again he tried to promote the Order of American Knights. He presided over a state council of the O.A.K. late in November and even got Bingham to play ball for a short time. Then, in December, he attended the national convention in Chicago and heard James A. McMaster of New York City characterize the order as a "humbug" and its architect as "a humbugger." Dodd realized that McMaster's critical comments had given the deathblow to the O.A.K.[30]

Disillusioned with the Order of American Knights, Dodd returned to Indianapolis to try to give shape to a dream of his own: he would devise a dark lantern society, the Sons of Liberty, upon the ruins of Wright's disintegrating organization. While giving shape to his dream, he attended his party's Sixth (Congressional) District convention, held in Indianapolis on January 8, 1863. The convention's responsibilities were to draft and adopt a set of resolutions expressing the sentiments of the Democrats present, and to select two delegates to represent the district at the forthcoming Democratic National Convention.

Dodd, seeking to be named one of the district's delegates, soon realized that antiwar sentiment dominated the mood of the hour. Given a chance to speak on the issues of the day, Dodd stated his propeace views with conviction. One word summed up his views, he said—*peace*. Yes, he wanted a "speedy, honorable, and permanent peace." Nor should the Democracy, in-

29. Indianapolis *Daily State Sentinel*, August 20, 1863.

30. The national convention of the O.A.K. in Chicago is treated more extensively in the previous chapter. Also see Joseph J. Bingham, testimony, October 28, 1864, in Proceedings of the Military Commission Convened in Indianapolis, General Courts Martial Records, Records of the Office of the Judge Advocate General, National Archives, and James A. McMaster, testimony before the Cincinnati Military Commission, March 25, 1865, in *House Executive Documents*, 39th Cong., 2nd Sess., 519–30.

fused with the spirit of Andy Jackson, allow forces representing the Lincoln administration to impose a president upon the people through "force, fraud, or violence." The majority of the convention members evidently agreed with Dodd's views and selected him one of the Sixth District delegates to attend the Chicago convention of July 4 and work for the nomination of a peace candidate, rather than George B. McClellan.[31]

During the following four weeks, Dodd spent considerable time giving shape to the Sons of Liberty, although he never used that name. He presented it as "an organization" or "our organization" and portrayed it as an auxiliary of the Democratic party, an association of conservatives devoted to the principles of the "founding fathers" of the Constitution. He composed a six-page booklet entitled *Constitution and Laws of the S.G.C.*—that is, Supreme Grand Council. Without mentioning the Sons of Liberty by name, Dodd listed the organization's goals in a single sentence: "Its object and purposes are the maintenance of constitutional freedom and States' rights, as recognized and established by the founders of our Republic." The booklet provided for national offices, headed by a supreme commander and a Supreme Grand Council, consisting of the grand commander and two elected delegates from each state.[32] Now that the outline and form were provided, all the new organization needed was officers and members.

Dodd intended to formalize his organization, still unnamed, at a February 16 meeting in Democratic party headquarters in Indianapolis. He contacted dozens of Democratic leaders, including members of the party hierarchy, and twisted arms as best he could. To some he emphasized the need for a meeting and an organization to promote peace and the nomination of a true peace man at the party's national convention in Chicago on July 4. To others he spoke of the need of a mutual protection society or a dark lantern auxiliary (to the Democratic party) devoted to winning elections and preserving civil rights. Occasionally he argued that the Democracy needed an organization similar to the Union League, a banding together of conservative men interested in preserving the fundamental principles of the nation. As a means to put his organization on a practical basis, he composed "an address" and had it printed as a pamphlet by his own press.

Thirty or forty attended the get-together, later characterized as a "state council meeting." There was a sprinkling of out-of-towners, including the ubiquitous William A. Bowles of French Lick, Horace Heffren of Salem, Thomas J. Blake of Terre Haute, and William Cushman of Fort Wayne. Bing-

31. Indianapolis *Daily State Sentinel*, January 9, 1864.

32. *Constitution and Laws of the S.G.C.* (n.p., n.d.), in General Courts Martial Records. This item and others were seized in a raid upon Dodd's office and were used to develop the case against Dodd and others during the Indianapolis treason trials.

ham, apprehensive about the whole thing, divided his time between the meeting place and his own newspaper office, dropping in and out.[33]

Dodd's address, cloaked in righteous rhetoric, repeated the usual Democratic contentions. The centralization of power in Washington and Governor Morton's high-handed tactics were deplored; freeing the slaves and promoting racial equality were affronts to the white man; peace must be achieved through an "honorable adjustment of the issues involved in this unholy and unnatural war"; men should not be taxed "to carry forward a war of emancipation, miscegenation, confiscation, or extermination"; and Democrats must be willing to fight to the bitter end for their rights as citizens and voters.[34]

The grand council adopted nine partisan resolutions expressing the sentiments usually stated at Democratic meetings. One of them warned authorities that Democrats would defend their rights, if need be, with force and vigor; "*Resolved*, That there is a point at which submission merges the man in the slave, and resistance becomes a duty. . . . We will resist by force any attempt to abridge the elective franchise, whether by the introduction of illegal voters, under military authority, or the attempt by Federal officers to intimidate the citizens by threats of suppression."[35]

Dodd engaged in a game of make-believe. The report of the grand secretary, presented by William M. Harrison, set state membership in "the organization" at twelve thousand. Dodd evidently wanted to convince those present that his dark lantern society was a going concern, and he wanted to overawe Republicans so elections would be free. Dodd's claim (in the secretary's report) that the order was active in other midwestern states as well as six eastern states was sheer pretense. The grand secretary's report ended with a hope and a prayer: "This is the first and only truly national organization the Democratic and Conservative men of the country have ever attempted, and we are assured that through it, and it only, can the peace, harmony and union of these States be restored."[36]

Dodd's excursions into the land of make-believe did not deceive most of

33. Bingham, testimony, October 28, 1864, in Proceedings of the Military Commission Convened in Indianapolis.

34. *Proceedings of the Grand Council of the State of Indiana, at Their Meeting, Held on the 16th and 17th of February* (Indianapolis, 1864), in General Courts Martial Records. Dodd was guilty of many pretensions, including that the meeting was a two-day rather than a one-day affair.

35. *Ibid.*

36. *Ibid.* These contentions regarding membership are unsubstantiated by any credible evidence. Certainly the papers and materials seized in raids upon Dodd's office and home and Harrison's quarters contain *no* evidence to prove that "the organization" was extensive or even existent. Only one of the letters seized even mentions a charter and this was more an inquiry than an assertion. I believe the grand secretary's report a fictitious one, intended more for Republican consumption than anything else. Yet this document serves as the base for the historical myth that 12,000 members belonged to Dodd's "organization," whatever its name, in February of 1864.

the Democrats present at the February 16 session. When Bingham asked Heffren what he thought of Dodd's organization, the Salem Democrat bluntly said it was "a humbug." Bingham agreed and soon told Dodd he wanted an "out."[37] Since Bingham was the most influential member of the Democratic party's hierarchy, it meant that Dodd's organization—still without a formal name—would not have the party's endorsement.

Nor were Bingham and Heffren the only doubters. Democrats who favored McClellan as the party's presidential nominee also questioned the motives of Dodd and his organization. Since Dodd and others close to him were out-and-out peace men, some Democrats feared that the new secret society would be an agency to prevent McClellan's nomination. "An active and determined minority," one apprehensive supporter of McClellan's candidacy wrote, "may by secret organization, control the State Convention, unless the majority is well organized."[38]

While Bingham was extracting himself from the quicksand, Dodd packed his bags for a trip to New York City to attend a semisecret get-together of propeace Democrats intent upon stopping the rumbling McClellan-for-president express. The conference, chiefly the work of two New York Democrats of the Fernando Wood wing of the party, Charles G. Gunther and John McKeon, was called to find means to nominate a peace man at Chicago.[39]

The New York semisecret conference of anti-McClellan men on February 22, 1864, evolved into an exercise in futility. Few Democratic leaders attended, and those who arrived on time adjourned and recessed while awaiting the laggards. The whole affair seemed disorganized and disheartening, with the members present realizing that no human power could prevent McClellan's nomination in Chicago on July 4. In time, the self-styled delegates turned to the question of endorsing or organizing some kind of secret Democratic society to work in behalf of nominating an out-and-out peace man and to counter the effective work of the Union League. With James A. McMaster leading the way, those present agreed that the Order of American Knights was a fantasy. McMaster called it "a humbug," and Phineas C. Wright was not present to defend his dying organization.[40] When McMaster said he might

37. Bingham, testimony, October 28, 1864, in Proceedings of the Military Commission Convened in Indianapolis.
38. A. Banning Norton to Samuel L. M. Barlow, February 8, 1864, in Samuel L. M. Barlow Papers, Huntington Library, San Marino, Calif.
39. Strangely, Edward C. Kirkland, *The Peacemakers of 1864* (New York, 1927), widely acclaimed in its day, makes no mention of the peace men's powwow. The call for the convention was by a printed circular letter, sent by the sponsors to known anti-McClellan Democrats. A copy, dated February 8, 1864, is in the Charles Mason Papers, State Department of History and Archives, Historical Library, Des Moines. It was also signed by William W. Eaton and John Cotton Smith of Connecticut and Daniel Holsman and Samuel Lilly of New Jersey.
40. McMaster, testimony before the Cincinnati Commission, March 25, 1865, in *House Executive Documents*, 39th Cong., 2nd Sess., 519–30.

accept a quasi-secret Democratic organization—without oaths and hocus-pocus—Dodd stepped forward and contended that he already had the skeleton of such an order in Indiana, with honorable objectives and supported by conservative men. When McMaster said he might accept one called "the States' Rights Association" or the "Sons of Liberty," Dodd fastened the latter name upon his society, and his new dark lantern society was then and there officially christened the Sons of Liberty.

Amos Green of Illinois and Dr. James A. Barret of Missouri proposed Clement L. Vallandigham as head of the Sons of Liberty. They had detoured through Windsor on their way to New York and had talked with Vallandigham about a secret political society to counter the work of the Union League and to help nominate and elect a peace man as president.[41] Although the assembled Democrats could agree upon no definite format, a number of the assembled delegates, including H. H. Dodd and Dr. Thomas C. Massey of Ohio, favored some such society, especially if Vallandigham would agree to head it.

On the way home, Dodd and Massey went to Windsor to visit with Vallandigham and report that he had been elected supreme commander of the Sons of Liberty. They showed him the partially drafted constitution and ritual, both evidently concocted between New York and Windsor. Vallandigham, reluctant at first, finally assented provided he was given a hand in revising the tenets and ritual. He vetoed much of the ritual and hocus-pocus that Dodd presented and added selections from the Virginia and Kentucky resolutions of 1798 as "lessons of the Inner Temple." He insisted that the membership oath include sustainment of the Constitution of the United States. In conclusion, Vallandigham agreed to "faithfully discharge the duties of the chief officer of the Sons of Liberty" for a year.[42]

Although Vallandigham became the nominal head of the Sons of Liberty, Dodd remained the organization's chief architect and apostle. Back home, after his trip to New York City and Windsor, he set out to formalize the society, composing four booklets of general laws, instructions, and rituals—each of which, it is assumed, was printed by H. H. Dodd & Company.

The first of the four, entitled *General Laws of the S.L.*, contained instructions on how to organize temples and how to conduct meetings. Then there were three small booklets, each with a different title, a different-colored cover, and a different purpose. The brown-covered one, entitled *S.L.*, dealt with the ritual and initiation procedures of the Sons of Liberty. The blue-covered one, entitled *I.*, for Innermost Temple, assured the initiate that his

41. Amos Green, testimony, April 3, 1865, *ibid.*, 183–87, 519–30; Clement L. Vallandigham, testimony before the Cincinnati Commission, March 29, 1865, published in the Cincinnati *Daily Enquirer*, March 30, 1865.

42. Vallandigham, testimony before the Cincinnati Commission, March 25, 1865, published in the Cincinnati *Daily Enquirer*, March 30, 1865.

obligations to the order "were not inconsistent with his duty to God, to his country, to his family, or to himself." The lessons of the Innermost Temple included three resolutions from those drafted by Thomas Jefferson and James Madison in 1798 and suggested by Vallandigham at Windsor in his conference with Dodd and Massey. The third tiny booklet, red-covered and entitled *G.C.I.*, outlined the constitution and structure of the Grand Council of Indiana. For good measure, Dodd composed a circular letter to accompany his packet of materials. The undated letter was addressed "Dear Sir" and signed "Office Grand Secretary, S.L." It urged interested parties to organize temples and stated that "material changes" in the ritual had been made by "the authority of the Supreme Council of the United States." The letter closed with this strange request: "You will please send an accredited member of your Temple here, as soon as possible for instruction, and with him you can send the amount due from your County, as the money is absolutely necessary and must be forthcoming."[43]

While Dodd was trying to give substance to his dream, the man who held the nominal title of supreme commander grew restless at Windsor and wanted to return to the United States, even at the risk of being arrested again. He hoped his friends would name him one of the delegates-at-large scheduled to be chosen at the March 23 state convention at Columbus, Ohio. "If he is chosen as a delegate," one supporter of Vallandigham wrote, "the Democracy of Ohio will see that he attends the Chicago Convention."[44]

Election as a delegate-at-large to the Democratic national convention was a prize that eluded Vallandigham at Columbus, however. He came close but lost by a hair. His loyal friends then set their sights upon the Third District convention, the site and date of which were yet unannounced, hoping he might redeem the honor there that he had lost at Columbus.

Meanwhile, the out-and-out peace Democrats searched for ways to prevent the nomination of General McClellan as their party's presidential candidate. A handful, representing five or six states, met with Vallandigham in mid-April to discuss strategy and tactics. As a result of the deliberations in the Hirons House, Vallandigham agreed to write an open letter for publication and circulation in the Democratic press. The letter would emphasize the need for peace and compromise and recommend the adoption of a peace plank and the nomination of a peace man at Chicago.[45]

43. The four booklets and the printed circular letter were seized in a raid upon Dodd's quarters, and are in the extensive materials of the General Courts Martial Records.

44. John A. Trimble to David A. Houk, April 14, 1864, in Alexander Boys Papers, Ohio Historical Society, Columbus.

45. Vallandigham, testimony before the Cincinnati Commission, March 29, 1865, published in the Cincinnati *Daily Enquirer*, March 30, 1865.

Later in the day, four of the Democratic hopefuls, including H. H. Dodd, met in Vallandigham's room to consider ways to make the Sons of Liberty a viable and effective organization and to continue the discussion of basic political issues. S. Corning Judd, seeking the Democratic gubernatorial nomination in Illinois, reported on conditions in his state. Democrats in Illinois, Judd asserted, would not give up their civil rights—especially free elections—without a struggle. Stretching the truth to the breaking point, Judd said that the Sons of Liberty were well established in Illinois, even possessing a de facto "military organization."[46]

Dodd then reported on affairs in Indiana. He condemned both President Lincoln and Governor Morton and argued that the Sons of Liberty, if organized extensively, could become the savior of civil rights. Self-styled patriots and soldiers, Dodd said, had set themselves above the law, serving as censors and resorting to vigilante action. They had destroyed the newspaper offices of the Vincennes *Sun* and the Franklin *Herald* and had tried to assault the building housing the Princeton *Democrat*.[47] Democrats needed a mutual protection society to check such dastardly acts, nullify the work of the Union League, salvage civil rights, ensure free elections, and check governmental usurpation.

When Dr. Thomas C. Massey talked about affairs in Ohio, Vallandigham bent an interested ear. The Ohio Democracy, Massey asserted, had not yet fully recovered from its defeat of the previous fall and was still factionalized and disheartened. The mobbing of the office of the *Crisis* in Columbus and the approach of the 1864 presidential election seemed to revive the party. Having done nothing to extend the Sons of Liberty into Ohio, Massey spent most of his time talking about the spreading peace sentiment. In Congress, Alexander Long of Cincinnati had openly espoused an armistice, while Samuel Medary of the *Crisis* continued to wave the white flag vigorously.[48]

Charles L. Hunt, who was being urged to head the Sons of Liberty in Missouri, added a note of discord to the séance. A friend of Phineas C. Wright, Hunt bluntly stated he preferred the old Order of American Knights to the Sons of Liberty. Furthermore, Hunt infuriated Vallandigham by saying that he favored an organization that would give both sympathy and aid to the rebels. Visibly angry, Vallandigham interrupted Hunt and the two engaged in a heated exchange. The nominal head of the Sons of Liberty not only gave Hunt a verbal castigation but bluntly asserted that he would have nothing to do with "the

46. S. Corning Judd, testimony, March 30, 1865, *ibid.*, April 2, 1865.
47. Melinda LaPlante to Charles B. Lasselle, March 21, 1864, in Charles B. Lasselle Papers, Indiana Division, Indiana State Library; Fort Wayne *Sentinel*, April 2, 1864.
48. *Congressional Globe*, 38th Cong., 1st Sess., 1501; (Columbus, Ohio) *Crisis*, April 20, 1864.

Missouri outfit." He might be a critic of Lincoln and the administration, but he was no traitor![49]

James A. McMaster, the annoyingly frank editor of the *Freeman's Journal* in New York, joined the heated debate. He openly endorsed secession as a principle and vehemently condemned President Lincoln for his unconstitutional acts. Another argument took place, with Judd supporting Vallandigham and Hunt defending McMaster. Sparks flew, tempers flared, and the meeting ended on a sour note of disagreement and disharmony.[50]

The clash of personalities and the heated arguments in a sense sealed the fate of the Sons of Liberty. The order died aborning at its so-called first national convention. The handful of supposed state leaders could not agree upon basic political principles, to say nothing of the ways and means to attain them. Nor could they agree as to the form and substance of the Sons of Liberty. The time and effort that Dodd had spent in giving shape to the order proved to be time wasted. It began to die even before it was officially established on a national level. The order became a paper organization and a Democratic pretense. As supreme commander, Clement L. Vallandigham never issued an edict or an order and never called a meeting. He held a title, not an office.[51] The self-styled grand commanders, who ostensibly headed the Sons of Liberty in their respective states, left for home aware that their organization was a dream rather than an actuality, pretense rather than reality.

The months of May and June, 1864, were a testing time for the nation. The peace crusade, which had lost its vigor the previous year after Gettysburg and Vicksburg, gained new converts following the blood baths experienced by the Army of the Potomac in the Wilderness (May 5–6), near Spottsylvania (May 8–12), and at Cold Harbour (June 3). Some disenchanted Republicans, dissatisfied with Lincoln on several counts, sponsored a convention, which met in Cleveland on May 31 and nominated John C. Frémont as a candidate. Democratic leaders, playing a political game, postponed their national convention, scheduled to meet in Chicago on July 4, hoping to capitalize upon the growing disillusionment with Lincoln and the war. The majority of Republicans, drawing the cloak of the National Union Convention over their actions, met in Baltimore on June 7, nominated Lincoln for a second term, and gave him Andrew Johnson as a running mate. Democrats, encouraged by the split in Republican ranks, pressed for an advantage in the political arena and appealed for votes in the areas of defeatism, racism, and self-service.

Dodd, holding the title of grand commander of the Sons of Liberty in In-

49. Judd, testimony before the Cincinnati Commission, March 30, 1865, published in Cincinnati *Daily Enquirer*, April 2, 1865.

50. *Ibid.*

51. Vallandigham, testimony, March 29, 1865, *ibid.*, March 30, 1865.

diana, did not discard the idea of a secret political party despite the fiasco at Windsor in mid-April. Without consulting Vallandigham, and on paper at least, he divided Indiana into four "military districts" and hand-picked the "major general" for each. Dodd's four "major generals," each supposedly commanding the military arm of the Sons of Liberty, were Dr. William A. Bowles of French Lick, Lambdin P. Milligan of Huntington, Andrew Humphreys of Bloomfield, and Dr. David T. Yeakel of Indianapolis. The military arm of the Sons of Liberty, however, existed more in Dodd's mind than in practice, for two of the four would later claim ignorance of any military appointment.[52]

Dodd evidently reported to Vallandigham on his promotional efforts, sending a courier with a message to Windsor. Since Dodd failed to provide a code to decipher the message, Vallandigham replied, "We cannot decipher the contents . . . spent an hour trying to understand the thing without any success."[53]

While trying, futilely, to put flesh on the Sons of Liberty skeleton, Dodd also spoke at several local Democratic rallies. He was especially concerned about the Democratic state convention, scheduled for July 12, for he had been elected a delegate at an earlier convention, and so he was interested in the views of his colleagues. He needed to know if there was support for a peace plank in the platform and the selection of a peace man as the party's presidential candidate.

Dodd was also interested in Vallandigham's immediate plans, for rumors continued to circulate that he would soon be returning to Ohio. The exile had repeatedly discussed with his friends the desirability of returning home. The martyr's halo that he imagined he was wearing had lost some of its glow. His ego required the spotlight, and continued absence from the scene could relegate him to oblivion. The admonitions of Wilbur F. Storey of the Chicago Times bothered Vallandigham; the editor had practically called the exile a coward for not returning to claim rights to which he was entitled.[54] There were other considerations. His wife, given to spells of melancholy, was not well, and his mother was gravely ill, perhaps upon her deathbed. Confederate agents in and around Windsor embarrassed him, giving President Lincoln's supporters a chance to say he was with his friends. Jacob Thompson, a Confederate commissioner on a mission to Canada, visited Vallandigham at the Hirons House. They discussed the question of peace and the possibility of

52. Lambdin P. Milligan, testimony in *Milligan* v. *Hovey*, quoted in Indianapolis *Daily Journal*, May 20, 1871; Harrison, testimony, in Pitman (ed.), *Trials for Treason at Indianapolis*, 80–81.

53. Clement L. Vallandigham to H. H. Dodd, May 1, 1864, in General Courts Martial Records.

54. Chicago *Times* (n.d.), quoted in Dayton *Daily Journal*, October 24, 1863.

compromise but disagreed upon the basics. Thompson represented a self-styled nation, which wanted peace and independence; Vallandigham, although an exile, favored peace, compromise, and reunion. Thompson, intrigued about the rumors concerning the Sons of Liberty and reports about disaffection in the upper Midwest, asked about the secret order's size and objectives. Vallandigham bluntly told the Confederate commissioner that he could give no information to a nonmember and turned to the discussion of other subjects. Rebuffed, Thompson tactfully asked no more about the Sons of Liberty and talked about such topics as reconstruction and the presidential election of 1864.[55] Vallandigham realized that Thompson's visit and the presence of an ever-increasing number of Confederate agents and draft-dodgers in Windsor would give his enemies a chance to stigmatize him and manufacture more political propaganda. He decided on a return to Ohio that would coincide with the Third District convention, where he hoped to be named a delegate to the Chicago convention, postponed until late August.

While awaiting word from his Ohio friends, Vallandigham wrote two very brief notes to Dodd. Neither made mention of the Sons of Liberty; both were concerned with the date of the Third District convention. Vallandigham's note of May 12 read: "Am awaiting to hear from Dayton as to the time of the District Convention; no announcement yet. Will give you notice immediately." The second, dated May 31, possessed a tone of urgency: "That District Convention is at last fixed—Hamilton, Butler County, June 15. Be there and bring friends and speakers."[56]

After Democratic leaders of the Third District set the date of the convention as June 15, four old friends from Hamilton—David W. Brant, Jacob Troutman, Edward Dalton, and Dr. John McElwee—made plans to escort Vallandigham from Windsor to their city. After dark, on June 14, Vallandigham and his escorts crossed from Windsor to Detroit on a ferryboat, walked to the railway depot, and boarded a sleeping car of the Toledo-bound train. They changed trains in Toledo and had an uneventful ride. The train passed through Vallandigham's hometown, Dayton, on its way southward, without its citizens becoming aware that a year of exile had come to an end.

55. Vallandigham, testimony before the Cincinnati Commission, March 29, 1865, published in Cincinnati *Daily Enquirer*, March 30, 1865. At a later date, Thompson claimed that Vallandigham had initiated him into the Sons of Liberty. Historians, thus, are faced with weighing Vallandigham's word against Thompson's. Vallandigham was under oath when he testified at Cincinnati. Furthermore he had a reputation for veracity, even with his enemies. Thompson, on the other hand, had his reputation tarnished by charges of corruption while holding public office. Since his Canadian mission had accomplished so little, he was wont to exaggerate his achievements. S. Corning Judd's testimony before the Cincinnati Military Commission, corroborated many (not all) of Vallandigham's statements about the Windsor get-together and about the Sons of Liberty.
56. Vallandigham to Dodd, May 12, 31, 1864, in General Courts Martial Records.

As the train slowed down on the outskirts of Hamilton, Vallandigham planned his dramatic reentry into public life. He was wearing two hats—one that of a citizen wondering if he would be rearrested, the other that of the nominal head of the Sons of Liberty with the title supreme commander.[57]

At his farm hideout, Vallandigham wrote a note to his nephew, John McMahon, a delegate from Montgomery County at the Third District convention. The onetime exile anticipated that the Montgomery County delegates would be meeting in caucus to consider resolutions and the delegate to the Chicago convention. Vallandigham's note said that he was "two miles from Hamilton" and that he "would speak at three o'clock." When McMahon read Vallandigham's note to the assembled delegates at the caucus, most were elated and promised to work for his election.[58]

When Vallandigham walked up the steps and onto the speakers' platform shortly before three o'clock, the excited audience "joined in one prolonged, furious, and overwhelming yell that lasted for several minutes."[59] "He came unheralded from his exile," a Hamilton disciple later recalled, "and this sudden appearance was like an apparition from the clouds."[60] H. H. Dodd, heading a small Indiana delegation, witnessed the exile's return to public life. The architect of the Sons of Liberty witnessed the return of the supreme commander.

After being informed that he had been named one of the Third District's two delegates to the Chicago convention, Vallandigham gave a carefully prepared speech. Posing as a martyr to freedom of speech, he denied he was guilty of any crime. He was willing, he said, to answer any charges in the civil courts, and he referred to the 186,000 Democrats who had voted for him the previous fall as his "sureties." "I am here," he said with emphasis, "for peace, not turbulence; for quiet, not convulsions; for law and order, not anarchy." Yet he contradicted his plea for law and order with the implication that he expected "the Democracy" to take "action" if he were arrested again and denied his rights.[61]

Vallandigham felt compelled to spend a few minutes talking about the Sons of Liberty. It was not, he asserted, a subversive society organized to aid the rebels and bring forth a northwestern confederacy, as Republicans contended. It was "a lawful Democratic" society, organized to counter the Union

57. Stephen D. Cone, *A Concise History of Hamilton* (2 vols.; Middleton, Ohio, 1901), II, 231.

58. Cone, *A Concise History of Hamilton*, II, 230–32; Dayton *Daily Empire*, June 16, 1864; Hamilton (Ohio) *True Telegraph*, June 23, 1864.

59. Dayton *Daily Empire*, June 16, 1864.

60. Stephen D. Cone, *Biographical and Historical Sketches: A Narrative of Hamilton and Its Residents from 1792 to 1896* (2 vols.; Hamilton, O., 1896), I, 198.

61. Dayton *Daily Empire*, June 16, 1864.

Leagues and to help win the 1864 presidential election.[62] He pretended that the society was extensively organized and intent upon preserving civil rights and keeping elections open and free. He evidently supposed that, if the Lincoln administration believed that the Sons of Liberty were numerous, federal officials would not trample upon civil rights or even rearrest him.

The political pot boiled as vigorously in Indiana as it did in Ohio. Dodd actively supported the candidacy of Lambdin P. Milligan, hoping for his nomination at the state convention scheduled for July 12. Rumors had made the rounds that Joseph E. McDonald, whom Morton had defeated in the 1860 gubernatorial contest, would not seek the honor of being defeated a second time. Milligan was a hardheaded, dogmatic, and often imprudent Huntington lawyer who had learned to detest New England "and all the isms" emanating from that section. He worshipped states' rights and the federal union, being one of the first to recognize that the central government was evolving into a national state in the crucible of war. He viewed Vallandigham as a martyr, Lincoln as a usurper, and Governor Morton as an unprincipled villain. He detested those who were less dogmatic than he and believed McDonald guilty of temporizing and fence-straddling. Milligan had put his concern into a personal letter which he wrote to H. H. Dodd on May 9:

> When men of so much seeming patriotism are willing for mere temporary purposes to abandon the great principles of Civil Liberty, what will those of less pretentions do when the real contest comes—when life and property all depend on the issue, when bullets instead of ballots are cast, and when the *halter* is a preamble to our platform. For unless Federal encroachments are arrest[ed] in the States by the efforts as well of the legislature as the executive, then will our *lives* and *fortunes* follow where our honors will have gone before.[63]

Milligan's and Dodd's fears that military decrees might replace civil law were shared by others. John C. Walker, an Indianapolis man on an assignment in New York City, expressed the same fears. It was necessary for "all true men" to "look and prepare [arm] for the day," Walker wrote, when it will be necessary "to redeem society, practical and moral, from the cauldron into which it will be thrown."[64] The fear that Lincoln might seize the polls was also expressed by the editor of the Lawrenceburg *Democratic Register*. He supposed that Governor Morton might "void the October elections" if they proved to be Democratic victories. "Old Abe will then issue a proclamation

62. *Ibid.*
63. Lambdin P. Milligan to Dodd, May 12, 1864, in General Courts Martial Records.
64. John C. Walker to Dodd, May 11, 1864, *ibid.*

Joseph K. C. Forrest made up tales about the Knights of the Golden Circle in Illinois.

Courtesy of the Illinois State Historical Library

Governor Richard Yates of Illinois encouraged the spread of rumors about
subversive societies and endorsed the Union League.
Courtesy of the Illinois State Historical Library

Governor Oliver P. Morton of Indiana repeatedly stated that a Copperhead
conspiracy existed.
Courtesy Indiana Historical Society

Colonel Henry B. Carrington composed a Golden Circle exposé in 1863 and a
Sons of Liberty exposé in 1864.

Courtesy Indiana Historical Society

Confederate General John Hunt Morgan's raid into Indiana and Ohio in 1863
became the basis for a variety of rumors about the Knights of the Golden
Circle.

Harper's Weekly

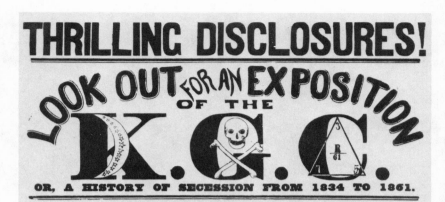

A flyer advertising Dr. James M. Hiatt's booklet about the Knights of the
Golden Circle
Courtesy Indiana Historical Society

George Harlow was the founder of the Union League in Illinois and helped spread it throughout the Midwest.

Judge Advocate General Joseph Holt prepared a report on secret societies and subversion for the secretary of war.
Harper's Weekly

Secretary of War Edwin M. Stanton asked Holt to prepare the report.
Harper's Weekly

Lafayette C. Baker, head of the War Department's spy network, could provide
Holt with only scant evidence of subversion.

Clement L. Vallandigham became nominal head of the Sons of Liberty in
February, 1864.

June 1864.

Felix G. Stidger

Felix G. Stidger was the chief witness against H. H. Dodd and the other
defendants in the Indianapolis treason trials.
Courtesy Indiana Historical Society

Some of the principals in the Indianapolis treason trials. *Clockwise from top*:
William A. Bowles, Andrew Humphreys, Stephen Horsey, Horace Heffren,
and Lambdin P. Milligan. Heffren became a witness. The other four were
found guilty of treason.

Major Henry L. Burnett presided at the Indianapolis and Cincinnati treason trials.

Harper's Weekly

Camp Douglas. In November, 1864, approximately eight thousand
Confederate prisoners were confined there.
Courtesy Albert Shaw, New York City

William A. "Deacon" Bross, financial editor of the Chicago *Tribune*, was the "discoverer" of the Camp Douglas conspiracy.

George St. Leger Grenfell, a central figure in the Cincinnati treason trial, was
a victim of chance and circumstance.
Courtesy Anthony H. Packe, Burnham, Slough, England

declaring Indiana in a state of rebellion," the distrusting editor wrote, "and proceed by force of arms and the proclamation aforesaid to subdue, conquer, and crush the same, giving us a military instead of a civil government." But Democrats, he stated defiantly, would not become willing serfs and would "wade through blood to the portals" to maintain open and free elections.[65] The fear expressed by these Democrats may have been ill-founded, and they may have been guilty of self-delusion, but it explains why some wanted to arm Democrats or organize them into a secret militia. The intent was not to wage a war of rebellion, but to be ready to combat military control of the polls.

Sometime in June, 1864, Milligan visited Indianapolis on business and attended a caucus of some peace-minded Democrats in Dodd's office, which was later characterized as a session of the "State Council" of the Sons of Liberty.[66] Andrew Humphreys, a respected Democrat from Green County, and William A. Bowles, always loquacious and often imprudent, attended. Most of the others were Indianapolis Democrats, including William M. Harrison, who held the title of grand secretary of the Sons of Liberty in his state. The discussion centered around three topics. The first was Vallandigham's return and the means to promote a peace plank and a peace man at the Chicago convention. The second dealt with Milligan's fading chances to gain the gubernatorial nomination; the party hierarchy favored Joseph E. McDonald, who had thrown his hat into the ring again. Finally, there was the controversial topic of the desirability of arming Democrats and organizing to keep the elections open and free.

After the departure of the principals, Dodd made a slight change in his paper-based organization. He dropped David T. Yeakel as one of the four "major-generals" and put John C. Walker, then in New York City as a state agent, in his stead. The postponement of the Chicago convention from July 4 to August 29 also produced a problem for Dodd. It had been agreed that the leading lights of the Sons of Liberty would meet in Chicago on the evening of July 3, the day before the meeting of the Democratic National Convention. S. Corning Judd, titled grand commander of the Sons of Liberty in Illinois, wondered if the proposed get-together of July 3 would proceed as originally scheduled. "The postponement of the National Convention disarranges matters," Judd wrote to Dodd, "but I suppose the S.C. [Supreme Council] will meet as proposed." But Vallandigham, evidently fearing arrest if he left the safety of Dayton, vetoed the suggestion. "I cannot go to C. [Chicago]

65. Lawrenceburg (Ind.) *Democratic Register*, June 17, 1864.
66. Felix G. Stidger, testimony, October 28, 1864, in Proceedings of the Military Commission Convened in Indianapolis.

now," Vallandigham stated tersely and without an explanation.[67] The proposed get-together of July 3 was postponed until the evening before the start of the rescheduled Chicago convention.

A day or two before receiving the brief notes from Judd and Vallandigham, Dodd had made a rather remarkable speech at a rally of Democrats in Hendricks County. He blamed the war upon Republicans, deplored the "unconstitutional acts" of President Lincoln and Governor Morton, and came out strongly for peace and compromise. He could not support McClellan, he said, because he wanted a nominee pledged to "stop the war and adopt compromise." He also repudiated the idea of a separate northwestern confederacy— a notion with which his name would be associated at the Indianapolis treason trials. "A Northwestern Confederacy may do for those who aspire to place and power," he said with an oratorical flourish, "but for me, I counsel against it . . . [and] I pray to God that all the States may again be happily united in one common fraternal bond, which may last while time endures."[68]

At the very time that Dodd was repudiating the idea of a northwestern confedracy, Brigadier General Henry B. Carrington was composing an exposé charging the Sons of Liberty with a conspiracy to establish one. Carrington, who had won a brigadier's star in March, had hired a coterie of detectives to seek information that would discredit such Democrats as Dodd, Milligan, Bowles, Bingham, and others. One of the detectives obtained copies of the five Sons of Liberty items that had come off the presses of H. H. Dodd & Company. Carrington selected much from the booklets for his exposé and added suppositions and rumors that presented the order in a bad light—as involved in treasonable activities culminating in a northwestern confederacy. Carrington's revelations, presented as a report to Governor Morton and dated June 28, 1864, appeared two days later in the Indianapolis *Journal*. The exposé filled six columns of fine print.[69]

Carrington had considerable experience in concocting revelations about subversive societies, having contributed mightily to the legend that Indiana was honeycombed with castles of the Knights of the Golden Circle. Perhaps he needed another revelation to keep his Indianapolis sinecure, to prove he deserved to be a brigadier, to discredit Vallandigham's return, or to check the Democratic revival that might prevent the reelection of Governor Morton.

67. Dodd to Lasselle, June 28, 1864, in Lasselle Papers; S. Corning Judd to Dodd, June 27, 1864, Vallandigham to Dodd, June 28, 1864, both in General Courts Martial Records. Judd apparently was promoting the Sons of Liberty more aggressively in Illinois than Dodd in Indiana. A sentence from Judd's letter to Dodd read: "Our G.C. [Grand Council] will meet a few days later, and a large supply of the circulars are wanted. I promised to write and urge you to have them with you at the S.C."
68. Dodd, quoted in Indianapolis *Daily State Sentinel*, June 27, 1864.
69. Indianapolis *Daily Journal*, June 30, 1864.

The Carrington exposé of June 28 correctly named Vallandigham as head of the Sons of Liberty. It also correctly identified Judd as heading the order in Illinois and Dodd in Indiana. Furthermore, the exposé was on firm ground when quoting extensively (sometimes in entirety) from the booklets or pamphlets Dodd had composed. This portion of the exposé gave it an aura of authenticity.

Most of Carrington's contentions, however, had no basis in fact, making the whole little more than political propaganda. Carrington asserted, for example, that the Sons of Liberty was the successor to the Knights of the Golden Circle, inheriting its commitment to treasonable activities. The members of the Sons of Liberty recognized the existing rebellion as "legitimate, legal, and just." They also believed that an uprising against "the present Government was not only a right, but a duty." There was more poppycock. The chief password of members was Nu-oh-lac, Calhoun spelled backwards. Members of Vallandigham's society were infuriated because General Morgan's raid had occurred "prematurely"; it was supposed to be timed with an uprising of the Sons of Liberty in the upper Midwest. Members of the secret order had had advance knowledge of General Nathan Bedford Forrest's excursion of March and April into Tennessee. The order was "well organized" in twelve states, with thirty thousand members in Indiana. The real objective of the Sons of Liberty was twofold: to establish a northwestern confederacy and to support the South in its rebellion.

Carrington's exposé made headlines in scores of newspapers. Republicans used it to taint the Democracy with treason and to stir the Union League to action in the fall election campaigns. Some Republican newspapers had made much of the supposed link between Vallandigham, at that time an exile in Canada, and Morgan's raid of July, 1863, into Indiana and Ohio. "The rumor," Murat Halstead of the Cincinnati *Commercial* stated, "that there was collusion between the friends of Vallandigham and Morgan seems possible." The surprise return of Vallandigham to Ohio just at the time that General Morgan was on another raid into Kentucky, seemed more than a coincidence to some rumormongers. Morgan's presence in Kentucky, one editor conjectured, might well have been a signal for a general revolt.[70]

Carrington's widely circulated exposé dealt the Sons of Liberty, which Dodd had been trying rather futilely to transform into a viable organization, a staggering blow from which it never recovered. S. Corning Judd, who had tried to establish this dark lantern society in Illinois, hurriedly dropped the

70. Cincinnati *Daily Commercial*, June 29, 1864; Indianapolis *Daily Journal*, June 28, 1864.

coals he was carrying to Newcastle. Realizing that Carrington's revelations discredited the order and nullified any chances for its usefulness, he left the Sons of Liberty to die by default in Illinois. Dodd, however, had invested too much time and effort in the Sons of Liberty to throw the project overboard. Although he was embarrassed by the exposé, he tried to salvage something by making "some material changes in the ritual." Not trusting the mails, he sent several letters by "accredited persons" to friends still interested in the original objectives of the secret political order. "Written communications are played out," he wrote to a trusted acquaintance, "as all letters are opened and read by Lincoln spies and hirelings during their transmission through the mails." [71]

While bemoaning the turn of events, Vallandigham stayed within the friendly confines of Dayton. He did not renounce his titular command of the Sons of Liberty but shrugged off the rumors circulating as a result of Carrington's exposé. Anticipating an arrest that never came, he made no speeches in July and August and said nothing about the order he nominally headed. He did not even go to New Lisbon to see his dying mother. "But while I feel perfectly secure *here*," he wrote to his mother "I think the Administration would be only too glad to find me at a distance from home." His mother never read the letter, for she died before it reached her. Nor did Vallandigham go to New Lisbon for the funeral. "Words cannot express the feelings of my heart," he wrote to an elder brother, "at the thought that I have not been in a position to be with her and with you all. . . . Though I could not see her in death, I rejoice that she lived to see my return to my own country and my home." [72]

Republicans, meanwhile, debated the question of rearresting Vallandigham. Governor Morton and editor Edgar Conkling of the Cincinnati *Gazette* typified those who wanted the onetime exile seized and hustled off to prison. Conkling even threatened to organize a posse and make a citizen's arrest if federal authorities failed to act. [73] Horace Greeley of the New York *Tribune* and Murat Halstead of the Cincinnati *Commercial* typified Republicans who argued that "the best thing to do is to let him alone," using his presence to discredit the Democracy. President Lincoln wryly stated that he had no offi-

71. Judd to Abraham Lincoln, March 3, 1865, in John Nicolay–John Hay Papers, Illinois State Historical Library; Judd, testimony before the Cincinnati Commission, March 31, 1865, published in the Cincinnati *Daily Enquirer*, April 21, 1865; "H" [Dodd] to W. I. Stewart, August 20, 1864, in General Courts Martial Records.

72. Vallandigham to "Dear Mother," July 7, 1864, in Clement L. Vallandigham Papers, Western Reserve Historical Society, Cleveland; Vallandigham to "Dear Brother" [James], July 10, 1864, published in part in James L. Vallandigham, *A Life of Clement L. Vallandigham* (Baltimore, 1872), 364.

73. Samuel P. Heintzelman Journal, June 15, 16, 1864 (MS in Samuel P. Heintzelman Papers, Library of Congress).

cial knowledge of Vallandigham's return and that he would do nothing unless the onetime exile was guilty of some objectionable act.[74]

Dodd, discredited in the eyes of some by the Carrington exposé, attended the Democratic State Convention, which met in Indianapolis on July 12. The Committee on Organization named him an assistant marshal, an honor he had deliberately sought. The delegates adopted resolutions condemning arbitrary arrests, violations of free speech and press, and Governor Morton's arbitrary practices. Dodd and the peace-at-any-price members lost their skirmish over the peace plank eventually adopted. Dodd's gubernatorial candidate, Milligan, lost out by an immense margin—1,097 to 160—to McDonald. Milligan then refused second place on the ticket, for he felt he was second "in talents and patriotism" to no one, especially McDonald.[75]

Although Dodd may have been disappointed with the convention's decisions, he did not sulk in his tent. He signed a call for a meeting of "the old Democratic club" of Indianapolis to ratify the actions of the state convention, even speaking briefly in behalf of McDonald's candidacy.[76] He took an active part in reorganizing and reactivating the Marion County Democratic organization. He even took one out-of-town trip to a local Democratic rally to remind the party faithful of their indebtedness to Jefferson and Jackson and of the need to cast their ballots during the fall elections.[77] Respected party leaders, however, shunned Dodd and the Sons of Liberty. He received no other invitations to speak at county or district party rallies. He was a pariah, whose presence discredited every meeting he attended. Carrington's exposé, like Banquo's ghost, haunted him at every turn, adding to his discomfiture and frustrations. An objective observer noticed that the exposé hung like a cloud over the Democratic party of Indiana. "There is trouble in the party," he wrote, "and this publishing the details of the secret organization is breaking it up."[78]

By the time the Republican press had squeezed all the juice it could out of the Carrington exposé, Colonel John P. Sanderson's revelations about the Order of American Knights made new headlines. He borrowed extensively from Carrington's exposé; he too claimed that Vallandigham was supreme com-

74. New York *Daily Tribune*, June 17, 1864; Murat Halstead to William Henry Smith, June 21, 1864, in William Henry Smith Papers, Indiana Historical Society Library; Lincoln to John Brough and Samuel Heintzelman, June 20, 1864, in Robert Todd Lincoln Papers. The envelope contains the notation "Not Sent."
75. Indianapolis *Daily State Sentinel*, July 12, 13, 1864; Milligan to Dodd, May 9, 1864, in General Courts Martial Records.
76. Indianapolis *Daily State Sentinel*, July 16, 1864.
77. William Holmes to "Dear Son" [Dr. John S. McPheeters], July 24, 1864, in John S. McPheeters Papers, Indiana Historical Society Library.
78. Heintzelman Journal, July 29, 1864.

mander, and that Dodd and Judd were fallen angels serving the devil, that the password of the Knights was Nu-oh-lac. No one paid much attention to the contradictions in the two revelations. The editor of the Indianapolis *Journal* believed that one supported the other; the exposé of the Order of American Knights, the editor averred, substantiated Carrington's contentions that evil was abroad in the land. Yes, "subversive organizations" were active in the Midwest, and the Democratic participants must be repudiated at the polls.[79]

If there ever was any chance that Dodd might transform his paper organization into a going concern, it evaporated with the publication and circulation of the Carrington and Sanderson exposés. Disheartened, discredited, and shunned, he looked afar for hope and grasped at straws. The peace movement seemed to be gathering momentum as General Grant's war of attrition cost many lives. The Republican party split over Lincoln and Frémont buoyed Democratic hopes. The dog days of August gave Lincoln reason to be pessimistic about his chances of reelection. Democrats hoped that Lincoln and Frémont would share the fate of the Kilkenny cats. Perhaps the Chicago convention might help to redeem the Democratic party and might listen to the siren song of peace.

While H. H. Dodd dreamt of what might have been, he tended his print shop and made plans to attend the Chicago convention, rescheduled to meet on August 29. Meanwhile, he became entangled in a web of his own making. It was a web that brought Dodd notoriety, discredited the Sons of Liberty, tainted the Democratic party, and provided the justification for the Indianapolis treason trials.

79. Indianapolis *Daily Journal*, August 1, 1864.

CHAPTER V

The Holt Report on Secret Societies

THE SO-CALLED Holt Report, a lengthy discourse about subversive societies, made the headlines during the presidential contest of 1864. Since it was the handiwork of a respected and well-known man who headed an arm of the government, it possessed an aspect of authenticity. Furthermore, it became an important historical document, often cited as evidence that evil-minded dark lantern societies were extensive and active during the Civil War.

The document's author, Joseph Holt, held the office of judge advocate general and possessed a reputation for patriotism and integrity. Secretary of War Edwin M. Stanton, the sponsor of the report, had proved himself a hard-working and able administrator who seemed more interested in military victories than in partisan politics. The names of Holt and Stanton lent credibility to the document usually labelled *Report of the Judge Advocate General on the Order of American Knights*.[1]

Joseph Holt, a lesser-known Kentucky politician of the 1850s, gained stature and something of a reputation during the closing months of President James Buchanan's administration, especially during the changing of cabinet members. Known as both an ardent Unionist and a supporter of compromise measures, Holt shifted ground and aligned himself with those responsible for stiffening Buchanan's backbone on the Fort Sumter and secession issues. When Secretary of War John B. Floyd resigned because Buchanan would not order Major Robert Anderson to move back to Fort Moultrie from Fort Sumter, Holt gave up the reins of the postmaster general's office to take over the War Department. He then promptly joined Edwin M. Stanton (the new attorney general), Jeremiah S. Black (the new secretary of state), and John A. Dix (who had replaced Howell Cobb as secretary of the treasury) to form the pro-Union bloc in the reorganized

---

1. Holt presented his untitled report, dated October 8, 1864, to Stanton in manuscript form. It has been published in *The War of the Rebellion: A Compilation of the Official Records of the Union and Confederate Armies* (128 vols.; Washington, D.C., 1880–1901), Ser. 2, Vol. VII, 930–53, hereinafter cited as *OR*. It was published as a pamphlet under the title *Report of the Judge Advocate General on the Order of American Knights*.

cabinet. Stanton boldly spoke out for the Union; Black endorsed coercion of the seceded states and the reinforcement of Fort Sumter; and Dix thrilled the hearts of patriots with his famous order to Captain John G. Breshwood, commanding the cutter USS *McClelland*: "If anyone attempts to haul down the American flag, shoot him on the spot."[2]

Stanton and Holt had ample opportunity to become better acquainted during the waning days of Buchanan's administration and to build a bridge of mutual respect. Stanton, although dogmatic and domineering at times, possessed boundless energy, excelled in organization, and pursued his responsibilities with a relentlessness bordering on malevolence. Holt proved to be hard-working, dependable, patriotic; he was also somewhat passive and flexible, able to compromise in the name of expediency and realism. Each went his own way when Buchanan left the White House and Abraham Lincoln moved in as his successor.

Events brought Stanton and Holt back together in 1862. After Simon Cameron left the War Department under a cloud in January, 1862, President Lincoln invited Stanton to take over the portfolio and assume its awesome responsibilities. In effecting the reorganization of the department, Stanton asked for the creation of a post to oversee military trials, review decisions of military commissions, and supervise military justice. Congress, in turn, passed an act on July 17, 1862, that authorized the appointment of the judge advocate general and several subordinate judge advocates, one for each military department or army in the field. Stanton offered Holt the important new title, and the latter assumed the office on September 3, 1862.[3]

Judge Advocate General Holt spent long hours at his desk reviewing the proceedings of courts-martial and passing on sentences, penalties, and pardons. Holt added to his reputation as a strong Unionist by supporting the numerous arbitrary arrests made during August of 1862 in Illinois, Indiana, and Ohio, many for supposed activity in the Knights of the Golden Circle. He also supported the summary treatment accorded Clement L. Vallandigham in May and June of 1863, evidently agreeing with Republican contentions that the Ohio curmudgeon was a traitor. In fact, Holt wrote the government's brief in *Ex Parte Vallandigham*, arguing that the United States Supreme Court did not have the authority, under either the Constitution or the Judiciary Act of 1789, to review the proceedings and decisions of a military commission. The Court's decision, borrowing heavily from Holt's argument, enhanced the reputation of

---

2. [Appleton's] *Annual Cyclopedia and Register of Important Events . . . 1861* (New York, 1862), 428–29.
3. Not until June 20, 1864, was the judge advocate general made the head of a bureau, the Department of Military Justice.

the judge advocate general and heightened his prestige with both Stanton and the President.[4]

Rumors and reports of subversive activity flooded Washington; the stories recited in midwestern newspapers appeared in briefer form in the *Chronicle* or *Intelligencer*. Most of the suppositions and exposés reached either Holt's or Stanton's desk. Governors Richard Yates of Illinois and Oliver P. Morton of Indiana repeatedly reported on subversive activity and asked for more arrests to stifle treason. Colonel Henry B. Carrington's reports on Golden Circle activity and the state of affairs in Indiana reached Stanton's desk as well as Lincoln's. Then, of course, Carrington's exposé of the Sons of Liberty in late June, 1864, and Colonel John P. Sanderson's revelations about the Order of American Knights a month later heightened rumors about subversive activity. Governor Morton visited Washington to impress officialdom with the seriousness of Carrington's contentions and to demand suppression of subversion. He even urged the arrest of the Indiana members of the Sons of Liberty as essential to "the success of the National cause in the autumn elections."[5] Governor Yates, more nervous and high-strung than Morton, besieged Washington with requests, reports, and rumors.

Morton evidently convinced Secretary of War Stanton that he had a responsibility to the Lincoln administration in political affairs as well as military ones. Governor Morton's allegations about subversive societies, the arrest of H. H. Dodd in Indianapolis, and the exposés concocted by Carrington and Sanderson prompted Stanton to order an investigation of the secret society reports and the treason charges. The intensity of the political campaign, the decline of faith in the Lincoln administration in August, 1864, and McClellan's rising popularity might also have served as incentives, for both Stanton and Holt had a vested interest in Lincoln's and Morton's reelection. "I feel that everything in our country," an assistant judge advocate had written to Holt on August 23, "depends upon the result of the approaching election."[6]

Stanton subsequently asked his judge advocate general to prepare a report on the so-called serpentine societies and promised Holt he would ask Lafayette C. Baker, head of the War Department's spy corps, to provide information for the proposed inquiry. Holt had no choice but to accept the assignment. He promptly sent telegrams to Carrington and Sanderson, asking them to forward information and evidence as soon as possible to his office. Such information, Holt assured Carrington, "would prove of great value to the Govern-

4. *Ex Parte Vallandigham*, 68 U.S. (1 Wallace), 243–54 (1864).

5. Morton's visit to Washington is reported in Henry B. Carrington, "Indiana War Documents Cleared of Error" (Typescript, n.d., in Henry B. Carrington Papers, Archives Division, Indiana State Library, Indianapolis), 8.

6. Col. William McKee Dunn to Joseph Holt, August 23, 1864, in Joseph Holt Papers, Library of Congress.

ment, by assisting it in arriving at correct conclusions, and in presenting the whole case for the consideration of the country."[7] Interestingly, Holt made his request of Carrington and Sanderson while the Democratic National Convention was meeting in Chicago, and his interest "in presenting the whole case for the consideration of the country" carried political implications.

Lafayette C. Baker, whom Stanton asked to provide information regarding secret societies and subversion to Holt's office, should have been the logical man to provide important evidence.[8] He had started his unusual career as a federal employee by serving as a detective—the word *spy* had a bad connotation—for Major General Winfield Scott during the early months of the war. When Scott retired as general-in-chief on November 1, 1861, Baker entered the employ of Secretary of State William H. Seward, still as a detective. On September 12, 1862, Stanton named Baker "special provost marshal" for the War Department, "to exercise the powers and to do and perform the functions pertaining to the office during the pleasure of the President." As special provost marshal, Baker's duties included investigating all cases concerned with disloyalty, treason, or espionage. Subversive dark lantern societies should have fallen within Baker's jurisdiction and responsibility. Although relieved of his title when he received a colonelcy, he continued his work as "a special agent," performing a variety of assignments for Stanton while serving as colonel of the First Regiment, District of Columbia Cavalry.[9]

Baker replied to Stanton's request most promptly with a one-page report replete with generalities, vagueness, and contradictions. Interestingly, Baker, who had access to the reports of scores of U.S. detectives active in the Midwest as well as Canada, had little to say. He had no document in hand that proved the existence of the Knights of the Golden Circle, the Order of American Knights, or the Sons of Liberty. He had no reliable evidence that substantiated the existence of any plot or conspiracy in the upper Midwest or elsewhere. His report, therefore, contained only a few general suppositions, which had circulated in the newspapers after Carrington and Sanderson had offered their exposés to the country at political altars.[10]

Most of Baker's meager report consisted of a list of forty-one names of persons supposedly belonging to the Sons of Liberty. The report made no men-

7. Holt to Henry B. Carrington, telegram, August 30, 1864, copy in Carrington MSS. entitled "Complications During the Draft, 1864" (13-pages, typewritten, n.d.), in Carrington Papers.

8. Stanton made his request of Baker through an assistant (Charles A. Dana), revealed in Lafayette C. Baker to Charles A. Dana, September 3, 1864, in Holt Papers.

9. Baker claimed that he and his bureau needed an in-case-of-emergency military force. Baker deserves an in-depth study by someone interested in historical detective work. Much of his correspondence appears in Lafayette C. Baker, *History of the United States Secret Service* (Philadelphia, 1867).

10. The report, undated, accompanied Baker's letter of September 3, 1864, to Dana. Both are in the Holt Papers.

tion of the Knights of the Golden Circle or the Order of American Knights. Nor did it refer to any conspiracy, like the "Northwest Confederacy" plot publicized by Carrington and Sanderson. The list of forty-one did not include the name of Clement L. Vallandigham, nominal head of the Sons of Liberty, or George Bickley, majordomo of the Knights of the Golden Circle, or Phineas C. Wright, whose Order of American Knights had disintegrated, or H. H. Dodd, who was then a prisoner in Indianapolis. Both Wright and Bickley were being held in federal prisons at the time, and both were bombarding Washington with letters demanding hearings. Nor did Baker's brief report include the names of Lambdin P. Milligan, William A. Bowles, and the others who would face a military commission later in the year in Indianapolis. The names of Dr. Thomas C. Massey of Ohio, Charles L. Hunt of St. Louis, and James A. McMaster of New York, all present the previous April in Vallandigham's hotel room in Windsor to discuss ways to sidetrack McClellan's candidacy and make the Sons of Liberty an auxiliary to the Democratic party, were not mentioned. Nor did the list include any residents of Ohio or Indiana. In a way, it repudiated Carrington's widely publicized revelations of June, 1864.

Of the forty-one listed in Baker's report, seventeen were Missourians (thirteen from Howard County), sixteen were from Illinois (most mentioned in Sanderson's exposé), and six were from New York City. The list did include "Mr. Judd, Grand Commander of the State, Lewiston, Fulton County" (Baker failed to supply the man's first name); "Story, Editor of the *Times*, Chicago, Ill." (Storey's surname was misspelled); and "Dr. R. H. Stevens, New York City" (Richard F. Stevens' leadership of the "McClellan Minutemen" in 1864 made him a prime target of Republicans).

Although Baker replied promptly, perhaps because he had little substance to offer, both Carrington and Sanderson procrastinated. Holt had to prod both to furnish the material and information asked of them. Holt reported to Stanton, and the latter sent a terse telegram to Carrington. "It is important," Stanton stated, "that the evidence and information asked for by the Judge Advocate General, in his letter to you of the thirtieth (30) ult., should be forwarded to him without delay." [11]

There was some justification for Carrington's delay. It took time for his clerk to make copies of the many letters and documents in his possession, especially those seized in the raids on the offices of H. H. Dodd and Daniel W. Voorhees. [12] Furthermore, Carrington wanted to consult his best detective,

11. Edwin M. Stanton to Carrington, September 19, 1864, in "War Telegrams of 1864," Carrington Papers.
12. Voorhees was a lawyer-congressman from Terre Haute. An office which he had in Indianapolis and seldom used also served Dodd.

then out of town on another assignment. The longhand report filled twenty-three pages of legal-sized foolscap, and in addition, Carrington wrote a long, long covering letter.

Carrington's long letter called Holt's attention to the nineteen reports written by detective Felix G. Stidger as well as the exposé, which had been published in the Indianapolis *Journal* of June 28, 1864. All of the assertions made in the report, Carrington assured Holt, could be substantiated by the stack of evidence he was forwarding to Washington. The letter showed that Carrington was pleased as Punch that his exposé of the Sons of Liberty "had demoralized the Peace party and the secret Order." Carrington suggested the arrest of William A. Bowles, "a man who should be the first tried before the Military Commission," if those already arrested were to be dealt with in such fashion. Interestingly, Carrington closed his covering letter with a plea to the War Department to honor his requisition of five thousand dollars "for expenditures and salaries" of the "numerous persons" employed to collect evidence against the subversive orders. "I have the personal contact and watch of this Order under my care," Carrington concluded with a show of satisfaction, "and the results speak for themselves." [13]

Carrington's twenty-three-page report was as much a justification of his command of the District of Indiana as it was an exposé of secret political societies and supposed subversion. He blamed "the subversive orders" and the spirit of defeatism for opposition to Federal conscription and emancipation. The "Copperhead Legislature" of 1863 had planned to take the state out of the Union. Most of the Indiana soldiers who had deserted belonged to the Knights of the Golden Circle, whose members had met secretly "at the Democratic Club Room in Indianapolis, twice weekly." He reviewed the so-called Constable Case, defending his arrest of the Illinois judge and criticizing Chief Justice Samuel E. Perkins of the Indiana State Supreme Court for censuring Carrington and Morton. Carrington justified the military edicts he had issued and the arrests he had made.

The second part of the report traced the origins of the Sons of Liberty to the Golden Circle, to an enigmatic organization called the Mighty Host, and to Democratic mutual protection societies. After he had exposed the Golden Circle in 1862, Carrington said, most members dropped out of the order and joined a new one, the Order of American Knights "during the summer of 1863." The new order extended itself "as far as practical" to all the states, forming a pyramid of county and state councils. But Carrington failed to explain how the Sons of Liberty evolved out of the Order of American Knights. To give substance to his suppositions, he quoted extensively from the four

13. Carrington's covering letter of September 16, 1864 is in General Courts Martial Records, Records of the Office of the Judge Advocate General, National Archives.

documents Dodd had prepared and had printed. Dodd's address, written to spur Democrats to organize local societies, provided considerable grist. So did the booklets explaining the ritual and the lessons of the "Third Degree." Carrington's star detective, who claimed to have attended the "grand council" meeting in Indianapolis in mid-February, also provided a report, which convinced Holt that treasonable projects were in progress.

The Sons of Liberty, Carrington argued, had met secretly in a national convention in New York City on February 22, 1864. Had not Vallandigham, in his June 11 speech in Hamilton, claimed that membership approximated 500,000? The order, Carrington added, had fixed August 15 as a date for an uprising ("some positive action"), but disorganization and prompt action by public authorities nullified the move to bring about a separate northwestern confederacy. Members of the subversive order in Indiana and Ohio knew in advance of General John Hunt Morgan's raid. "The whole history of the secret order, under whatever name," the report concluded, "has been one of local disorder, abuse of the government, its acts and its agents, arming to overawe the elections, opposition to recruiting and the war—and subtle secret attempts to bring about anarchy and bloodshed, in the interests of the rebellion." [14]

Colonel John P. Sanderson, like Carrington, failed to respond to the first request for information and evidence of subversive society activity. It was necessary for the War Department to prod him again. Holt had a slight acquaintance with Sanderson. The War Department, concerned about arbitrary arrests Sanderson had made, had sent Holt on a mission to St. Louis in early July, 1864.[15] At the time, Sanderson complained about subversive activity and defended the arrests that he had made for "treasonable activity." He claimed that the Order of American Knights was involved in a plot to establish a northwestern confederacy.

Eventually, Sanderson sent Holt copies of his four reports to Major General William S. Rosecrans. He also sent selections from some of the compositions his detectives had provided. It was a basketful of interesting material, many contentions, and little substantive evidence. Interestingly, Sanderson claimed that Clement L. Vallandigham was head of the Order of American Knights; Carrington claimed that Vallandigham commanded the Sons of Liberty. Both, however, claimed that each of the two societies wished to establish a separate confederation in the upper Midwest!

14. Carrington, "Outline of Disloyal Organizations, 'O.A.K.' and 'O.S.L.' in Indiana, and Adjoining States" (report, n.d., *ibid.*).
15. (St. Louis) *Missouri Republican*, August 2, 1864; Gen. William S. Rosecrans to John Nicolay, November 5, 1889, in John Nicolay-John Hay Papers, Illinois State Historical Library, Springfield.

Since Lafayette C. Baker and the War Department's spies had little to offer, it was necessary for Holt to compose his report from the evidence and suppositions provided by Carrington and Sanderson, two politically conscious army officers. Each had earlier prepared his own exposé of secret societies and had circulated it in the public press, aware of its propaganda value.

Judge Advocate General Holt, anxious to complete the assignment that Secretary of War Stanton had thrust upon him, sifted and studied the stack of evidence. In time, he composed and completed a fourteen-thousand-word report.[16]

Holt divided his report into eight sections, proving he was an adept organizer. A preamble stated the reason for the study: "It has been deemed proper to set forth in full the acts and purposes of this organization, and thus to make it known to the country at large its intensely treasonable and revolutionary spirit." The first section dealt with the origin and history of "the subversive order." Holt, like Carrington and Sanderson before him, traced the order back to the Knights of the Golden Circle. He then repeated Sanderson's suppositions that the dark lantern society had changed its name but not its devious objectives. Vallandigham, Holt asserted, had "founded" the Order of American Knights while in exile in Dixie "upon consultation at Richmond with [President] Davis and other prominent traitors."[17] Holt repeated Sanderson's timeworn contention that Confederate General Sterling Price commanded the southern branch of the order, while Vallandigham headed the northern half. Holt also presented Mary Ann Pitman, one of Sanderson's supposed informers, as "a most intelligent witness." She supposedly had seen the names of Davis, Vallandigham, and General George B. McClellan on an official list of members of the Order of American Knights in Richmond. Holt wove in Sanderson's allegations that the "McClellan Minutemen," Democratic activists in New York City, were actually "a branch of the O.A.K."[18]

Holt depended mainly upon Carrington's report and supplementary documents for the second section, which was devoted to the "organization and officers" of the supposed society. The organizational pattern, Holt wrote, approximated a pyramid, with "temples" being the basic units on the lowest level, "state councils" on the state level, and a "supreme council" on the national level. Having to decide whether Phineas C. Wright or Vallandigham headed the subversive order, Holt struck a compromise, writing that the former had headed the order until his arrest, and Vallandigham in the days that followed. Holt dwelt at length on the order's "military arm." "But when it is

16. Holt to Stanton, report, October 8, 1864, published in *OR*, Ser. 2, Vol. VII, 930–53.
17. Interestingly, Vallandigham never visited Richmond while he was an exile in the Confederacy; neither did he meet with Davis.
18. Holt to Stanton, report, October 8, 1864, in *OR*, Ser. 2, Vol. VII, 931.

understood," he added with a flourish, "that the order comprises within itself a large army of well-armed men, constantly drilled and exercised as soldiers, and that this army is held ready at any time for such forcible resistance to our military authorities and such active cooperation with the public enemy as it may be called upon to engage in by its commanders, it will be perceived that the titles of the latter are not assumed for a mere purpose of display, but that they are chiefs of an actual and formidable force of conspirators against the life of the Government."[19]

After this excursion into the world of make-believe, Holt was ready to estimate the subversive order's "extent and numbers"—the third section of the lengthy document. Some estimates, Holt wrote, put the number of members at a million. He estimated that 500,000 was "nearer the true total." He listed approximate totals for key states: Indiana, 75,000 to 125,000; Illinois, 100,000 to 140,000; Ohio, 80,000 to 108,000; Kentucky, 40,000 to 70,000; Missouri, 20,000 to 40,000; and Michigan and New York, about 20,000 each. "It is to be noted that the order, or its counterpart," Holt added, "is probably much more widely extended at the South than even the North, and that a large proportion of the officers of the rebel army are represented by credible witnesses to be members." Judge Advocate General Holt did not say that his chief "credible" witness was Mary Ann Pitman, a questionable source at best.

Holt was on firmer ground when composing the section entitled "Its Rituals, Oaths, and Interior Forms." He had at hand the various ritual and degree booklets that H. H. Dodd had composed when trying to transform the Sons of Liberty from an abstraction into a reality in February, 1864. Holt included nearly the entirety of the booklets in his report. For good measure, he added two time-tested myths. One was that the password was Nu-oh-lac. The other was that General John H. Morgan, on his excursion into Indiana and Ohio, had bypassed the homes of members of "the Order" because they had displayed a five-pointed star on their farmhouse doors.

The judge advocate general drew most of his material for section six, entitled "Its Written Principles," from Wright's "Occasional Address of the Supreme Grand Commander" and Dodd's *Constitution and Laws of the S.G.C.* Some of Wright's and Dodd's statements had a revolutionary ring; they could have been viewed as "treasonable" had they ever been transformed from rhetoric to reality. Holt digressed in this section to incorporate his own views on the nature of the national government and to criticize John C. Calhoun's states' rights theories. "The thorns which now pierce and tear us," Holt wrote, "are of the tree he planted." He characterized Calhoun as "a man who,

19. *Ibid.*, 934.

baffled in his lust for power, with gnashing teeth turned upon the Government that had lifted him to its highest honors." [20]

In the section entitled "Its Specific Purposes and Operations," Holt listed eleven "objectives" of "the Order" as he understood them: encouraging and aiding desertion and harboring and protecting deserters, discouraging enlistments and resisting the draft, circulating disloyal and treasonable publications, communicating with and giving intelligence to the enemy, aiding the enemy by recruiting for them, furnishing the rebels with arms and ammunition, cooperating with the enemy raids and invasions (as in the case of Morgan's raid), destroying government property, destroying personal property and persecuting loyal men, assassinating and murdering, and establishing a northwestern confederacy. [21]

The final section, entitled "The Witnesses and Their Testimony," gave high praise to Sanderson and Carrington for furnishing sheaves of documentary information. Yes, they had furnished "the great mass of testimony" incorporated into the fourteen-thousand-word report. Holt paid a special compliment to Mary Ann Pitman for her courage, resourcefulness, intelligence, and patriotism. The concluding paragraphs in the final section censured the Indiana "Copperhead Legislature" of 1863 as "strongly tainted with treason," the institution of slavery as the "fountain" of intolerance and treason, and northern Democrats who endorsed peace and compromise. Dipping his pen in acid ink, Holt closed his long report with a literary flourish: "Judea produced but one Judas Iscariot, and Rome, from the sinks of demoralization, produced but one Catiline; and yet, as events prove, there has arisen in our land an entire brood of such traitors, all animated by the same parricidal spirit, and all struggling with the same relentless malignity for the dismemberment of the Union." [22]

After receiving Holt's report on secret societies, Secretary of War Stanton promptly turned it over to the press and to the Union Congressional Committee. Republican newspapers published summaries or portions of the report, with the New York *Tribune* and Washington *Chronicle* leading the parade. Editorials implied that a vote for Lincoln was a vote against serpentine societies and Democratic leaders who flirted with treason. Horace Greeley of the *Tribune* wrote an editorial most critical of Dr. Richard F. Stevens, head of "McClellan's Minutemen" in New York, dressing him in a traitor's garb. Joseph Medill of the Chicago *Tribune* not only published sections of Holt's report but held all Illinois Democrats guilty by association. [23] Republican

20. *Ibid.*, 940–42.
21. *Ibid.*, 942–51.
22. *Ibid.*, 953.
23. New York *Daily Tribune*, October 15, 1864; Chicago *Daily Tribune*, October 15, 1864.

newspaper editors evidently recognized the propaganda value of Holt's timely document and made the most of it.

The Union Congressional Committee published Holt's report in its entirety, giving it the title *Report of the Judge Advocate General on the "Order of American Knights," alias "Sons of Liberty": A Western Conspiracy in Aid of the Southern Rebellion*. The committee ordered ten thousand copies of the pamphlet and distributed them through the Union Leagues. The purpose of the document, one Republican worker wrote, was to bolster Lincoln's stock and depress McClellan's.[24]

Democrats countered by venting their wrath upon Judge Advocate General Holt, as well as his controversial document. Some termed him a renegade and rascal, a Judas whose services had been purchased for thirty pieces of silver. "A man, who, *once* a Democrat and who has received so many favors and high honors at the hands of the Democracy as *you* have, and will stoop to such depths of infamy to curry favor with the despot in power . . . ," a Democrat wrote disdainfully, "merits the scorn, contempt, and ignomy which will for-ever after attach to the name of Joseph Holt." Another Democratic critic saw Holt as "a modern Titus Oates" who was "a scavenger for the despicable masters he services." Henry N. Walker, competent but partisan editor of the Detroit *Free Press*, thought that Holt had been bribed by Lincoln's party and had become a "puppet" and "a man who is ready to commit any folly to please his employers." One Midwestern Democratic editor fished in a slough off the main river, suggesting that Holt's report was a bid to gain an appoint-ment to the U.S. Supreme Court. Another saw Holt as a victim of "Washing-ton poison," "Republican pollution," and "the malaria of Radicalism."[25]

While coining new epithets for Holt, Democratic editors reserved their most savage criticism for his report. Most saw it as "a partisan electioneering document," "political propaganda," and "transparent demagoguery." Edi-torials, full of venom and bitterness, bore such titles as "A Despicable Slander Against the Friends of McClellan" and "The Fabrication of a Defamer and Scoundrel."[26] Charles H. Lanphier of the *Illinois State Register*, for example, characterized Holt's handiwork as "a conglomeration of falsehoods," "a de-liberate and atrocious lie," and "a precious pottage" cooked in the cauldron of the judge advocate general's imagination.[27]

24. D. N. Cooley to Elihu B. Washburne, October 20, 1864, in Elihu B. Washburne Papers, Library of Congress.

25. Anonymous letter, October 15, 1864, in Holt Papers; (Springfield) *Illinois State Regis-ter*, October 18, 21, 1864; Detroit *Free Press*, October 23, 1864; *Illinois State Register*, October 18, 1864; *Missouri Republican*, October 18, 1864.

26. *Missouri Republican*, October 18, 1864; (Madison) *Wisconsin Patriot*, November 3, 1864; Cincinnati *Daily Enquirer*, October 20, 1864; Detroit *Free Press*, October 18, 1864; Bos-ton *Post*, October 17, 1864; New York *World*, October 20, 1864; Cleveland *Plain Dealer*, Octo-ber 24, 1864; (Columbus, Ohio) *Crisis*, October 26, 1864.

27. *Illinois State Register*, October 18, 21, 1864.

James J. Faran of the Cincinnati *Enquirer* also called the report "a lie" and its author "a liar." It "deserves simply to be classed among the ante-election falsehoods of a dishonest party," the angry editor continued, "using the authority of the Government for its own purposes." It was, he added, "a cold-blooded piece of campaign propaganda, printed and circulated at public expense" and needed to arouse "the rather flagging energies of the Republican masses." Looking into his crystal ball, Faran predicted that the Lincoln administration would use the Holt report as an excuse to station troops at the polls, screen voters, and elect Republican candidates.[28]

Manton Marble of the New York *World* was as critical of the Holt report as his Democratic brethren. He was especially critical of efforts to discredit the "McClellan Minutemen." It was a disgraceful bit of Republican propaganda. "The rigmarole mealtub plot of Holt has seemed so monstrously absurd," Marble wrote contemptuously, "that we have not thought it worth while to attempt seriously to defend the Democratic party from the charges contained in it." Despite his claim that the report might be ignored, Marble felt compelled to denounce it again and again. Once he wrote:

> Judge Holt has rendered himself a laughing stock to the country by allowing his name to be used to give currency to a long partisan rigmarole intended to effect the election, in which it is charged that 500,000 Democrats are enrolled in a society to aid rebellion and form a northwestern confederacy. If it were true that five hundred thousand voters at the North were in favor of the Davis government, then LINCOLN is fighting a clear majority of his countrymen in waging war; but of course it is a lie, and so stupid a one that it will deceive none but boobies. It is positively insufferable that the members of the Democratic party, who have had to bear their share of the blood, expense, and suffering of this dreadful war, should be insulted by these scoundrelly charges, emanating as they do from the fanatics and fools who got the country into its present troubles, and do not know how to get it out of them. We ask no better Democratic campaign document than this cock-and-bull story of HOLT, for no fair-minded man can read it without being moved to indignation against the officials who would dare give it currency.[29]

After criticizing both Judge Advocate General Holt and his "ridiculous report," the editor of the Detroit *Free Press* wrote disparagingly of Mary Ann Pitman, praised in the composition as "a person of unusual intelligence and force of character." Editor Walker, exuding malice, characterized the "wit-

28. Cincinnati *Daily Enquirer*, October 16, 20, 1864.
29. New York *World*, October 20, October 17, 1864.

ness" in slanderous terms: "We are informed by one who knows that MARY ANN PITMAN, the 'Southern lady' referred to in Judge Holt's infamous report, is a mulatto girl, and was taken from a plantation about ten miles from Fort Pillow. She drinks, chews tobacco, smokes, dresses in men's clothing when necessary, and is addicted to all the vices of a woman who is a regular camp follower. She is shrewd, unscrupulous and vicious to the last degree; she will not hesitate at anything for pay." [30] Walker's tactic, evidently, was to repay slander with slander and misrepresentation with misrepresentation.

Dr. Richard F. Stevens, the respected head of "McClellan's Minutemen" in New York, denounced Holt and his "scurrilous" documents and denied involvement in any subversive activities. He vindicated himself in a letter that was published in the New York *World*. Holt's report, Dr. Stevens argued, was little more than "campaign fodder," intended to discredit Democrats. "None of the members of the association [the "McClellan Minutemen" or "Minute Guard"] ever held a secret meeting," Stevens wrote, "and nothing of a secret or traitorous nature was ever connected with it." It was no more than "an association for ordinary political campaign work." It had no secrets and no ritual. Each man wore or carried the American flag on public occasions. Holt's assertions linking him and his association to the Knights of the Golden Circle or any subversive society, Dr. Stevens concluded with an air of finality, were pure bunkum and "absolute and entire falsehoods." [31]

Clement L. Vallandigham, depicted in Holt's report as head of "the Order" that plotted treason, also stated his indignation and denials in a letter intended for publication. Feeling maligned, Vallandigham showed no restraint in attacking Judge Advocate General Holt and his "malicious and fiendish report." He ridiculed the conspiracy charges and he repudiated the slanderous allegations. "As far as to the 'conspiracy' set forth in Judge Advocate General Holt's pamphlet and the eleven specifications summed up by Horace Greeley," Vallandigham wrote with indignation, "I have only to say that, as far as I am concerned, they are absolute falsehoods and fabrications from beginning to end. They are false in the aggregate and false in detail. More than that, they are [as] preposterous and ridiculous as they are without foundation; and all this Mr. Judge Advocate Holt, Mary Ann Pitman, and Mr. Horace Greeley know very well." [32]

Vallandigham also made his explanations and denials in several public speeches. He talked at length about the Sons of Liberty in two different ad-

---

30. Detroit *Free Press*, October 26, 1864.
31. Stevens to "Editor," October 17, 1864, published in New York *World*, October 19, 1864.
32. Clement L. Vallandigham to "Editor," October 22, 1864, published in New York *Daily News*, October 26, 1864, New York *Daily Tribune*, October 26, 1864, and Dayton *Daily Empire*, October 29, 1864.

dresses. Each time he related the ideals and the objectives of the order as he understood them. The aims, he said, were most honorable—to counter the work of the Union Leagues, "promote Jeffersonian doctrine," "protect individual rights," and ensure Democratic victories at the polls. It was, he concluded, merely "a militant Democratic group within the great national [Democratic] party," comparable in patriotism to the Sons of Liberty of pre–Revolutionary War days.[33]

Phineas C. Wright, awaiting vindication in a cell in Fort Lafayette, also felt compelled to deny implication in any traitorous plans. He begged for a chance to clear his name and brush away the web of conspiracy that Holt had woven around him and the Order of American Knights. "You have brought me before the public," he wrote plaintively to the judge advocate general, "in a character that is not *mine*. In the name of justice let me be heard and then let the public judge." Wright begged for a jury trial—a right guaranteed by the Constitution, he said.[34]

But the imprisoned man, once founder of the Order of American Knights, could not gain the ear or sympathy of any public offical. Holt and Stanton did not want his denials publicized, their exposé repudiated, and the rumors about "the Order" imperiled. Disheartened, Wright wrote to a lawyer friend in Detroit: "Of these matters which have been ventilated in Indiana, Illinois, and Missouri, I know nothing whatever save through the public press. I deny that any organization with which I am connected has had any part in plots and conspiracies. Why then am I denied the opportunity to exculpate myself?"[35] The answer to this question lies in the field of conjecture. By keeping Wright entombed in Fort Lafayette, his denials could be quashed and Holt's impressive report could remain a vital and important campaign document.

While federal authorities turned a deaf ear to Wright's pleas, the presidential campaign continued into its last month. Holt's report found thousands of readers as Union Leagues made the pamphlet available from Maine to Missouri. It also paid handsome dividends at the polls on November 8. Lincoln defeated McClellan by 400,000 votes, gaining 212 electoral votes to McClellan's 21. More important, Republicans gained control of every state legislature of the upper Midwest and Governors Oliver P. Morton of Indiana and Richard Yates of Illinois won reelection and a sort of vindication. "I suppose," a friend wrote to Holt, "the discovery of a conspiracy will go far to account for the great majority with which the West voted for the Union."[36]

Actually, Lincoln would have defeated McClellan handily even without

33. Chicago *Times*, October 22, 1864; Dayton *Daily Empire*, November 7, 1864.
34. Phineas C. Wright to Holt, October 17, 1864, in Holt Papers.
35. Wright to Theodore Romeyn, November 27, 1864, in Holt Papers.
36. William B. Lord to Holt, November 3, 1864, in Holt Papers.

Holt's report. Its contribution was more in the area of Civil War mythology. Holt's noted document gave respectability to the politically motivated exposés earlier concocted by Carrington and Sanderson. It was ironic that the War Department's spy system, headed by Lafayette C. Baker, had so little to offer Holt while two politically minded army officers offered so much. So in the end, Holt and Stanton joined Carrington and Sanderson in slandering the Democracy, stigmatizing such men as Vallandigham and Dr. Stevens as traitors, and contributing to a myth that survived the war and remained in circulation for more than a hundred years.

CHAPTER VI

The Northwestern Confederacy Scheme and the Indianapolis Treason Trials

THE STRANGE drama that unfolded in Indiana in 1864 featured three principal characters, a large supporting cast, and a discernible if disarranged plot. It possessed some of the qualities of a melodrama and some of the features of medieval mystery and morality plays. The situation existing in the Hoosier State in 1864 provided a near-perfect setting for the drama.

There was no moratorium on partisanship in Indiana in 1864. Governor Oliver P. Morton sought reelection and vindication. A victory at the polls would appear to indemnify his rather arbitrary actions, taken in the name of necessity and patriotism. The presidential contest added fuel to the partisan fires. Political differences degenerated into personal animosities, sometimes warping the judgment of once reasonable men. Lambdin P. Milligan's hatred of Governor Morton was matched by Morton's hatred of Milligan. H. H. Dodd's detestation of Republicans was matched by Brigadier General Henry B. Carrington's contempt for the Democracy. Governor Morton, aggressive leader of his party in Indiana, asked no quarter and, in turn, offered none to Democrats whom he had learned to detest and distrust.

Oliver P. Morton, one of the three principal characters in the 1864 drama, was a formidable political foe. He was, without question, "the ablest and most energetic of the war governors of the Western states."[1] He had the zeal and energy to transform his causes into crusades. His magnetic qualities, administrative skills, and political astuteness gave his party an advantage in the political wars in Indiana; Democrats had no leader of his ability. In fact, the Democrats were split into factions, with only the party loyalty of the rank and file making the Indiana Democracy a viable political force. Morton's almost fanatical devotion to the Republican party, his fervent patriotism, and his

1. James Ford Rhodes, *History of the United States from the Compromise of 1850 to the McKinley-Bryan Campaign of 1896* (7 vols.; New York, 1893–1906), V, 182.

tendency toward self-righteousness led him to believe that he was providentially commissioned to quash Copperhead hopes and Democratic stratagems.

In a way, Morton had a valid reason to detest Democrats, for they had played partisan politics viciously while the nation's life was at stake. The Democratic-dominated state legislature of 1863 had pursued partisan goals with a vengeance, trying to usurp the governor's military power and to embarrass him with ill-timed investigations. The Democratic legislators also made an attempt to redraw congressional district lines and delayed passing a budget bill.

Morton countered Democratic shenanigans with effective tactics. He solicited letters and petitions from Republican-officered regiments, revitalized the Union League, raised the Golden Circle bugaboo, and tainted the Democratic party with treason. When the Democratic-smelling committees failed to find any evidence of fraud or maladministration, some party members tried other tactics, but Governor Morton outfoxed them at every turn.

Rash acts of individuals, most of whom claimed to be Democrats, played into Morton's hands. In Terre Haute, a bastion of the Democracy, misguided individuals threw stones at soldiers home on furlough. In some backwoods areas, there was open resistance to the draft. There was a vague plot, perhaps more rumor than fact, to assassinate the governor. Occasionally someone openly expressed a preference for the Confederate president over Lincoln or cheered for Jeff Davis after tarrying in a tavern.

Despite their disadvantages, Democrats effected a resurgence during the summer of 1864. Grant's defeats before Richmond provided a base for the renewed peace crusade. War weariness undermined northern morale. Furthermore, the Republicans seemed to be on the verge of an open rupture; they quarreled over reconstruction in Congress and John C. Frémont received the nomination of a radical faction of the party at a convention in Cleveland on May 31. Even Carrington's exposé of the Sons of Liberty, first published in the Indianapolis *Daily Journal* of June 29, failed to stop the Democratic resurgence.

Governor Morton was fully aware that his record and reputation lay on the line. If the Democracy obtained the governorship and control of the state legislature, his reputation would suffer and his administration would be discredited. On the other hand, reelection could be viewed as a vindication and as a repudiation of Judge Samuel E. Perkins' critical decisions and public pronouncements. Morton's future and reputation, obviously, rested in the hands of the electorate.

Morton, with everything at stake, took the offensive. He tipped his hand at Greencastle where he lambasted the Democratic gubernatorial nominee, Joseph E. McDonald, and his "treason-inclined supporters." "Every open and avowed secessionist—every worshipper of Jeff Davis—every Knight of the Golden Circle and Son of Liberty—every Southern spy who is lurking through our borders," Morton shouted with malevolence and a show of patriotism, "is his [McDonald's] warm and earnest advocate."[2] The governor revealed his plan of attack: Democrats would be tainted with treason, and patriots must repudiate them.

As one of the principals in the developing drama, Morton had some competent helpers. William R. Holloway, the governor's brother-in-law and private secretary, borrowed money from Morton and purchased the Indianapolis *Journal* and its printing plant on August 28, 1864. He spent much time in the weeks that followed discrediting the Democracy and presenting Morton as patriotism personified. William H. H. Terrell, whom Morton had earlier named adjutant general of Indiana, often provided information that could be used for partisan ends. His integrity might be questioned, for he later doctored a general's official report to absolve a friend of wrongdoing and to impugn the loyalty of Democrats.[3] Brigadier General Henry B. Carrington, whose earlier exposés had tied Democrats to supposedly subversive dark lantern societies, hired a swarm of detectives to link Democrats to treason. General Alvin P. Hovey, who replaced Carrington in late August, 1864, as commander of the District of Indiana, stumbled onstage rather belatedly, but he served Morton well by making the arrests the governor wanted and by acquiescing in the use of a military commission to try civilians in an area where the civil courts were open and operating.

H. H. Dodd was the second of the three principals in the drama that unfolded in Indiana in 1864. He became the villain in the mystery play, of which parts of the story are still clouded and unclear. Dodd's star seemed in the ascendency early in 1864. He had enticed a few Democratic bigwigs into the Sons of Liberty early in the year, and he had become the organization's chief architect and promoter. He had always presented the Sons of Liberty to his partisan colleagues as a legitimate organization, dedicated to keeping the elections free, serving as a mutual protection society, countering the work of the Union League, and aiding in the nomination and election of a peace man as president of the country. Dodd had gloried in the resurgence of the peace movement during the first six months of 1864, had been selected by his constituents as a delegate to the Democratic national convention, and had openly espoused the nomination of Lambdin P. Milligan as the party's gubernatorial nominee.

2. Oliver P. Morton, quoted in Indianapolis *Daily Journal*, July 28, 1864.

3. After the war Holloway presented his partisan views in an oft-cited work, *History of Indianapolis and Marion County* (Philadelphia, 1884). Terrell doctored General Milo S. Hascall's report of September 25, 1865 before it was published as "Document No. 80" in *Report of the Adjutant General of Indiana* (8 vols.; Indianapolis, 1869), I, 276–77. Interested readers can

Then, in July of 1864, Dodd's house of cards collapsed. Carrington's exposé of the Sons of Liberty rang the death knell of the dark lantern society that Dodd had tried to transform from a paper tiger into a viable political force. Dodd's anger and bitterness at being depicted as a traitor affected his judgment and good sense. He received another setback to his dreams at the Democratic State Convention of July 12; the delegates sidetracked Milligan's candidacy, named Joseph E. McDonald as the party's gubernatorial candidate, and repudiated the unequivocal peace men. Two weeks later, Colonel John P. Sanderson's exposé of the Order of American Knights rubbed more salt into Dodd's open wounds.

During these days of dejection and disappointment, Dodd learned that Confederate agents in Canada had money available to subsidize the peace movement, elect Copperheads to office, arouse discontent, and support a vague scheme to foment rebellion and bring about a northwestern confederacy. Since both Carrington and Sanderson had implicated Dodd and Confederate agents in Canada had given credence to the "revelations," Jacob Thompson, the chief Confederate agent in Canada, and his helpers were most willing to pass a bundle of cash in Dodd's direction. Coincidently, Dodd's printing firm needed money to bring out the 1864 city directory and to pay creditors who had loaned money to purchase several new steam-operated printing presses. The temptation to take ten thousand dollars without giving any security and with only vague commitments to subsidize rebellion was much stronger than Dodd could resist. But taking rebel-tainted money was much more than an indiscretion, whether Dodd's intent was to milk a cooperative cow or to subsidize an uprising in some mysterious way.[4] Dodd's act of imprudence transformed a second-rate politician with a good public record into a miscreant willing to take the low road. Those who cooperate with the enemy and take thirty pieces of silver, whatever the intent, become villains in a nation's history.

---

compare Hascall's manuscript report, in the Archives Division, Indiana State Library, Indianapolis, with the printed version.

4. Godfrey J. Hyams, "Toronto Report" (MS, May 8, 1865, in Halmer H. Emmons Papers, Burton Historical Collection, Detroit Public Library); Indianapolis *Daily Journal*, August 21, September 21, 1864; Joseph J. Bingham, testimony, October 28, 1864, in Proceedings of the Military Commission Convened in Indianapolis, General Courts Martial Records, Records of the Office of the Judge Advocate General, National Archives. See also Thomas H. Hines [really written by John B. Castleman and W. W. Cleary], "The Northwestern Conspiracy," *Southern Bivouac: A Monthly Literary and Historical Magazine*, n.s., II (June, 1886–May, 1887), 437–45, 500–10, 567–74, 699–704; John B. Castleman, *Active Service* (Louisville, 1917), 145–47; Jacob Thompson to Judah P. Benjamin, report, December 3, 1864, published in *The War of the Rebellion: A Compilation of the Official Records of the Union and Confederate Armies* (128 vols.; Washington, D.C., 1880–1901), Ser. 1, Vol. XLII, 930–31, hereinafter cited as *OR*. I believe that the Hines-Castleman account of the Northwest conspiracy was based upon Edmund Kirke [James R. Gilmore], "The Chicago Conspiracy," *Atlantic Monthly*, XVI (July, 1865), 108–20,

Wittingly or otherwise, Dodd involved others in his schemes. Without taking them into his confidence, he named four acquaintances as the "major generals" of four imaginary military districts in the reorganized Sons of Liberty. Without their consent, he made them, on paper at least, leaders of a military arm of the Sons of Liberty. Dodd evidently envisioned the military arm as an agency to oppose Republican takeover of the polls in the fall elections. He and a few other Democrats had convinced themselves that the threat was real, that the polls might be taken over by the soldiery as had happened in Kentucky. It is possible, on the other hand, that Dodd actually hoped to effect a revolutionary scheme or that he wanted Confederate agents in Canada to believe that he was really living up to his vague promises.[5]

Each of the four whom Dodd selected as his "district commanders" became involved in the drama destined to develop in Indiana. Milligan, the best known of the four, detested Morton with a passion and believed that the Lincoln administration had trespassed beyond constitutional limits. Andrew Humphreys, of Greene County, sometimes became intemperate when expressing views on such subjects as Morton, Lincoln, and the war. John C. Walker, who also took money from Confederate agents in Canada and walked down the low road with Dodd, was cut from the same cloth as Humphreys and Milligan; he once called Governor Morton "a common liar," who was as "false as his own heart is black, as villainous as his own nature is cowardly and infamous."[6] William A. Bowles, the fourth "major general," had mastered the art of mixing loquacity with imprudence in a ratio that galled Republicans; he even claimed that he had more respect for Jefferson Davis than for Lincoln, defended slavery as an institution, and talked too much too often.

In addition to the four "major generals," five other Democrats stood in Dodd's shadow on the stage. Joseph J. Bingham, editor of the Indianapolis *State Sentinel* and chairman of the Democratic State Central Committee, became involved because he was an acquaintance of Dodd and had lent money to H. H. Dodd & Company. Horace Heffren, once described as "a disgusting compound of whiskey, grease, vulgarity, and cowardice" by a Republican editor, also became a victim of circumstance.[7] Although Heffren had earlier told Bingham that he regarded the Sons of Liberty as "a humbug," Dodd's paper-based organization still listed the Salem Democrat as a "deputy grand com-

---

and the published proceedings of the Cincinnati treason trial rather than the facts in the case. A copy of the Gilmore article, with notes written in the margin in Hines's own hand, is in the Thomas H. Hines Papers, University of Kentucky Library, Lexington.

5. *Argument of John R. Coffroth in Defense of Col. L. P. Milligan . . .* (Indianapolis, 1864), 4–6.

6. John C. Walker to "Editor," June 25, 1863, published in Indianapolis *Daily State Sentinel*, June 25, 1863.

7. Indianapolis *Daily Journal*, August 6, 1864.

mander," without Heffren's knowledge or approval.[8] William M. Harrison, who had earlier accepted favors at Dodd's hands, held the title of grand secretary of the Sons of Liberty in Indiana, without realizing that this assignment would place him in the spotlight. Stephen Horsey, who belonged to a loosely organized mutual protection society called the Circle of Honor in Martin County, seems to have attended one meeting in Indianapolis where Dodd talked politics and promoted the Sons of Liberty. David T. Yeakel, a dentist from Lafayette, had his fingers in the Order of American Knights pudding when Dodd tried to serve it in 1863, and retained close contact with him throughout 1864. These five, along with the four "major generals," would become involved in the Indianapolis treason trials in one way or another.

Felix G. Stidger, a perceptive fellow who practiced self-service and excelled in the art of expediency, became the third principal character in the melodrama that would be staged in Indianapolis. Stidger's early career gave no indication that he would evolve into a superstar in the Morton-staged production. Starting life as a farm boy near Taylorsville, Kentucky, the plucky lad moved with his family to the Mattoon area of Illinois in 1853. He drifted back to Kentucky to work as a carpenter for two years before trying his hand as a clerk in a drygoods store in Fairfield and moving to Louisville at the start of the war. He volunteered for service in the Union army, being mustered into the Fifteenth Kentucky Infantry Regiment at Chaplain Hills in 1862.[9] His ability to write and cipher brought him a clerk's assignment at divisional headquarters, but he tired of his work as a soldier-clerk. Feigning illness, he obtained "a fraudulent discharge"—a bit of deceit and misrepresentation about which he later bragged.[10] After his "recovery," he became a civilian clerk in the office of Captain Stephen E. Jones, provost marshal general of the District of Kentucky, and Lieutenant Colonel Thomas B. Farleigh, who commanded the Louisville subdivision. After a stint of effective service, Stidger noted that a government detective earned six times as much as a clerk; so he begged Captain Jones for an opportunity to try on Sherlock Holmes's cap for size. Acquiescing, Captain Jones put Stidger's name on his list of "special agents."

Captain Jones subsequently sent Stidger into southern Kentucky to check

8. Bingham, testimony, October 28, 1864, in Proceedings of the Military Commission Convened at Indianapolis.

9. Felix G. Stidger, testimony, November 3, 1864, *ibid*. Also see the Felix G. Stidger Papers, in Records of the Adjutant General's Office, Records of the Office of the Judge Advocate General. Statements that Stidger later made in his book, *Treason History of the Order of the Sons of Liberty, Formerly Circle of Honor, Succeeded by the Knights of the Golden Circle, Afterwards Order of American Knights: The Most Gigantic Treasonable Conspiracy the World Has Ever Known* (Chicago, 1903), do not square with some of the testimony that he gave before the Indianapolis-based military commission.

10. Stidger, *Treason History of the Sons of Liberty*, 30–31, 41, 52–53, 63–65, 105–106, 114.

out rumors of an impending Confederate invasion. Using a pseudonym, Stidger reported on the rumors and suppositions then circulating in southern Kentucky. The following day, Captain Jones, a close personal friend of Governor Morton, received a request for "an agent" to investigate "a plot" of some secret society members of the Kentucky-Indiana area. One of Carrington's chief agents, Samuel P. Coffin, had tried to blackmail his employers (asking for five thousand dollars for information in hand) and had bungled an assignment by unwittingly revealing his identity. Desperately, Carrington telegraphed Captain Jones, asking him to "loan" a responsible detective. Jones, in return, "loaned" Stidger to Carrington.[11]

Carrington's new detective took a hurried trip into southern Indiana, visiting Salem, Paoli, and French Lick. He learned little about Democratic dark lantern societies, but he discovered that Horace Heffren detested Lincoln and his emancipation policy and that William A. Bowles was bitter about the war. To Stidger, Bowles looked like a man who would engage in traitorous activity. "He has one of the worst countenances I near ever saw a man have," Stidger reported; "he cannot look *anyone* in the face for one minute, I don't believe."[12]

Several days later, Stidger had an opportunity to visit with Bowles. Suspecting that Stidger was a spy, Bowles gave him an earful, exaggerating as best he could. He talked about the extensive membership of a Democratic secret society and bluntly said that civil war would come to Indiana if the government stifled civil rights and tried to seize the polls on election day. After returning to Louisville from his week-long trip into southern Indiana, Stidger sat down to compose a nine-page report, transforming Bowles's rhetoric into treason and trying to impress his employers with his sleuthing.[13]

Stidger also joined a local Louisville Democratic club, with Dr. Henry F. Kalfus as his sponsor. Kalfus, once a major in the Union army, had been Stidger's superior during his stint with the Fifteenth Kentucky. Dr. Kalfus had written a letter of resignation, stating his conviction that the war was being fought "for the elevation of the negro race, or rather for the *degradation of the white man . . .* and for the subversion of the rights and institutions of the states." Angered, General William S. Rosecrans promptly dismissed Kalfus

11. J. T. Farris [Felix G. Stidger] to Col. Thomas B. Farleigh, May 4, 1864, "Additional Statement of Edward T. Hoffman," May 29, 1864, both in Reports on the Order of American Knights, Records of the Office of the Judge Advocate General; Stidger, testimony, October 24, 1864, in Proceedings of the Military Commission Convened at Indianapolis.

12. J. J. Eustiss [Stidger] to Capt. Stephen E. Jones, May 13, 1864, in Reports on the Order of American Knights. Interestingly, other witnesses were impressed by Bowles's appearance. He was well proportioned, over six feet tall, and possessed attractive personal qualities. One of Bowles's acquaintances wrote, "He was one of the finest looking men I ever saw." See the comments of A. J. Rhodes in Indianapolis *Daily News*, December 30, 1901.

13. Eustiss [Stidger] to Jones, May 13, 1864, in Reports on the Order of American Knights.

from the service, with dishonor, and ordered his provost marshal "to arrest" him and "place him in irons for his disloyalty." After his release, Kalfus returned to Louisville to express his bitterness openly and return to local Democratic party activity.[14] Stidger, feigning disaffection, gained Kalfus' confidence and the secretaryship of the Democratic Reading Club of Louisville. With Dr. Kalfus' blessing, he also served as acting state secretary of the badly disorganized Democratic party in Kentucky.[15] In his reports, Stidger transformed these Democratic meetings on the local and state level into "sessions" of the Sons of Liberty—clearly a misrepresentation.[16]

At a meeting of local Louisville Democrats, Stidger first learned of the unmasking of Morton's spy (Coffin); he also learned that Clement L. Vallandigham planned to return from exile in Canada, and that party members were anxious to set up a state Democratic convention to select delegates to the Chicago convention, then scheduled for July 4.[17] Stidger also became acquainted with other Louisville Democrats, including Joshua F. Bullitt, who was most critical of Lincoln, the war, and military misrule in Kentucky.

Posing as Bullitt's personal secretary and carrying a forged letter of introduction from Dr. Kalfus, Stidger took a most rewarding trip to Indianapolis. Claiming that he had held conversations with Dr. Bowles and that Louisville members of the city's Democratic club wished to form a "castle" of the Sons of Liberty, Stidger gained H. H. Dodd's confidence. Dodd, as grand commander of the order in Indiana, gave Stidger a packet of Sons of Liberty material, containing Dodd's previously published address, initiation booklets and other items. Dodd also took Stidger to the office of the Indianapolis *State Sentinel*, where the "emissary from Louisville" met Joseph J. Bingham. Stidger related what he had earlier told Dodd, that Judge Bullitt was then under arrest, perhaps compromised by agent Coffin.[18]

Before returning to Louisville with the items Dodd had given him, Stidger visited Carrington and showed him his interesting packet of Sons of Liberty material. Elated, Carrington hurriedly made a copy of each item, and these became the chief source of information for his exposé of late June, 1864.[19]

14. Maj. Henry F. Kalfus to Major Goddard, February 26, 1863, and Rosecrans' endorsement on this letter, in Packet No. 825, Volunteer Service Branch, War Department Records, National Archives.
15. Sitdger to Farleigh, June 29, 1864, in Reports on the Order of American Knights.
16. Eustiss [Stidger] to Jones, June 2, 1864, Stidger to John J. Felix, July 19, 1864, both *ibid*.
17. Unsigned [Stidger] to Jones, June 2, 1864, *ibid*.
18. Kalfus and W. K. Thomas to H. H. Dodd, June 13, 1864, *ibid*. This letter, in Stidger's own hand, is a forged document. Also see Stidger to Jones, June 28, 1864, *ibid*.; Bingham, testimony, October 28, 1864, Stidger, testimony, October 24, 1864, both in Proceedings of the Military Commission Convened at Indianapolis.
19. The Carrington exposé of June 28, 1864 was published in the Indianapolis *Daily Journal*, June 29, 1864.

Back in Louisville, Stidger learned that General Stephen G. Burbridge, commander of the District of Kentucky, had released Joshua F. Bullitt, arrested a week earlier. General Burbridge, evidently, had no evidence that implicated Bullitt in any questionable activity. Bullitt then called together a handful of partisans who constituted themselves the Democratic State Central Committee. On June 27 Bullitt presided over a meeting of sixteen or seventeen men in the Galt House, with Stidger serving as interim secretary. The men, half of them from outside Louisville, named a slate of four delegates— Bullitt one of them—to represent the Kentucky Democracy at the Chicago convention, rescheduled for late August. They drew up a statement denouncing the military dictatorship in Kentucky. They also planned to meet again on July 18 to plan and promote the election of state and national Democratic nominees.[20]

In his lengthy report of June 29, which dealt in a large measure with the Democratic gathering at the Galt House, Stidger was again guilty of misrepresentation. He transformed the political session into a meeting of the grand council of the Sons of Liberty, assigned the title of grand commander to Bullitt and grand secretary to himself, and pretended that the meeting was subversive in nature, proposing an insurrection and an alliance with the Confederacy.[21]

Stidger's contention that the Sons of Liberty planned an insurrection as a means to establish a northwestern confederacy was not his own invention. Governor Morton had expressed that fear again and again. It was the central theme of Carrington's exposé of June 28, 1864, and Sanderson's exposé a month later.

The rumor that Copperheads—that is, Democratic critics of the Lincoln administration—planned an uprising and dreamt of establishing a separate confederacy had intangible historical roots. One of the roots fed upon the widespread discontent existing in the upper Midwest. Another drew sustenance from the spirit of western sectionalism, opposed to "Puritan domination in religion or morals or literature or politics."[22] A third root reached into Missouri, where J. W. Tucker, one of General Sterling Price's devotees and editor of the *Mississippi Army Argus* and the Jackson (Mississippi) *Argus*, feeling that Richmond had failed to give western Confederates the supplies and support due that section, wrote several articles favorable to the establishment of a northwestern confederacy. Some Confederate officials, guilty of ac-

20. Stidger, testimony, October 24, 1864, in Proceedings of the Military Commission Convened at Indianapolis; Eustiss [Stidger] to Jones, June 29, 1864, in Reports on the Order of American Knights.
21. Eustiss [Stidger] to Jones, June 29, 1864, in Reports on the Order of American Knights.
22. Samuel S. Cox, *Puritanism in Politics: Speech of Hon. S. S. Cox Before the Democratic Union Association, Jan. 13, 1863* (New York, 1863), 12.

cepting Copperhead rhetoric at face value, convinced themselves that dis-affected midwesterners might withdraw from the war and ally themselves with the South. Henry S. Foote of Mississippi, for example, introduced a res-olution in the Confederate congress providing for recognition of a north-western confederacy. General Pierre G. T. Beauregard contemplated a cam-paign into Kentucky and Ohio to help the Midwest throw off the yoke of "the accursed Yankee nation." One of the main roots drew its nourishment from Republican political propaganda spread to discredit Democratic dissenters when they threatened to gain political power in 1862. Rumors about the Knights of the Golden Circle, little more than a straw man devised for politi-cal gain, linked that dark lantern society to midwestern discontent and some strange confederacy scheme. An affiant, who claimed that there were 1.5 mil-lion Golden Circle members in the country, swore that one of the goals of the subversive society was to establish a northwestern confederacy. Quite as ab-surd was a story which appeared in a Philadelphia newspaper; the tall tale linked Clement L. Vallandigham to a Copperhead-minded organization called the Brothers of the Great West, founded to resist the draft and promote the idea of a separate western confederacy. Governors Oliver P. Morton and Richard Yates repeatedly railed against Copperheadism and treasonable plots, preparing the public mind for the exposés and charges that would gain head-lines during the last year of the war. Carrington helped to develop the myth that General John H. Morgan's raid of July, 1863, into Indiana and Ohio was intended to correspond with a Copperhead-sponsored insurrection.[23]

The roots of rumors about such an insurrection also reached into Canada. Suppositions that Confederates, either fugitives or agents in the Windsor or Toronto areas, intended to seize the USS *Michigan* and release prisoners held within stockades on Johnson's Island in Sanduskey Bay were repeated now and then.[24] The suppositions improved in the retelling and came to include the capture of Detroit and an invasion from Canada, "with tens of thousands of sympathizers everywhere in ambush to rise up and join them."[25]

23. Pierre G. T. Beauregard to Charles J. Villere, May 23, 1863, published in *OR*, Ser. 1, Vol. IV, 955; Eli Wells, affidavit before J. J. Hayden, J.P., January 12, 1863 (copy in General Courts Martial Records); Philadelphia *Evening Bulletin*, March 20, 1863; Indianapolis *Daily Journal*, July 15, 22, 25, 1863. Interestingly, Carrington's report ("Memorandum of Condition of Public Affairs in Indiana, to Be Submitted to the President and the Honorable Secretary of War" [MS, March 19, 1863, in Robert Todd Lincoln Papers, Library of Congress]) contains no expression of fear *re* a northwestern confederacy.

24. New York *Times*, November 13, 1863; Detroit *Free Press*, November 13, 14, 15, 1863; *OR*, Ser. 2, Vol. VI, 368, 402, 415; N. W. Brooks to "Dear Son," November 19, 1863, in N. W. Brooks Papers, Burton Historical Collection.

25. Detroit *Advertiser & Tribune*, November 12, 13, 1863; (Columbus, Ohio) *Crisis*, No-vember 18, 1863; Detroit *Free Press*, December 29, 1863.

Rumors about conspiracies became more prevalent with each passing week as Democrats and Republicans squared off for the fall elections. Colonel Carrington, still glorying in the popularity of his exposé of the Sons of Liberty, predicted that a revolution might occur during the Democratic State Convention of July 12. To convince the skeptical, he issued an order to have federal troops in readiness; he also tightened control of the Confederate prisoners held at Camp Morton and alerted the howitzer battery at Burnside Barracks.[26]

Governor Morton, believing that treason existed in certain circles and worrying about his reelection, wanted the leaders of the Sons of Liberty arrested. He believed that the Carrington and Sanderson exposés would lead the public to accept such drastic action. "The Governor," Carrington later wrote, "urged the arrest of the Indiana members [of the Sons of Liberty] as essential to the success of the National cause in the autumn election."[27] Governor Morton and Carrington took their request to Major General Samuel P. Heintzelman, commanding the Northern Department.[28] Heintzelman did not consider the evidence that Morton and Carrington offered conclusive, for no overt act had been committed by Dodd or Bowles. Nor did Heintzelman share Morton's sense of urgency. Practicing prudence, Heintzelman earned Morton's enmity by refusing to make the arrests without authority or instructions from Washington.[29]

Morton continued to insist upon the arrest of Dodd and Bowles, for he believed both to be traitors. He solicited support from General Stephen G. Burbridge, then commanding in Kentucky. General Burbridge, in turn, asked the War Department to authorize the arrest of "these men in Indiana." Exaggerating the state of affairs, Burbridge added, "I would also suggest that the prisoners at Rock Island and Indpls. be removed to some safe place farther north, there being great danger of their being released and armed by traitors at home."[30]

In public Governor Morton charged that some secret society members were guilty of treason and deserved to be arrested.[31] In private he put pressure upon Carrington to come up with more substantive evidence. He was not

26. Henry B. Carrington, "Special Order No. 81," July 9, 1864, in Henry B. Carrington Papers, Archives Division, Indiana State Library.

27. Carrington, "Indiana War Documents Cleared of Error" (typescript, n.d., in Carrington Papers).

28. When the western departments were reorganized, the Department of the Ohio (which Gen. Burnside had commanded) gave way to the Northern Department.

29. Samuel J. Heintzelman Journal, July 29, 1864 (MS in Samuel J. Heintzelman Papers, Library of Congress); Carrington, "Indiana War Documents Cleared of Error."

30. Gen. Stephen G. Burbridge to Edwin M. Stanton, August 6, 1864, in *OR*, Ser. 1, Vol. XXXIX, Pt. 2, p. 228.

31. Indianapolis *Daily Journal*, August 4, 1864.

pleased with Carrington's failure to convince General Heintzelman that arrests ought to be made. Carrington wrote to Heintzelman again, expressing "great alarm about a copperhead outbreak," and asked for more troops. Heintzelman evidently believed that Carrington was exaggerating the state of affairs. He feared that a rash of arbitrary arrests might bring a public reaction, perhaps even mob violence. In such a case, ten thousand soldiers would be needed to overawe the public. Since his office in Columbus was across the street from Governor David Tod's quarters in the statehouse, Heintzelman walked over "to get his opinion as to the propriety of arresting the leaders in Ind." Tod felt "a delicacy in giving his opinion," at first endorsing such arrests and then backtracking as he talked. Heintzelman, therefore, decided that he would not permit the arrests to be made in Indiana unless he had a force strong enough "to prevent an outbreak."[32]

While General Heintzelman hedged, nettling Governor Morton, Carrington intensified his search for evidence that would incriminate Democratic leaders, especially H. H. Dodd. Carrington, watching Dodd's every movement, noticed that the suspected Democrat frequently visited Daniel W. Voorhees' empty law office in Indianapolis. Desperately in need of evidence and under pressure from Governor Morton, Carrington and others broke down the door to the empty law office on August 4 and carted off some letters, as well as a stack of Sons of Liberty material. The action evidently pleased Governor Morton, for his adjutant general wrote, "We are now very busy with hunting up 'Sons of Liberty' and exposing them. A lot of rituals etc. were found in Dan Voorhees' office yesterday and there is a general flounder among them." The raid failed to provide Carrington with any more information about the Sons of Liberty than he already had, but it did show that some of Congressman Voorhees' friends were bitter and outspoken in their opposition to President Lincoln, Governor Morton, and the war. It also gave the editor of the Indianapolis *Journal* a chance to compose headlines that the headquarters of the Sons of Liberty had been raided and treasonable materials confiscated.[33]

As far as H. H. Dodd was concerned, Carrington's raid on Voorhees' office was the last straw. It was further evidence that Governor Morton would go to any lengths to discredit his critics and win the election—even to the extent of using soldiers to control the polls and election returns. Dodd lost his last shred of forbearance. Recent events had heaped frustration upon frustration. Carrington's exposé of June 28 had discredited him and pricked his Sons of Lib-

32. Heintzelman Journal, August 5, 9, 1864; William Henry Smith, "Private Memorandum: Wartimes," notation of August 8, 1864, in William Henry Smith Papers, Ohio Historical Society, Columbus.
33. Lazarus Noble to "Dear [John T.] Wilder," August 5, 1864, in John T. Wilder Papers, Indiana Division, Indiana State Library; Indianapolis *Daily Journal*, August 6, 1864.

erty bubble. Old friends avoided him; he was no longer invited to address Democratic rallies; his once bright political star had plummeted. Instead of blaming himself for his misfortune, he blamed others. He rationalized that Governor Morton was simply seeking excuses to seize the polls and control the elections.

Dodd's fear that free elections might disappear was shared by other Indiana Democrats, for whom Kentucky was an object lesson. "The Democracy of this region of the state," a Rush County dissenter wrote, "are apprehensive that we will not be allowed a fair election, that an attempt will be made to enforce a draft for the purpose of arousing the people to desperation, and thereby giving the powers that be an excuse to declare martial law, and investing the election precincts with bayonets sufficient to patrol the election as they have done in other states." At least one current historian who assessed the situation in Indiana concluded that Democratic fears were reasonable. He wrote, "Considering the record of election interference compiled by the [Lincoln] administration thus far, Democratic fears do not appear entirely groundless." Joseph J. Bingham, recognized as a reasonable and conservative Democrat, shared the apprehensions of the hour. Even he urged party members to arm "for the protection of the political rights" that the Constitution guaranteed them.[34]

The fear that Morton and the Lincoln administration might use force to control the elections, led Dodd to try to devise a new organization on the foundations of the old. Carrington's exposé of the Sons of Liberty not only had discredited that dark lantern society but had made it impossible to transform Dodd's paper-based organization into a viable one. Dodd, therefore, banded together a few friends, most of whom had been nominal members of the Sons of Liberty, into a new society called the Order of American Cincinnatus. Those who belonged considered it "a defensive organization," willing to repel force with force if the administration tried to close the polls or set up a dictatorship. They viewed their chief objective as proper and noble—"to maintain the Constitution and the laws of the United States in their purity."[35] The fact that Dodd had accepted money from Confederate agents in Canada could taint every organization to which he belonged, be it the new Order of American Cincinnatus, the old Sons of Liberty, or the Democratic party.

Frustrated because Carrington's exposé had discredited him and boiling

34. William H. Hall to Charles B. Lasselle, August 4, 1864, in Charles B. Lasselle Papers, Indiana Division, Indiana State Library; Gilbert R. Tredway, "Indiana Against the Administration, 1861–1865" (Ph.D. dissertation, Indiana University, 1962), 59; Indianapolis *Daily State Sentinel*, August 7, 8, 10, 1864.
35. David T. Yeakel, *To the People of Indiana* (Printed flyer, October 28, 1864, in Lasselle Papers).

with indignation that the office he was using had been raided, Dodd convinced himself that the public would support "an uprising" against the administration. On August 6, at a council meeting of the Order of American Cincinnatus, Dodd shocked the assembled few by proposing open resistance. Those present, recognizing that Dodd was guilty of more than an indiscretion, pronounced the proposition "monstrous" and immediately set to work to prevent him from carrying out "any ambitious or criminal projects of his own." [36]

Undeterred, Dodd visited editor Bingham in his office in the *State Sentinel* Building, pledged him to secrecy, and said that a "council of sixteen" had agreed upon "revolution." The uprising, Dodd continued, had been set for August 16, the date of a proposed Democratic rally in Indianapolis. Emotional speeches might transform the multitude into a mob and pave the way for radical action. Arrangements had been made, Dodd continued, to release Confederate prisoners held in Camp Morton (outside of Indianapolis), Camp Chase, Camp Douglas, and Johnson's Island. At the same time there would be an uprising at Louisville, where government stores would be seized, and at several other points. [37]

Dodd's audacity and naïveté shocked Bingham, a patriotic and practical fellow. He stood astonished, and could not believe his ears. "Mr. Dodd," Bingham finally said, "do you know what you are proposing to undertake? Do you know the position of military affairs at this post? Do you think you can accomplish this scheme with any number of unarmed and undisciplined men you can bring here? How is this revolution to take place and nobody know anything about it?" It was, as far as Bingham was concerned, a harebrained and treasonable scheme. "I told him," Bingham later reported, "I would consent to nothing of the kind and would be a party to no such move." [38]

Bingham was anxious to find out if any other Democrats purportedly belonging to Dodd's secret circle were involved in the proposed scheme. He hunted up Joseph Ristine, state auditor, and Oscar B. Hord, an Indianapolis resident. Neither had heard of Dodd's proposition. The next morning, Bingham contacted Joseph E. McDonald, the Democratic gubernatorial candidate. "I told Mr. McDonald," Bingham testified several months later, "all that Dodd told me." McDonald agreed with Bingham that something must be done—but what? The two decided to sleep on it and exchange ideas the next morning. But on the way home Bingham met Michael C. Kerr, a respected

36. *Ibid.* In this flyer, Yeakel explains his version of the so-called council meeting and subsequent events, throwing new light upon the Order of American Cincinnatus.

37. Bingham, testimony, October 28, 1864, in Proceedings of the Military Commission Convened at Indianapolis.

38. *Ibid.*

party member and Democratic congressional candidate in the Second District. Excitedly, Kerr told Bingham that Democrats in Washington, Harrison, and Floyd counties were spreading rumors about "a revolution impending." He recited the plans for the uprising, and they seemed to match what Dodd had related to Bingham. Both were aghast. Bingham asked Kerr to accompany him back to McDonald's quarters and tell his story there. After arriving at McDonald's, Kerr recounted what he had heard, adding that Governor Morton "would be captured or taken prisoner" and Dr. James A. Athon, a Democrat and state treasurer, installed as "provisional governor." [39]

Bingham, with Kerr in tow, then walked over to Dr. Athon's house, although it was nearly midnight. He got the doctor out of bed and related what he had heard from Dodd's and Kerr's lips. Athon labeled the reports rubbish, mere rumors deserving no credence. "It's all gas," Athon said; "such a scheme cannot be entertained by sensible men." Nevertheless, Athon agreed to meet next morning at McDonald's office to discuss a plan of action. [40]

Bingham, chairman of the Democratic State Central Committee, invited every prominent Democrat he could find to attend the meeting in McDonald's office. Ten or eleven were there by midmorning the next day, including Joseph Ristine, Aqilla Jones, Samuel H. Buskirk, William Henderson, and Oscar B. Hord, as well as David Yeakel and Colonel Robert Caldwell of Lafayette. Bingham induced Kerr to relate his story once more. The consensus of opinion was that Dodd's project, if still in process, must be stopped then and there. [41]

After a while, Dodd and John C. Walker, who had returned from New York City earlier that morning, dropped in on the gathering in McDonald's office. Bingham had evidently asked Dodd to attend the informal affair. Kerr made a speech that the project must be stopped and that it was the responsibility of every deserving Democrat to stop it at once. Bingham seconded Kerr's statements forcefully. "If it can not be stopped in any other way," he concluded resolutely, "it is our duty to inform the authorities." [42]

Dodd, after listening to Kerr's and Bingham's comments, neither affirmed nor denied that "a revolutionary plan" was in process. Instead, both Dodd and Walker, who had also taken money from Confederate agents in Canada, spoke earnestly about "the state of affairs," adding that an appeal to the ballot was "folly," that the public would not accept another draft, that the people were prepared for "a revolution," and that it was better to direct the revolution than be directed by it. Nevertheless, at the insistence of the Democrats assembled

39. *Ibid.*
40. *Ibid.*
41. *Ibid.*
42. *Ibid.*

in McDonald's office, Dodd and Walker pledged that "the thing" would be stopped through orders, messengers, and good sense—a quality Dodd had not demonstrated in recent weeks.[43]

Bingham's failure to reveal Dodd's vague and visionary scheme to authorities plagued his conscience. He recognized that it could discredit him and the Democratic party. On the other hand, exposing it to authorities could be the death of McDonald's candidacy. He would be damned if he did and damned if he did not. Furthermore, public disclosure would violate his pledge to Dodd and might be just the excuse authorities needed to introduce martial law and control the elections. Maybe Dodd's aberration was already dead, a thing of the past. Carrington and Morton, Bingham rationalized, must surely have heard about the supposed scheme in one way or another.

Bingham and the members of his political circle breathed more easily as the days passed by. No arrests had been made. Dodd and Walker were around and seemed to be tending to routine business. Bingham looked forward to August 12 and the scheduled meeting of the Indiana State Central Committee.

The committee met as scheduled. Bingham had invited a few prominent local Democrats to sit in on the proceedings. First, the committee selected candidates to fill the vacancies on the state ticket. Next, members discussed "basic issues" as a prelude to framing some resolutions. Several members expressed concern with General Burbridge's dictatorial practices in Kentucky. Some commented upon the Carrington and Sanderson exposés, dismissing them as political propaganda and wondering if they had been devised as a justification to declare martial law and control the elections. Members expressed concern with the governor's practice of arming the Union Leagues.

In time, the members gave shape to several resolutions. The first, based upon "well founded apprehensions," expressed Democratic fears that authorities might interfere in the coming elections and advised loyal party members to arm and organize themselves in order to protect their rights. The other resolutions stated the traditional party principles and concerns. Then Bingham and Kerr brought up "the whole affair" regarding Dodd, Walker, and the proposed insurrection. Everyone agreed, without a dissent, that if Dodd had not already shelved his scheme, "it must be stopped."[44]

Discussion carried over to a second day. John C. Walker put in an appearance to assure the committee members that "the project" had been suspended and shelved—"that it was stopped—that nothing of the kind should take place." The members then agreed that an address to the people should be pre-

43. *Ibid.*
44. Indianapolis *Daily State Sentinel*, August 15, 1864; Bingham, testimony, October 28, 1864, in Proceedings of the Military Commission Convened in Indianapolis.

pared immediately to urge them not to resist the draft but to seek redress at the polls. "To all these acts," Yeakel later wrote, "Dodd was a party and expressed himself satisfied."[45]

While the Democrats were fumbling the football, Governor Morton and Brigadier General Carrington heard about Dodd's "proposition." William A. Bowles, informed by Dodd of the proposed uprising and the negative reaction of the "supreme council" of the Order of American Cincinnatus, passed the information on to detective Stidger when he came to French Lick on August 7. Stidger, in turn, informed Carrington and added his own elaborations. "The members in council," Stidger stated, "protested that this [Dodd's order for "a demonstration" on August 16] was a violation of the [previous] order 'not to rise in arms until a Confederate force crossed the Ohio' or 'opened up in Kentucky.'"[46]

Carrington, under pressure from the governor to arrest Dodd and others, promptly wrote to General Heintzelman, telling him of the proposed "insurrection" and urging him to make arrests lest the situation get out of hand. Exaggerating again, Carrington blamed "guerrilla activities" in Sullivan and Greene counties upon Andrew Humphreys, "a major general of the secret order."[47]

Supposing that the trail was getting hotter, Carrington watched Dodd even more closely. About five o'clock on Saturday afternoon, August 20, several boxes marked "J. J. Parsons" arrived from New York City. The express agent promptly notified Carrington who immediately asked the commandant at Camp Morton to lend a detail of soldiers to seize the shipment which had been delivered to H. H. Dodd & Company, 18 East Washington Street. Only an engineer was present at the printing plant when the drayman delivered the boxes and stored them in the engine room. Almost immediately, a squad of soldiers arrived, opened the boxes, noted that they contained revolvers and ammunition, and confiscated the whole shipment. Carrington next raided and ransacked Dodd's office, carrying off a stack of material. Since both Dodd and John C. Walker, who had contracted for the arms while he was in New York City, were out of town on a trip to Chicago, they escaped arrest at the time. Shortly after midnight, however, a squad of soldiers visited the residence of William M. Harrison, once secretary of the Sons of Liberty. They arrested Harrison, searched the premises, and carted off a few items. Next

45. Bingham, testimony, October 28, 1864, in Proceedings of the Military Commission Convened in Indianapolis; Indianapolis *Daily State Sentinel*, August 13, 1864; Yeakel, *To the People of Indiana*.
46. Henry B. Carrington to Samuel P. Heintzelman, August 9, 1864, published in *OR*, Ser. I, Vol. XXXIX, Pt. 2, pp. 236–38.
47. *Ibid*.

morning the military detail called at the homes of J. J. Parsons and Charles P. Hutchinson, two of Dodd's partners in the printing and book-binding business, searched every room, and arrested both. In the afternoon military officials released Parsons and Hutchinson—the former after he signed an affidavit saying that he knew nothing about the shipment of revolvers and the latter after signing an oath of allegiance—but Carrington kept Harrison in custody.[48]

The revolvers and cartridges that Carrington seized had evidently been purchased by Walker from W. J. Symes, 300 Broadway, New York City. The firm was an agent for the Savage revolving firearm, manufactured in Middleton, Connecticut. Money for the purchase had presumably come from Confederate agents, perhaps Clement C. Clay, then in Canada.[49]

Governor Morton and his aides recognized the seizure of the Dodd-Walker revolvers and ammunition and the letters and miscellaneous papers as a political windfall. William H. H. Terrell, adjutant general of Indiana, promptly contacted the commandant at Camp Morton, asking for one of the captured revolvers and "a paper of cartridges" so he could send an officer to New York City to investigate the purchase. Terrell also asked for all "papers and documents captured in Dodd's office," so they could be copied and turned over to the press to be published at once "to show the treasonable character of the secret order."[50]

Terrell fed the information to the press, and Carrington embroidered upon the story, stating that the revolvers and ammunition seized had been shipped in boxes marked "Sunday school books." Carrington not only greatly exaggerated the number of revolvers taken but implied that an uprising had been nipped in the bud. The Indianapolis *Journal* carried the headline "Rampant Treason in Indianapolis," stated that a traitorous plot had been uncovered, and asserted that prominent Democrats were involved. Authorities had obtained the membership rolls of the Sons of Liberty, the editor added, as well as the great seal of the society, a "strange banner," and a lot of "treasonable correspondence."[51]

The next day, at Morton's prompting, Republicans sponsored a public indignation meeting so that the governor would have a chance to lash out at

48. Adoniram J. Werner, "Memorandum of Statement of the Drayman Who Hauled the Boxes of Arms" (MS, August 21, 1864, in Adoniram J. Werner Papers, William P. Palmer Collection, Western Reserve Historical Society, Cleveland); Indianapolis *Daily Journal*, August 22, 23, 1864; Indianapolis *Daily State Sentinel*, August 22, 23, 1864. The *State Sentinel*, August 22, 1864, stated that Dodd was in New York, but evidence indicates that he and Walker were in Chicago.

49. Indianapolis *Daily Journal*, August 22, 23, 1864; Indianapolis *Daily State Sentinel*, August 22, 23, 1864; Hines, notation on margins of Kirke [Gilmore], "The Chicago Conspiracy," 108–20, in Hines Papers.

50. William H. H. Terrell to Col. Adoniram J. Werner, August 22, 1864, in Werner Papers.

51. Indianapolis *Daily Journal*, August 22, 23, 1864.

traitors and Democrats. He hammered home the message that the seizure of weapons at Dodd's printing plant substantiated his oft-made charge of domestic treason. He bore down heavily upon the Democratic leadership, claiming that Dodd was but the tool of prominent party members bent upon leading Indiana down the low road. "It is all one thing to Jeff Davis," Morton concluded with a show of emotion, "whether we shall fall by means of a defeat at the coming elections or by the overthrow of the Union armies in the field." [52]

Stunned and demoralized, Democrats tried to salvage some honor. Joseph J. Bingham protested his innocence and repudiated efforts to impugn his loyalty to his country and the Constitution. [53] Others also professed their innocence. Morton, having his adversaries at a disadvantage, trumpeted his charges of treason at every opportunity. Republican newspapers repeated the governor's charges and helped seal the fate of the Democracy in Indiana.

Carrington believed that Dodd had run off to St. Paul. Several days after the raid upon Dodd's offices, he reported, "Dodd has disappeared, but intercepted letters show him to be in St. Paul, Minn." Actually, the two culprits in the case stayed on in Chicago, fearing arrest if they returned to Indianapolis. Dodd, elected a delegate to the Democratic National Convention, could claim he was staying on for the sessions slated to begin August 29. Walker wrote from Chicago to Governor Morton, openly claiming ownership of the revolvers that had been seized and brazenly demanding the return of his property. He had purchased the revolvers and ammunition "for the purpose of supplying the orders of friends in Indiana." He had violated no law, he insisted, either in "the purchase or shipment of this property," and he wanted all of it returned! [54]

Several days later Democrats began to gather in Chicago to choose their presidential candidate and write a party platform. Clement L. Vallandigham, still pretending he was the supreme commander of the Sons of Liberty, arrived to promote a peace candidate and write a peace platform. S. Corning Judd, who had headed the Sons of Liberty in Illinois before its demise, came as a delegate. The Indiana delegates, headquartered at the Richmond House, were more concerned with events back home than with the business of the convention. Dodd's presence cast a cloud over their delegation, for some anticipated his arrest when he returned to Indianapolis.

Some pro-McClellan delegates, headed by Samuel S. Cox and Amos Kendall, met on the eve of the convention under the Conservative Union Na-

---

52. *Ibid.*, August 24, 1864.
53. Indianapolis *Daily State Sentinel*, August 23, 27, 1864.
54. Carrington to Col. S. H. Lathrop, telegram, August 23, 1864 in "Telegrams of 1864" (typescript in Carrington Papers); Walker to Oliver P. Morton, August 25, 1864, in General Courts Martial Records; Indianapolis *Daily State Sentinel*, August 30, 1864.

tional Convention umbrella and proclaimed the controversial general as their presidential candidate. Peace Democrats, on the other hand, sponsored a series of antiwar rallies on the eve of the convention as a means to promote their candidate and proposals; Vallandigham and Fernando Wood were featured speakers.

Vallandigham, introduced as "the Honorable Exile and Patriot," proved he had not forgotten how to handle an audience. First he appealed to the pride of the audience as he traced the historic role of the Democratic party. Then he recited the sins of the Lincoln administration. Next he dwelt at length on the need for peace, compromise, and reunion. Finally, he felt the need to discuss the Sons of Liberty, discredited by Carrington's exposé. He defended the organization as an auxiliary of the Democratic party with the honorable purposes of electing Democrats to office, countering the work of the Union League, and protecting rights threatened by Lincoln's "minions." Yes, the Sons of Liberty were engaged in "a conspiracy" as Republican propagandists contended; this "conspiracy" was an open attempt to beat Lincoln's party in the coming elections. The leader of the "conspiracy," Vallandigham said with a twinkle in his eye and a smile on his face, would be known to all when the Democrats nominated him as their party's presidential candidate.[55]

Vallandigham's room in the Sherman House became the informal headquarters for the avowed peace men. The door was never locked, and friends and delegates walked in and out all evening. Such committed antiwar Ohioans as Dr. Edson B. Olds and Alexander Long, both delegates, stopped by. So did H. H. Dodd and S. Corning Judd, once the nominal heads of the Sons of Liberty in their respective states. Even General Samuel P. Heintzelman, at heart a Democrat but present as the commander of the Northern Department, stopped in to visit, smoke cigars, and exchange political banter.[56]

The informal meeting in Vallandigham's smoke-filled room did not end until long past midnight.[57] It proved that Vallandigham, despite being tainted with treason, had a host of friends who respected him and regarded him as the leader of the peace movement. It also proved that the peace men had no strong candidate who could challenge McClellan and that they were quite disorganized and leaderless, for some regarded Vallandigham as the party's pariah.

Late the next morning, on August 29, delegates and well-wishers drifted into the convention hall, soon filled to overflowing. Vallandigham received scattered applause as he strode down the aisle to take his seat with the Ohio

55. Chicago *Times*, August 29, 1864; Dayton *Daily Empire*, August 30, 1864.
56. Samuel P. Heintzelman Diary, August 27, 28, 1864 (MS in Heintzelman Papers); Heintzelman Journal, August 30, 31, September 1, 1864, in Heintzelman Papers. Some historians have described the meeting in Vallandigham's room as a session of the "Supreme Council" of the Sons of Liberty.
57. Clement L. Vallandigham, testimony before the Cincinnati Military Commission, March 29, 1865, published in Cincinnati *Daily Enquirer*, March 30, 1865.

delegation. Dodd sat with the Indiana delegation. The temporary chairman banged his gavel at exactly twelve-thirty. After some preliminaries, Amos Kendall, who had been a Democrat since the days of Andrew Jackson, won recognition from the presiding officer. He asked for permission to report "the recommendations" of the Conservative Union National Convention, which had met the previous evening. The Cox-Kendall stratagem caught the peace men by surprise, and they sat stunned while the gray-haired party patriarch read a resolution recommending the nomination of McClellan as the convention's candidate. Cox, quickly and according to plan, moved that "the report and recommendations" be referred to the newly established Committee on Recommendations.[58]

While Kendall was reading, a handful of peace men huddled to devise counterstrategy. Dr. Edson Olds obtained the floor. As spokesman for the handful, he said that "another body" of delegates, those representing the Sons of Liberty then "in session in Chicago," would also have a candidate to recommend to the convention. If Kendall's report became part of the convention's minutes, so should the recommendation of the Sons of Liberty, even though the "communication" of the "other body" was neither ready nor formalized.[59] Pressed for further information, Dr. Olds, caught bluffing, said he would drop the matter.

In time, the Democratic delegates completed their work. They adopted a party platform that included a resolution calling the war a failure and asking for "a cessation of hostilities, with a view to an ultimate convention of the States." This so-called peace plank was Vallandigham's chief contribution to the proceedings of the Chicago convention.[60] Then, on the first ballot, the delegates named McClellan as the party's presidential candidate. Vallandigham capped his work at the convention with a motion that McClellan's nomination be declared unanimous.

While the Democrats were choosing their presidential candidate, Governor Morton moved to center stage in the developing drama. Already a principal actor, he now took steps to assume the roles of director and playwright as well. In the first place, he acquired the unequivocal support of the Indianapolis *Journal* for his plans to arrest Dodd and others and try them before a military commission by having his brother-in-law buy the paper and become its new editor.[61] In the second place, Morton secured changes of military commanders, removing those who were hesitant to make arrests and use military

58. Dayton *Daily Empire*, August 29, 30, 31, 1864; Chicago *Times*, August 30, 31, 1864. One can draw comparisons between the tactics used by the Cox-Kendall men and the Union League role before and during the convention that nominated Lincoln.

59. Chicago *Times*, August 30, 31, 1864.

60. *Ibid.*, August 30, 1864.

61. Indianapolis *Daily Journal*, August 30, 1864.

commissions to try civilians. Carrington, reluctant to arrest prominent Democrats, was the first to be sloughed aside. At Morton's insistence, the War Department created a new military district encompassing the state of Indiana, with headquarters at Indianapolis, and put General Alvin P. Hovey in charge of it.[62] Soon General Heintzelman too would be sent elsewhere.

After the Chicago convention adjourned, the members of the Indiana delegation returned home. On Saturday, September 3, soon after Dodd returned to his residence, a squad of soldiers arrived to arrest him and escort him to a military prison. John C. Walker, whom Morton also wanted arrested, did not return to Indianapolis from Chicago, heading for Canada instead. Dodd's arrest and the resultant headlines hurt the Democratic cause in Indiana. The party's candidates for state office denied membership in any treasonable organization, but "The exposure of the Sons of Liberty is tearing the ranks of the Democracy all to flinders," one of Morton's jubilant secretaries wrote. "McClellan stock is not quoted at all. McDonald's stock is fast going down."[63]

Morton was most anxious that the trial of Dodd and William M. Harrison begin in September, in time to influence the October elections. General Hovey cooperated with the governor, enjoining a military commission "to meet at the United States Court Rooms in the City of Indianapolis on the nineteenth (19) day of September, 1864, at ten o'clock a.m., or as soon thereafter as practicable, for the trial of Harrison H. Dodd and such other prisoners as may be brought before it." Shortly after he issued the order setting up the military trial, Hovey proved he was allied with the governor in defeating the Democracy. "As for myself," he said in an out-and-out partisan and patriotic public speech, "this peace party never can or shall triumph, at the polls or anywhere else, while I have the power to prevent it."[64]

Hovey had the power to prevent it by convening a military commission in an area where the civil courts were open and by publicizing this as the trial of "conspirators," the Sons of Liberty, and Democratic perfidy. After all, he had little more than his political views to qualify him for his military office. During the political campaign of 1862, he had taken time out to campaign for the Republican slate. He saw events through partisan spectacles, and unlike Heintzelman, he was more than willing to make arrests and use military courts to secure convictions.

Major Henry L. Burnett, judge advocate of the Northern Department,

62. Henry W. Halleck to Heintzelman, telegram, August 22, 1864, copy in Records of the Office of the Judge Advocate General; *OR*, Ser. 1, Vol. XXXIX, Pt. 2, pp. 281, 289.
63. Indianapolis *Daily Journal*, September 5, 1864; Terrell to Wilder, September 6, 1864, in Wilder Papers.
64. Alvin P. Hovey, "Special Orders, No. 129" (MS, copy, September 17, 1864, in General Courts Martial Records); Hovey, quoted in the Indianapolis *Daily Journal*, September 19, 1864.

came to Indianapolis to direct Governor Morton's show. Carrington, who was still in Indianapolis although shorn of his command, had formulated the charges and specifications against Dodd and Harrison, but General Hovey was not satisfied with them.[65] He instructed Burnett to prepare a new set. The major promptly complied and the new charges and specifications were immediately distributed to the press.

The first specification stated that Dodd and others "did conspire against the Government and duly constituted authorities of the United States, joining and organizing a subversive society for the purpose." Another specification stated that Dodd and others had conspired "to seize by force, the United States arsenals [at Indianapolis and Columbus], to release rebel prisoners at Camp Douglas, Camp Morton, Camp Chase, and Johnson's Island, to arm said prisoners, and then march into Kentucky to cooperate with the rebels." The final specification accused Dodd of arousing "hostility to the Government of the United States" through public addresses and of secretly arming subversive society members "for the purpose of resisting the laws of the United States." Mentioning by name the Sons of Liberty and the Order of American Knights, Major Burnett declared that the two organizations had as their main objectives the purposes of overthrowing the government, holding communication with the enemy, conspiring to seize munitions of war stored in arsenals, freeing the rebel prisoners held in northern compounds, and attempting to establish a northwestern confederacy.[66]

Dodd, from behind bars, sought to counter the efforts of Hovey, Morton, and the Republican press to adjudge him guilty of treason even before the trials were scheduled to begin. He turned to the columns of the Indianapolis *State Sentinel* to deny some of the allegations circulating as rumors and newspaper reports. The boxes seized by the posse of soldiers, Dodd stated, were not marked "Sunday school books" as Carrington had alleged. Carrington's contention that he had confiscated a "rebel prisoner list" in the raid on Dodd's office was "a baseless fabrication," he insisted. "No such list was ever in my possession." The "roll of members of the Sons of Liberty" taken at Harrison's house was the list of members of the Marion County Democratic Club, of which Harrison was secretary. The "strange banner" Carrington had captured had nothing to do with the Sons of Liberty; it was a regimental banner captured by a Republican colonel on a Civil War battlefield and entrusted to Dodd for safekeeping. Dodd criticized "political tricksters" interested in political propaganda at the expense of justice. Had not William M. Harrison,

---

65. Carrington, "Indiana War Documents Cleared of Error."
66. Maj. Henry L. Burnett, "Charges and Specifications Preferred Against Harrison H. Dodd" (printed copy, n.d., in Union Provost Marshals' File of One-Name Papers *re* Citizens, Records of the Office of the Judge Advocate General).

still in prison, been offered his "release and freedom" if he would make "revelations" that would show that a conspiracy existed and give substance to Republican propaganda? Nor did Dodd think that the letters, which Carrington had seized in Voorhees' office and his own quarters and which the Indianapolis *Journal* had promptly published as proof of treason, contained any evidence of treason or a conspiracy. Some Democrats shared Dodd's view of the letters. "We can find more treason in speeches in Congress, some by Republicans," wrote the respected editor of the Louisville *Daily Democrat*, "than there is to be found in these productions." [67]

While Dodd, still possessing considerable confidence, secured Martin M. Ray and John W. Gordon as counsel, General Hovey sent a detail to French Lick to arrest William A. Bowles. Over the years the good doctor had been guilty of a series of indiscretions. Early in the war a letter to his brother, in which he had expressed a desire "to go South," had fallen into the hands of the censors. Worse than that, he had given an acquaintance a letter of introduction to a Confederate general with whom he had fought in the Mexican War, and this too had fallen into government hands. He had often and openly expressed sympathy for the South and had repeatedly spoken contemptuously of the Lincoln administration, abolitionists, and Governor Morton. He had boasted about the strength and influence of the Sons of Liberty. By June of 1864 Carrington had expressed the opinion that he could make "a clear case" against Bowles for "enlisting men for the rebel army, secreting rebel officers, and plotting war against the government." [68]

Although Carrington, as usual, was guilty of gross exaggeration, Bowles's hands certainly were not clean. After his arrest, the aged and gray-haired doctor was brought to Indianapolis, lodged in a cell in the Federal Building, and listed as a coconspirator, although he was not arraigned for several weeks.

General Hovey, meanwhile, was eager to get the show on the road. He selected seven Indiana army officers as the military commission that would try Dodd and others, and he set September 22 as the opening day for the proceedings. In a sense, the cards were stacked against Dodd, for several members of the commission were partisan Republicans who believed that all advocates of peace and compromise were traitors. Colonel Benjamin F. Spooner, one of the seven, had publicly expressed his contempt for all Copperheads, Butternuts,

---

67. Dodd, "Card" (letter), September 3, 1864, published in Indianapolis *Daily State Sentinel*, September 5, 1864; *ibid.*, August 22, September 8, 1864; Lousiville *Daily Democrat*, August 26, 1864. Carrington turned over much of the confiscated material to editor Holloway, who published a dozen letters to or from Voorhees in the Indianapolis *Daily Journal*, August 24, 1864.

68. Indianapolis *Daily Journal*, September 5, 1864; William A. Bowles to "Dear Brother," May 31, 1861, Bowles to Gen. Gideon J. Pillow, August 18, 1861, both in Union Provost Marshals' File of One-Name Papers *re* Citizens; Carrington to Capt. Carroll M. Potter, report, June 5, 1864, published in *OR*, Ser. 2, Vol. VII, 340.

and Democrats. Worse than that, Major Burnett, selected to direct the proceedings, had called Democratic leaders "tools of the South," who were "in league with the rebellion, and assisting it by all means in their power."[69]

Through counsel, Dodd denied that a military commission had a right to try him. He was a civilian, subject to the civil courts; the civil courts were open, and Indiana was not under martial law. The commission brushed aside Dodd's objections, directed the trial to proceed, and then recessed for five days to give the prisoner's counsel a chance to develop a defense.

On September 27, the court reconvened. Major Burnett put Felix G. Stidger, who later characterized himself as "the star witness" and "the spy complete," upon the witness stand. Stidger related the details of Dodd's contemplated "insurrection," relying largely upon the secondhand information that the talkative Bowles had given him. He exposed the Sons of Liberty yet could not demonstrate that the order was a conspiracy *per se*, although this was a fundamental assumption of Major Burnett, Governor Morton, and the prosecution. Nor could he offer clear evidence of any overt act, required in the Constitution for a conviction of treason. Nor could Stidger offer any tangible evidence that the Sons of Liberty was more than a paper tiger, a figment of Dodd's imagination.[70]

Other witnesses followed Stidger, but their testimony concerned the Sons of Liberty rather than Dodd's plot. One witness, of questionable credibility, related rumors about a conspiracy to assassinate Governor Morton. A witness who came from neighboring Illinois contributed questionable revelations about the Sons of Liberty in his state. The judge advocate, supervising the parade of witnesses, tried to ask questions and elicit answers that would parlay the hearsay, rumors, and suppositions into acceptable evidence.

Meanwhile, Governor Morton was at last able to push aside General Heintzelman's restraining hand. On September 28, shortly after Dodd's trial had gotten underway, Major General Joseph Hooker arrived to replace Heintzelman in command of the Northern Department. Heintzelman recognized that he had been reassigned because he "did not make enough arrests." Later he was to write, "I have not been radical enough—won't arrest people without orders [from Washington]—would not take the responsibility of doing what Mr.

69. Burnett, quoted in the Indianapolis *Daily Journal*, August 19, September 5, 9, 22, 1864.

70. Stidger, testimony, September 27–30, 1864, in Proceedings of the Military Commission Convened at Indianapolis. Stidger's testimony is also recited in Benn Pitman (ed.), *The Trials for Treason at Indianapolis, Disclosing the Plans for Establishing a North-western Confederacy: Being the Official Record of the Trials Before the Military Commission Convened by Special Orders No. 129, Headquarters, District of Indiana* (Cincinnati, 1865), 19–37. Gilbert R. Tredway, author of a worthy book entitled *Democratic Opposition to the Lincoln Administration in Indiana* (Indianapolis, 1973), is one of the first to compare the manuscript proceedings with the mangled version Pitman produced.

Stanton would not do without Mr. Lincoln's orders. They can't make me a radical. I will do what I think best for the country & not for the party. I have served my country too long to now commence to serve a party." General Hooker was not so scrupulous. He promptly gave General Hovey permission to make more civilian arrests—permission that Heintzelman had refused to give without orders from Washington.[71]

In the days that followed, Hovey arrested seven rather well-known Democrats. On October 5 military details took Joseph Bingham, chariman of the Democratic State Central Committee; David Yeakel of Lafayette; and Dr. James B. Wilson of Salem into custody. Early the next morning, a squad of soldiers called at Lambdin P. Milligan's residence in Huntington, where he was confined to bed, having had an operation on one of his legs the day before. The soldiers placed him on a couch and carried him to a special train, which conveyed him to Indianapolis. Authorities arrested Horace Heffren of Salem the same day. On October 7 they took Andrew Humphreys of Greene County and Stephen Horsey of Martin County into custody. Hovey assigned all of the new prisoners except Milligan to cells in the Federal Building. He placed Milligan, still bedridden, under guard in the temporary soldiers' hospital. After Milligan's condition improved, he too was placed in a cell in the Federal Building and a stool pigeon was assigned as a cell-mate.[72]

While the early October roundup was in process, Dodd convinced his captors that he should be transferred from his cell in the military prison to a second-floor room in the post office, giving his word of honor that he "would not go beyond the limits assigned nor attempt to escape." Mrs. Dodd had brought her husband a pie the evening before, apparently including some twine in the supposed delicacy. Violating his pledge, Dodd crawled out of his window "shortly before four o'clock" and used the twine "to draw up to his window a large rope furnished by some parties outside who assisted in the escape."[73]

Dodd's escape four days before the October 11 election proved a political bonanza for Republicans. The escape and the new arrests gave a semblance of respectability to the rumors and charges of treason. The Indianapolis *Journal* featured bold and incriminating headlines about Dodd's escape and the "nefarious conspiracy." Carrington, still in Indianapolis awaiting a new assignment, prepared a stirring statement for the *Journal*: "The exposure of the

71. Heintzelman to Gov. Andrew G. Curtin, December 9, 1864, in Heintzelman Papers; Heintzelman Journal, September 30, 1864; *OR*, Ser. 1, Vol. XXXIX, Pt. 2, pp. 515–16.

72. John A. Marshall, *American Bastile: A History of the Illegal Arrests and Imprisonment of American Citizens During the Late Civil War* (Philadelphia, 1878), 73–74.

73. Werner to Capt. Andrew C. Kemper, report, October 7, 1864, in Union Provost Marshals' File of One-Name Papers *re* Citizens. The twine-in-the-pie story is family tradition and was passed on to me by H. H. Dodd's grandson.

Sons of Liberty has been made, every word is true. Harrison H. Dodd, Grand Commander of Indiana, has been on trial. Proof was overwhelming. Night before last he escaped. . . . Innocent men do not do so. The act confesses guilt. . . . Citizens, every day shows that you are upon the threshold of revolution. You can rebuke this treason. The traitors intended to bring war to your homes. Meet them at the ballot box while Grant and Sherman meet them in the field." The Republicans made the most of the opportunity Dodd's flight had handed them. They viewed it as proof that a conspiracy existed and proof of Dodd's guilt. The Indianapolis *Journal* found it to be absolute and "conclusive proof of his guilt."[74] A vote for Morton was a vote for patriotism and propriety; a vote for McDonald was a vote for treason, deviousness, and the Confederacy.

Democrats, at a disadvantage, defended themselves weakly and ineptly. Two days before Dodd's escape and his own arrest, Bingham had called "the so-called conspiracy trial" a political act—"a mockery" and "a farce" that was "gotten up for political purposes." After Dodd's escape Bingham was unable to plead his case, for he was behind bars. Someone in the *Sentinel*'s office composed an editorial in Bingham's absence, offering the theory that Dodd's escape had been engineered by the authorities to discredit the Democracy and to justify the arrests made. The purpose, the theorist wrote, was "to get up a show of conspiracy against the Government, to be exposed upon the eve of the election, and afford a fund of political claptrap to assist the Republicans in carrying the State."[75] Democrats evidently refused to face the fact that Dodd had proposed an insurrection and had accepted money from Confederate agents in Canada. To admit such things would be to tar themselves with the same brush. Furthermore, Bingham and other Democratic leaders were guilty of trying to cover up Dodd's rash acts because they feared political repercussions.

Dodd's escape gave Judge Advocate Burnett a chance to recess the trial so that he and several of the members of the military commission could go out into the political hustings. Then, on October 10, the day before the election, Burnett reconvened the commission and asked the seven members to return a verdict. Dodd's lawyer again challenged the jurisdiction of the military court and argued that all the evidence presented against the fugitive was hearsay and supposition. Burnett, showing partiality and partisanship, expressed scorn for the plea of the defense and practically instructed the commissioners to bring in a verdict of guilty. "No argument of the counsel, or finally drawn sophistries," Burnett said with conviction, "can change the perilous and treasonable

74. Indianapolis *Daily Journal*, October 8, 10, 1864; Stidger, *Treason History of the Sons of Liberty*, 152–53.
75. Indianapolis *Daily State Sentinel*, October 3, 10, 1864.

nature of the circumstances. . . . There exists in this State an organization numbering fifty to eighty thousand men, military in character, and about two-thirds armed, ready to be called out to obey the orders of their superiors, regardless of the law and authority of the United States."[76] Burnett, thus, joined Carrington, Sanderson, and Morton in developing the myth that an extensive dark lantern society, subversive in nature and involved in a conspiracy, existed in the upper Midwest.

The military commission found Dodd guilty of every charge and specification and sentenced him to be hanged by the neck until he was dead. Generals Hovey and Hooker quickly approved the verdict and sentence, as did Judge Advocate General Joseph Holt, still serving at a desk in the War Department.[77]

The Republican party swept the election of October 11 in Indiana. Governor Morton, elected for a second four-year term, won vindication. Sherman's capture of Atlanta early in September and Sheridan's successes in the Shenandoah helped. So did war prosperity and the effective work of the Union League. And so did the circumstances surrounding H. H. Dodd. Morton's brother-in-law estimated that the exposé of the Dodd "conspiracy" had added "10,000 votes to the Union party majority." The jubilant governor stated that the election returns "dealt the rebellion a staggering blow."[78]

After celebrating the election results, Judge Advocate Burnett prepared the charges and specifications against the other prisoners. Each of the nine was accused of five counts: "Conspiracy against the government of the United States," "Affording aid and comfort to the rebels against the authority of the United States," "Inciting insurrection," "Disloyal practices," and "Violations of the laws of war."[79] The prisoners were brought before the military commission on October 16 to hear the charges and specifications. Then Judge Advocate Burnett set October 21 as the starting date of the second treason trial.

In the days that followed, the prosecution bargained with some of the prisoners, seeking witnesses and offering absolution. Bingham, whose hands were clean except for the fact that he had not reported Dodd's proposition to the authorities, had no choice but to appear as a witness. He could give damaging evidence against Dodd, a fugitive in Canada. William M. Harrison, as onetime secretary general of the Sons of Liberty in Indiana, also chose to be a witness rather than a defendant; he was in a position to verify some of Stidger's

76. Burnett's plea, October 10, 1864, in Proceedings of the Military Commission Convened at Indianapolis.

77. Joseph Holt to "The Secretary of War for the President," report, December 12, 1864, published in *OR*, Ser. 2, Vol. VII, 1214–17.

78. Indianapolis *Daily Journal*, October 27, 10, 1864.

79. "General Courts Martial Orders, No. 214" (printed copy, n.d., in Records of the Adjutant General's Office).

second- and thirdhand suppositions. Dr. James B. Wilson, present at the session of the Order of the American Cincinnatus when Dodd suggested his "monstrous proposition," also expressed a willingness to tell what he knew in exchange for his freedom; Burnett needed his testimony in order to tie Dodd's secret societies to the purported plot. Dr. David T. Yeakel, eager to discredit the allegations and specifications, was released because Burnett did not want his side of the story presented to the commission.

Felix Stidger, scheduled to open the testimony against the five remaining prisoners, balked and asked for a goodly sum of cash—"a sufficiency to live hereafter"—before returning to the witness stand.[80] Morton and Carrington twisted Stidger's arm, made promises, and eventually acquiesced to the blackmail demands. Meanwhile, Morton, Carrington, and Burnett rounded up a dozen more witnesses. Several were government detectives, a few were out-and-out scoundrels, and others were personal or political enemies of the accused. Governor Morton, now more self-assured, was most anxious for the trial to get under way and grind grist for the November election.[81]

Hovey added five more members to the military commission for the second trial, raising the number to twelve. The political prisoners, meanwhile, arranged for counsel and weighed the merit of a report that several members of the commission had expressed the view that the accused ought to be hanged.[82]

While Hovey and Morton were setting the stage for the second act, Clement L. Vallandigham quit sulking in his tent, and returned to the political wars to campaign for McClellan. He pretended that the Sons of Liberty still existed, and could be a dynamic force in the election. On October 21, in a speech in Monmouth, Illinois, Vallandigham felt compelled to contradict assertions made in Judge Advocate General Holt's report on secret societies. The aims of the Sons of Liberty were honorable, he said, not treasonable. It was "a militant Democratic group" within "the great national [Democratic] party." He compared it to its namesake of pre-Revolutionary War days. Its purpose, he repeated again, was to promote Jeffersonian principles, protect the rights of individual Democrats, and counteract the work of the Union Leagues.[83]

80. Indianapolis *People*, March 10, 1883 (clipping in Indiana Scrapbook Collection, compiled by George S. Cottman, in Indiana Historical Society Library, Indianapolis), III, 33–34.

81. Kenneth M. Stampp recognizes that the trials were more political than judicial and says the affair resembled *opera bouffe* far more than a trial for treason. See Stampp, *Indiana Politics During the Civil War* (Indianapolis, 1949), 246–54, and "The Milligan Case and the Election of 1864 in Indiana," *Mississippi Valley Historical Review*, XXXI (1944), 41–58. Also see Winfred A. Harbison, "Indiana Republicans and the Re-election of Lincoln," *Indiana Magazine of History*, XXXIV (1935), 267–76, and William F. Zornow, "Treason as a Campaign Issue in the Re-election of Lincoln," *Abraham Lincoln Quarterly*, V (1949), 348–63.

82. Indianapolis *Daily Journal*, November 1, 1864.

83. Chicago *Times*, October 22, 1864; Heintzelman Journal, November 4, 1864.

On his way to Peoria, Vallandigham stopped over in Chicago. While there, he wrote a letter to the editor of the New York *Daily News* to debunk Holt's report and some of the complementary allegations that had appeared in Horace Greeley's New York *Tribune*. Then, at Peoria he repeated some of the statements about the Sons of Liberty that he had made at Monmouth. This auxiliary of the Democratic party, Vallandigham said, was organized to stymie the threat to free elections posed by armed Union Leaguers. Yes, the order was real and extensive, organized to preserve civil rights, preach traditional Democratic doctrine, and elect Democrats to office.[84]

While Vallandigham was on the campaign trail, the military commission convened again on October 21. Attorneys for the five political prisoners again challenged the jurisdiction of the military court over civilians in an area where the civil courts were open, citing both English and American precedent. One of William A. Bowles's attorneys made a point of arguing that belonging to the Sons of Liberty did not constitute participation in a conspiracy. Milligan's lawyer argued that the trial possessed political overtones, being designed, in the main, to influence the election returns. He even felt obligated to defend Milligan's anti–New England views and states' rights principles.

Major Burnett, acting as both judge and prosecutor, brushed aside the arguments of the defense attorneys. He spoke of the "overpowering necessity of military interference" to combat subversion and nullify a conspiracy. He borrowed heavily from Judge Humphrey H. Leavitt's justification of the summary treatment accorded Vallandigham in Cincinnati seventeen months earlier.

After brushing aside the arguments of the defense attorneys, Burnett brought out his first witness, Felix G. Stidger. The onetime detective gave voluminous testimony, some of it based upon what Bowles had told him and some drawn from Carrington's exposé of the Sons of Liberty and Holt's report on secret societies. Some of Stidger's allegations were outright falsehoods. He stated, for example, that the Sons of Liberty had regular communication with Richmond as well as with Confederate military forces operating in Kentucky and Tennessee. Stidger's testimony that Confederate authorities had agreed to pay secret society members 10 percent of the value of any Federal property that they destroyed was lifted directly from Holt's famous report.

Defense attorneys cross-examined Stidger, revealing some contradictions in his testimony. He admitted that he had urged men to incriminate themselves. He admitted that he had tried to entrap some Democrats by offering to murder a detective whom they suspected of double-crossing them. Whenever

---

84. Vallandigham to "Editor," October 22, 1864, published in New York *Daily News*, December 29, 1864; Dayton *Daily Empire*, November 7, 1864.

the cross-examination tended to destroy Stidger's credibility, however, Judge Advocate Burnett intervened to prevent the defense attorneys from discrediting the testimony.[85]

Both William M. Harrison and Joseph J. Bingham testified extensively, and their testimony seems the most credible of the lot. Some of their statements, very critical of Dodd's actions and judgment, were more favorable to the defendants than the prosecution. Since much of Stidger's testimony and many of his assumptions were secondhand, Harrison contradicted it frequently, especially regarding the presence of Milligan and Humphreys at meetings of the "state council" and the meaning of the title "major general."

During the second week of the trial the prosecution decided to drop the charges against Horace Heffren and use him as a witness too. Hovey and Burnett evidently concluded that changing Heffren's status from prisoner to witness might bolster their weak case against the remaining four, especially if they could develop the supposition that he had turned state's evidence. The editor of the Indianapolis *Journal* cooperated by reporting that Heffren had decided to escape the noose by "peaching on his comrades and accomplices." Heffren, at a later date, tried to refute the myth, claiming it "another first class falsehood."[86]

Democrats, of course, made an attempt to discredit the summary proceedings. "Why introduce witnesses in prosecution only," Dr. Yeakel asked, "and no rebuttal witnesses?" And Democrats invariably denied that a military commission had the right to try civilians in an area where the civil courts were open. "It is a precedent," one Democratic editor stated, "which, if unresisted, places every man in this country, innocent or guilty, at the mercy of the creatures of the President." Others referred to the proceedings as "a farce," intended to provide political propaganda and affect the election returns. "These trials," Dr. Yeakel wrote, "are a mockery and a sham, for base political purposes, so conducted as to conceal their base objects and ignomy, and to prejudice the light of all parties against the Democratic party and the Order." He meant the Order of the American Cincinnatus rather than the Sons of Liberty. Dr. Yeakel wanted to testify in the proceedings to discredit Stidger's testimony; denied the opportunity, he had a flyer printed and circulated.[87]

85. Stidger, testimony, October 24–25, 1864, in Proceedings of the Military Commission Convened at Indianapolis. Tredway, *Democratic Opposition to the Lincoln Administration in Indiana*, is most critical of Burnett's direction of the military proceedings. Burnett was interested in securing convictions, not justice.

86. Horace Heffren, quoted in Indianapolis *People*, March 10, 1883 (clipping, in Indiana Scrapbook Collection), III, 33–34.

87. Yeakel, *To the People of Indiana*; Henry N. Walker, in Detroit *Free Press*, January 1, 1865.

Dr. Yeakel, who had been as close to Dodd as anyone, regarded most of Stidger's testimony as a maze of conjecture and contradictions. Some of the witnesses, Yeakel pointed out, did not know the difference between the Knights of the Golden Circle, the Order of American Knights, and the Sons of Liberty, for they used the terms interchangeably. Even Stidger knew nothing about the Order of American Cincinnatus, created informally by a handful upon the ashes of the Sons of Liberty, which disintegrated and died after Carrington's well-publicized and effective exposé of June 28, 1864. Yeakel also noted that Governor Morton and Judge Advocate Burnett had utilized the principle of guilt by association, linking Dodd to the Sons of Liberty and that dark lantern society to the Democratic party. Small wonder, then, that Dr. Yeakel regarded the military proceedings as a means to "perpetuate a falsehood," stigmatize the Democracy, and develop treason as the central campaign issue.[88]

Joseph J. Bingham, after testifying before the commission, returned to his desk in the *Sentinel* Building to write restrained editorials; he did not want to be behind bars again. Bingham supposed that Governor Morton "was coldly calculating how much party and personal capital he could make out of the errors of a few reckless men." Government authorities, with a swarm of detectives in the field, knew more about "the supposed conspiracy," Bingham wrote, than any of the four men still being tried. "The whole affair," Bingham concluded, "was confined to a very few men, and they had no right to speak or act for anyone but themselves."[89]

While Democrats made their rather feeble efforts to discredit the treason trial, Governor Morton's and Lincoln's supporters ground out sheaves of campaign propaganda for the November 8 presidential election. Governor Morton's brother-in-law, as editor of the Indianapolis *Journal*, provided an example for others. Several days before the election he brought out an extra, which selected testimony from the trial and developed the thesis that Democrats and the Sons of Liberty had planned a gigantic and infamous conspiracy. He laid the base for the legends that Heffren had turned state's evidence and that Bingham's testimony was "a confession." The extra reached reading rooms maintained by the Union League, and it was quoted by scores of Republican newspapers all over Indiana. Even Carrington, still grieving for a child who had died, made a worthy contribution to the propaganda campaign. He composed an article entitled *The Great Northern Conspiracy of the 'S.O.L.': Resistance to Tyrants Is Obedience to God*. It was published and circulated as a pamphlet on the eve of the election.[90]

88. Yeakel, *To the People of Indiana*.
89. Indianapolis *Daily State Sentinel*, October 31, November 8, 1864.
90. Indianapolis *Daily Journal*, extra, November 1, 1864; [Henry B. Carrington], *The Great*

The propaganda campaign paid dividends. Indiana voters contributed nobly to Lincoln's reelection victory, giving him a 150,238 to 130,233 majority over McClellan. Lincoln received 53.59 percent of the votes cast, almost identical to Morton's percentage of 53.68 in the October 11 election. The division of partisans into patriots and traitors helped immeasurably. One of Governor Morton's supporters, a millionaire banker, predicted that posterity would treat all who had voted for McClellan ignobly. "To tell the grandson or child that his father voted for a candidate for president who was running upon the issue that the war was a failure & we should make peace with the enemy," Calvin Fletcher wrote in his diary, "will be a disgrace to such a descendant." [91]

After celebrating Lincoln's reelection and the repudiation of the Democrats, General Hovey and Judge Advocate Burnett returned to the task of finding the four political prisoners guilty of the charges registered against them. Several of the lesser witnesses stained their own reputations while testifying against the defendants. One admitted that he had offered to testify against Stephen Horsey as a means to evade military service. Another, who came in as a witness and walked out a liar, had his story of Andrew Humphreys' involvement in an incident turned upside down, for the Greene County Democrat had prevented a riot rather than started one. Henry L. Zumro, the chief witness against Lambdin P. Milligan, also walked off the witness stand with dirty hands. As one of Carrington's detectives, he had repeatedly tried to compromise the outspoken and churlish Huntington Democrat. Zumro had arranged to have himself arrested for preaching pro-Confederate sentiments; he used "the most vile and harsh epithets against the government and Mr. Lincoln" to try to get Milligan to make some unfavorable remarks. He tried to hire Milligan as counsel as a means of entrapping him and putting him in a bad light. Milligan, wary and suspicious, avoided the various traps Zumro tried to set to justify the hundred-dollar-per-month salary Carrington had promised him. When Zumro testified, he had little more than some suppositions and third-hand accounts of Milligan's "disloyalty" to present as evidence. [92]

Democrats were not far off the mark when they characterized the second phase of the Indianapolis treason trials as "a farce." None of the four defen-

---

Northern Conspiracy of the S.O.L.: Resistance to Tyrants Is Obedience to God (n.p., n.d.). It evidently came off the same presses as the Indianapolis *Daily Journal*. The Cincinnati *Daily Commercial* and the Cincinnati *Daily Gazette* exemplify out-of-state newspapers that copied extensively from the *Journal*.

91. Calvin Fletcher Diary, November 9, 1864 (MS, in Calvin Fletcher Papers, Indiana Historical Society Library).

92. Stephen Tenney, testimony, November 18, 1864, Elisha Cogwill, testimony, November 22, 1864, Henry L. Zumro, testimony, November 15, 1864, all in Proceedings of the Military Commission Convened at Indianapolis; Lambdin P. Milligan, testimony in *Milligan* v. *Slack et al.* (1871), reported in Indianapolis *Daily Journal*, May 22, 1871.

dants was allowed to take the stand to deny the witnesses' contentions or relate his own accounts or views. The twelve commissioners held the view that Copperheads (antiadministration Democrats) were traitors; all equated criticism of the Lincoln administration with giving aid and comfort to the enemy. Morton wanted Milligan's blood and expected a favorable verdict. In fact, he had publicly declared the prisoners guilty of treason even before the trial had begun. Judge Advocate Burnett wanted a colonelcy. Serving in the dual role of judge and prosecutor, he violated the principles of justice time and time again. He protected prosecution witnesses from the probing of defense counsel, and he browbeat witnesses trying to discredit the testimony of government detectives. He allowed much hearsay and questionable evidence in order to build the case against the accused, even admitting thirdhand reports and rumors. Burnett functioned more like a biased partisan and one who had made up his mind even before the trial got under way than like a judge in charge of the scales of justice.[93]

The trials ended on December 1, ten weeks after an auspicious beginning. The commissioners, after hearing the concluding arguments of both the prosecution and defense, agreed to meet on December 10 to announce the verdicts and pass sentence. On that day they found each of the four prisoners guilty of every charge. "The testimony . . . was so convincing," Rueben Williams, one of the commissioners, recalled at a later date, "that there was not a dissenting vote on the first ballot." He should have added that not one of the twelve was a Democrat. The commissioners sentenced Milligan, Bowles, and Horsey to be "hanged by the neck until . . . dead, at such time and place as the commanding officer [Hovey] of the district shall designate." Since the case against Humphreys was especially weak, he received a lesser sentence—confinement at hard labor for the duration of the war. Rueben Williams attributed the lighter sentence to the fact that Humphreys had intervened to prevent draft resistance in June of 1863 in Sullivan County, advising an assemblage of four hundred angry men to go home and depend upon the courts for justice.[94]

Three weeks later, General Hovey modified Humphreys' sentence, allowing him to go home but confining him to two townships of Greene County and adding the condition that he "take no part, directly or indirectly, against the prosecution of the present war." Hovey's superior, General Hooker, challenged the commutation of Humphreys' sentence, questioning the propriety of changing a sentence once approved. President Lincoln sided with Hovey in

93. Tredway, "Indiana Against the Administration," concludes that Judge Advocate Burnett conducted the trials "in a manner which left little doubt as to either their outcome or his purposes."
94. Rueben Williams, quoted in the Indianapolis *Daily Journal*, January 8, 1900; Alvin P. Hovey, "General Orders, No. 27," May 9, 1865, published in *OR*, Ser. 2, Vol. VIII, 543–49.

the controversy, and Humphreys, in the days that followed, spent his time on his farm, counting his blessings.[95]

Although General Hooker promptly approved the execution of Milligan, Bowles, and Horsey, Governor Morton seemed to have a change of heart. He had used the arrests and trial as a stratagem to ensure his reelection, but he did not want their blood upon his hands. Political expediency called for clemency. "From the political point of view," an advisor wrote to the governor, "it can do our party no good to shed more blood; but on the contrary, if we are merciful, the child is not yet born who will see the defeat of the Republican party."[96]

Since Hooker had turned his back upon clemency, the defense appealed its case to President Lincoln, busy with winding down the war. Judge Advocate General Holt, in charge of the Bureau of Military Justice, reviewed the proceedings of the Indianapolis-based military trial. He summarized the case for the secretary of war and the president, adding his own observations and recommendations. Since Holt believed the verdict and sentences right and proper, he added his conclusion that "any other decision than that to which they arrived would be a violation of their oaths." He wrote with eloquent flourish, "The coolness and audacity with which they plotted their treason, and the heartless indifference with which they meditated acts which would have drenched the Northern homes with the cries of widows and orphans seem to demand their punishment as an atonement for the sufferings of patriots, whose struggles in the field for the liberties of their country, they would have rendered fruitless." Before President Lincoln had a chance to rule on the sentences of the condemned men, an assassin's bullet put a new occupant in the White House. Governor Morton, campaigning for clemency, claimed that Lincoln, before his death, had privately assured counsel for the three remaining prisoners that he would free them as soon as the war was over.[97]

Milligan, Bowles and Horsey spent the remaining days of the war in cells in the Federal Building in Indianapolis, hoping for favorable news from Washington. The wives of the accused had visitation rights and they occasionally brought delicacies and good cheer. Those charged with the safekeeping of the

95. Hovey, "General Orders, No. 1," January 2, 1865, published in *OR*, Ser. 2. Vol. VIII, 11; Abraham Lincoln to Joseph Hooker, telegram, January 11, 1865, copy in Robert Todd Lincoln Papers.

96. Silas F. Miller to Morton, May 15, 1865, in Miscellaneous Letter File, Indiana Historical Society Library.

97. Holt, "To the President," February 15, 1865, in General Courts Martial Records; Morton, statement in a speech made in Richmond, Indiana, September 29, 1869, quoted in William Dudley Foulke, *Life of Oliver P. Morton, Including His Important Speeches* (2 vols., Indianapolis, 1899), I, 430–31. Milligan, on the other hand, contended that such an "understanding" existed from the very beginning between Morton, Lincoln, and the commissioners. See an article, based upon an interview with Milligan, in the Huntington *Herald*, December 15, 1899.

prisoners regarded Mrs. Bowles as "a dangerous woman." When she visited her aging husband on December 17 she had spoken "contemptuously" and in "an insulting manner" to the guards. Two days later, when she came for another visit, she brought a package which the guards confiscated. It contained $1250 in greenbacks.[98]

Felix G. Stidger, the star witness in the Indianapolis proceedings, was also interested in greenbacks. On December 13, just a few days after the four defendants had been sentenced, Carrington begged Secretary of War Stanton to pay Stidger the sum of six hundred dollars for six months' work (May 5 to December 5) at one hundred dollars per month. Carrington wrote that the amount asked for Stidger's services was fully justified by "the value of his work, and the risk incurred."[99] The sum was but a pittance compared to the fortune Morton and Carrington had invested in detective work to expose conspiracies. On March 23, 1863, Morton had assigned forty thousand dollars from his funds to secret service work, and on September 7, 1864, he added ten thousand dollars more. Four days later Secretary of War Stanton advanced five thousand dollars from a special fund, and on January 29, 1865, the federal government refunded Morton twenty-five thousand dollars.

While Stidger waited for his pay and the condemned men awaited favorable word from Washington, Henry B. Carrington left Indianapolis for a new assignment—field service with his old regiment, then with the Army of the Cumberland. He left Indiana believing he had played an important role in discovering and exposing a plot to establish a northwestern confederacy. "I feel that the state of Indiana," he wrote to one of his former superiors, "was saved by the discoveries."[100]

98. O. Hewitt to Werner, report, December 20, 1864, in Union Provost Marshals' File of One-Name Papers *re* Citizens.

99. Carrington, quoted in George Fort Milton, *Abraham Lincoln and the Fifth Column* (New York, 1942), 318.

100. Carrington to Heintzelman, November 11, 1864, in Heintzelman Papers.

CHAPTER VII

The Camp Douglas Conspiracy and the Cincinnati Treason Trial

THE STORY of the Camp Douglas conspiracy and the Cincinnati-based treason trial developed as a sequel to the Indianapolis-based drama. Although all of the principal characters were new, the script possessed many similarities. In each case, the script writers were more interested in political propaganda than in simple justice, perhaps deceiving themselves while they deceived others.

The so-called Camp Douglas conspiracy had the same historical setting as its Indianapolis counterpart. Its background included aspects of western sectionalism and the idea of a separate confederacy, Democratic disaffection and the fear that the Lincoln administration might seize the polls, vague rumors about Confederate agents and operations in Canada, and the approach of the 1864 state and presidential elections.

Some Illinois residents, usually Democrats, were as adept at uttering sectional sentiments as their Indiana and Ohio brethren. One Chicago editor thought of the agrarian West and industrial-minded Northeast as "two distinct and warring sections." He did not want "the great Northwest" to become "a vassal to New England" and predicted that the sections would be "cut in twain on the line of Pennsylvania and Ohio." Orlando B. Ficklin, a Democrat from Coles County who had served in the state legislature with Lincoln, repeatedly expressed his distrust of the Yankee Northeast both before and after Fort Sumter. He was thankful, he once said, "that God [had] made the world before He had made the Yankees, for they would have interfered with His business and destroyed the beautiful world in which we live." [1]

After the coming of the war and the closing of the trade down the Mississippi, some sectionalist-minded Democrats blamed the Republicans for their economic woes. An Illinois Democratic editor told the farmers who were his readers that they were the victims of national policy. In an article entitled "Western Farmers,

1. Chicago *Times*, December 10, 1860; Orlando B. Ficklin, quoted in (Springfield) *Illinois State Journal*, January 9, 1863.

187

What Are Your Interests[?]," he asked, "Will the fighting farmers of the Upper Mississippi ever find that it is the Lincoln Blood-and-murder party who has killed their 'goose with the golden eggs'?"[2]

The repudiation of Lincoln and the Republican party, expressed through the election returns of 1862 in Illinois, emboldened Democratic critics and intensified western sectionalism. General John A. McClernand, assigned by President Lincoln to tour Illinois and report on public opinion, wrote that much of the Democratic disaffection had economic and sectional roots. The Illinois "Copperhead Legislature" of 1863 expressed prowestern sentiments, even sowing the seeds of grangerism while practicing disgraceful partisan politics and plumping for peace.[3]

Democratic critics of President Lincoln frequently overstepped the bounds of propriety. Some residents of southern Illinois expressed sympathy for the southern cause; occasionally a resident might leave to join the Confederate army. A Jefferson County farmer supposedly told a federal marshal that if Confederate raider John H. Morgan came to Illinois, some residents would feed his horses and not charge him a cent. Such Copperhead rhetoric, which sometimes seemed to border on treason, misled Confederates. Major General Pierre G. T. Beauregard, for example, thought that a Confederate military expedition into Ohio would pave the way for a popular uprising. Insurgents of the upper Midwest, Beauregard believed, might establish a northwestern confederacy and perhaps sign "a treaty of alliance, defensive and offensive," with the Confederacy.[4]

Governor Richard Yates criticized Democrats who hid their partisanship behind anti-Yankee rhetoric. "Palsied be the hand," Yates once wrote, "that would sever the ties that bind the East and the West." Jittery, he imagined he was sitting on the edge of a volcano in which disaffection was the boiling lava. He apparently believed that the threat of revolution was real. He expressed the fear that the Democratic state convention of June 17, 1863, might "inau-

2. Carlyle (Ill.) *Constitution and Union*, October 3, 1863.

3. John A. McClernand to Abraham Lincoln, November 10, 1862, published in *The War of the Rebellion: A Compilation of the Official Records of the Union and Confederate Armies* (128 vols.; Washington, D.C., 1880–1901), Ser. 1, Vol. XVII, Pt. 2, pp. 332–33, hereinafter cited as *OR*. The theme that the elections of 1862 repudiated the Lincoln administration is developed in such articles as Harry E. Pratt, "The Repudiation of Lincoln's War Policy in 1862—Stuart-Swett Congressional Campaign," *Journal of the Illinois State Historical Society*, XXIV (1931), 129–40, and Winfred A. Harbison, "The Election of 1862 as a Vote of Want of Confidence in President Lincoln," *Michigan Academy of Sciences, Arts, and Letters Papers* (1930), 499–513.

4. David I. Board, statement, n.d., forwarded with David Phillips to Edwin M. Stanton, August 11, 1862, in Lafayette C. Baker–Levi C. Turner Papers, Records of the Adjutant General's Office, Records of the Office of the Judge Advocate General, National Archives; Pierre G. T. Beauregard to Charles J. Villere, May 26, 1863, published in *OR*, Ser. 1, Vol. XIV, 955.

gurate direct opposition to the Government"—perhaps leading to an effort to establish a separate confederacy.[5]

Rumors about disaffection were mixed with reports about the nefarious plots of the Knights of the Golden Circle. Brigadier General Henry B. Carrington's exposé of the Sons of Liberty and Colonel John P. Sanderson's revelations about the Order of American Knights seemed to give substance to the rumors that Democratic dissidents were planning to effect a revolution which would lead to the establishment of the northwestern confederacy.

There were also widespread rumors about rebel activity in Canada and about schemes hatched in Windsor or Toronto. Some of the rumors centered around plots to free rebel prisoners held in Camp Chase near Columbus, Ohio, and Camp Douglas on the outskirts of Chicago. The rumors gained some credence on September 19, 1864, when a handful of Confederate refugees in Canada, led by John Yates Beall, boarded and seized the *Philo Parsons* to try their hand at piracy. After the ship had left Detroit and was well out in Lake Erie, these ex-Confederate ragtags took over the ship. After robbing the crewmen, they put all in the hold except the engineer and headed for Bass Island, about twenty-five miles northwest of Sandusky. While loading on wood at Bass Island, the *Island Queen*, a smaller ship, also docked for fuel. The amateur pirates seized the *Island Queen* as well, robbing the crew and plundering the ship. After unloading their prisoners, mostly crew members of the two ships, the gritty would-be pirates raised anchor and sailed off aboard the *Philo Parsons*, with the *Island Queen* in tow. Finding that the *Island Queen* slowed their efforts to get back to Canada, the adventurers scuttled and sank the small craft. After arriving at the mouth of the Detroit River, near Canada, they cut the feeder pipes, set the *Philo Parsons* adrift, and scrambled for land and safety.[6]

United States officials tried to implicate Jacob Thompson, then on a mission in Canada, in the *Philo Parsons* affair. Some newspaper editors also assumed that the capture of the *Philo Parsons* fitted into a rebel conspiracy "to release the prisoners on Johnson's Island." The story improved with each retelling into a "gigantic conspiracy" not only to free the three thousand rebel prisoners on Johnson's Island but to raid and burn American cities along the Great Lakes and seriously cripple the Union war effort.[7]

5. Richard Yates, quoted in Chicago *Daily Tribune*, January 7, 1863; Richard Yates to Edwin M. Stanton, June 15, 1863, published in *OR*, Ser. 3, Vol. XXVII, 140.

6. Detroit *Free Press*, extra, September 20, 1864.

7. Samuel P. Heintzelman Journal, September 20, 23, 24, 1864 (MS in Samuel P. Heintzelman Papers, Library of Congress); Detroit *Free Press*, September 20, 1864. Andrew W. Renfrew, "Copperheads, Confederates, and Conspiracies on the Detroit-Canadian Border" (M.A. thesis, Wayne State University, 1952), gives credence to the rumors.

Confederates in Canada attracted even more attention through a widely publicized raid and bank robbery in the Vermont border town of St. Albans. On October 19, 1864, Bennett H. Young led a raid of nonuniformed Confederates across the Canadian border, looted three St. Albans banks of more than $200,000, killed one citizen of the town, and left Vermont and New Hampshire residents jittery for months.

The rumors resulting from the St. Albans raid and the *Philo Parsons* affair caused some to suppose that the Confederate prisoners being held in Camp Douglas or Chicago itself might become targets of Canadian-based conspiracies. U.S. agents in Canada passed on every rumor that came their way, irrespective of its credibility. Former Confederates in Canada tried to sell information, real or imagined, to U.S. authorities and increased the number of rumors in circulation. Secretary of State William H. Seward helped to transform some of the rumors into newspaper headlines. "This Department," he telegraphed the mayor of Detroit, "has information from the British Provinces to the effect that there is a conspiracy on foot to set fire to the principal cities in the Northern States on the day of the Presidential election."[8]

Illinois provided one of the more dramatic conspiracy stories on the eve of the 1864 presidential election. Six different individuals, some almost strangers to Chicago, became the central figures in the bizarre story.

William A. "Deacon" Bross was credited with being most "instrumental in discovering the Confederate conspiracy at Camp Douglas."[9] Bross was president of the Chicago *Tribune* Company, as well as the Republican newspaper's commercial and financial editor. His newspaper was the first in the country to propose Abraham Lincoln for president. Bross became a bigwig in Republican circles, and as the years passed, became more and more partisan and less and less tolerant of the Democracy. He described Democrats, gathering for their party's 1864 national convention in Chicago, as "blear-eyed, bottle-nosed, whiskey-blotched vagabonds—the very excrescence and sweepings of the slums and sinks of all the cities of the nation" and as "a horde of cutthroats, and bloated, beastly wretches, spoiling for free whiskey and a free fight." Revealingly, he added, "I sat often at my window on Michigan Avenue, and saw the filthy stream of degraded humanity swagger along to the wigwam [meeting place of the Democratic convention] on the lake shore and wondered how the city could be saved from burning and plunder, and our wives and daughters from a more dreadful fate."[10]

8. William H. Seward to "Mayor of Detroit," November 2, 1864, published in Detroit *Free Press*, November 4, 1864.

9. [Appleton's] *National Cyclopedia of American Biography* (54 vols.; New York, 1933), XXIII, 374–75.

10. William A. Bross, *Biographical Sketch of the Late General B. J. Sweet [and] History of*

In time, Bross dreamed up a way to save "the wives and daughters" and to get Governor Yates and President Lincoln reelected as well. The means was a well-tested formula: improvise a conspiracy and then expose it.

After the war Deacon Bross told a number of different and conflicting tales of how he first learned of "the plot" to free Confederate prisoners being held at Camp Douglas, burn Chicago, and expand the insurrection over the Midwest. At first he claimed that he had inadvertently overheard a couple of conspirators discussing their scheme on a streetcar. Later, he claimed that he was standing on a street corner in front of the Tremont House when an acquaintance who was passing by stopped to say that conspirators had "ten thousand stands of arms secreted in cellars and basements" in the vicinity.[11]

Bross, as chief deviser of the conspiracy, brought the names of two other men into the plot, and each became a principal in the Camp Douglas story. Colonel Benjamin J. Sweet was an army officer and the commandant of Camp Douglas, where more than eight thousand Confederate prisoners were being held in confinement.[12] Colonel Sweet had been a controversial figure long before he came to Chicago in May, 1864, to supervise the prison camp. He brought a blemished military record with him, partly because his ambition overruled his judgment and exceeded his abilities. While serving as second in command of the Sixth Wisconsin, Sweet tried to discredit his superior so he could take over the regiment. He "apparently stated openly to his fellow officers that one of Colonel [Lysander] Cutler's written orders contained a falsehood."[13] The commander countered by accusing Sweet of insubordination and filed written charges against his ambitious, politically minded subordinate. The brigade commander avoided the trial by persuading Sweet to return to Wisconsin and raise his own regiment, the Twenty-first Wisconsin. Colonel Sweet and his regiment were then assigned to the western sector and the army of Major General Don Carlos Buell.

The army blundered into a battle near Perryville, Kentucky, on October 8, 1862. Sweet's regiment, ineptly trained and led, "behaved badly." When the untried soldiers found themselves in a cornfield in advance of the Union line under crossfire, they "left quickly for a safer spot" in the rear of the Union line. The regiment suffered 179 casualties, including 42 killed. Colo-

---

Camp Douglas: A Paper Read Before the Chicago Historical Society, June 18, 1878 (Chicago, 1878), 18.

11. Tracy E. Strevey, "Joseph Medill and the Chicago *Tribune* During the Civil War Period" (Ph.D. dissertation, University of Chicago, 1930), 188–89; Bross, *Biographical Sketch of B. J. Sweet*, 17.

12. E. B. Tuttle, *The History of Camp Douglas: Including Official Report of Gen. B. J. Sweet; and Anecdotes of the Rebel Prisoners* (Chicago, 1865), 2, 7, 27.

13. Alan T. Nolan, *The Iron Brigade* (New York, 1961), 52.

nel Sweet's elbow and chest wounds, greatly exaggerated by friends, served as an excuse to stifle an investigation of his errors of judgment on the battlefield. Authorities wisely gave Sweet a behind-the-lines assignment, relegating him to the Veterans' Reserve Corps and putting him in charge of Camp Douglas. There he could seek the publicity and glory that had escaped him on the battlefield.[14]

Sweet spent considerable time mending his political fences in Wisconsin and making new Republican friends in Chicago, including Deacon Bross and Joseph Medill of the Chicago *Tribune*. Like Bross and Medill, Sweet believed that Copperheads were traitors and that Governor Yates and President Lincoln *must* be reelected.

It time, after Bross had convinced himself that there was a Copperhead-sponsored conspiracy afoot, he called upon Colonel Sweet at Camp Douglas, related his "suspicions and facts," and encouraged the surveillance of "every leading rebel that arrived from the South or from Canada." Some fourteen years later Bross wrote, "I saw Gen. [then a colonel] Sweet frequently, and I found that his detectives tracked like sleuth-hounds every scent and rumor to its source."[15] Brought into the central cast of characters by Bross, Sweet became the chief architect of the conspiracy. Bross provided the idea; Sweet devised the conspiracy. Then the two exposed it.

Deacon Bross also brought Isaiah Winslow Ayer into the act. Ayer was a strange character, with a shady reputation and a shadowy past. He claimed to be a graduate of Howard University and to have diplomas from two respected medical schools. Later evidence proved him to be an imposter, liar, and charlatan, whose diplomas had been forged. Acquaintances questioned Ayer's moral standards, for he kept a concubine in his quarters, consisting of an office and a bedroom in the McCormick Building, and introduced her as his sister.[16] He was evidently a fellow without moral scruples, willing to serve anyone in any way for money.

Having trouble eking out a living as a patent-medicine vendor and would-be doctor, Ayer turned toward more devious channels. He claimed to have found "a key which would disclose to the Government what appeared to be . . . a fearful conspiracy which threatened the most disastrous results for the

14. Sweet's brief service receives cursory treatment in William D. Love, *Wisconsin in the War of Rebellion* (Chicago, 1866), 611–12, and Edwin B. Quiner, *The Military History of Wisconsin* (Chicago, 1866), 323–25.

15. Bross, *Biographical Sketch of B. J. Sweet*, 17–18.

16. John M. Scudder [dean of the Eclectic Medical Institute of Cincinnati] to Robert Hervey, April 1, 1865, in General Courts Martial Records, Records of the Office of the Judge Advocate General; I. Winslow Ayer, Charles Patten, Charles C. Copeland, testimony before the military commission convened at Cincinnati, February 8–10, April 7, March 22, 1865, all in *House Executive Documents*, 39th Cong., 2nd Sess., 196–230, 359–60, 472–76.

country." He offered his services to the government at a hundred dollars per month but later admitted that he had expected to earn five thousand dollars for his sleuthing.[17]

In mid-July the would-be sleuth hunted up Isaac N. Arnold, a congressman from Chicago, and tried to interest him in "a most fearful conspiracy." Ayer said that he could expose the traitorous plot if he were paid handsomely for his efforts. Congressman Arnold doubted that such a conspiracy existed. Furthermore, he distrusted the glib and shifty-eyed visitor. Ayer next turned to prominent men in the office of the Chicago *Tribune* with his proposition. There he gained the sponsorship of Deacon Bross, who instructed the pretender to see Governor Yates and promised his endorsement.

Armed with Bross's letter of recommendation—as well as several forged ones, including one purportedly written by congressman Arnold—Ayer met with Yates and assured him that he could expose "a gigantic scheme of treason to aid Southern Rebels, to create a further secession and to establish a Northwestern Confederacy, and to carry the election by arms." Governor Yates, concerned about his own reelection, wrote to Brigadier General Halbert E. Paine, commanding the military District of Illinois, declaring that Ayer's services as a detective "would be duly appreciated by the Government." General Paine, in turn, put Ayer "in communication" with Colonel Sweet, commandant at Camp Douglas. In this roundabout fashion, Ayer entered upon his service to the government.[18]

There were some rumors that dissidents might use the meeting of the Democratic National Convention in Chicago as the occasion for an uprising. It was also reported that the Sons of Liberty would be meeting in Chicago at the same time. Furthermore, Clement L. Vallandigham, purported head of the Sons of Liberty and a delegate to the convention, would be there. Colonel Sweet was apprehensive and asked his superior for more troops; he wanted to place some reinforcements in the center of the city and some at Camp Douglas—just in case.

Major General Samuel P. Heintzelman, in command of the Northern Department (headquartered in Columbus, Ohio), came to Chicago to check on some of the rumors. He met with Colonel Sweet, toured Camp Douglas, and visited Democratic politicians in their hotel rooms. He found no evidence to support apprehension that an uprising was in the offing. In fact, everything was unusually quiet, and it was a case of politics as usual.[19]

17. Jabez Howard, testimony, March 14, 1865, *ibid.*, 416.
18. I. Winslow Ayer to Yates, December 2, 1864, in Governor Richard Yates Papers, Illinois State Historical Library, Springfield.
19. Samuel P. Heintzelman Diary, August 27, 28, 1864 (MS in Heintzelman Papers); Heintzelman Journal, August 30, 31, 1864.

The Democratic national convention attracted others than delegates to Chicago. There were many Democratic celebrities—Vallandigham, Horatio Seymour, George Francis Train, and Amos Kendall, the "fossilized relic" of Andrew Jackson's day—all eager for the chance to strut across the stage. There were those who wanted a glimpse of one of these famous men. There were small-time and small-town Democrats who came to buoy their spirits and drink anew at the well. Even several dozen former Confederates, hanging on in Canada, crossed the border to see if popular dissension was as widespread as they had been led to believe or to set the stage for further mischief.

Two of the former Confederates, Godfrey J. Hyams and Thomas H. Hines, were typical of those who had special reason to visit Chicago during the sessions of the Democratic convention. Hyams sought information he could sell for a price to the gullible, while Hines was paymaster of a group of soldiers, some of them deserters and some escaped prisoners of war, who were returning to the South to rejoin the army. Hines may also have been checking to see if money paid to Copperheads like H. H. Dodd and John C. Walker had been well spent or wasted. Hyams stayed at the Richmond House, along with some other "southerners." Hines found a chasm between rumors of Copperhead perfidy and reality. He also found that such Democrats as Harrison H. Dodd, John C. Walker, and William A. Bowles had taken Confederate money and given little in return.[20]

The Democratic national convention passed off quietly enough and without violence. Even Deacon Bross, invariably critical of everything said or done by Democrats, admitted it was a routine affair. "The Democratic convention of 1864," Bross said fourteen years later, "was as quiet and respectable as any other political body that ever assembled in the city." Instead of crediting Democratic propriety for the absence of conspirational activity, however, Bross gave his own explanation. Colonel Sweet's precautionary measures, he insisted, simply made any planned revolutionary action infeasible. Sweet "had small squads of men with signs and pass-words in all the alleys in the central portions of the city ready to concentrate at the point of danger at any moment." The "wily New York politicians," not willing to be associated with an uprising doomed to fail because of Sweet's precautions,

---

20. Godfrey J. Hyams to Halmer H. Emmons, statement, September 24, 1864, in Halmer H. Emmons Papers, Burton Historical Collection, Detroit Public Library. The accounts of the Chicago convention in Thomas H. Hines [John B. Castleman and W. W. Cleary], "The Northwestern Conspiracy," *Southern Bivouac: A Monthly Literary and Historical Magazine*, n.s., II (June, 1886–May, 1887), 506–10, and John B. Castleman, *Active Service* (Louisville, 1917), 144–48, simply do not square with the facts. Inconclusive evidence indicates that Dodd, Walker, and Bowles took Confederate funds (perhaps about ten thousand dollars apiece) either to purchase arms or to stage an uprising. Some money also went to help elect the Democratic state ticket in Illinois.

gave "orders" to the "rabble" to call off the proposed and planned insurrection. Bross proved himself adept as a storyteller.[21]

While Bross spent time at his office in the *Tribune* Building, I. Winslow Ayer started his search for evidence of a conspiracy. He joined a local Democratic club, in which Irish-Americans predominated and which most of the members called an "Invincible Club." Its intent was to generate enthusiasm at the local level, police the polling places on election day, and counter the work of local Republican politicians. The meetings were open to all interested Democrats and club activity always intensified as elections approached.[22]

Posing as a Kentucky fugitive who held strong pro-Democratic and pro-Confederate views, Ayer became one of the most active members of the Invincible Club. He constantly criticized President Lincoln and seemed to detest Republicanism. He kept company with L. A. Doolittle, an irresponsible young lawyer who was entranced with his own oratory and was prone to make radical statements. Doolittle's anti-Lincoln tirades usually exceeded the bounds of propriety and embarrassed the more moderate members. Ayer applauded whenever any member damned Lincoln or Governor Yates or the war; he also liked to refer to the Invincible Club as a chapter of the Sons of Liberty.[23]

Buckner S. Morris, a former judge whom Lincoln had met during his circuit-riding days, appeared frequently at the local Democratic club, usually as a speaker. Judge Morris, biased in his political views, always spoke critically of the Lincoln administration, condemning the suspension of habeas corpus, use of federal troops to control elections in Kentucky, and the arming of the Union Leagues. Morris, like others, feared "that the purity of the polls would be disturbed by the Republican party." Yet he always counseled obedience to the law, fitting advice from one who was once a circuit judge.[24]

Ayer also became well acquainted with two other members of the local Democratic club. Thomas Edward Courtney, a mason and contractor, served on the club's executive committee. Like the typical Irish-American, Courtney voted the straight Democratic ticket. He also belonged to the Society of the Illini, organized by "the conservative citizens of Chicago" in 1863 "to secure the triumph of Democratic principles." Led to believe that the administration might patrol the polls, "as in Kentucky, Maryland, Missouri, and other places," Courtney was bold enough to talk of repelling force with force, if necessary, to keep the elections free. In fact, he "bought a revolver some three weeks previous to the election." At a later date Courtney would testify

21. Bross, *Biographical Sketch of B. J. Sweet*, 18–20.
22. Thomas Edward Courtney, testimony, March 1, 1865, in *House Executive Documents*, 39th Cong., 2nd Sess., 292–301.
23. Charles W. Patten, testimony, April 7, 1865, *ibid.*, 348.
24. Courtney, testimony, March 1, 1865, *ibid.*, 292–301.

that the local Democratic club was not really a secret society. It was "open to everybody," and had no passwords, grips, or "anything of that kind." [25]

Ayer also became acquainted with Charles Walsh, the most active and important member of the local Democratic club. He lived on the fringe of the city—in the "Irish section"—and operated a prosperous dray business. His house was too small for his large family of ten children, the eldest a comely lass of nineteen and the youngest a three-year-old toddler. Walsh, addicted to politics, considered himself a patriot, for he had fought for his adopted country twice, first in the Florida War against the Seminoles and then in the Mexican War. Once, he had futilely sought an elective office, being nominated as the Democratic candidate for sheriff of his county. He had also served as sergeant-at-arms during one session of the state legislature. [26]

Early in the war Walsh talked like a patriot, helping to raise an all-Irish regiment. When Lincoln turned to emancipation as a moral issue, Walsh became a bitter critic. Like so many others, he also feared that Governor Yates was arming the Union Leagues in order to seize and control the 1864 election. His fear became an obsession, and he collected a stack of arms and turned his house into a virtual arsenal. Walsh once told members of his local Democratic club that he expected them to become "an armed patrol" at the polls and that he would provide all with arms if the need arose, "but he hoped there would be no occasion to use them." He added that "these arms," which he expected to lend to forty or fifty Democratic poll watchers, "must be returned after the election." [27]

At some meetings of the local Democratic club, Ayer not only took the lead in castigating Lincoln and the Republicans but urged his fellow members to take questionable action. He wanted arms collected, of course, and distributed to members "to protect themselves." Once he pulled a small revolver from his pocket and showed it to the members, saying he did not think it "sufficient." He wanted one that would shoot straight and far. He wanted all Democrats armed and readied. The Union Leagues, he said, were armed; "they were disciplined men and drilled nightly." Ayer repeatedly tried to get the arms that Charles Walsh had in his home moved to local Democratic head-

25. *Constitution and By-laws of the Society of Illini* (Chicago, 1863), 1–2. A copy of this printed document is in General Courts Martial Records; Courtney, testimony, March 1, 1865, in *House Executive Documents*, 39th Cong., 2nd Sess., 292–301.

26. Francis C. Sherman [mayor of Chicago], testimony, March 10, 1865, in *House Executive Documents*, 39th Cong., 2nd Sess., 377–81; Alice Kay Pendleton to "My dear Mr. Blair," April 24, 1865, in Union Provost Marshals' File of One-Name Papers *re* Citizens, Records of the Office of the Judge Advocate General. Mrs. Pendleton wrote to Jacob B. Blair, a congressman from West Virginia, seeking a pardon for Charles Walsh. Three of Walsh's daughters also testified before the Cincinnati-based military commission.

27. William Hull, Courtney, Samuel Remington, testimony, February 14, March 1, 3, 1865, in *House Executive Documents*, 39th Cong., 2nd Sess., 263–66, 292–301, 319–21.

quarters, recognizing that their seizure by federal authorities at the club building would be damaging evidence of a conspiracy. The secretary of the Invincible Club, however, opposed the transfer, thus preventing Ayer from forging one of the links in his chain of the conspiracy.[28]

Colonel Sweet added four more detectives to his staff, who also became members of the local Democratic club. These four urged the collection of a cache of arms and tried to lead well-intentioned Democrats down the road to treason. Since average attendance at the weekly meetings varied from twelve to fifteen, the five detectives formed a goodly porton of the activists. At one of the weekly meetings, only eight members were present, four of them Colonel Sweet's detectives.[29]

Two of Sweet's detectives and Ayer's allies, John T. Shanks and Maurice Langhorne, also helped to develop the conspiracy. Shanks's record as a rascal, long before Sweet put him on his payroll, would have made a knave blush. His record of dishonesty extended back to his days in Texas, where he was employed in a state land office in Austin. Caught forging land warrants and stealing state money, Shanks was indicted on five counts. Found guilty, the "convicted felon" secured a release from "confinement" by enlisting in the Confederate army. He deserted after a brief stint as a private in the Fifteenth Regiment Texas Cavalry and drifted to Mississippi where he became a salaried clerk for Major John F. Mellon near Aberdeen and Tupelo. He made "false entries on the books," defrauded civilians who had sold supplies to the army, "appropriated" a fine saddle as his own, and married a Mississippi woman even though he already had a wife in Texas. He was court-martialed and found guilty of all charges. In addition, his superiors accused him of bigamy and asked that he be turned over to civil authorities for indictment and trial.[30] Escaping, he was a fugitive, vagabond, and horse thief. Eventually he found his way to central Tennessee where he joined General John H. Morgan's cavalry raiders. He was captured on Morgan's raid into Indiana and Ohio in July, 1863, and assigned with a contingent of other prisoners to quarters behind the stockade surrounding Camp Douglas.

Detailed as a clerk in the Camp Douglas prison, Shanks stole thirty dollars from a fellow prisoner by falsifying a signature. Although the evidence was unimpeachable, he brazenly denied the crime. In spite of Shanks's record—or

28. *Ibid.*

29. James L. Rock, testimony, March 8, 9, 1865, *ibid.*, 360–76; Chicago *Times*, February 20, 1865.

30. "Record of Court Martial of John T. Shanks, Tupelo, Mississippi" (MS, August 23, 1862, in Confederate Papers Relating to Citizens or Business Firms, National Archives); John T. Shanks Papers, in Compiled Service Records of Confederate Soldiers Who Served in Organizations from Texas, Microfilm Section, National Archives.

perhaps because of it—Colonel Sweet smuggled the Texas miscreant out of the prison compound and put the glib fellow on his payroll as a detective.

Shanks launched his career as a detective by trying to entrap S. Corning Judd, Democratic nominee for the second spot on the state ticket, and Buckner S. Morris. Pretending he was an escapee from Camp Douglas, Shanks asked Judd for food, shelter, clothing, and money. Suspicious, Judd expressed indignation and threatened to call the police. Shanks then hunted up Morris in his office and made the same request. Morris also turned his back upon the entrapper, who then went over to the Morris home and made his request of Mrs. Morris. Touched by his tale of woe, the kind-hearted woman gave him some clothes and money.[31] This well-intentioned act of charity later led to her arrest and incarceration. As for Shanks, he had begun a career as Sweet's detective, and in time he would become one of the chief witnesses in the treason trials held in Cincinnati.

Maurice Langhorne's reputation was only slightly less reprehensible than Shanks's. Langhorne had also served a stint in General Morgan's cavalry before deserting and making his way to Canada. There he found a dozen former Confederates anxious to sell "information" or their services as detectives to the U.S. government. Eager to make the hundred-dollar-a-month payroll, Langhorne "got up a pretended conspiracy to sack and destroy the city of Detroit." He tried to sell his "invaluable information," including some forged documents, to U.S. authorities for a thousand dollars.[32] He had several nibbles but failed to find a buyer. While in Toronto, he learned that such Confederate emissaries as Jacob Thompson wanted to subsidize discontent in the upper Midwest, even dreaming of the establishment of a northwestern confederacy. Thompson evidently took Copperhead rhetoric at face value and believed there was substance to the Carrington and Sanderson exposés.

Langhorne was one of more than a dozen former Confederates in Canada whom Thomas H. Hines recruited to return to the Confederacy via Chicago at the time of the Democratic national convention. Langhorne registered at the Richmond House as Walter Hunt, took handouts from Hines, picked up some scuttlebut here and there, and listened to reports about the Democratic convention. He played hookey when Hines led his contingent of Confederates southward and stayed behind in Chicago. Hines felt that Langhorne had double-crossed him and later wrote, "A blacker-hearted villain never lived."[33]

31. S. Corning Judd, testimony, April 7, 1865, in *House Executive Documents*, 39th Cong., 2nd Sess., 541–45; John A. Marshall, *American Bastile: A History of the Illegal Arrests and Imprisonment of American Citizens During the Late Civil War* (Philadelphia, 1878), 104; Robert Hervey, "Observations upon the Testimony Affecting G. St. Leger Grenfell, One of the Accused" (MS, May, 1865, in General Courts Martial Records).

32. Hervey, "Observations upon the Testimony Affecting Grenfell"; memorandum, January 17, 1865, in Emmons Papers.

33. Thomas H. Hines, marginal note on a magazine article, Edmund Kirke [James R. Gil-

In Chicago, Langhorne claimed he had information to sell and found his way to the office of Colonel Sweet. Believing that the glib and brazen Rebel had connections that might be exploited, Sweet put him on his payroll at the usual hundred dollars a month.[34] Briefed by Sweet and Ayer, Langhorne was in a unique position and able to link Hines to the conspiracy in the offing.

Two "strangers," George St. Leger Grenfell and Vincent Marmaduke, in Chicago for different reasons early in November, 1864, became entangled in the web of conspiracy. Each of the two possessed pro-Confederate sympathies and had a past enshrouded in mystery. Grenfell, a self-styled English gentleman-adventurer, seemed more like a character out of a romantic novel than a true historical figure. He claimed to have been a soldier of fortune who had fought with a French cavalry regiment in Algeria, engaged the Riffe pirates in encounters off the coast of Morocco, campaigned as a colonel in the Crimean War, tramped with Garibaldi's legions over parts of South America to bring new republics into being, and participated in the suppression of the Sepoy Mutiny in India. As with many adventurers, Grenfell's tales improved with each retelling. His tawdry and gaudy past actually included some military service and some storybook adventures but also considerable intrigue, speculation, travel, smuggling, and prevarication. He devised his own definition for such words as *honor* and *propriety*, always claiming to be an English gentleman, *bon vivant*, and soldier of fortune.[35]

Early in 1862, Grenfell visited with John Slidell, emissary of the Confederate government to France, told of his desire to serve the South, and received letters of recommendation to Generals Robert E. Lee and Pierre G. T. Beauregard. Carrying a packet of letters and memorabilia, Grenfell crossed the Atlantic, visited Charleston, and headed for Richmond, where he met General Lee. After a lengthy interview, Lee wrote to Beauregard in Grenfell's behalf. The English adventurer set out for the Tennessee area, but chance and circumstance led him to join Colonel John Hunt Morgan's command, actually serving as assistant adjutant general during the July, 1862, raid into Kentucky.[36] Grenfell accompanied Morgan on several other raids, including the Hartsville expedition where 1,250 Confederate effectives surprised and captured 2,400

---

more], "The Chicago Conspiracy," *Atlantic Monthly*, XVI (July, 1865), 108–20, in Thomas H. Hines Papers, University of Kentucky Library, Lexington.

34. Maurice Langhorne, testimony, January 25–26, 1865, in *House Executive Documents*, 39th Cong., 2nd Sess., 84–100.

35. Grenfell's adventures varied with each retelling. See, for example, Basil W. Duke, *Reminiscences of General Basil W. Duke, C.S.A.* (New York, 1911), 50; Walter Lord (ed.), *The Freemantle Diary* (New York, 1960), 127; and John Minor Botts to Joseph Holt, June 17, 1865, in *House Executive Documents*, 39th Cong., 2nd Sess., 637.

36. R. E. Lee to Beauregard, April 26, 1862, George St. Leger Grenfell to Beauregard, May 30, 1862, both in G. St. Leger Grenfell Papers, War Department Records, National Archives. Grenfell's adventures and experiences in the Confederacy are related superbly in Stephen Z. Starr, *Colonel Grenfell's Wars: The Life of a Soldier of Fortune* (Baton Rouge, 1971).

Federal troops because an incompetent colonel, Absalom B. Moore of the 104th Illinois Regiment, had failed to detail pickets and outposts. (The disgraced colonel later secured a measure of revenge by testifying that Grenfell was a fiend incarnate at the Cincinnati treason trial.) Later, while on his way to join General Braxton Bragg's army, Grenfell encountered a deserter-renegade named John T. Shanks, whom Grenfell would meet again during the Cincinnati treason trials. Shanks and four companions stole five of Grenfell's horses. Like an avenging angel, Grenfell pursued the horse thieves, vented his wrath upon them, and recovered his horses.

After a series of other adventures, Grenfell decided to quit the Confederate service and head for England or Canada. He ran the blockade to Bermuda and missed the Halifax-bound mail steamer. Tired of waiting for another boat to Canada or England, he caught a ship sailing for New York City. There he called upon General John A. Dix, in charge of the Department of the East, to clarify his status and get permission to travel in the North. Dix sent the adventurer to Washington where he had an interview with Secretary of War Stanton and related his service in the Confederacy. Grenfell promised to give no further support to the Confederacy and signed an oath that he would "faithfully support, protect, and defend" the Constitution of the United States. He received permission to go unattended wherever and whenever he pleased.[37]

As a gentleman of leisure, Grenfell visited Baltimore and New York City, took a hunting and fishing trip into the Adirondacks, and ended up at the Clifton House, on the Canadian side of Niagara Falls. He was there when Horace Greeley and Jacob Thompson met for "peace negotiations," which fizzled. He renewed his acquaintance with Thomas H. Hines with whom he had formed a bond of respect when the two served under General Morgan in 1862.

After the peace efforts failed, Jacob Thompson became interested in subsidizing an insurrection in the upper Midwest. The Confederate agents in Canada evidently believed that the Order of American Knights and Sons of Liberty were more than paper-based organizations. Thompson passed out seed money to such dissenters as H. H. Dodd, John C. Walker, and William A. Bowles, who took the easy money simply because it was there for the taking and cloaked their avarice behind vagueness and bad faith. Through Hines, Grenfell was led to believe that there would be action and excitement in Chicago at the time of the Democratic national convention. Thompson's hopes for an insurrection, with Confederates in Canada involved in one way or another, prompted Grenfell to write to his daughter: "You will not see me in England for the present. There is still work to be done and I am awaiting events." Thompson's ability to distort reality was bound to bring disappoint-

37. Loyalty oath, signed by Grenfell, June 15, 1864, in Letters Received by the Adjutant Generals' Office, 1861–1870, National Archives.

ment. Even Hines, after the war, remarked on Thompson's gullibility; he was, Hines wrote, "inclined to believe much that was told him, trust too many men, doubt too little and suspect less."[38]

While the Confederates in Canada were seeking ways to subsidize discontent across the border, Grenfell spent most of August on an extended hunting and fishing safari in the Georgian Bay area. He returned to Toronto just in time to accompany Hines and his contingent of former Confederates to Chicago to see if there was an opportunity for mischief. The Chicago setting during the convention would allow strangers to go unnoticed. Grenfell wanted to see the Democratic national convention in action, for such sessions were regarded by Englishmen as a distinctly American phenomenon. Furthermore, Hines had led Grenfell to believe that they would be "engaged in rather dangerous speculations."[39]

When Hines and his contingent arrived in Chicago, he realized that the opportunity for "mischief" simply did not exist. No plans had been made to raid Camp Douglas, free the Confederate prisoners held there, and engineer a revolt. The Democratic convention proceeded without incident. Hines and Grenfell parted, the former with his soldier-recruits heading for the Confederacy and the latter, for another hunting safari. Addicted to hunting, Grenfell headed for south central Illinois to shoot prairie chicken, quail, plover, and gray squirrel for six weeks. He made the acquaintance of some Clinton County residents, both Republicans and Democrats, one of whom later testified that Grenfell had "engaged in no unlawful enterprise of any kind during his stay here."[40]

As the colder weather set in and hunting lost some of its pleasure, Grenfell headed back for Chicago as a stopover on his way to Canada and England. He arrived in Chicago early on the morning of November 6, a Sunday, and registered at the Richmond House, where the Prince of Wales had stayed on his hunting expedition during September, 1860. He registered as "Col. G. St. Leger Grenfell, Great Britain" without assumed name, secrecy, deceit, or disguise, and he signed in his own hand.[41] When Colonel Sweet's detectives learned of Grenfell's presence at the Richmond House, they entangled him in their faulty and yet unfinished web.

Vincent Marmaduke, the second "stranger" entangled in the web, had not led Grenfell's adventurous life. Young Marmaduke's greatest sin was being

38. Grenfell to Marie Pearce-Seracold (daughter), July 18, 1864, in Mabel Clare Weaks (ed.), "Colonel George St. Leger Grenfell," *Filson Club Historical Quarterly*, XXXIV (1960), 9; Hines [Castleman], "The Northwestern Conspiracy," 502.

39. Grenfell to William Maynard, August 31, 1886, in Weaks (ed.), "Colonel George St. Leger Grenfell," 11.

40. Hervey, "Observations upon the Testimony Affecting Grenfell."

41. *Ibid.*

a brother to a brigadier general serving in the Confederate army. General John S. Marmaduke, a Missouri-born West Pointer, gained notoriety by leading successful raids into his home state from Arkansas bases. Brother Vincent, an avowed secessionist, had attended the "state convention" that had tried to exercise constituent powers. Since he had cast his lot with the Confederate cause, Unionists labeled young Marmaduke a *persona non grata* and Major General John M. Schofield ordered him banished from the state for the duration of the war. Young Marmaduke then left for Europe, "to avoid taking sides in the civil war in Missouri." When his father died, he returned to the United States, arriving about August 1, 1864. After reaching Chicago, he hunted up some old acquaintances to ask about affairs in Missouri. They advised him not to return to his native state, at least not until after the November elections.[42] Since his funds were low and his income limited, he stayed at a rooming house rather than a hotel. While pondering his future and awaiting the evolution of events in Missouri, Vincent Marmaduke, like Grenfell, became caught up in the web of conspiracy.

The approach of the November 8 election made it necessary for Colonel Sweet to transform his charade into a conspiracy, even though his evidence was unconvincing. Early on Sunday morning, November 6, he sent out three squads of soldiers to make arrests. One went to the Charles Walsh home to arrest the man of the house and seize the arms and ammunition stored there. One of the searchers also stole $550 and a pocketbook from Walsh's bedroom. Bross, repeating what Colonel Sweet wrote in his report, claimed that the squad seized "two cart loads of large-sized revolvers, loaded and capped, and two hundred muskets and a large quantity of ammunition." However, Lieutenant Colonel Lewis C. Skinner, who led the detail that arrested Walsh and seized the arms, said he saw no revolvers, muskets, or shotguns that were capped.[43] Another squad went to Judge Buckner S. Morris' home, awakened him at two o'clock in the morning, and carted him off to Camp Douglas as a prisoner. A third squad, the largest, headed for downtown Chicago to pick up suspicious-looking visitors, for there was a rumor that hundreds of Butternuts ("the most desperate class of bushwacking vagabonds") had come from southern Illinois to cast Democratic votes in the November 8 elections.[44] The downtown squad arrested twenty-seven suspects at the Donaldson House and

42. Maj. Gen. John M. Schofield, "Special Orders, No. 171," June 27, 1863, Department of the Missouri, in *House Executive Documents*, 39th Cong., 2nd Sess., 600; Vincent Marmaduke to Maj. Gen. Joseph Hooker, December 22, 1864, in Citizens' File, War Department Records.

43. Letitia Walsh, Margaret Walsh, testimony, March 2, 3, 1865, in *House Executive Documents*, 39th Cong., 2nd Sess., 301–11; Bross, *Biographical Sketch of B. J. Sweet*, 24; B. J. Sweet to Brig. Gen. James B. Fry, November 23, 1864, in *OR*, Ser. 1, Vol. XLV, Pt. 1, pp. 1077–80; Lewis C. Skinner, testimony, February 2, 1865, in *House Executive Documents*, 39th Cong., 2nd Sess., 160, 164. Skinner's testimony is much more trustworthy than Sweet's (or Bross's). Writers of fiction prefer Sweet's for it gives more substance to the conspiracy story.

44. Bross, *Biographical Sketch of B. J. Sweet*, 24.

another lot on North Water Street. By evening, the number arrested exceeded one hundred, all of whom were eventually escorted to Camp Douglas for interrogation. After Grenfell's arrival at the Richmond House (suspicion falls on Shanks as the one who noticed the Englishman's name on the register) another squad of soldiers hurried there to claim him as a prisoner. For good measure, some soldiers arrested Shanks too and put him in Grenfell's cell. Sweet evidently hoped that Shanks might pry some incriminating evidence from Grenfell or that the detective might get him to make some damaging remarks. The strategy failed. Sweet's men also seized and searched all of Grenfell's baggage, but failed to find a single scrap of evidence of any kind that would implicate the adventurer in any plot or conspiracy.[45]

Soon after the arrests, detectives Ayer and Langhorne took the lead in calling for a "special meeting" of the local Democratic club to which they, Walsh, and others belonged. Both Ayer and Langhorne tried to convince the timid members that they should rescue Walsh and Morris "by violence." But the members believed such drastic action imprudent, and the baited trap caught no one.[46]

While Colonel Sweet arrested others here and there, Deacon Bross put the scanty evidence together as the basis for an election eve exposé. The imaginative story, published under the banner headline "Camp Douglas Conspiracy!," was a tangled tale about the proposed release of Confederate prisoners held in Camp Douglas, the burning and plunder of Chicago, and a planned insurrection intended to establish a northwestern confederacy. Bross brought both George B. McClellan, Democratic presidential nominee, and Clement L. Vallandigham, nominal head of the Sons of Liberty, into the plot. The Knights of the Golden Circle, the Order of American Knights, and the Sons of Liberty were all involved. Only prompt action by Colonel Sweet, the exposé in the Chicago *Tribune* stated, had nipped the conspiracy in the bud, prevented the burning of Chicago, and nullified the plans of traitors to take over the polls and revolutionize the upper Midwest.[47]

The arrest of the principals, Bross's *Tribune* insisted, was *prima facie* evidence that a conspiracy existed. Actually, the *Tribune*'s exposé borrowed heavily from Judge Advocate General Holt's report on secret societies and incorporated some of the flimsy evidence that Sweet's corps of detectives had gathered. Other Republican editors, especially those in Illinois, also gave publicity to the election eve exposé.

Democratic editors, of course, ridiculed the *Tribune*'s election eve revela-

45. Hervey, "Observations upon the Testimony Affecting Grenfell."
46. Rock, testimony, March 1, 1865, in *House Executive Documents*, 39th Cong., 2nd Sess., 384.
47. Chicago *Daily Tribune*, November 8, 9, 1864. The same story is detailed in Bross, *Biographical Sketch of B. J. Sweet*, 16–17, and in Ayer to Yates, December 2, 1864, in Yates Papers.

tions, grumbling that their denials and rebuttals would not be read until after the votes were cast. Most Democratic editors regarded the *Tribune*'s story as just another "roorback of huge dimensions." James W. Sheahan of the Chicago *Morning Post* considered it just another "trick" to influence the voters. Henry N. Walker of the Detroit *Free Press* added words of disbelief and derision, stating that the whole story was "too ridiculous to be given a moment's credit." The editor of the Louisville *Democrat* called the *Tribune*'s revelations a "contrivance," which would be accepted as fact only by those who wanted to be deceived. "Preposterous as it is," the disgusted editor wrote, "there are fools enough to believe it." He concluded rather cynically, "We would like to know how many greenbacks it takes to make a conspiracy."[48]

Wilbur F. Storey, the doubting Thomas who edited the Chicago *Times*, eventually expressed his opinion of the so-called conspiracy. He believed it a "hoax" and suspected it had been devised in the offices of the Chicago *Tribune* rather than the back rooms of some dark lantern society. "We do not mean," he wrote perceptively, "that a few fools calling themselves 'Sons of Liberty,' or something of the sort, did not hold mysterious conclaves in mysterious places, and spout preposterous nonsense and utter direful threats which they were as likely to execute as they would a military assault on the moon. It is possible that there were such conclaves, one of which, according to testimony, consisted of six persons, while there were present four detectives! Four detectives leading on two fools!"[49] Storey's suppositions were not far off the mark. Bross and Sweet had taken questionable evidence and transformed it into a gigantic conspiracy.

While Democrats were condemning the *Tribune* and the exposé and Republicans were celebrating the reelection of Governor Yates and President Lincoln, Colonel Sweet was composing a report that summarized the evidence and came up with the desired result—giving the outlines of the Camp Douglas conspiracy. He found it necessary to free or parole all but 8 of the 150 men whom his posses had arrested on November 7 and the days that followed. While releasing the many, he ordered two more arrests. On November 17 a squad arrested Richard I. Semmes, a fledgling lawyer whose elder brother belonged to Judge Morris' law firm. Several days later he arrested Mrs. Morris, who had given clothes and money to Shanks when he was posing as an escapee from Camp Douglas. Arresting Mrs. Morris seemed to make the case against her husband more plausible, even though the technique was guilt by association. Colonel Sweet ordered the distraught woman confined to a dungeon—"a dark, damp, filthy place swarming with vermin." However,

48. Chicago *Morning Post*, November 9, 1864; Detroit *Free Press*, November 11, 1864; Louisville *Daily Democrat*, November 9, 1864.
49. Chicago *Times*, February 20, 1865.

Sweet's subordinate, a less ambitious and more humane man, had the Morrises transferred to a room in his own quarters, even permitting them to bring in their own bedding and furniture. Mrs. Morris was never told why she and her husband were arrested, nor were any charges ever filed against her.[50]

General Joseph Hooker, in whose department the arrests had been made, sent his judge advocate, Major Henry L. Burnett, to Chicago to see Colonel Sweet, interrogate the prisoners and detectives, and prepare the charges and specifications. With conviction of the four so-called traitors at Indianapolis to his credit, Major Burnett had another chance to hold center stage and get another leg on the promotion he coveted. Colonel Sweet also expected that bringing the Camp Douglas conspiracy to light would get him a promotion. "If things were all right," a confidant stated, "he expected to be made a brigadier."[51]

Major Burnett took his stenographic aide, Benn Pitman, with him to Chicago, where he spent five days talking to Sweet and his detectives and interrogating the ten prisoners. After completing his preliminary investigation, Burnett ordered the release of Mrs. Morris and William C. Walsh, the eldest son of Charles Walsh, supposedly one of the central figures in the conspiracy. The judge adovcate then compiled the charges and specifications against the remaining eight prisoners and recommended that they be transferred to McLean Barracks near Cincinnati, where the military commission would be convened.

While the Burnett-Sweet team was setting the stage for another treason trial by a military court in an area where the civil courts were open, several of the principals wrote interesting and important letters. One of the letter writers was I. Winslow Ayer, one of the more important detectives, who wanted more money for his sleuthing and for testifying before the military commission. He wrote a long letter to Governor Yates, bragging about his accomplishments as a detective. It was he who had discovered "the gigantic conspiracy," and he seemed to think that Colonel Sweet was getting too much of the credit. "To unravel the plot and lay bare to the authorities the extent of the treasonable design," Ayer wrote, "was a work as arduous and complicated as it was full of peril." He also asked that he be reimbursed "several hundred dollars" of his own money, which he had spent on "incidental matters connected with the work."[52] If it was not blackmail, it was something very similar. It was also in keeping with Ayer's character.

Vincent Marmaduke, one of the "Chicago eight," also wrote a long letter.

50. Marshall, *American Bastile*, 101, 625.

51. Obadiah Jackson, testimony, March 17, 1865, in *House Executive Documents*, 39th Cong., 2nd Sess., 451.

52. Ayer to Yates, December 2, 1864, in Yates Papers.

The former Missourian had trouble finding out why he was arrested. After he was finally told that he was involved in a conspiracy to free the Confederate prisoners held in Camp Douglas and revolutionize the upper Midwest, Marmaduke promptly put his denials down on paper. He wrote to General Hooker and presented his side of the story. At first, soon after he was arrested, Marmaduke said, he was told that he was "an officer in the rebel army." This he denied, saying he had never served in the Confederate army, navy, or government. Two days later, Colonel Sweet told him that he was involved in "a plot to attack Camp Douglas or the city of Chicago." This second charge, Marmaduke wrote to Hooker, was as ridiculous as the first. He was but biding time in Chicago, waiting for the war to end so he could return to Missouri to reestablish his law practice. He had reliable and respected references to substantiate all of his contentions and prove his innocence. He was guilty of nothing, he concluded in his letter to Hooker, being the victim of chance and circumstance and a frame-up.[53]

While Ayer and Marmaduke wrote long letters, G. St. Leger Grenfell wrote two short ones. Held incommunicado for twenty-seven days, the Englishman finally received permission to write a note to the British consul in Chicago; he hoped, evidently, that the consul would intervene in his behalf. After claiming to be a British subject, Grenfell added, "I have been hitherto allowed to communicate with no one, not even a lawyer, and I am in ignorance of the charges against me." Grenfell's second letter, to a friend in England, stated that he had taken the liberty of drawing a letter of credit for fifty pounds sterling upon the friend's account to cover, in part, the cost of his defense.[54]

On December 23, federal authorities transferred the "Chicago eight" to Cincinnati. Grenfell had heavy leg irons fastened to his ankles during the move. The military detail directing the transfer, ineptly led, failed to provide any food to the prisoners either on the train or after their arrival in Cincinnati. It was the coldest day of the winter. In time, the benumbed prisoners were lodged in the McLean Barracks. The guards then replaced Grenfell's leg irons with a sixty-pound ball and chain.[55]

The eight prisoners were a motley crew. Because Grenfell seemed to be the prime catch, Colonel Sweet and his detectives concocted the myth that he was to be the leader of the forces assaulting Camp Douglas to free the prisoners held there. Since he had actually served in the southern army, Grenfell provided a link with the Confederacy.

53. Marmaduke to Hooker, December 22, 1864, in Citizens' File, War Department Records.
54. Grenfell to "My Lord," December 2, 1864, in Letters Received by the Adjutant General's Office; Grenfell to Maynard, December 5, 1864, quoted in Starr, *Grenfell's Wars*, 210.
55. Marshall, *American Bastile*, 626; Grenfell to "British Ambassador, Washington," January 23, 1865, cited in Starr, *Grenfell's Wars*, 210.

In addition to Grenfell, four other prisoners had Confederate links. Vincent Marmaduke's brother was a Confederate general. Benjamin Anderson had once fought with a Kentucky rebel regiment before becoming a deserter, a Canadian resident, and a hanger-on in Chicago. No matter how Sweet and Burnett juggled their few facts about Anderson, they had no incriminating evidence against the moody and rather unstable fellow. Charles T. Daniel, who had once served in the Confederate ranks before coming to Chicago, eked out a meager living as a workman while courting one of Charles Walsh's pretty daughters. George E. Cantrell, like Daniel, was a nobody; he had once lived in Kentucky, drifted to Chicago, and shared Democratic views with Walsh while dating another daughter. Daniel and Cantrell, both sympathetic to the southern cause, had occasionally attended meetings of Walsh's Democratic club to curry his favor and his daughters' good will.

The other three prisoners had solid Copperhead and Democratic ties. Judge Buckner S. Morris, whose name topped the list, had evolved into a steadfast anti-Lincoln man, sometimes guilty of "violent and absurd harangues" against the war and the government. His wife, also Kentucky-born, had relatives who had been avowed secessionists and rebel soldiers. She had betrayed her sympathies by taking baskets of provisions to the Confederate soldiers confined within the Camp Douglas compound.[56]

Charles Walsh had unclean hands. A year earlier, he had sold some sugar to Confederate agents, receiving cash in return. He was a prominent Democratic leader in his ward but talked and bragged too much to win the respect of his colleagues. He also drank too much too often, for he liked his liquor and his Democratic politics straight and unadulterated. He let two detectives, Ayer and Langhorne, push him to the brink of treason. They helped to convince him, although he needed little convincing, that Democratic rights were endangered and that Republicans intended to seize the polls. They encouraged him to collect a store of arms and ammunition in case it was desirable to arm the forty or fifty Democratic poll watchers. So Walsh collected arms and ammunition openly and fearlessly, letting Republicans know that they would pay the piper if Union Leaguers tried to take over the polls by force of arms. Respectable witnesses heard Walsh say that "he hoped to God it would not be necessary to use them (the arms)." Another witness testified in like vein, hearing Walsh say that he would pass out arms if need be, but that he hoped that the election would go off peaceably with Democratic victories in the local, state, and national elections.[57]

56. Chicago *Times*, February 20, 1865; Mary Morris to Hooker, February 13, 1865, published in Cincinnati *Daily Gazette*, February 14, 1865.

57. Charles Walsh, "Statement" (MS, n.d., in Charles Walsh Papers, Citizens' File, War Department Records); Courtney, Remington, testimony, March 1, 3, 1865, in *House Executive Documents*, 39th Cong., 2nd Sess., 292–95, 319–22.

Richard T. Semmes possessed the weakest political credentials of the three Chicago Democrats caught in the Sweet-concocted web. He was not, as some have claimed, the brother of Confederate Admiral Raphael Semmes. Semmes's family ties reached back to Cumberland, Maryland, where his father was a respected lawyer. Young Semmes grew to manhood amidst the bitter feuds over slavery and secession that split the Cumberland community. Early in the war, young Semmes left for Chicago to read law in his brother's office and to escape the hatreds that divided families in Cumberland. He had not served in the armed forces of either the Confederacy or the United States. After 1863, he set up his own practice. He tried to widen his circle of acquaintances by joining literary and political clubs, evidently hoping that acquaintances would become clients. He joined the neighborhood Democratic club patronized by Sweet's detectives. This local club, which Semmes occasionally attended and which Ayer and Langhorne claimed was a castle of the Sons of Liberty and the center for plotting the Camp Douglas conspiracy, held only seven meetings.[58]

While the eight prisoners arranged for counsel, Judge Advocate Burnett prepared the charges and specifications. The two charges read: "Charge 1st—Conspiracy, in violation of the laws of war, to release the rebel prisoners of war, confined by authority of the United States, at Camp Douglas, near Chicago, Illinois. Charge 2nd—Conspiring, in violation of the laws of war, to lay waste and destroy the city of Chicago, Illinois." The specifications detailed the charges and brought in the name of Thomas H. Hines, "alias Doctor Hunter," as a co-conspirator in the scheme "to release the rebel prisoners of war . . . by suddenly attacking said Camp [Douglas] on or about the evening of the eighth of November [1864] . . . with a large number of armed men, overpowering the guard and forces then and there stationed, seizing the cannon and arms in possession of said guard . . . forcibly opening the gates of said prison camp and removing all the obstructions to the successful escape of said prisoners confined within its limits." Captain Hines was listed in the specifications as one of the accomplices in the plot to capture the arsenal in Chicago, cut the telegraph wires, burn the railway depots, take possession of the banks and public buildings, and sack and burn the city.[59]

Including Hines's name in the specifications meant that he would, in effect, be tried in absentia—all in an effort to make a weak case more convincing. Hines had had a checkered career. A Kentuckian, he had ridden off to war soon after the start of hostilities and had had some storybook adventures. In June of 1863 he and a handful of Confederates went on a horse-stealing expedition into southern Indiana. Pursued aggressively, Hines and the others es-

58. Courtney, testimony, March 1, 1865, in *House Executive Documents*, 39th Cong., 2nd Sess., 292–95.

59. "General Orders, No. 30 (1864)," April 2, 1865, in General Courts Martial Records.

caped across the Ohio River, but without honor or horses. In mid-July Hines led one of the companies in General John Hunt Morgan's cavalry command. Captured near Salinville, Ohio, Morgan, Hines, and several other officers were confined in the State Penitentiary Building in Columbus, supposedly for the duration of the war. Morgan, Hines, and four others tunneled out of their cell block, scaled an outer wall, and escaped back to Kentucky.[60]

After returning to Kentucky, Hines accompanied Morgan on a journey to the Confederate capital. There Hines received a new assignment. He was to proceed to Canada and put himself at the service of James P. Holcombe, a Confederate commissioner sent there in 1864. Hines's special assignment seemed to be "to collect and organize . . . all the Confederate soldiers in Canada, most of whom were escaped prisoners," and to subsidize their return to the South. He could also carry out operations not contrary to the "neutral obligations" of the British provinces. James A. Seddon, as secretary of war, assigned two hundred bales of cotton to Hines, with proceeds of the sale to be used to finance Hines's Canadian responsibilities. After President Jefferson Davis sent Jacob Thompson to Canada to head "the peace mission" that participated in the "July fiasco," Seddon sent word to Hines to put himself in the service of the new head man in Canada.[61]

Hines recruited a handful of onetime Rebels to return to the Confederacy via Detroit and Chicago, subsidizing their travel expenses out of the funds secured by selling the two hundred bales of cotton. Hines and his contingent arrived in Chicago on the eve of the meeting of the Democratic national convention. If they had any dream of partaking in an insurrection to be staged by insurgent Copperheads, the dream dissipated after arriving in Chicago. Hines, as paymaster for his contingent, was using the convention as a screen for his mission.[62] A federal detective (Thomas H. Keefe) trailed Hines from Toronto to Chicago but lost him in the city. Realizing that the idea of an insurrection was sheer fantasy, Hines and most of the members of his contingent then left for Kentucky where Hines married his fiancee on November 16, 1864.[63] Hines's known presence in Chicago as a man with money and responsibilities during the time of the so-called conspiracy gave Colonel Sweet room

60. William E. Wilson, "Thunderbolt of the Confederacy or 'King of Horse Thieves' (General John H. Morgan)," *Indiana Magazine of History*, LIV (1958), 119–30, summarizes the story of Morgan's raid in superb fashion. Some students of Civil War history offer the supposition that Morgan *et al.* escaped by bribing guards and walked out of the prison.

61. James A. Seddon to Hines, March 16, 1864, Seddon to Leonidas Polk, order, March 16, 1864, copies of both in Hines Papers.

62. Hyams to Emmons, statement, September 24, 1864, in Emmons Papers.

63. Rev. Paul E. Ryan to Most Rev. William T. Mulloy, April 22, 1955, in my possession. This letter resulted from the author's inquiry (to the Bishop of Covington, Ky.) as to the date of the marriage and why a Catholic priest would marry two non-Catholics. In his book, *Confederate Agent: A Discovery in History* (New York, 1954), James D. Horan mistakenly gives November 10, 1864, as the day of the marriage.

to envision him as a principal. So Judge Advocate Burnett included Hines's name in his specifications.

The shifting of the trial of the supposed conspirators from Chicago to Cincinnati made it more difficult for the accused to secure adequate counsel. In the first place, none of the eight had the financial resources to hire topflight legal talent. In the second place, no respectable lawyer wanted his reputation tainted by defending clients the Republican press had already convicted or by being a party to a summary procedure he believed unconstitutional and improper.

Nevertheless, General Hooker convened a military commission and set January 11, 1865, as the opening day of the trial. Judge Advocate Burnett, who had run the show expeditiously at Indianapolis, again served as both judge and prosecutor. Burnett had a "servile jury," for most of the nine members of the military commission had been active in Republican circles before the war. Several had even blatantly paraded their partisanship as army officers and three had served on the military commission in Indianapolis. Aware of the political connotations of the case, Judge Advocate Burnett directed that the trial be open to the press and the public. The Cincinnati *Gazette* and the Cincinnati *Commercial* took it for granted that the "Chicago eight" were guilty of the charges against them. The editor of the *Gazette*, for example, urged the public to attend "and look upon distinguished specimen of the bold and desperate men who have plotted evil to our government and the people of our sister-city."[64]

After the trial opened, the two sides sparred for advantage. Judge Advocate Burnett read the special orders convening the court. The attorneys for the defendants promptly presented long formal papers denying the jurisdiction of a military court over their clients in an area where the civil courts were open. The judge advocate, in turn, presented a long, long reply to the challenge of jurisdiction; it filled more than a hundred pages of legal-size foolscap. After the question of jurisdiction was settled, at least as far as the judge advocate was concerned, each of the eight defendants entered a plea of not guilty. Through attorneys, each of the eight also introduced a motion for a separate trial. The court denied each of the motions except George Cantrell's. He had become ill and was granted severance "on ground of his evident inability to be present during the trial."[65]

John T. Shanks, Colonel Sweet's prized if unprincipled detective, led the parade of witnesses whom Judge Advocate Burnett produced for the court. Shanks made a convincing witness, presenting a "carefully rehearsed story,"

64. Cincinnati *Daily Gazette*, January 9, 1865.
65. Judge Advocate Henry L. Burnett, "Reply" (MS, January 11, 1865, in General Courts Martial Records).

while the judge advocate asked leading questions to fill in the details and reiterate key points.[66] The inept lawyers for the defendants spent more than two days probing contradictions, but Shanks more than held his own. Finally it was attorney Robert Hervey's turn; he was one of the lawyers for Morris and Grenfell. Hervey had uncovered evidence, brought up from Texas, that Shanks had been convicted of forgery. "Were you, Mr. Shanks," Hervey asked politely, "ever arrested, tried, convicted and sentenced for the crime of felony in Texas?" The judge advocate intervened to protect his star witness, saying that the question was immaterial and irrelevant. Shanks, however, blurted out, "I never was." Hervey then produced documentary evidence that proved Shanks to be a brazen liar, without scruples or conscience. The judge advocate felt the need to try to erase the stain upon his star witness by presenting him to the court as a man of great courage and devotion to country, implying that courage should be associated with truthfulness.[67] Shanks's chief contribution lay in linking Grenfell to the Chicago conspiracy, although his evidence was strictly conjecture.

Maurice Langhorne, another of Colonel Sweet's star detectives, followed Shanks on the witness stand. Langhorne had deserted Hines's contingent of returning soldiers in Chicago. He wove a fancy tale, implicating Hines, Grenfell, Marmaduke, Anderson, and Walsh in the conspiracy to free Confederate prisoners held in Camp Douglas, burn Chicago, and sponsor a revolution. The lawyers for the defense subjected Langhorne to a vigorous cross-examination and revealed that his past record, like Shanks's, made his testimony suspect. Under questioning, Langhorne admitted that he had tried to sell some "revelations" to Colonel Bennett H. Hill, the assistant provost marshal of the District of Michigan, for one thousand dollars.[68] Judge Advocate Burnett again came to the defense of the witness, implying that the credibility of a witness had no bearing on the worth of his testimony. Burnett said that the testimony implicating Langhorne in forgery and blackmail also was immaterial and inapplicable, and the nine commissioners sustained his contentions.

I. Winslow Ayer, another of Colonel Sweet's prize detectives and Judge Advocate Burnett's star witnesses, offered damaging testimony against Charles Walsh and other members of the local Democratic club that he had joined. Ayer always referred to the ward organization as a castle of the Sons of Liberty, doing more than any other to present the Camp Douglas conspiracy as the work of the dark lantern society H. H. Dodd had tried to establish. Under the probing of several defense attorneys, however, Ayer also left the witness stand with his reputation tarnished and his veracity questioned. He had to

66. The quoted phrase is borrowed from Starr, *Grenfell's Wars*, 222.
67. *House Executive Documents*, 39th Cong., 2nd Sess., 68, 580–81.
68. *Ibid.*, 90–92.

admit that in times past he had been both liar and imposter and that he expected to get five thousand dollars for his work as detective and witness.[69]

Charles C. Strawn and Peter Alexander, two more of Colonel Sweet's detectives, substantiated many of Ayer's contentions, adding little new to the scrambled testimony. Both always referred to the local Democratic club as a castle of the Sons of Liberty, and both contended that the arms stored at the Walsh home were to be used in the assault on Camp Douglas.

Nineteen other prosecution witnesses took turns on the witness stand. William Walsh admitted that his father had some arms and ammunition stored in the basement and in a bedroom in his house. Obadiah Jackson, the president of the local Democratic club, admitted that some members were anti-Lincoln and antiwar. It was brought out, however, that the average attendance at club meetings varied from twelve to fourteen, and that the detective-members led the way in talking up treason and an insurrection.

Felix G. Stidger, the star witness during the Indianapolis treason trials, took the stand to link Dodd's Sons of Liberty with the Camp Douglas conspiracy. Judge Advocate Burnett also put several prominent midwestern Democrats on the witness stand to connect the Democratic party to treason. Amos Green, a resident of Edgar County, Illinois, had a link to both the Order of American Knights and the Sons of Liberty. Editor Joseph J. Bingham of the Indianapolis *State Sentinel* repeated some of the testimony he had earlier given at the trials of H. H. Dodd and others. Absalom B. Moore, onetime colonel of the 104th Illinois Regiment, was the strangest of the prosecution witnesses. He had surrendered rather disgracefully to Confederate General John H. Morgan at Hartsville, Tennessee. Grenfell had accompanied Morgan as an aide, and now Moore was eager to paint both Grenfell and Morgan as villains. He offered secondhand evidence that Grenfell was a heartless wretch and ruffian, ready to raise the black flag of no mercy, willing to exterminate "the whole Yankee force."[70]

On February 25, after the judge advocate announced that the prosecution was resting its case, the attorneys representing Richard T. Semmes and Vincent Marmaduke put them at the mercy of the court after contending that the evidence linking them to a conspiracy was flimsy, inadequate, and "unworthy." After considering the matter, the nine commissioners acquitted Marmaduke but found Semmes guilty on every count. The court ordered Marmaduke discharged from custody and sentenced Semmes to prison for three years.[71] Then the commission adjourned for eight days, in part to give the defense attorneys a chance to line up a string of witnesses.

69. Ayer, Howard, testimony, March 8–9, 14, 1865, *ibid.*, 196–213, 416–17.
70. Absalom B. Moore, testimony, February 14, 1865, *ibid.*, 269–70.
71. *House Executive Documents*, 39th Cong., 2nd Sess., 272–73.

Democratic newspapers used the recess as a chance to criticize and discredit the summary proceedings and to convince readers that the so-called trial was unconstitutional, phony, and disgracefully partisan. "The trials have turned out to be simply a solemn farce," Wilbur F. Storey stated in the Chicago *Times*, "and the sooner they are brought to a close the more creditable to those who have gotten them up. There never was the slightest danger of an attack upon Camp Douglas. That such an attack was contemplated by a half dozen rebels is probable, but that they could have relied upon any local assistance in the undertaking is wholly improbable." [72] Editor Storey, in this case at least, hit the nail squarely on the head.

Even respected Republicans had doubts about the whole affair and about the propriety of using military commissions to try civilians. Some recognized that the chief witnesses in the case—men like Shanks, Langhorne, and Ayer—offered fallible testimony. Schuyler Colfax, Speaker of the House of Representatives, put his doubts on paper. Writing to Judge Advocate General Joseph Holt, Colfax said he mistrusted the summary proceedings, which relied upon the testimony of individuals "on whose evidence I would not hang a cat." [73]

On the afternoon of February 23, Judge Advocate Burnett reconvened the court. He felt compelled to announce formally what everyone present already knew. Charles T. Daniel had escaped, giving the slip to the guard charged with his custody, and Benjamin Anderson, another of the prisoners, had committed suicide in prison. The prosecution chose to regard both acts as admissions of guilt. [74]

Then it was the turn of the defense lawyers to bring on their witnesses. Charles Walsh's three eldest daughters, pretty and concerned, presented "a deeply affecting scene." The defense attorneys implied in their questioning that the father of such comely and devoted daughters could hardly be guilty of heinous crimes. Letitia, Margaret, and Mary Walsh denied they had ever seen Langhorne before, despite his earlier testimony that he had been at the house to help pack powder and cast bullets. [75]

Several members of the local Democratic club, especially Thomas Edward Courtney, Samuel Remington, and Richard Patten, contradicted some of Ayer's testimony. They explained that their local Democratic club possessed only honorable motives. The Invincible Club had "open" membership and was devoid of secret trappings. It was like a thousand local Democratic and Republican associations organized in the months preceding elections, espe-

72. Chicago *Times*, February 20, 1865.
73. Schuyler Colfax to Holt, January 28, 1865, in Joseph Holt Papers, Library of Congress.
74. *House Executive Documents*, 39th Cong., 2nd Sess., 274.
75. Letitia, Margaret and Mary Walsh, testimony, March 2–3, 1865, *ibid.*, 301–11, 399.

cially presidential contests. It was not a castle of the Order of American Knights or the Sons of Liberty. The arms and ammunition stored in Walsh's home were not intended for subversive purposes but were to be loaned to Democratic poll watchers only if Republicans or Union Leaguers made an attempt to seize the polls and screen the voters. L. A. Doolittle's various statements at club meetings often embarrassed members. He was an erratic young man who liked the sound of his own voice. His statements, if taken out of context, could incriminate those present. Yes, once he had said that, if Republicans overpowered Democrats at the polls by force, fellow members should counter by releasing the Confederate prisoners held within the confines of Camp Douglas. One member of the local Democratic club, disgusted by Doolittle's silly suggestions, had said, "God damn him; I wish he would sit down."[76]

Three residents of the Carlyle, Illinois, area, where Grenfell had spent nearly two months hunting and loafing, contradicted testimony of Shanks and Langhorne. The two detectives had insisted that the English adventurer had gone there to recruit and drill the Copperheads who would assault Camp Douglas and lead the subsequent insurrection. A Texan who had once shared a cell with him in a state penitentiary in Austin identified Colonel Sweet's prize detective as a forger, a felon, and a liar—a rascal whose every word was suspect.[77]

Three prominent Democrats offered testimony intended to vindicate the Sons of Liberty. Clement L. Vallandigham denied that any organization with which he was connected had had anything to do with the Camp Douglas conspiracy or any other traitorous project. Yes, he had headed the Sons of Liberty as supreme commander, but the organization had only political aims—to win elections for the Democratic party, counter the work of the Union Leagues, keep elections free and open, and protect the property and civil rights of Democrats. Yes, he had received a call while in exile in Windsor from Jacob Thompson, the peace emissary who had met with Horace Greeley at Niagara Falls. The two had discussed the possibilities of peace, compromise, and reconstruction. When Thompson had asked Vallandigham about the Sons of Liberty, the latter curtly said he could give no information about the order to one who was not a member. Rebuffed, Thompson turned the conversation to other topics.[78]

Vallandigham's testimony, the editor of the Cincinnati *Enquirer* stated, re-

76. Courtney, Remington, Richard Patten, testimony, March 1, 3, 7, 1865, *ibid.*, 292–301, 319–21, 348–49.
77. J. P. Knapp, John Kendall, James Mullen, Morris S. Davis, testimony, March 8, 13, 29, 1865, all *ibid.*, 355–59, 502–18.
78. Clement L. Vallandigham, testimony, March 29, 1865, *ibid.*, 502–18.

pudiated testimony made by prosecution witnesses and vindicated both him and "the secret order to which he belonged." The Republican Dayton *Daily Journal*, on the other hand, wrote of his testimony: "It seems carefully prepared for effect. Those who read it will be amazed at the atmosphere of outraged innocence which pervades his evidence. His ignorance of the wicked conspiracy, and the bloody objectives of his confederates in the order, of which he confesses himself the Supreme Commander, is astounding, but it is more astonishing that the able and wicked villains who controlled the order, should have consented so long to retain such an ignoramus in command— especially since he confesses, that if he had known they contemplated anything evil, he would have told on them. The tears that will be shed for sorrow over such outraged innocence as his, will be found in an onion." [79]

S. Corning Judd, who headed the Sons of Liberty for a time in Illinois, perhaps because of his respect for Vallandigham, seconded much of what the Ohio curmudgeon had said. Most of the evidence presented by the prosecution, in the main by Colonel Sweet's detectives, was mere conjecture and sheer speculation. The Sons of Liberty, as he understood it, was little more than a mutual protection society with partisan goals. Such a matter as releasing the prisoners held in Camp Douglas, Judd asserted forcefully, "*was never proposed.*" [80]

James A. McMaster, editor of the *Freeman's Journal* in New York, reviewed his brief flirtation with the Order of American Knights and Sons of Liberty. He corroborated what Judd and Vallandigham had said about the dark lantern society, which was supposed to be an auxiliary of the Democratic party. Its objectives, McMaster insisted, were honorable and political.

After the last of the string of witnesses for the defense stepped off the stand on April 6, Judge Advocate Burnett declared a three-day recess to give both sides a chance to review the evidence and prepare the final pleas. When the military commission reconvened, attorney Robert Wilson gave his closing argument in behalf of Charles Walsh. Thomas W. Bartley, counsel for Buckner S. Morris, presented a convincing plea in behalf of his client. Finally, the young and erratic Robert Hervey gave his closing arguments in defense of G. St. Leger Grenfell. He challenged the credibility of John T. Shanks and Maurice Langhorne, who had linked Grenfell to the Chicago conspiracy. Shanks, Hervey contended, had lied when he denied he was a convicted forger. All of his testimony, therefore, should be doubted. The only facts established against Grenfell were that he happened to be in Chicago in late August and early No-

79. Cincinnati *Daily Enquirer*, March 30, 1865; Dayton *Daily Journal*, March 31, 1865.
80. Judd, testimony before the Cincinnati Military Commission, March 31, 1865, published in the Cincinnati *Daily Enquirer*, April 2, 1865. See also S. Corning Judd to Lincoln, March 3, 1865, in John Nicolay–John Hay Papers, Illinois State Historical Library.

vember, on his way to and from a hunting safari in central Illinois. Really, Grenfell's chief crime was that he was an Englishman and had fought in the Confederate army. He was associated with no plot, no conspiracy, and no "overt act."[81]

Judge Advocate Burnett ended the formal session with a lengthy summary of the evidence, selecting those bits of evidence that seemed essential to obtaining a conviction. He felt compelled to defend the reputations of his coterie of detectives, especially Shanks, Langhorne, and Ayer. He praised them as men of ability and courage, motivated by a devotion to duty. He saved his most demeaning and damning remarks for Grenfell, depicting him as an unprincipled villain, adept at deceiving, betraying, and conspiring. He closed with a patriotic plea. The blood of fallen Union soldiers could be redeemed by convicting those who would conspire, divide, and destroy.[82]

On the evening of April 18, the commission held its final session, meeting to announce the verdicts. No sentences would be announced publicly, however, until General Hooker approved them. The commission found Buckner S. Morris and Vincent Marmaduke not guilty on each of the charges and specifications. It found Charles Walsh guilty and sentenced him to a five-year prison term, although seven of the nine commissioners signed a recommendation that he be pardoned. And it declared both G. St. Leger Grenfell and Richard T. Semmes guilty on each charge and specification; the commissioner sentenced Semmes to three years "at hard labor" and Grenfell to be hanged by the neck until dead.

General Hooker promptly approved the verdicts and sentences. Then he ordered Morris released from confinement "upon taking the oath of allegiance." He instructed that Walsh and Semmes be confined in the state penitentiary building in Columbus, Ohio. He approved the death sentence for Grenfell but set no date for the execution. Finally he ordered the military commission adjourned after thanking the members for their service. Hooker then forwarded the trial record and his recommendations to Washington.

The trial ended rather abruptly and inconspicuously in Cincinnati. Of the 150 or more originally arrested in Chicago, only 8 were held over for trial. One of the "Chicago eight," George Cantrell, succumbed to mental illness and so was never really tried. Charles T. Daniel escaped, and Benjamin M. Anderson committed suicide. Morris and Marmaduke were acquitted. Walsh and Semme were found guilty but later pardoned. Only one of the "Chicago eight," an Englishman at that, was sentenced to death.

G. St. Leger Grenfell, however, escaped the hangman's noose. An array of

---

81. Hervey, "Observations upon the Testimony affecting Grenfell."
82. Burnett's summation, in *House Exeuctive Documents*, 39th Cong., 2nd Sess., 594–620.

letters, asking for clemency, reached President Johnson's desk. Colonel Sweet wrote one of the letters in Grenfell's behalf, not wanting the innocent man's blood upon his hands. Even General Hooker had the good sense to realize that there was reason to question whether Grenfell had been involved in the Camp Douglas conspiracy; so he asked for the mitigation of Grenfell's sentence.[83]

Respected citizens, including some Republicans, added their voices to the chorus asking mercy. They pointed out that those declared guilty in Cincinnati were not guilty of the "overt act" that the Constitution deemed essential for conviction of treason. In a sense, they had been found guilty of intent to commit a crime—if, indeed, there had actually been a plot, rather than just a cock-and-bull story. President Johnson, listening to reason, commuted Grenfell's sentence to "imprisonment for life, at hard labor, at the Dry Tortugas, or such other place as the Secretary of War may designate."[84]

All in all, it was a rather strange turn of events. It was also an admission that "the great conspiracy" was based upon flimsy and questionable evidence that no civil court would have found acceptable. S. Corning Judd, a man whom President Lincoln trusted, had correctly characterized the evidence as "*suppositions* and *understandings* and *guesses* and *loose generalities*." The charges and the trial provided a means for Colonel Sweet to get a brigadier's star and Burnett a colonelcy. Grenfell knew he had been railroaded, for Judge Advocate Burnett had "openly announced in court his conviction of our guilt before a single witness had been examined."[85]

Deacon Bross sketched the Camp Douglas conspiracy format, foreseeing its possibility as political propaganda on the eve of an important election. Colonel Sweet and his corps of detectives put flesh on the bones. It was a fantasy passed off as fact, a travesty of justice, a political stratagem made respectable by historians.

83. Holt to "The President" [Andrew Johnson], June 29, 1865, in *OR*, Ser. 2, Vol. VIII, 684–89.

84. George Fries to Johnson, May 13, 1865, in General Courts Martial Records; Johnson, executive order, July 22, 1865, in "General Courts Martial Orders, No. 452," *ibid.*

85. Judd to Lincoln, March 3, 1865, in Nicolay-Hay Papers; Grenfell to Samuel L. M. Barlow, January 13, 1865, in General Courts Martial Records.

CHAPTER VIII

Epilogue: Postwar Potpourri

EACH OF THE principals involved in the founding of a Democratic dark lantern society or tried for treason at Indianapolis or Cincinnati followed a different path during the postwar years. Some enjoyed a measure of worldly success; others drifted into oblivion. One, Lambdin P. Milligan, had his name linked to a famous U.S. Supreme Court case, which a well-known historian characterized as "one of the bulwarks of American civil liberty."[1]

The practice of exposing "treason" and using the revelations as political propaganda took a different tack during the postwar years. "Waving the bloody shirt" proved a most effective technique for twenty years. Furthermore, a considerable amount of the political propaganda about subversive secret societies and wartime conspiracies gained respectability and was written into history textbooks and imprinted upon the American psyche.

Secret Society and Treason Trial Principals After the War

George Bickley, who created the Knights of the Golden Circle and saw

it evolve into a legend, remained in prison for six months after Appomattox symbolized the war's end. Shortly before Lincoln's assassination, federal authorities transferred Bickley from Fort Lafayette to Fort Warren in Boston Harbor. After Lincoln's death some suspected that the Golden Circle was involved in one way or another in the assassination plot. Judge Advocate General Joseph Holt sent a subordinate to interview Bickley in his prison cell and find out if the Knights of the Golden Circle had had a hand in the dastardly deed.[2]

After the war's end, Bickley made another bid to gain his release from prison. First he told supervisory personnel that he was willing to defend himself against any accusations of disloyalty; he claimed that he was totally unaware of any charges filed against him. Failing to get a sympathetic ear, he took up his pen again. He wrote a five-page letter to Secretary of State William H. Seward, reviewing his record as a civilian and a prisoner of state. His letter asked

1. James G. Randall, *The Civil War and Reconstruction* (Boston, 1937), 398.

2. Washington (D.C.) *Evening Star*, n.d., quoted in Dayton *Daily Journal*, April 16, 1865; James R. Gilmore to Joseph Holt, April 22, 1865, in Joseph Holt Papers, Library of Congress.

Seward to review his case and subject it "to such action as its merits justify."[3]

The wheels of justice turned slowly. In mid-July the case reached the desk of Judge Advocate General Holt, head of the Bureau of Military Justice. Holt's assistant reviewed the Bickley case and wrote a comment for his chief. The assistant defended Bickley's arrest and incarceration, characterizing him as vainglorious and dangerous. "As the chief of the treasonable association of the Knights of the Golden Circle, as an officer of the rebel army, as a conspicuously disloyal individual, and as a false, bad man," the aide stated, "he must necessarily have proved, as indeed he had already commenced to be, a most mischievous as well as dangerous character; and to have heretofore granted him an exchange as a prisoner of war, would, it is conceived, have been a mistake and hazardous policy." Since the war was over, however, and the chances of mischief remote, his release seemed desirable. His confinement, however, should not "be terminated" unless he takes an oath of allegiance and a promise of "future loyal behaviour toward the Government."[4]

Delay followed delay. Finally, on October 14, 1865, George Bickley gained his conditional freedom. Before being released, however, he had to sign an oath of loyalty and promise not to prosecute the government for arresting him and keeping him behind bars for twenty-seven months. No specific charges were ever filed against him.[5]

Soon after his release from Fort Warren, Bickley took a trip to England, where he tried to capitalize upon his notoriety and garrulity. Evidently, he expected to give a series of lectures and collect lucrative fees, but there was no magic in his name, and the lecture tour never materialized. Plagued by ill health and shunned by the English, Bickley returned to his native land to drift into oblivion. He died in Baltimore on August 10, 1867, less than two years after his release from Fort Warren. Baltimore newspapers carried no notice of his death, and the Cincinnati papers did little better. The Cincinnati *Gazette*, which had done so much to develop the Golden Circle legend, gave the onetime resident a two-sentence obituary: "G. W. T. [*sic*] Bickley died in Baltimore on Saturday. Bickley flourished in Cincinnati fourteen or fifteen years ago."[6]

Bickley's son made a feeble and futile effort to find out why his father had been arrested and imprisoned during the war. In 1888 Charles S. Bickley wrote to President Grover Cleveland: "Am trying to trace his career for family

3. Maj. Harvey A. Allen, notations and enclosures, May 18, 1865, in George Bickley Papers, George Bickley to William H. Seward, May 18, 1865, both in Reports on the Order of American Knights, Records of the Office of the Judge Advocate General, National Archives.

4. Maj. Addison A. Hosmer to Edwin M. Stanton, July 17, 1865, *ibid.*

5. Stephen V. Benet (acting secretary of war) to Charles S. Bickley, March 15, 1888, in Bickley Papers.

6. Cincinnati *Daily Gazette*, August 16, 1867.

information, and appeal to you, Hon. Sir, as the head of our Goverment [*sic*] and my nation for such facts as you may see fit to lay before me concerning his imprisonment in Columbus, Ohio, Ft. Lafayett [*sic*], N.Y., and Fort Warren, Boston." [7]

President Cleveland passed the letter on to the War Department. William O. Endicott, who headed the department at the time, tabulated the record of Bickley's incarceration without saying why the arrest was made or if any charges had been filed. Angered at the evasion, Charles S. Bickley wrote tartly: "I ask the Department the cause of my father's arrest. It gives me the dates of his imprisonment and transfers. Why, Gents, I have known what you tell me for years. If you do not wish to tell the truth, say so." [8]

Young Bickley's tart letter brought a response from the secretary of war. The elder Bickley, Secretary of War Endicott stated, had been arrested and confined because he had been "the Chief of a treasonable association of the Knights of the Golden Circle, an officer of the rebel army, a conspicuously disloyal person," and "a most mischievous as well as a dangerous character." The secretary added that Bickley had never been tried and that the judge advocate general had finally recommended that he be released upon taking the oath. [9]

Young Bickley had the courtesy to express his appreciation for the information received, despite its critical connotations. "I thank you most kindly for your considerate courtesy," he wrote, "and beg to affirm that with a friendly Administration, the son will never have to endure the humiliation of the father." [10]

Phineas C. Wright had no son who could ask questions about a father's arrest and incarceration during the postwar years. After Wright's arrest in Michigan on April 27, 1864, he was carted off to Fort Lafayette. Failing to receive adequate explanations as to why he was arrested and imprisoned, Wright wrote a letter to President Lincoln. Uncontrite, he demanded justice. "I am not a *criminal*, begging for mercy," he wrote pointedly, "but a *free citizen* demanding *justice*, to know whereof I am accused, and who is my accuser, to be confronted with the witnesses against me, tried by the law, and by it to be convicted or acquitted." [11]

Lincoln never answered the letter, nor did any of his subordinates tell Wright why he had been arrested or when he would be tried. The publication

7. Charles S. Bickley to President Grover Cleveland, January 30, 1888, in Reports on the Order of American Knights.
8. Charles S. Bickley to "Sir" [War Department], n.d., copy, *ibid.*
9. William O. Endicott to Charles S. Bickley, April 17, 1888, *ibid.*
10. Charles S. Bickley to "Sir" [War Department], n.d., copy, *ibid.*
11. Phineas C. Wright to Abraham Lincoln, August 30, 1864, in John A. Marshall, *American Bastile: A History of the Illegal Arrests and Imprisonment of American Citizens During the Late Civil War* (Philadelphia, 1878), 227–28.

of Judge Advocate General Holt's report on secret societies and subversion distressed Wright, for it cast him in the role of scoundrel and traitor. He therefore wrote to Holt asking for a public trial and simple justice.[12] The judge advocate general, however, ignored the plea.

Failing to obtain a hearing through regular channels, Wright tried a ruse. He pretended that he had something very important to say if he had a hearing. "I can tell you that which you never dreamed of," he wrote to a lawyer. He followed with a second letter in which he said, "It is in my power to do much for my country, and it shall be done if I am permitted." This tactic brought results. Judge Advocate General Joseph Holt authorized an interview with Wright in his cell in Fort Lafayette, "with the understanding that the latter [Wright] would make a full confession of his connection with certain treasonable organizations." During the interview, Wright related his role in founding and heading the Order of American Knights. He claimed that the order had honorable objectives and was guilty of no treasonable activities. Disappointed that Wright offered no substantial information, the interviewer asked him to prepare a written statement about himself and the American Knights.[13]

Wright subsequently composed a twelve-page report, which presented the Order of American Knights as a worthy organization glorifying states' rights principles and concerned with preserving civil rights. The organization and Wright himself, the report stated, had been involved in no treasonable activities or conspiracies. Federal authorities, however, refused to accept Wright's statement as "a full disclosure."[14] They let him languish in his cell in Fort Lafayette until March 13, 1865, when he was tranferred to Fort Warren.

After Lincoln's assassination, an interrogator visited Wright to ask if he or his order were involved in any way. The questioner asked the meaning of the statement Wright had made earlier: "I can tell you that which you have never conceived or dreamed of." The statement, Wright admitted, had been only a ruse—"merely a request for an opportunity to explain . . . the true purposes of the Order of American Knights." Wright denied any knowledge of Lincoln's assassination or of the plot to kill the president. Nor did he have any knowledge of treasonable activities in the upper Midwest or elsewhere. The Order of American Knights, he insisted once more, had had worthy objectives and had been unfairly maligned in the exposés and the newspapers.[15]

12. Wright to Holt, October 17, 1864, in Holt Papers.
13. Wright to "Friend [Theodore] Romeyn," November 27, 1864, Wright to Romeyn, February 13, 1865, quoted in Romeyn to Charles A. Dana, March 11, 1865, both *ibid.*; Gen. John A. Dix to Stanton, March 12, 1865, in Lafayette C. Baker–Levi C. Turner Papers, Records of the Adjutant General's Office, Records of the Office of the Judge Advocate General.
14. Wright to Romeyn, statement, March 1, 1865, Dix to Stanton, March 12, 1865, both in Baker-Turner Papers.
15. Maj. John A. Bolles, "Examination of P. C. Wright, Fort Warren, April 27, 1865" (MS in Holt Papers).

Wright remained a prisoner in Fort Warren for nearly four more months. He was finally released "about the first of August, 1865." He returned to St. Louis and drifted back into obscurity. But his filibustering scheme of prewar days gave way to a "settlement project" after the war. It provided in Central America "a place of refuge and an asylum for the multitudes in military service whom the speedy close of the war would through [*sic*] upon this world, with their families destitute and unprovided for." [16]

H. H. Dodd and Clement L. Vallandigham, the two principals associated with the Sons of Liberty, enjoyed more success during the postwar years than Wright or Bickley. Dodd, the chief architect of the Sons of Liberty, surfaced in Hamilton, Canada West, after escaping during the Indianapolis treason trials. One U.S. detective reported that Dodd's hideout in Hamilton was well known and that it was possible to arrest him and bring him back anytime Indiana or federal authorities gave the word. Authorities, however, let him be, for he was more valuable as a fugitive than as a prisoner back in the United States. After the war ended, Dodd transferred his place of residence to Windsor, for a Confederate agent reported: "H. H. Dodd—North end of Frank Smith's Brick House, Three squares east of post office." [17]

In 1869 H. H. Dodd's two brothers-in-law persuaded the exile to return to the United States to head an American Express Company office in Fond du Lac, Wisconsin. The two brothers-in-law, who owned and operated the American Express Company as if it were a personal fief, set him up as an agent in the small city whose population was less than 2,500. [18] His wife and four children came up from Indianapolis to join him.

The onetime fugitive pulled the curtain down on his past and started life anew. In time, he became "one of Fond du Lac's most honored and highly respected residents." In fact, he became the city's number one citizen. He was twice mayor; twice exalted ruler of Lodge No. 57, B.P.O.E.; central figure in the Royal Arcanum, a secret benevolent society, perhaps properly characterized as a mutual life insurance association, that paid the heirs of deceased members a sum of three thousand dollars. He was also commodore of the local yacht club, and newspaper accounts invariably referred to him as Commodore Dodd. The former fugitive even reentered the political arena and attended one or two state conventions of the Democratic party. The editor of the

16. Wright's account, in Marshall, *American Bastile*, 231.
17. S. W. Scott [alias S. Carson] to Col. Adoniram J. Werner, April 22, 1865, in Adoniram J. Werner Papers, William P. Palmer Papers, Western Reserve Historical Society, Cleveland; Thomas H. Hines, memorandum in diary, 1865, in Thomas H. Hines Papers, University of Kentucky Library, Lexington. The Indianapolis *Daily Journal*, November 4, 17, 1864, reported that some Democrats believed that Governor Morton had arranged for Dodd's escape to make it seem as if he were guilty of the charges against him.
18. Julia Dodd, reminiscences, in possession of Mrs. John Gaffin, 371 E. Division Street, Fond du Lac, Wisconsin.

Milwaukee *Sentinel*, proficient at waving the bloody shirt, tried to discredit the Democratic party by reciting events out of Dodd's past, reviewing his role in the Sons of Liberty and the Indianapolis treason trials.[19] But in Fond du Lac, at least, the citizens ignored the smear campaign and took Dodd to their hearts, giving him their respect and adulation.

The Republican attack upon the Democracy as "a onetime party of treason" intensified in 1876, especially after Dodd endorsed Samuel J. Tilden, running for the presidency against Rutherford B. Hayes. Dodd also spoke out against the Republican congressional candidate, a Civil War general named Edward S. Bragg. The Republican press attacked Dodd and the Democrats as mongers of treason during the war.[20] The following year Dodd gained political respectability through a conversion to Republicanism, and that party's newspaper editors buried the hatchet and endorsed his good judgment.[21]

Both of H. H. Dodd's sons became successful and popular businessmen. One of his daughters served for many years as the reference librarian and cataloguer at the Fond du Lac Public Library. Her "Children's Hour" had a countywide reputation.[22]

Commodore Dodd, much in demand as an after-dinner speaker, lived to a ripe old age. He died on June 2, 1906, several months after celebrating his eighty-second birthday. He had headed the city's highly successful American Express agency for thirty-seven years.[23] He left no personal papers that throw any light upon his Civil War years or upon whether he had accepted money from Confederate agents in Canada.

While Dodd rehabilitated his reputation in Fond du Lac, Clement L. Vallandigham sought vindication in Dayton, Ohio. The man who had worn the mantle of supreme commander of the Sons of Liberty for a year continued to believe that his wartime views were correct and that Father Time would make it clear that he had been a prophet. During the Reconstruction era he opposed the Thirteenth, Fourteenth, and Fifteenth amendments, and he sought election to the U.S. Senate as a reward for his "martyrdom" during the war.[24] He was a central figure at the Philadelphia convention of 1866 organized by President

19. Fond du Lac *Daily Reporter*, June 2, 1906; Milwaukee *Sentinel*, September 15, 18, October 27, 1875.

20. Milwaukee *Sentinel*, August 9, 10, 22, September 2, 8, 1876.

21. The sole exception seems to have been the Republican author and editor, Clark S. Matteson, who used the fact that Dodd lived in Wisconsin as an excuse to weave into his book a tangled tale about the Knights of the Golden Circle, the Order of American Knights, the Sons of Liberty, and the Indianapolis treason trials. See Clark S. Matteson, *The History of Wisconsin from Prehistoric to Present Periods* (2 vols.; Milwaukee, 1893), II, 439–55.

22. Julia Dodd, reminiscences.

23. Fond du Lac *Daily Reporter*, June 2, 1906.

24. Clement L. Vallandigham to Horace Greeley, April 20, 1865, in Horace Greeley Papers, New York Public Library; Dayton *Daily Journal*, June 8, 1865; Dayton *Daily Empire*, August 25, 1865.

Johnson's supporters to develop public acceptance of his policies. Some of those attending feared that Vallandigham's presence as a delegate would stigmatize the convention. After a backstage agreement, Vallandigham promised not to attend the formal sessions, although Confederate generals and government officials were welcomed with open arms.[25]

As a delegate to the Democratic national convention of 1868, he worked in the cloakrooms for the nomination of Salmon P. Chase, believing that his candidacy would give the Democracy a chance to regain the White House. Outmaneuvered, his effort to play the role of Warwick came to naught.[26]

Denied the vindication he sought through election to the U.S. Senate, Vallandigham concentrated upon law. He formed a partnership with a former judge, Daniel A. Haynes, and the new team soon proved "one of the best and ablest in the West." During the following several years, the firm was involved in some of the state's most notorious criminal cases. One of these inadvertently led to Vallandigham's death. Using a pistol, which he did not realize was loaded, he was demonstrating to a fellow lawyer how the man whom his client was accused of murdering had really shot himself.[27] The controversial Copperhead was buried on June 20, 1871, never gaining the U.S. Senate seat he wanted so desperately nor the vindication he was so sure that Father Time and Clio would give him.

Unlike Vallandigham, the four principals found guilty in the second of the Indianapolis treason trials achieved a measure of vindication after the war. At the time of Lincoln's death, Andrew Humphreys was confined to two townships of Greene County, Indiana, under the restrictions of his parole. The other three, Lambdin P. Milligan, Stephen Horsey, and William A. Bowles, were confined to dreary rooms in the Soldiers' Home prison, under sentence of death. Hopes for commutation of the sentence ebbed when Andrew Johnson replaced Lincoln in the White House. Nevertheless, a flood of petitions poured into Washington. Most were sponsored by friends of the convicted men or by important members of the Democratic party. Some of the petitions, though, were pleas for vengeance. Some endorsed "death to the traitors." One vindictive citizen wrote: "Hang them! and if necessary raise the gallows more than 500 cubits high! Let the people know—let all the world know—that *Treason* is a crime, the deepest, darkest, and most damnable crime in the

25. Philadelphia *Enquirer*, August 16, 1866; Dayton *Daily Empire*, August 15–20, 1866. Thomas Wagstaff, "The Arm-in-Arm Convention," *Civil War History*, XIV (1968), 101–19, treats the convention in scholarly fashion.

26. William W. Armstrong, "Personal Recollections," in Cincinnati *Daily Enquirer*, March 20, 1886.

27. Dayton *Evening Herald*, December 30, 1869, June 19, 1871; Dayton *Daily Journal*, June 17, 1871.

whole catalogue of crime. Hang them and we and our children will bless your name and revere your memory for ever and ever."[28]

Milligan personally appealed to Secretary of War Stanton, asking him to intercede. His acquaintance with Stanton dated back to 1836, when both were members of a class of nine being examined by a committee of the state supreme court as to their qualifications to the bar. Milligan, ironically, made the best impression of the nine and received the top rating in the class. Mrs. Milligan even visited the War Department to remind Stanton that he and her husband were longtime acquaintances, but she received rather uncivil treatment.[29]

The hopes of the three condemned men shrank in early May when Major Henry L. Burnett instructed a subordinate to put the prisoners "in irons." A jailer subsequently fastened a heavy iron contrivance around one of each man's ankles. Lock, ball, and chain together weighed approximately forty pounds. On May 8 President Johnson, seemingly bent on pursuing a vindictive policy toward Rebels and Copperheads, approved the death sentences of Milligan, Horsey, and Bowles. The War Department, with Stanton involved in the decision making, promptly instructed General Hovey, who had charge of the prisoners, to carry out the executions "without delay" and set May 19 as the date of the hangings.[30]

Milligan, through his lawyer, had filed a petition for a writ of habeas corpus on May 10 in the U.S. Circuit Court for the District of Indiana; he claimed that the military commission had had no right to try a citizen in an area where the civil courts were open. Judge David Davis, sitting in the circuit court, promptly conferred with Governor Morton. Apparently, he was able to convince Morton that the prisoners had been tried illegally and to persuade the governor to make an appeal for commutation to President Johnson. Judge Davis also wrote a forceful letter to the president, asking him to stay the execution until the civil courts passed upon the case. "The Court which pronounced the sentence," Judge Davis stated, "is a new tribunal unknown to the common law. . . . Would it not be wiser to defer the execution of these men until the Supreme Court of the United States passed on the question of the jurisdiction of the court that tried them?"[31]

28. W. H. Fogg to Johnson, May 23, 1865, in General Courts Martial Records.

29. Lambdin P. Milligan to Stanton, December 28, 1864, in General Courts Martial Records, Records of the Office of the Judge Advocate General.

30. Henry L. Burnett to Alvin P. Hovey, May 1, 1865, in *The War of the Rebellion: A Compilation of the Official Records of the Union and Confederate Armies* (128 vols.; Washington, D.C., 1880–1901), Ser. 2, Vol. VIII, 523, hereinafter cited as *OR*; Alvin P. Hovey, "General Orders, No. 27, District of Indiana," May 19, 1865, *ibid.*, 548–49.

31. Marshall, *American Bastile*, 79; Judges David Davis and David McDonald to Andrew Johnson, May 11, 1865, in General Courts Martial Records.

Governor Morton, caught up in the general reaction against the death penalty for the three condemned men and not wishing to have their blood upon his hands, also wrote to President Johnson. The Indianapolis *Journal*, owned and edited by Morton's brother-in-law, reversed its endorsement of execution and asked for postponement of the sentence until the case could be tested in the federal courts.[32]

Milligan, meanwhile, spent time visiting with his twelve-year-old grandson and preparing his own case for the civil courts. Then, as May 19 approached and hopes for a stay of execution evaporated, he made arrangements for his own funeral and wrote out an address, which he expected to deliver before the noose was set in place. Milligan's fellow prisoners, Bowles and Horsey, sat haplessly and hopelessly, evidently resigned to their fate.

President Johnson decided to bow to the pressure for commutation exerted by Judge Davis, Governor Morton, and a host of others. Furthermore, a number of important people began to question the practice of substituting military trials for civil ones in areas where the courts were open. The previous March, during the closing days of the session of Congress, both houses had passed by large margins resolutions challenging the trial of civilians by military tribunals. "No person shall be tried by a military commission," one of the resolutions read, "in any State or Territory where the courts of the United States are open."[33]

Three days before the scheduled execution, President Johnson commuted the sentence of Andrew Humphreys and postponed the fateful day for Milligan, Horsey, and Bowles to June 2.[34] Attorneys for the convicted Copperheads, meanwhile, had appealed to the federal judges sitting in the Indiana district of the circuit court to assume jurisdiction to discharge the prisoners. Counsel for the prisoners filed petitions for their release under terms of a congressional act, passed in 1863, which had provided that civilians arrested by military authorities should be released if they were not indicted by a grand jury. A federal grand jury had met in Indianapolis shortly after the arrest of Milligan and others but had brought forth no indictment. The two judges hearing the petitions in the Indiana district, David Davis and Thomas Drummond, disagreed in order that the case could be certified to the U.S. Supreme Court *in banco*. After the petition for release was filed, a hurriedly convened grand jury met and indicted Milligan, Horsey, Bowles, and Humphreys, charging

32. Oliver P. Morton to Johnson, telegram, May 12, 1865, in Telegram Dispatch Books, Oliver P. Morton, 1861–1865, Archives Division, Indiana State Library, Indianapolis; Silas F. Miller to Morton, May 15, 1865, in Miscellaneous Letter File, Indiana Historical Society Library, Indianapolis; Indianapolis *Daily Journal*, May 13, 14, 1865.

33. *Congressional Globe*, 38th Cong., 2nd Sess., 1323–30.

34. Johnson to Hovey, May 16, 1865, in *OR*, Ser. 2, Vol. VIII, 587.

them and other members of the Sons of Liberty with conspiracy—this in June, 1865. While the case moved to the Supreme Court, officials kept the indictments alive.

On May 30, two days before the scheduled date of execution, President Johnson commuted the sentences of Milligan, Bowles, and Horsey to life imprisonment. Secretary of War Stanton relayed Johnson's decision to General Hovey: "The President orders that the sentence of death heretofore passed against Horsey, Bowles, and Milligan, be commuted to imprisonment of each at hard labor, in the Penitentiary [Columbus], duration his life." Stanton's instructions, marked "Strictly confidential," ended with a rather sadistic request; he asked Hovey to keep the order secret "until the day of execution arrives."[35] Perhaps Stanton secured some special satisfaction in letting the three condemned men believe until the last moment that they would be hanged.

While the three condemned men bided time in their cells in Columbus, some Republicans tried to bargain with the prisoners, promising a presidential pardon if Milligan would withdraw his suit from the U.S. Supreme Court. These go-betweens evidently feared a decision that might be damaging to their party. Milligan, still as defiant and self-righteous as ever, insisted that he had no reason to seek a pardon since he had been guilty of no crime. Bowles, ill and more pliant, asked his attorney to petition for the dismissal of his case, but the attorney ignored the instructions.[36]

At length the case came up for argument before the U.S. Supreme Court, both sides having added counsel. Jeremiah S. Black, Joseph E. McDonald, and David Dudley Field represented Milligan; U.S. Attorney General James Speed, Henry Stanbery, and Benjamin F. Butler represented the government. Black argued eloquently and eruditely that the trial of civilians by a military commission in an area where the civil courts were open was unhistorical, unconstitutional, and contrary to democratic precepts. In due time, on April 3, 1866, the Court handed down its decision in *Ex Parte Milligan*, rejecting the government's plea of necessity and, in effect, repudiating Governor Morton's use of a military commission to achieve political ends. Reprimanding those who had utilized military commissions where the civil courts were open, the Supreme Court said: "A citizen, not connected with the military service, and resident in a State where the courts are all open, and in the proper exercise of their jurisdiction, cannot, even when the privilege of habeas corpus is suspended, be tried, convicted or sentenced otherwise than by the ordinary courts of law." Judge David Davis, who wrote the decision for the Court, added:

35. Johnson to Stanton, May 30, 1865, Stanton to Hovey, coded telegram, May 30, 1865, both in *OR*, Ser. 2, Vol. VIII, 637, 583–84.
36. Milligan's account, in Marshall, *American Bastile*, 82–83.

"The Constitution of the United States is a law for rulers and people, equally in war and peace, and covers with the shield of protection all classes of men, at all times and under all circumstances. No doctrine involving more pernicious consequences was ever invented by the wit of man than that any of its great provisions can be suspended during any of the great exigencies of Government." [37]

After laying down the constitutional guidelines, the Court ordered that Milligan, Bowles, and Horsey "be discharged from custody." Milligan's lawyers promptly asked President Johnson to discharge the prisoners, pointing out that indictments were "pending against them in one of the United States Courts in Indianapolis." [38] The indictments, however, were later dropped and the three men were never tried in the civil courts.

Somewhat tardily, the War Department ordered the discharge of the three prisoners. The warden of the Ohio State Penitentiary opened the cell doors on the afternoon of April 12, 1866, and Milligan, Bowles, and Horsey walked out as free men. [39] After eighteen months behind bars, the three departed for their respective homes, still viewing themselves as the victims of a malignant political persecution and malevolent arbitrary action. Sometime later, federal officials released Andrew Humphreys from the boundary restrictions that had been imposed upon him. The four were then free to seek solace or vindication, each in his own way.

Humphreys was the first to turn to the civil courts for a measure of revenge against those who had arrested him. On February 1, 1866, he filed a complaint in the circuit court of Sullivan County, seeking damages from Samuel McCormick, captain of the army unit that had arrested him, and ten others for "assault and battery and false imprisonment." The presiding judge, Delana R. Eckles, had been a wartime Copperhead, serving as the first grand commander of the Order of American Knights in Indiana in 1863. Moreover, Sullivan County was a Democratic stronghold. Humphreys had every reason to expect a favorable verdict as well as his own pound of flesh in such a place before such a judge. The jury, as Humphreys anticipated, found McCormick *et al.* guilty of the charges and awarded the plaintiff $25,000 in damages.

McCormick and his fellow defendants refused to accept the decision and their counsel took steps to have the case transferred from the state to the federal courts. The judge of the state circuit court, also a former Copperhead, overruled the transfer motion. The defendants then made an effort to appeal

37. *Ex Parte Milligan*, 71 U.S. (4 Wallace), 431–32.
38. Thomas A. Hendricks and William E. Niblack to Johnson, April 11, 1866, in General Courts Martial Records.
39. Edward E. Townsend to "Warden of the Ohio State Penitentiary," order, April 10, 1866, John A. Prentice [warden], report, April 12, 1866, both *ibid.*

their case to the state supreme court, but that body avoided a decision and the case bogged down on legal technicalities. In the end, Humphreys failed to collect any of the damages the state circuit court had awarded him. His victory was only a partial one—one of spirit rather than specie.[40]

Republicans, in control of the Indiana state legislature, took prompt steps to close the door to damage claims and retaliatory measures of Democrats who had been arbitrarily arrested. In March, 1867, the legislature passed an act that offered indemnity or protection to state or federal officials when they were defendants in suits brought against them. The act provided that the state would furnish free counsel, and it limited awards for damages (excluding costs) to five dollars, especially if the plaintiff were associated with "any society or organization . . . in sympathy with the rebellion."[41]

Congress also closed the doors to Democrats or others seeking vindication and damages for arbitrary arrests and wrongful imprisonment. In 1866 it amended the Indemnity Act of March 3, 1863, by forbidding the hearing of such cases in state courts, while providing that damages and double costs could be levied against state judges accepting such cases in defiance of the federal law. In effect, the state and federal indemnity acts protected the federal officials responsible for the arbitrary arrests from the consequences of their actions. The new law, perhaps wittingly, endorsed "the doctrine of necessity" and slammed the door against those who had been arbitrarily arrested during the war and hoped that the civil courts might provide vindication and damages in the postwar years.

With the door to legal recourse closed, Humphreys sought a veneer of vindication in the arena of politics. In 1868 he tried for a seat in the upper house of the state legislature but lost by a narrow margin to a Republican rival. Six years later, in 1874, he ran for the state senate, again as a Democratic candidate, and defeated a Republican opponent. Two years later, he resigned to run for a congressional seat, won the election, and served in the 44th Congress from December 5, 1876, to March 3, 1877. In 1878 he again won election to the state senate, taking over the chairmanship of the Ways and Means Committee during the following session of the state legislature. He retired to his farm at the end of the session but attended nearly every Democratic state convention in the years that followed. In 1896 his party drafted him to run for the state senate again, although the seventy-four-year-old former Copperhead was most reluctant to make the race. His victory never fully erased the stigma of treason fastened to his name in the Indianapolis treason trials. He lived to the

40. Indianapolis *Daily Journal*, February 19, 1867, newspaper clipping in the Werner Papers.

41. *Indiana House Journal*, 1867, Vol. II, pp. 684, 834, 1044, 1077; William H. H. Terrell, *Report of the Adjutant General of Indiana* (8 vols.; Indianapolis, 1869), I, appendix, 267–68.

age of eighty-three, dying at his home in Linton on June 24, 1904, nearly forty years after his arrest for involvement in a "conspiracy."[42]

Unlike Humphreys, neither William A. Bowles nor Stephen Horsey succeeded in vindicating himself or gaining any measure of revenge. Bowles's health deteriorated after his release from prison, and he became an irritable, dour, and surly fellow. His wife sued him for divorce in 1868, charging him with battery and mistreatment. The seventy-two-year-old doctor countered with a suit charging his wife with adultery. The jury that heard the case decided in Mrs. Bowles's favor and awarded her $25,000 in alimony. Stubborn and defiant, Bowles refused to pay and the haggling continued until Mrs. Bowles's death when a boiler exploded on a river steamer on which she was a passenger. Confined to his home because of ill health, Bowles hung onto life until March 28, 1873. History remembers him more for his role in the Indianapolis treason trial than for establishing a health resort at French Lick Springs.[43]

Stephen Horsey's last years were as tragic as those of Bowles. The summary treatment accorded him and the threat of hanging broke his spirit. Indebtedness and lawyers' fees hung over his head and consumed his meager savings. Convinced that he had been wronged by political enemies and perjurers, he retreated from society and sought solace in solitude. For a time he worked in a wagon-making establishment until infirmities impaired his usefulness. Then he retired to the hills in Martin County, operated a brandy-making still, grew a full beard, and became known as "the wild man of the woods." In time, relatives consigned him to a "poor farm," where he lived out his last days, forgotten and quite forlorn.[44]

Lambdin P. Milligan, unlike Horsey and Bowles, built up a fortune and secured some revenge in the courts. After his release from his cell in the state penitentiary in Columbus on the afternoon of April 12, 1866, Milligan walked over to the Neil House to await the departure of the next day's train to Huntington. That night a host of friends, all Democrats, gathered at the hotel to celebrate his release, excoriate all Republicans, and review the wrongs perpetrated by Governor Morton and President Lincoln. Milligan took the lead in denouncing Morton and his use of a military commission to achieve political ends. He also criticized Judge David Davis for taking six months to write a one-hundred-page decision. It had meant a longer stay in a prison cell. Milligan claimed that Justice Stephen J. Field confided to him that the justices had

---

42. *Biographical Memoirs of Greene County, Indiana* (3 vols.; Indianapolis, 1908), I, 693–95.

43. Indianapolis *Daily Journal*, April 2, 1873; (Paoli, Ind.) *American Eagle*, April 26, 1868.

44. Most of the information in this paragraph is gleaned from Gilbert R. Tredway, "Indiana Against the Administration, 1861–1865" (Ph.D. dissertation, Indiana University, 1962), 377–78.

reached their decision in October, 1865, six months before the Court rendered its decision.[45]

When Milligan reached Huntington, he found that the Democratic mayor and his old cronies had arranged a gala homecoming. Cannons boomed as a mob welcomed home "the hero and martyr." Emotional speeches followed the impressive parade. In his brief reply, Milligan forthrightly denied that he was guilty of any wrongdoing, either to his country or to his fellowmen.[46]

In his next public appearance, Milligan was as self-righteous and defiant as ever. He laid the verbal lash upon those whom he held accountable for his arrest and incarceration. He gave Morton more than a fair share of the abuse. As for Lincoln, Milligan said he had been "summoned to the bar of retributive justice with his sins unrepented."[47]

Milligan, like Humphreys, also turned to the courts to seek personal revenge. On March 13, 1868, he filed suit in the Huntington County court against James R. Slack, a Huntington resident and Republican attorney who had urged the arrest of Milligan; Governor Morton; General Hovey; and twenty others whom he implicated in his arrest and imprisonment, including the twelve members of the military commission that had found him guilty and sentenced him to death. Milligan asked for damages totaling a half million dollars.

The case, *Milligan* v. *Slack et al.*, dragged on for three years without a hearing, while attorneys for the defense used delaying tactics. At the request of Governor Morton, the War Department searched its files for evidence and correspondence that would implicate Milligan in some conspirational scheme. It found none.

The case finally evolved into *Milligan* v. *Hovey*, as Slack's name and a dozen others were dropped from the original suit. It went to trial in May of 1871 in the federal circuit court in Indianapolis. Thomas J. Hendricks, much abused during the war years for his Copperhead views, served as chief counsel for the plaintiff. Hendricks, anxious to vindicate the Democratic party of the disloyalty charges, condemned Governor Morton for his arbitrary practices. He handled Morton and his coterie roughly and discredited Brigadier General Henry B. Carrington, as well as the detectives who served as witnesses at the Indianapolis trial. Furthermore, under oath, Milligan testified that he had never belonged to the Sons of Liberty, much less functioned as one of the order's major generals. Defense attorneys failed to make him change his contentions.

45. Huntington (Ind.) *Herald*, December 15, 1899.
46. Huntington (Ind.) *Democrat*, n.d., quoted in Marshall, *American Bastile*, 87–91.
47. Huntington *Democrat*, May 26, 1866, quoted in Tredway, "Indiana Against the Administration," 373.

A sympathetic jury found for Milligan, awarding him five dollars in damages—the maximum allowed by state law—and costs, estimated at one thousand to twelve hundred dollars. One juror, despite explicit instructions from the presiding judge and the well-known intent of the state law, held out for an award of twenty-five thousand dollars until he finally bowed to the reasoning of the majority.[48]

Disciples of Governor Morton tried to discredit the verdict. Turning to sarcasm, they said that five dollars was more than Milligan's life was worth. The Indianapolis *Journal*, edited by Morton's brother-in-law, said that the case had been brought by a "scoundrel" anxious to "filch money from the pockets of brave men who had justly condemned him to death."[49]

Milligan's friends, on the other hand, lauded the verdict, recognizing that the five-dollar-award limitation had been set by a Republican-controlled state legislature. They regarded the verdict as another vindication of Milligan, a rebuke to Morton, and a repudiation of summary treatment of civilians. The state's leading Democratic newspaper, the Indianapolis *State Sentinel*, pointed out that the court had reached a pro-Milligan decision despite the fact that the presiding judge, Thomas Drummond, was a Republican, as were all of the court officials and ten of the twelve jurymen. Furthermore, federal officials had thrown the full weight of the government on the side of the defendants.[50]

Milligan next made an effort to overturn the congressional act that decreed that such cases as his must be tried in federal rather than state courts. He tried to appeal his case through the court of common pleas to the state supreme court, hoping that this body would declare the congressional act unconstitutional. His case, however, "was barred by the statute of limitations," and the Huntington curmudgeon failed to get a test of the constitutional question.[51]

Milligan, meanwhile, recovered his health, rebuilt his law practice, and regained respectability in the Huntington community. He remained as outspoken, as independent, and as intrepid as he had always been. To his dying day, he believed that he had been wronged by vengeful and conniving men. He died on December 21, 1899, at the age of eighty-seven. Even Huntington's Republican newspaper, which had slandered and bedeviled him during the war years, spoke well of him at the end. "He was," the repentant editor wrote, "a good citizen, a kind neighbor, and an honorable and upright business man. He was an able and conscientious lawyer, and his record at the Huntington bar was of great credit. He did much for Huntington and Hunting-

48. Indianapolis *Daily Journal*, May 31, 1871; Samuel Klaus (ed.), *The Milligan Case*, American Trials Series (New York, 1929), 40–45.
49. Indianapolis *Daily Journal*, May 31, June 1, 1871.
50. Indianapolis *Daily State Sentinel*, May 31, June 1, 1871.
51. Jonathan W. Gordon to Holt, report, July 1, 1869, in General Courts Martial Records.

ton County, and the community sorrows at the death of a man whose heart was devoted to its interests."[52]

George St. Leger Grenfell, the only one sentenced to death by the Cincinnati military commission, had no chance to redeem himself or clear his name. Even after his trial and conviction, he continued to deny that he had been involved in any plot or conspiracy. Such a scheme as the burning of Chicago, he wrote to a former congressman from Virginia, was "abhorrent" to an English gentleman. He tried to interest former acquaintances in his case. "I can only say," he wrote to a southerner at whose home he had once been a guest, "that I was accused and convicted of having conspired with six other individuals, five of whom I had never seen or heard of in my life, the sixth [Benjamin Anderson] was formerly in Morgan's Command but left it in Sept. '62, since which time I never heard from him or of him."[53]

Grenfell escaped the hangman's noose because Judge Advocate General Holt and a host of others interceded, asking President Johnson to commute the sentence. Colonel Benjamin J. Sweet, who had filled in the Camp Douglas conspiracy format, asked the president to remit the death penalty. It is possible that he did not want innocent blood, even of an Englishman, upon his hands. Even Archbishop John B. Purcell wrote in behalf of the redoubtable prisoner: "He is hardly guilty of the crime alleged against him, being an enthusiast of the Don Quixote style and all his life a reckless unthinking adventurer. Now that all the others engaged in the foolish work at Chicago are, in one way or another, out of jail, it seems to be this poor fellow's turn to be set at liberty. He can do no harm, and clemency to him, under such circumstances, will be punishment and mercy combined."[54]

President Johnson, acquiescing in the recommendations of subordinates, changed Grenfell's sentence to "imprisonment for life."[55] Secretary of War Stanton, in turn, assigned the English soldier of fortune to spend the rest of his life at Fort Jefferson and the U.S. military prison on Garden Key, largest of the chain making up the Dry Tortugas. By sending him there, Stanton effectively placed him beyond the pale of the civil courts.

Life on Garden Key became nigh intolerable for Grenfell. The blazing sun and summer heat seared his spirit. The thirty-pound ball-and-chain welded to

52. Huntington *Herald*, December 22, 1899.
53. Grenfell to John Minor Botts, May 19, 1865, in General Courts Martial Records.
54. Holt to President Johnson, June 29, 1865, in *OR*, Ser. 2, Vol. VIII, 684–89; John M. Botts to Holt, June 17, 1865, in Holt Papers. Archbishop Purcell to William Dennison [then Postmaster General], July 4, 1865, Col. Benjamin J. Sweet to Johnson, June 27, 1865, both in Letters Received by the Adjutant General's Office, 1861–1870, National Archives.
55. President Johnson, executive order, July 22, 1865, published as "General Court Martial Orders, No. 452," in General Courts Martial Records.

a leg manacle restrained his movements and served as a constant reminder that he was "a convicted felon." The daily fare evolved into "loathsome food."[56] Grenfell's petition for clemency fell upon deaf ears.

The U.S. Supreme Court's decision in *Ex Parte Milligan* cast the cloak of illegality over the military proceedings in Cincinnati as well as those in Indianapolis and gave Grenfell a ray of hope. Then, Samuel L. M. Barlow, an influential and respected Democrat, interested himself in Grenfell's case. Barlow wrote to President Johnson in Grenfell's behalf, concluding, "I am convinced of his innocence." Barlow also pointed out that Grenfell's conduct during his confinement had been exemplary and that his volunteer work during the yellow fever epidemic at Fort Jefferson had prompted officers at "that God-forsaken prison" to petition for his discharge.[57]

Grenfell wrote a long letter protesting his innocence to Barlow, giving him ammunition for his case. The imprisoned Englishman again denied any involvement in the plot to free Confederate prisoners held in Camp Douglas and to burn the city of Chicago. "My conscience is as white as snow of any knowledge whatever of the conspiracy," he wrote to Barlow. "As he [God] is my judge, I am innocent of the charges made against me." But neither President Johnson nor Judge Advocate General Holt seemed to have any sympathy for the adventurer spending his declining years at a prison off the Florida keys.[58]

In March, 1868, Grenfell and several other prisoners made an attempt to escape. Carrying their balls-and-chains, they commandeered a small boat on a stormy night and disappeared into the darkness. The boat must have foundered in the turbulent waters, for the would-be escapees were never heard from again. George St. Leger Grenfell, the only man sentenced to death in the Camp Douglas conspiracy, escaped the hangman's noose and the blazing sun on Garden Key but gave his life to the shark-infested waters off the coast of Florida.

The Evolution of Subversive Society and Conspiracy Myths

The anti-Copperhead crusade and the wartime exposés, important as political propaganda, had their counterpart in the postwar practice of "waving the bloody shirt." Both techniques were cut from the same political cloth—ap-

56. Dr. Samuel A. Mudd to "My dear Jere" (brother), November 11, 1865, published in Nettie Mudd (ed.), *The Life of Dr. Samuel A. Mudd* (Saginaw, Mich., 1962), 141. Grenfell's days at Fort Jefferson are superbly chronicled in Stephen Z. Starr, *Colonel Grenfell's Wars: The Life of a Soldier of Fortune* (Baton Rouge, 1971), 267–326.

57. Samuel L. M. Barlow to Johnson, January 2, 1868, in General Courts Martial Records.

58. George St. Leger Grenfell to Barlow, January 13, 1868, *ibid.*; Grenfell to Marie Pearce-Seracold [daughter], February 26, 1868, in Mabel Clare Weaks (ed.), "Colonel George St. Leger Grenfell," *Filson Club Historical Quarterly* XXXIV (1960), 19–20.

pealing to the emotions—and were utilized on the eve of important elections.

The bloody-shirt era, little more than an extension of the "loyalty crusade" of the war years, lasted into the 1880s and helped Republicans maintain a twenty-year monopoly of the presidency. Democratic candidates of the 1870s and even the 1880s were linked to Copperheadism and the so-called subversive societies that had made headlines during the war. When Thomas A. Hendricks, governor of Indiana and a prominent Copperhead during the Civil War, ran as Samuel J. Tilden's vice-presidential partner in 1876, the ghosts of the past haunted him. One renegade, who claimed that he had belonged to the Knights of the Golden Circle during the war, produced a letter stating that Hendricks had been a major general of that subversive society.[59]

The practice of linking Democrats to wartime "treason" gained headlines when Grover Cleveland sought to break the Republican stranglehold upon the presidency in 1884. Some referred to the Democracy as the party of "Rum, Romanism, and Rebellion" and to Cleveland as a wartime Copperhead. The issue clouded the confirmation of Melville W. Fuller as chief justice of the U.S. Supreme Court in 1888.

In the same year, John W. Ingalls, a U.S. senator from Kansas, attacked Daniel W. Voorhees of Indiana for having been a Copperhead and traitor during the war. Voorhees reacted emotionally, too, calling Ingalls "a great liar and dirty dog." The editor of the New York *Times* labeled the Ingalls-Voorhees feud "fatal nonsense" and reprimanded Ingalls for using the bloody-shirt stratagem. The editor called the practice outdated, unfair, and irresponsible. "It is well enough in political warfare to rake over the past for all the weapons that can be fairly used," the New York editor wrote, "but it is also to be remembered that it is the past and that the issues on which the next election is to be decided are not those of a quarter century ago."[60]

While Republicans were waving the bloody shirt during the postwar era, they also set to work with their pens to write their contentions into history. Horace Greeley, Whitelaw Reid, and Berry R. Sulgrove exemplified wartime Republican editors who turned into authors of "history" books, which devoted space to the so-called subversive societies and conspiracies of the war years.

Greeley, whose New York *Tribune* had given widespread publicity to the wartime "conspiracies" and exposés, repeated most of his wartime allegations about the secret societies in a two-volume work entitled *The American Conflict*. He accused the Knights of the Golden Circle of leading Texas down the road to secession, exerting pressure upon Kentucky to join the Confederacy, and spreading antiwar sentiment in the upper Midwest. Greeley also ex-

59. Baltimore *Sun*, August 11, 1876.
60. New York *Times*, May 2, 1888.

pressed his scorn for Clement L. Vallandigham and Lambdin P. Milligan. He believed both to be guilty of sympathy for the rebels, devoid of patriotism and good sense, and involved in one way or another in dark lantern societies and treasonable plots.[61]

Whitelaw Reid followed in Greeley's footsteps. Characterized as "a passionate Union man" while editing the Cincinnati *Gazette* and serving a tour as a war correspondent and a Washington-based librarian and clerk, Reid wrote his views into the record in a two-volume work, *Ohio in the War*. No northern editor had exhibited less tolerance of Democrats during the war. He had helped to fasten the smear term *Copperhead* upon Democratic critics of the Lincoln administration, had linked them to treason, and had given space to exposés of the Golden Circle and the so-called conspiracies. He carried his political bias over into his book, fastening myths about the Golden Circle and the conspiracies into his history.[62]

Berry R. Sulgrove bent Indiana's wartime history in the same direction as Reid and Greeley had. He had edited the Indianapolis *Journal* during most of the war, publishing the exposés of the Knights of the Golden Circle, Order of American Knights, and Sons of Liberty. In his oft-quoted book, *History of Indianapolis and Marion County*, Sulgrove repeated many of the allegations he had made during the war. He claimed, for example, that members of the Golden Circle were most numerous in Indiana, that Democratic traitors had sought to establish a northwestern confederacy, and that the treason trials at Indianapolis had properly convicted conspiracy-minded men.[63]

Sulgrove had the help of four other Hoosiers in weaving partisan contentions into the fabric of history. Benn Pitman, shorthand reporter at the trial of the "conspirators" at Indianapolis, edited the proceedings in a widely circulated book entitled *The Trials of Treason at Indianapolis*. Pitman, blatantly partisan, even falsified the transcript at times and misrepresented testimony in order to put the prosecution in a good light. He sometimes deleted statements and sentences in the name of economy and space saving, giving readers wrong impressions and false information. He eliminated Judge Advocate Henry L. Burnett's intemperate remarks, prejudicial statements, and abuse of defense witnesses to mask the partisan conduct of the trials and to bolster the case against the accused.[64]

61. Horace Greeley, *The American Conflict: A History of the Great Rebellion in the United States of America, 1860–1865* (2 vols.; Hartford, Conn., 1867), I, 350, 492–93, II, 18–19, 556–58.

62. Whitelaw Reid, *Ohio in the War* (2 vols.; Cincinnati, 1868), *passim*.

63. Berry R. Sulgrove, *History of Indianapolis and Marion County* (Philadelphia, 1886), *passim*.

64. Benn Pitman (ed.), *The Trials for Treason at Indianapolis, Disclosing the Plans for Establishing a North-western Confederacy: Being the Official Record of the Trials Before the Mili-*

William H. H. Terrell, Pitman's compatriot, also had a hand in coloring Indiana's history. As adjutant general of his state and as Governor Morton's loyal servant, Terrell had the chance to attach the stigma of treason to the Democracy. Soon after the war, he compiled an eight-volume work, *Report of the Adjutant General of Indiana*. He incorporated a generous measure of partisan propaganda into the record. By mixing statistics, reports, facts, and suppositions in an interesting proportion, he passed on to posterity slanted documentary material that would be cited by historians for more than a century. He portrayed Governor Morton as patriotism personified and his critics as treason-minded men. He even expunged the references to Colonel Henry B. Carrington's arrest for "drunkenness and inefficiency" from General Hascall's report, displaying loyalty to a friend while falsifying the record.[65] Since Terrell's eight-volume report was published at state expense, the taxpayers, some of whom had been wartime Copperheads, subsidized a distorted version of Civil War history.

Felix G. Stidger, perhaps more a transient than a Hoosier, also helped to discredit the Sons of Liberty and some Democrats later in life. Styling himself "the spy complete" and "the star witness at Indianapolis," Stidger told an engaging story entitled *Treason History of the Order of the Sons of Liberty*. Stidger relied heavily upon his fanciful memory, Terrell's and Pitman's works, Holt's famous report, and Carrington's exposé of the Sons of Liberty to give shape to his account. Dodd and Milligan emerged as villains; Governor Morton and super-spy Stidger, as the heroes.[66] The book sold like the proverbial hotcakes and became a source for the writing of Civil War history.

William D. Foulke, a devotee of Governor Morton, put the frosting on the partisan cake. Foulke wrote the "official" biography of Governor Morton, depicting him as the Sir Galahad of his day and his Copperhead critics as the Sir Modreds. Foulke, a lawyer turned biographer, designed traitor's cloaks for Dodd and Milligan, justified Morton's one-man rule in Indiana, and incorporated much myth about the supposedly subversive societies into his blend of biography, history, and conjecture. Foulke's account, which a later historian characterized as "overly laudatory and not well documented," gave respectability to some of the subversive society legends, transformed a small inci-

---

tary Commission Convened by Special Orders No. 129, Headquarters, District of Indiana (Cincinnati, 1865). Ironically, Pitman termed his book "the official record of the trials." For a comparison of Pitman's version to the original transcript, see Tredway, "Indiana Against the Administration," and the revised and moderated book that resulted, *Democratic Opposition to the Lincoln Administration in Indiana* (Indianapolis, 1973).

65. Terrell, *Report of the Adjutant General of Indiana*, I, 278–93.

66. *Treason History of the Order of the Sons of Liberty, Formerly Circle of Honor, Succeeded by the Knights of the Golden Circle, Afterwards Order of American Knights: The Most Gigantic Treasonable Conspiracy the World Has Ever Known* (Chicago, 1903).

dent into "the Battle of Pogue's Run," and gloried in Morton's victory over "the forces of evil." Foulke borrowed heavily from Terrell's reports, the Pitman-edited proceedings, Carrington's compositions, and the highly partisan pages of the Indianapolis *Journal*.[67]

The so-called Camp Douglas conspiracy received as much postwar publicity as the treason tales emanating from Indiana. James R. Gilmore wrote the first account and it became the base upon which others built their castles.

Gilmore had a varied career before writing his tall tale about the Chicago-based conspiracy. During the war he had dealt in confiscated cotton; had written *Among the Pines*, professedly a picture of southern life; had journeyed to Richmond on an ill-fated peace mission; and had digested legends and exposés dealing with the subversive secret societies. He suspected that the Order of American Knights had somehow been involved in the assassination of Lincoln and searched for evidence to support his suppositions.[68]

Using the Chicago *Tribune* exposé of the Camp Douglas conspiracy and Colonel Benjamin J. Sweet's report as a basis, Gilmore composed a thrilling tale entitled "The Chicago Conspiracy" and it appeared under a pseudonym in the July, 1865, issue of the *Atlantic Monthly*. Gilmore's account popularized the suppositions that had been largely confined to a courtroom in Cincinnati. It was an interesting mixture of facts, half-truths, and outright fiction, and it became, in the main, the shallow well from which a dozen others drew water.[69]

I. Winslow Ayer's account of the so-called Camp Douglas or Chicago conspiracy appeared in the same year as Gilmore's. Ayer, one of Colonel Sweet's detectives and a witness at the Cincinnati treason trial, made an effort to capitalize upon his notoriety. His story appeared as a booklet entitled *The Great Northwestern Conspiracy in All Its Startling Details*.[70]

William A. "Deacon" Bross, who had outlined the format of the Camp Douglas conspiracy, mixed reminiscence, history, and myth in his account, composed as an eulogy for Brigadier General Benjamin J. Sweet, who re-

67. William Dudley Foulke, *Life of Oliver P. Morton. Including His Important Speeches* (2 vols.; Indianapolis, 1899); Emma Lou Thornbrough, *Indiana in the Civil War Era, 1850–1880*, History of Indiana, III (Indianapolis, 1965), 723.

68. Gilmore to Holt, April 22, 1865, in Holt Papers.

69. Edmund Kirke [James R. Gilmore], "The Chicago Conspiracy," *Atlantic Monthly* XVI (July, 1865), 108–20. Also see Sweet to Brig. Gen. James B. Fry, report, December 23, 1864, in *OR*, Ser. 1, Vol. XLV, Pt. 1, pp. 1077–80; Chicago *Daily Tribune*, November 7, 1864.

70. I. Winslow Ayer, *The Great Northwestern Conspiracy in All Its Startling Details; The People's Union Book; The Plot to Plunder and Burn Chicago—Release of All Rebel Prisoners—Seizure of Arsenals—Raids from Canada—Plot to Burn New York—Piracy on the Lakes—Parts for the Sons of Liberty—Trial of Chicago Conspiracy—Inside Views of the Sons of Liberty—Names of Prominent Members* (Chicago, 1865). Revised slightly, it was republished thirty years later under the title *The Great Treason Plot in the North During the War; Most Dangerous, Perfidious, Extensive, and Startling Plot Ever Devised; Imminent Hidden Perils of the Republic; Astounding Development Never Before Published* (Chicago, 1895).

ceived his star after the war, having earned it by exposing the Camp Douglas conspiracy. Deacon Bross presented his twice-told tale as a paper at a meeting of the Chicago Historical Society in 1878. Bross took credit for discovering the plot in process and convincing Sweet that an exposé could serve a useful purpose. Bross also characterized Sweet as "the Savior of Chicago." [71]

Thomas H. Hines's account, entitled "The Northwestern Confederacy," seemed to give some substance to the imaginative tales told by Bross, Ayer, and Gilmore. After all, he was supposedly one of the chief plotters and participants. Circumstances surrounding the composition of the account, however, make it suspect.

When Basil W. Duke took over the responsibility of reviving the *Southern Bivouac: A Monthly Literary and Historical Magazine*, he begged Hines to contribute an article. The two had served in General John H. Morgan's command, sharing the glory of victory and the agony of defeat together. Duke's *History of Morgan's Cavalry*, published soon after the war, had heaped lavish praise upon his young friend. [72] Hines evidently felt compelled to compose an article of historical worth.

Instead of basing the article upon his personal knowledge and experiences, Hines sought information elsewhere. First of all, he obtained a copy of Gilmore's composition, "The Chicago Conspiracy," which had appeared in the *Atlantic Monthly*—a copy with the margins filled with annotations in Hines's hand is available to historians. [73] Then Hines wrote to his congressman, asking him to provide a copy of Judge Advocate General Holt's report on secret societies, as well as a copy of the proceedings of the Indiana military commission. Borrowing heavily from Gilmore's article and Holt's report, Hines concocted a fanciful tale. He gave the public the impression that only betrayal by a couple of turncoats—he put his finger upon Maurice Langhorne as the chief renegade—had prevented the success of the northwestern confederacy scheme. [74]

Historians took over where the participants left off. James Ford Rhodes, bestirred by the nationalism of the 1890s, presented Democratic critics of the

71. William A. Bross, *Biographical Sketch of the Late General B. J. Sweet [and] History of Camp Douglas: A Paper Read Before the Chicago Historical Society, June 10, 1878* (Chicago, 1878). Allan Nevins, *The Organized War to Victory, 1864–1865* (New York, 1971), 132, Vol. IV of Nevins, *The War for the Union*, 4 vols. characterizes Bross's account as "a melodramatic and doubtless weirdly exaggerated story of the Camp Douglas plot."

72. Basil W. Duke, *History of Morgan's Cavalry* (Cincinnati, 1866).

73. Hines Papers.

74. Thomas H. Hines to John W. Caldwell, July 28, 1882, in General Courts Martial Records; Thomas H. Hines [John B. Castleman and W. W. Cleary], "The Northwestern Conspiracy," *Southern Bivouac: A Monthly Literary and Historical Magazine*, n.s., II (June, 1886–May, 1887), 437–45, 500–10, 567–74, 699–704. Actually, John B. Castleman, who served with Hines in Morgan's command, wrote the article for Hines and it was passed off to readers as Hines's handiwork. Hines's account was later supplemented by the works of two other former Confederates: John W. Headley, *Confederate Operations in Canada* (New York, 1906); John B.

Lincoln administration in a bad light, assigned untold numbers of Copperheads to subversive societies, and put his stamp of approval upon the treason trials held in Indianapolis and Cincinnati.[75]

U.S. entry into World War I engendered renewed nationalism and revived an interest in Civil War subversion and treason tales. Mayo Fesler, an Indianapolis newspaperman who had been weaned on Civil War myths and suppositions, responded to the war psychosis of his day and decided to seek more information about the Knights of the Golden Circle and secret wartime activities of the 1860–1865 era. After taking notes from newspapers and wartime exposés, he decided to question survivors of Civil War days before Father Time gathered the full harvest. He formulated a questionnaire seeking information about the Golden Circle and secret society activities and sent it to five hundred old-timers, including many Indiana Democrats who had been accused of belonging to some secret political societies. In addition, Fesler interviewed two hundred other old-timers, putting his questions orally.

Not a single Democratic respondent admitted membership in the Golden Circle or in any subversive society. Nor did any know of a single council or lodge existing in their neighborhood or county. Republican respondents, on the other hand, repeated their assumptions about the Golden Circle and the subversive society rumors that had circulated during the war.

Instead of accepting Democratic denials at face value, Fesler developed an interesting rationale to support his suppositions. Democratic respondents who had once belonged to the Golden Circle lied, denying any knowledge of subversion, because they regarded their secret society vows binding for life and superior to any civil oath. In other words, Fesler used the lack of tangible evidence as further proof that subversive societies existed, spewing treason on the home front during the war. "Many who were known to be members of the order," he lamented, "refused to give any information whatever concerning its operation."[76]

Rejecting the denials of Democrats, Fesler then winnowed the responses of Republicans. He found their suppositions convincing, for they reinforced his own beliefs about subversive societies of Civil War days. Unable to distinguish between the Knights of the Golden Circle, the Order of American Knights, and the Sons of Liberty, Fesler lumped them all together, asserting they were really one and the same thing—an assertion that should have made

Castleman, *Active Service* (Louisville, 1917). One of the federal detectives who trailed Hines from Toronto to Chicago and lost his quarry there also wrote an interesting tale for public consumption: Thomas H. Keefe, "How the Northwest Was Saved: A Chapter from the Secret Service Records of the Civil War," *Everybody's Magazine*, II (January, 1900), 82–91.

75. James Ford Rhodes, *History of the United States from the Compromise of 1850 to the McKinley-Bryan Campaign of 1896* (7 vols.; New York, 1893–1906), *passim*.

76. Mayo Fesler, "Secret Political Societies in the North During the Civil War," *Indiana Magazine of History*, XIV (1918), 183–286.

his work suspect. "These secret associations," the single-minded newspaper-man concluded, "bore different names in different sections in different peri-ods of the war." He also repeated the old saw that hundreds of thousands of Democrats joined "the subversive orders" and that the prime purpose of the serpentine societies was to overthrow the government, thus "lending assis-tance to the southern rebels." [77]

The editor of the respected *Indiana Magazine of History* published Fesler's long composition, for it bore the trappings of scholarship, including an array of footnotes. Although Fesler's pseudo-scholarly work incorporated his own suppositions as well as much historical hogwash, it won acceptance in the best historical circles. Fesler's contentions entered the college textbooks, and his notable article became gospel during the 1920s and 1930s. [78]

A generation later, when World War II stoked the fires of nationalism and patriotism again, renewing an interest in dissent and subversion associated with previous wars, George Fort Milton composed a poorly researched and hurriedly written potboiler entitled *Abraham Lincoln and the Fifth Column*. Accepting much of the political propaganda of Civil War days as historical fact, Milton blamed the Knights of the Golden Circle, the Order of American Knights, and the Sons of Liberty for draft disturbances, widespread discon-tent, and wartime conspiracies. Adept at drawing word portraits and drama-tizing historical events, Milton wrote a book that read like a detective thriller. In the end, according to Milton, truth triumphed over evil and Lincoln over the purveyors of treason. Not only had Lincoln been elected for a second term in the November elections of 1864, Milton concluded with a literary flourish, "but he also won a complete victory over the secessionists' fifth column in the Loyal States." [79]

Important people endorsed Milton's book, inadvertently sanctioning his retelling of Civil War rumors and myths in readable fashion. President Frank-lin D. Roosevelt, as a favor for a friend, arranged to be photographed holding the book preparatory to boarding a plane for one of his conferences with Joseph Stalin and Winston Churchill. Roosevelt also gave the book a plug by equating dissenters of his own day with those of the Civil War era, applying the term *Copperhead* to both. Homer S. Cummings, FDR's attorney general, also endorsed Milton's book, pointing out that it dealt with "the appeasers, the seditionists, and the faint-hearted of another day when the nation was in peril." Even Henry Steele Commager, one of the country's most respected

77. *Ibid.*, 184–85, 189, 214, 224.
78. During the 1920s Curtis H. Morrow wrote a doctoral dissertation entitled "Politico-Military Societies in the Northwest" (Clark University, 1927), covering much of the same ground as Fesler and reaching similar conclusions. Portions of the dissertation were published in five installments in *Social Science*, IV (November, 1928–August, 1929), 9–31, 222–42, 348–61, 363–76, and V (November, 1929), 73–84.
79. George Fort Milton, *Abraham Lincoln and the Fifth Column* (New York, 1942), 334.

historians, wrote warmly in Milton's behalf. The timely tale, Commager averred, was "a stirring and on the whole, heartening story of how Lincoln outmaneuvered and confounded the appeasers, the defeatists, and the fifth columnists of the Civil War era." [80]

The same year that saw the publication of Milton's popular potboiler also witnessed the appearance of Wood Gray's scholarly and overly footnoted book, *The Hidden Civil War*. The book evolved out of Gray's doctoral dissertation, which had gathered dust for nearly a decade before World War II reawakened an interest in subversion, defeatism, and conspiracies in previous wars. More scholarly than Milton's, it nevertheless pursued a nationalistic and anti-Copperhead course. Gray collected hundreds of quotations from Copperheads and their critics and hung them on the line of treason. Expressing the patriotism of the hour, Gray characterized the Copperhead leaders as "a type that is dangerous in a democracy"—dissenters who "must be guarded against in time of crisis among a free people." [81]

Writers of college textbooks borrowed from Wood Gray, George Fort Milton, and Mayo Fesler, presenting Democratic dissenters of Civil War days as members of subversive dark lantern societies that were involved in treasonable plots. John D. Hicks's widely used one-volume textbook, *A Short History of American Democracy*, followed the nationalistic line. The textbook, which reputedly sold more than a million copies, depicted Democratic critics of Lincoln's day in a bad light, implying that they deserved to be equated with the poisonous snake after which they were named. Hicks portrayed Copperheads as peace-at-any-price men who joined subversive societies like the Knights of the Golden Circle and gave aid and comfort to the Confederacy. [82]

Hicks' acceptance of political propaganda of Civil War days as historical fact encouraged others to do likewise. Mark M. Boatner III, for example, incorporated myths about Copperheads into his popular and frequently used reference work, *The Civil War Dictionary*. Boatner's book, regarded as a bible by some Civil War cultists, devotes three and one-half sentences to the best-known of the secret societies of the war years:

> *Knights of the Golden Circle*. A secret order in the North of Southern sympathizers. Originally starting in the South, its purpose was the extension of slavery in the 1850's, and as the movement spread into other parts of the country, it became the organization of the Peace Democrats, who disapproved of the war. In the latter part of 1863, the name was changed to the Order of American Knights, and in 1864 to the Sons of

80. Homer S. Cummings, Henry Steele Commager, both quoted on the dust jacket of Milton's *Abraham Lincoln and the Fifth Column*.

81. Wood Gray, *The Hidden Civil War: The Story of the Copperheads* (New York, 1942), 224.

82. John D. Hicks, *A Short History of American Democracy* (Boston, 1943), 403.

Liberty. Vallandigham was the Supreme Commander of this last-named order, having been active in the original organization as well.

The three and one-half sentences contain eight errors of fact—more than two errors per sentence—and helped to popularize some of the myths and suppositions that evolved out of Civil War political propaganda of the 1860s.[83]

Writers of historical novels borrowed from academe, transforming Civil War myths and suppositions into folklore. William Blake mixed sex and intrigue in a ratio that made his book, *The Copperheads*, a best seller. Blake began his historical novel with the assumption that all Copperheads were traitors and that many had joined the Knights of the Golden Circle. The story featured a pretty New York miss, Maria Meinhardt, and three suitors. The first was a wealthy and corrupted scion of an old New York family; he was also a Copperhead and a member of the Golden Circle. He sought the heroine's hand while engaged in illegal trade with the Confederacy and while taking part in subversive activities. The second suitor, a fervent Unionist, possessed the finesse of Falstaff in the art of wooing a fair maiden. The third suitor wore the hero's mantle, being a staunch patriot, a brave soldier, a gentleman's gentleman, and an ardent lover wrapped up in one. After he had won the fair maiden's heart and served a stint in the Union army, the War Department sent him on a spying mission into the upper Midwest to ferret out a plot of the Knights of the Golden Circle to subsidize a rebellion and establish a northwestern confederacy. The hero foiled the plot and returned to New York to marry his beloved only to find her already married to suitor number two. Like a gallant gentleman and in the manner of Tennyson's Enoch Arden, the sad suitor tiptoed off into the night.[84]

Constance Robertson's historical novel, *The Golden Circle*, also made the best-seller lists. It featured less sex and more drama, with true historical characters playing minor roles in the tale of intrigue and counterintrigue. The story had its setting in Dayton, hometown of Clement L. Vallandigham, famous Ohio Copperhead and onetime supreme commander of the Sons of Liberty. It centered around a conspiracy scheme devised by the Knights of the

83. Mark M. Boatner, *The Civil War Dictionary* (New York, 1959), 175. Some of the same errors of fact appear in the *Encyclopaedia Britannica*, 1951 edition, XIII, 441–42. The acceptance of the subversive society interpretation is also revealed in such works as Logan Esarey, *History of Indiana* (2 vols.; Fort Wayne, 1942); Daniel W. Snepp, *Evansville's Channels of Trade and the Secession Movement, 1850–1865*, Indiana Historical Society *Publications* (Indianapolis, 1928); Arthur C. Cole, *The Era of the Civil War, 1848–1870* (Chicago, 1922), Vol. III of the *Centennial History of Illinois*; Edward C. Smith, *The Borderland in the Civil War* (New York, 1927); Nathaniel Weyl, *Treason: The Story of Disloyalty and Betrayal in American History* (Washington, D.C., 1950); Bethania Meradith Smith, "Civil War Subversives," *Journal of the Illinois State Historical Society*, XLV (Autumn, 1952), 220–40; and Stephen Z. Starr, "Was There a Northwest Conspiracy?" *Filson Club Historical Quarterly*, XXXVIII (October, 1964), 328–41.

84. William Blake [Blech], *The Copperheads* (New York, 1941).

Golden Circle. Zachary Granger, the hero, arrived in Dayton to investigate subversion, and he soon met Asa Ormerod, the villain who headed the local chapter of the Golden Circle and who had devised the scheme to revolutionize the upper Midwest and bring a northwestern confederacy into being. Not only did the two work backstage at cross purposes, but both sought the hand of a vivacious, astute, and wealthy young widow. In the end, Granger foiled the treasonable scheme, exposed the villain (he was arrested and carted off to prison), and ended up in the widow's arms. Patriotism, truth, honor, and virtue triumphed over villainy, treason, Copperheadism, and the Golden Circle.[85]

Three other historical novels helped to popularize Civil War dissenters, subversive societies, and supposed conspiracies. Ernest Haycox, who is now being rediscovered as a worthy western writer, entitled a story *The Long Storm*. It dealt with the Knights of the Golden Circle and a treason plot centered in the Pacific Northwest. Phyllis A. Whitney wrote a romantic story, *The Quicksilver Pool*, that also dealt with the Golden Circle and a conspiracy. Mary Tracy Earle wrote a young people's tale about an orphaned teen-ager with prorebel sympathies, his Union-minded uncle, and a Golden Circle plot. The uncle, a doctor kidnapped by Golden Circle members, showed such pluck that he converted the nephew to Unionism and caused the subversive society to disintegrate in south central Tennessee.[86]

Storytellers as well as academic historians have continued to depict Copperheads as pure-and-simple traitors who joined subversive societies like the Knights of the Golden Circle to wreak havoc on the war effort in the North. They have continued to quote Joseph Holt's famous report on secret Copperhead societies as a worthy source. They have continued to link Lambdin P. Milligan to an Indianapolis-based conspiracy and have recited the tall tale about a Camp Douglas plot. Even Allan Nevins, in his monumental four-volume work, *The War for the Union*, repeated Civil War myths about the Golden Circle and supposed Copperhead-sponsored conspiracies.[87] Legends and myths nurtured by nationalism and based upon wartime political propaganda remain a part of consensus history.

The acorns that George Bickley, Phineas C. Wright, H. H. Dodd, John B. Sanderson, Henry B. Carrington, Joseph Holt, Oliver P. Morton, and William A. Bross planted grew into postwar oaks, deformed and diseased hybrids of questionable worth.

85. Constance Robertson, *The Golden Circle* (New York, 1951).

86. Ernest Haycox, *The Long Storm* (Roslyn, N.Y., 1946); Phyllis A. Whitney, *The Quicksilver Pool* (Greenwich, Conn., 1955); Mary Tracy Earle, *Flag on the Hilltop* (Boston, 1902).

87. Allan Nevins, *War Becomes Revolution, 1862–1863* (New York, 1960), 318, 318 n, 389–90, 391 n, *The Organized War, 1863–1864* (New York, 1971), 162, *The Organized War to Victory*, 131–35, Vols. II, III, and IV of Nevins, *The War for the Union*, 4 vols.

BIBLIOGRAPHICAL ESSAY

Chapter I

The George Bickley Papers, a portion of a collection called Reports on the Order of American Knights, in the Records of the Office of the Judge Advocate General, National Archives, provide a starting point for research centering around Bickley and the Knights of the Golden Circle. The Bickley Papers include the items taken from his trunk after his arrest and, in a way, show the wide gap between pretense and reality. The Records of the Office of the Judge Advocate General contain other relevant materials besides the Bickley Papers—for example, the General Courts Martial Records, the Union Provost Marshals' Files, and the Records of the Adjutant General's Office (especially the Lafayette C. Baker–Levi C. Turner Papers). The Civil War Political Prisoners' Records, State Department Files, National Archives, also contain some relevant items.

The Robert Todd Lincoln Papers, Library of Congress, not only contain two letters Bickley wrote to the president, but also Colonel Henry B. Carrington's letters and reports as well as a dozen other items bearing on the story of the Golden Circle. The Henry B. Carrington Papers, Archives Division, Indiana State Library, Indianapolis, reveal Carrington's role in building the Golden Circle legend. Since the states of Indiana and Illinois contributed considerably more to developing the subversive society story than any other states, the Governor Oliver P. Morton Papers in the Indiana State Library and the Governor Richard Yates Papers, Illinois State Historical Library, contain many invaluable letters and documents. Other manuscript collections that bear upon the Golden Circle story are revealed in the footnotes.

Six Republican newspapers, all published in the upper Midwest, proved to be the richest sources for rumors and information about the K.G.C. These were Chicago *Daily Tribune*, (Springfield) *Illinois State Journal*, Cincinnati *Gazette*, Cincinnati *Commercial*, and the Cleveland *Leader*. The Dubuque *Weekly Times*, April 17, 1862, contained a K.G.C. exposé which filled three columns of fine print. The Democratic rebuttal, in the main, was provided by the (Springfield) *Illinois State Register*, Indianapolis *State Sentinel*, Cincinnati *Daily Enquirer*, (Columbus) *Ohio Statesman* and (Columbus, Ohio) *Crisis*. The New York *Tribune* and the Louisville *Daily Journal* also proved invaluable. The Louisville *Daily Journal*, July 18, 1861, published the first exposé of the Golden Circle.

Six different K.G.C. exposés were published during the war years. Joseph W. Pomfrey's forty-seven-page booklet carried the title *A True Disclosure and Exposition of the Knights of the Golden Circle, Including the Secret Signs, Grips, and Charges, of*

245

the Third Degree as Practiced by the Order (Cincinnati, 1861). It was followed by James M. Hiatt's composition, published anonymously by C. O. Perrine and entitled *An Authentic Exposition of the K.G.C., Knights of the Golden Circle; or, A History of Secession from 1834 to 1861* (Indianapolis, 1861). Hiatt's exposé provided much of the material that appeared in *K.G.C.: A Full Exposure of the Southern Traitors; The Knights of the Golden Circle: Their Startling Schemes Frustrated: From Original Documents Never Before Published (Five Cent Monthly)* (Boston, 1861). Two shorter exposés, prepared to justify and stimulate the organization of the Union League, reached print in 1862, one published in Louisville and the other in Indianapolis. Charles G. Leland, "The Knights of the Golden Circle," *Continental Monthly*, I (May, 1862), 573–79, contains more conjecture than historical fact.

Ollinger Crenshaw, "The Knights of the Golden Circle: the Career of George Bickley," *American Historical Review*, XLVII (1941), 23–50, dealt primarily with Bickley's prewar years. Charles M. Dustin, "The Knights of the Golden Circle," *Pacific Monthly*, XXVI (1911), 152–65, develops the myth of K.G.C. activity in California during the war years. This myth was debunked in two articles written by Benjamin F. Gilbert, namely "California and the Civil War," *California Historical Society Quarterly*, XL (1961), 160–85, and "The Mythical Johnston Conspiracy," *ibid.*, XXVII (1949), 165–73.

I have treated aspects of the Golden Circle story in a series of articles: "Franklin Pierce and the Treason Charges of 1861–1862," *Historian*, XXIII (1961), 436–48, and "The Hopkins Hoax and Golden Circle Rumors in Michigan, 1861–1862," *Michigan History*, LXVII (1963), 1–14, deal with Michigan's contributions to the tall tales arising in the Midwest. Joseph K. C. Forrest's contribution to myth-making is discussed in "Copperhead Secret Societies in Illinois during the Civil War," in *Journal of the Illinois State Historical Society*, XLVIII (1955), 152–80. The Iowa story is treated in "Rumors of Golden Circle Activity in Iowa during the Civil War Years," in *Annals of Iowa*, XXVII (1965), 523–36. The role of Colonel Henry B. Carrington and Governor Morton in developing the subversive society myth in Indiana appears in "Carrington and the Golden Circle Legend in Indiana during the Civil War," *Indiana Magazine of History*, LXI (1965), 31–52. Ohio's considerable contributions are debunked in "Ohio and the Knights of the Golden Circle: The Evolution of a Civil War Myth," *Cincinnati Historical Society Bulletin*, XXXII (1974), 7–27.

Chapter II

The published proceedings of the Union Leagues, on both the national and the state levels, provide a starting point for a study of the organization. The proceedings of the three national conventions held during 1863 and 1864, are invaluable primary sources: *Proceedings of the National Convention, Union League of America, Held at Cleveland, May 20 and 21, 1863, with Reports, Etc., Etc.* (Washington, D.C., 1863); *Proceedings of the Annual Meeting of the Grand National Council, Union League of America, Held at Washington, December 9, 10, and 11, 1863* (Washington, D.C., 1863); and *Proceedings of the Union League of America, June 6, 1864* (Washington, D.C., 1864). The executive committee of the U.L.A. brought forth one other important and interesting document, namely, *Resolutions Adopted by the National Union League of America at Its Annual Session Held in Washington City, D.C., December 14 and 15, 1864, and Directed to be Laid Before the President* (Washington, D.C., 1864).

The published proceedings of two state councils proved of greater value than the dozens of others. The early history of the Union League in Illinois is reviewed in detail in *Proceedings of the State Grand Council of the U.L.A., of Illinois, at Its Second Annual Session, Held at Springfield, Wednesday, September 2nd, A.D. 1863. . . .* (Springfield, 1863). The *Proceedings of the State Grand Council of the U.L.A. of Michigan at Its Special Meeting Held at Detroit . . . March 2, 1864* (n.p., n.d.) also contained relevant information.

A microfilm copy of the record book of George H. Harlow, founder of the Union League of Illinois and grand state secretary, is in the State Historical Society of Wisconsin. The Henry W. Bellows Papers (Massachusetts Historical Society, Boston) failed to provide much information although Bellows was one of the founders of the league in New York City. U.S. Senator John Sherman was an influential leader of the league and his papers (in the Library of Congress) contain several invaluable letters. The Robert Todd Lincoln Papers (Library of Congress) contain the president's reply to the committee of Union Leaguers who met with him on June 9, 1864, some letters from James M. Edmunds, and other important items. Revealing letters can also be found in the papers of Salmon P. Chase, Elihu B. Washburne, Edwin M. Stanton, and Lyman Trumbull—all in the Library of Congress. Of the governors' papers, those of Richard Yates (Illinois State Historical Library) are most valuable, for Harlow worked hand-in-glove with the Illinois governor.

Prominent persons involved in the founding of the Union Leagues of New York, Philadelphia, and Boston later wrote accounts that were both memoirs and history. Henry W. Bellows, *Historical Sketch of the Union League Club of New York: Its Origin, Organization, and Work, 1863–1879* (New York, 1879), is the best of the lot. George P. Lathrop, *History of the Union League of Philadelphia* (Philadelphia, 1884), provides information and insights. Samuel L. Thorndike, *The Past Members of the Union Club of Boston and a Brief Sketch of the History of the Club, July, 1893* (Boston, 1893), is still another parochial and uncritical account.

Four doctoral dissertations deal with the Union League. Clement M. Silvestro, "None but Patriots: The Union Leagues in Civil War and Reconstruction" (University of Wisconsin, 1959) sees the league as the strong right arm of the Republican party. Guy J. Gibson's "Lincoln's League: The Union League Movement During the Civil War" (University of Illinois, 1957), is much more detailed but sees the league as a patriotic society pure and simple. It proved invaluable, both for information provided and for bibliographical aids. George Winston Smith, "Generative Forces of Union Propaganda: A Study of Civil War Pressure Groups" (University of Wisconsin, 1940), devotes considerable space to the Union League. Ann Smith Hardie, "The Influence of the Union League of America on the Second Election of Lincoln" (Louisiana State University, 1937), deals with one phase of the league's history. Guy Gibson, "The Union League Movement in Illinois during the Civil War" (M.A. thesis, University of Illinois, 1953) served as a springboard for his doctoral dissertation.

E. Bently Hamilton, "The Union League: Its Origin and Achievements in the Civil War," *Transactions of the Illinois State Historical Society* (1921), 110–115, is based largely upon a section entitled "Union League of America" in Newton Bateman and Paul Selby (eds.), *Historical Encyclopedia of Illinois* (2 vols.; Chicago, 1905), II, 538–39. Maxwell Whiteman, *Gentlemen in Crisis: The First Century of the Union League of Philadelphia, 1862–1962* (Philadelphia, 1962), is a recent scholarly study that devotes considerable space to the Civil War years.

Other sources, such as the diaries of George Templeton Strong and Calvin Fletcher, the memoirs of William O. Stoddard, an article by Frank Freidel, and newspapers like the Chicago *Tribune* and the *Illinois State Register* are cited in the footnotes.

Chapter III

The John P. Sanderson Papers (Ohio Historical Library) and the extensive materials in the Reports of the Order of American Knights, Records of the Office of the Judge Advocate General, National Archives, are the basic sources for any research centering around Phineas C. Wright and the organization he founded.

The National Archives houses other documents that provide important information for the story of American Knights. Letters Received, 1861–1867, Department of the Missouri, U.S. Army Commands, are cited a dozen times in this chapter. Other collections include: Union Provost Marshals' File of One-Name Papers *re* Citizens; Citizens' File, 1861–1865, War Department Collection of Confederate Records; and the Lafayette C. Baker–Levi C. Turner Papers.

The Joseph Holt Papers, Robert Todd Lincoln Papers, and John Hay Papers in the Library of Congress contained pertinent information relating to Wright or the O.A.K.

The proceedings of the military commissions that tried Indiana "conspirators" at Indianapolis and men supposedly involved in the "Camp Douglas Conspiracy" at Cincinnati provide much information, some of it contradictory. The testimony of James A. McMaster, John J. Bingham, S. Corning Judd, and William S. Ewing seems to be more credible than that of other witnesses.

The (St. Louis) *Missouri Republican*, a Democratic newspaper, and the (St. Louis) *Missouri Democrat*, a Republican newspaper, provided sources of information as well as quotations for the text. Sanderson's exposé was first published in the *Missouri Democrat*, July 28, 1864.

Official Records, Ser. 2, Vol. VII, 228–366, 626–60, 717–54, contains many of the items that form the Reports on the Order of American Knights.

Phineas C. Wright's account of his arrest and imprisonment appears in John A. Marshall, *American Bastile: A History of the Illegal Arrests and Imprisonment of American Citizens During the Late Civil War* (Philadelphia, 1878).

George Fort Milton, *Abraham Lincoln and the Fifth Column* (New York, 1942), maligns Phineas C. Wright and the Order of American Knights, often substituting conjecture and myth for historical fact. My article, "Phineas C. Wright, the Order of American Knights, and the Sanderson Exposé," *Civil War History*, XVIII (1972), 5–23, provides an antidote.

248

Chapter IV

Material seized in raids on H. H. Dodd's home and offices in August, 1864, makes up a small portion of the documents comprised in the Records of the Office of the Judge Advocate General, National Archives. The Dodd material includes his correspondence as well as the pamphlets or booklets printed to promote the Sons of Liberty. The manuscript reports of the proceedings of the treason trials held in Indianapolis and Cincinnati also form a part of the Judge Advocate General's records. The testimony of James A. McMaster, S. Corning Judd, Joseph J. Bingham, and Clement L. Vallandigham proved the most valuable (and the most dependable). The proceedings of the Indianapolis military commission were later edited by Benn Pitman, shorthand reporter at the trials, and published under the title *The Trials for Treason at Indianapolis, Disclosing the Plans for Establishing a North-western Confederacy: Being the Official Record of the Trials before the Military Commission Convened by Special Orders No. 129, Headquarters, District of Indiana* (Cincinnati, 1865). The proceedings of the Cincinnati military commission were published in *House Executive Documents*, 39 Cong., 2nd Sess., pp. 120–600.

Several other manuscript collections bear upon the H. H. Dodd–Henry B. Carrington story. The Carrington Papers, Archives Division, Indiana State Library, are most important. The Charles B. Laselle Papers, Indiana Division, Indiana State Library, also provided some invaluable information. S. Corning Judd's letter of March 3, 1865, to President Lincoln, in the John Nicolay–John Hay Papers, Illinois State Historical Library, deserves more attention than it has received.

The Indianapolis *Daily State Sentinel*, edited by Joseph J. Bingham, and the Indianapolis *Daily Journal*, always the organ of Governor Oliver P. Morton, proved of greater value than any other newspaper, although twenty more are cited. The so-called Carrington Report appeared in its entirety in the Indianapolis *Daily Journal*, June 30, 1864.

The Indiana political setting, which prompted Democrats to think of organizing a secret political society, is discussed in a variety of secondary works. Emma Lou Thornbrough, *Indiana in the Civil War Era, 1850–1880*, History of Indiana, III (Indianapolis, 1965) has received excellent reviews. Kenneth Stampp, *Indiana Politics During the Civil War* (Indianapolis, 1949), serves as an antidote to such patriotic mishmash as William Dudley Foulke, *Life of Oliver P. Morton, Including His Important Speeches* (2 vols.; Indianapolis, 1899). Gilbert R. Tredway, "Indiana Against the Administration, 1861–1865" (Ph.D. dissertation, Indiana University, 1962) should be balanced by Lorna Lutes Sylvester, "Oliver P. Morton and Hoosier Politics During the Civil War" (Ph.D. dissertation, Indiana University, 1968). Tredway's dissertation, slightly revised, evolved into a book, *Democratic Opposition to the Lincoln Administration in Indiana* (Indianapolis, 1973).

H. H. Dodd, chief architect of the Sons of Liberty and head of the organization in Indiana, has been bypassed by historians and biographers. Clement L. Vallandigham's role as nominal head of the Sons of Liberty is treated briefly in my "Vallandigham as an Exile in Canada, 1863–1864," *Ohio History*, LXXIV (1965), 151–68, 208–10, and *The Limits of Dissent: Clement L. Vallandigham and the Civil War* (Lexington, Ky., 1970). Footnotes provide clues to other sources.

Chapter V

The so-called Holt Report, presented to Secretary of War Edwin M. Stanton, appears in *Official Records*, Ser. 2, Vol. VII, 930–53. It was based upon reports and materials furnished by Colonel John P. Sanderson, Brigadier General Henry B. Carrington, and Lafayette C. Baker—materials available in General Courts Martial Records, Records of the Office of the Judge Advocate General, National Archives, or the Joseph Holt Papers, Library of Congress. Clement L. Vallandigham's views on Holt's handiwork appear in the New York *Daily News*, October 26, 1864, and Dr. Richard F. Stevens' rebuttal appears in the New York *World*, October 19, 1864.

Two doctoral dissertations deal with aspects of Holt's public life. Roger Bartman, "The Contribution of Joseph Holt to the Political Life of the United States" (Fordham University, 1958), treats his role as judge advocate general in cursory fashion. Mary B. Allen, "Joseph Holt, Judge Advocate General, 1862–1875: A Study in the Treatment of Political Prisoners by the U.S. Government During the Civil War" (University of Chicago, 1927), provides no analysis of the so-called Holt Report.

Incidental information and newspaper comments come from widespread sources, revealed in the footnotes.

Chapter VI

The manuscript transcript of the Indianapolis-based treason trials and related materials fill two dozen boxes in a collection called General Courts Martial Records, Records of the Office of the Judge Advocate General. Items in the Records of the Order of American Knights, in the Union Provost Marshals' File of One-Name Papers *Re* Citizens, and in the Records of Adjutant General's Office contain supplementary information. All are in the National Archives. Serious scholars should use the manuscript proceedings, for the published version was heavily edited and altered at times to make the defendants appear in a more unfavorable light. See Benn Pitman (ed.), *The Trials for Treason at Indianapolis, Disclosing the Plans for Establishing a North-western Confederacy: Being the Official Record of the Trials Before the Military Commission Convened by Special Orders No. 129, Headquarters, District of Indiana* (Cincinnati, 1865).

The Henry B. Carrington Papers (Archives Division, Indiana State Library), the Adoniram J. Werner Papers in the William P. Palmer Collection (Western Reserve Historical Society) and the Samuel P. Heintzelman Papers (Library of Congress) rate as some of the more important sources for additional information about the principals and the Indianapolis trials. The only known copy of David T. Yeakel's flyer *To the People of Indiana*, October 28, 1864, is in the Charles B. Lasselle Papers, Indiana Division, Indiana State Library.

The Indianapolis *Journal* served as Governor Oliver P. Morton's mouthpiece, while the Indianapolis *State Sentinel* presented Democratic views. Both are available in bound volumes and on microfilm.

Felix G. Stidger, *Treason History of the Order of the Sons of Liberty, Formerly Circle of Honor, Succeeded by Knights of the Golden Circle, Afterwards Order of American Knights: The Most Gigantic Treasonable Conspiracy the World Has Ever Known* (Chicago, 1903), is more important to a student of Civil War political propaganda than to a historian trying to unscramble the events of 1864 in Indiana. Henry B. Carrington's exposé of the Sons of Liberty evolved into a campaign document entitled *The Great Northern Conspiracy of the "S.O.L.": Resistance to Tyrants Is Obedience to God* (n.p., n.d.).

The historical background for Indiana politics of 1864 and the treason trials is provided by Kenneth M. Stampp, *Indiana Politics During the Civil War* (Indianapolis, 1949), Lorna Lutes Sylvester, "Oliver P. Morton and Hoosier Politics During the Civil War" (Ph.D. dissertation, Indiana University, 1968), and Gilbert R. Tredway, "Indiana Against the Administration, 1861–1865" (Ph.D. dissertation, Indiana University, 1969). Sylvester saw events of 1864 through Morton's eyes, while Tredway took a hostile approach to Governor Morton and President Lincoln. Tredway's dissertation contains a superb analysis of the proceedings of the trials.

Darwin Kelley, *Milligan's Fight Against Lincoln* (New York, 1973), is a thin book with too little substance—a golden opportunity gone astray.

Footnotes refer to other books, to articles, and to other sources, none deserving special mention in an abbreviated bibliographical note.

Chapter VII

A mine full of information dealing with the Camp Douglas conspiracy and the Cincinnati treason trials is available in the National Archives. General Courts Martial Records, Records of the Office of the Judge Advocate General, provided the richest lode. Prospectors should also consult: Letters Received by the Adjutant General's Office, 1861–1870; Citizens' File, War Department Records; and the Lafayette C. Baker–Levi C. Turner Papers. The proceedings of the military commission that convened in Cincinnati on January 11, 1865, have been published and are available in *House Executive Documents*, 39 Cong., 2nd Sess.

Since Major General Samuel P. Heintzelman commanded the Northern Department during most of 1864, his papers (in the Library of Congress) must be perused by anyone interested in the Camp Douglas story. The Halmer H. Emmons Papers (Burton Historical Collection, Detroit Public Library), the Governor Richard Yates Papers (Illinois State Historical Library), and the Thomas H. Hines Papers (University of Kentucky Library, Lexington) contain relevant and interesting items.

Contemporaries, involved in one way or another in the Camp Douglas conspiracy story, wrote reminiscences or "historical accounts" during the postwar years. I. Winslow Ayer, a renegade turned detective, wrote two unreliable booklets. The first, *The Great Northwest Conspiracy . . .* (Chicago, 1865), misleads more than it informs. The second, published thirty years later and entitled *The Great Treason Plot in the North During the Civil War . . .* (Chicago, 1895), also contains more propaganda than fact. Thomas H. Hines [John B. Castleman and W. W. Cleary], "The Northwestern Conspiracy," *Southern Bivouac: A Monthly Literary and Historical Magazine*, n.s., II

(June, 1886–May, 1887), 437–45, 500–10, 567–74, 699–704, John W. Headley, *Confederate Operations in Canada and New York* (New York, 1906), and William A. Bross, *Biographical Sketch of the Late General B. J. Sweet [and] History of Camp Douglas: A Paper Read Before the Chicago Historical Society, June 18, 1878* (Chicago, 1878), usually serve as the base for the traditional story of the Camp Douglas conspiracy. Edmund Kirke [James R. Gilmore], "The Chicago Conspiracy," *Atlantic Monthly*, XVI (July, 1865), 108–20, and Thomas H. Keefe, "How the Northwest Was Saved: A Chapter from the Secret Service Records of the Civil War," *Everybody's Magazine*, II (January, 1900), 82–91, also serve as cornerstones.

The Chicago *Times*, Chicago *Tribune*, and Detroit *Free Press* provided more footnotes for this chapter than other newspapers.

Lewis B. Clingman, "History of Camp Douglas" (M.A. thesis, DePaul University, 1942), is a respectable account, although Clingman accepts aspects of the myth. It is based, in the main, upon E. B. Tuttle, *The History of Camp Douglas: Including Official Report of Gen. B. J. Sweet; with Anecdotes of Rebel Prisoners* (Chicago, 1865), John M. Copely, *A Sketch of the Battle of Franklin, Tenn., with Reminiscences of Camp Douglas* (Austin, 1893), and Chicago newspapers. Joseph L. Eisendrath, Jr., "Chicago's Camp Douglas," *Journal of the Illinois State Historical Society*, LIII (1960), 37–63, contains much information on the prison and its management. E. B. "Pete" Long, "Camp Douglas: A Hellish Den?" *Chicago History*, I (1970), 83–95, has some excellent illustrations and deserves more attention.

William C. Cochran, "The Dream of a Northwestern Confederacy," *Proceedings of the State Historical Society of Wisconsin, 1916* (Madison, 1917), 213–53, is badly outdated. James D. Horan, *Confederate Agent: A Discovery in History* (New York, 1954) contains as much conjecture as fact. George Fort Milton, *Abraham Lincoln and the Fifth Column* (New York, 1942) is a potboiler that accepts the conspiracy stories uncritically. Stephen Z. Starr, "Was There a Northwest Conspiracy?" *Filson Club Historical Quarterly*, XXXVIII (1964), 328–41, Frederic S. Klein, "The Great Northwest Conspiracy," *Civil War Times Illustrated*, IV (June, 1965), 21–26, and Dee Alexander Brown, "Northwest Conspiracy," *Civil War Times Illustrated*, X (May, 1971), 10–19, are examples of articles that do a disservice to history by perpetuating subversive society and conspiracy myths.

Interesting letters, written by the soldier of fortune who was found guilty at Cincinnati, appear in Mabel Clare Weaks (ed.), "Colonel George St. Leger Grenfell," *Filson Club Historical Quarterly*, XXXIV (1960), 5–23. Stephen Z. Starr, *Colonel Grenfell's Wars: The Life of a Soldier of Fortune* (Baton Rouge, 1971), treats the English adventurer's life as a Confederate soldier superbly, but errs in accepting the traditional story of his involvement in the so-called Chicago plot.

Chapter VIII

As in the previous chapters, the National Archives provided more information on the postwar careers of the persons tried at Indianapolis and Cincinnati than any other depository. The George Bickley Papers, Reports on the Order of American Knights, and General Courts Martial Records, Records of the Office of the Judge Advocate General furnished considerable data. The Joseph Holt Papers, Library of Congress, and the Adoniram J. Werner Papers, William P. Palmer Collection, Western Reserve Historical Society, Cleveland, supplemented the material in the National Archives. The Thomas H. Hines Papers, University of Kentucky Library, Lexington, provided too little substance and raised more questions than they answered.

The Fond du Lac *Daily Reporter*, June 2, 1906, contained an H. H. Dodd obituary. Milligan's postwar years can be traced in the columns of the Huntington (Indiana) *Herald* and the Huntington *Democrat*. Other newspapers, cited in the footnotes, have provided a tidbit here and there.

The *Official Records*, as usual, provided letters and reports which bear on the story. John A. Marshall, *American Bastile: A History of the Illegal Arrests and Imprisonment of American Citizens During the Late Civil War* (Philadelphia, 1878), had a long account of Lambdin P. Milligan and a brief one of Phineas C. Wright. Samuel Klaus (ed.), *The Milligan Case*, American Trials Series (New York, 1929), contained the editor's excellent introduction as well as the arguments and decisions in this famous Supreme Court case.

Edmund Kirke [James R. Gilmore], "The Chicago Conspiracy," *Atlantic Monthly*, XVI (July, 1865), 108–20, provided the framework copied by others. Thomas H. Hines [John B. Castleman and W. W. Cleary], "The Northwestern Conspiracy," *Southern Bivouac: A Monthly Literary and Historical Magazine*, n.s., II (June, 1886–May, 1887), 437–45, 500–10, 567–74, 699–704, was based more upon Gilmore's account than upon reality. Furthermore, the article was not written by Hines, but by John B. Castleman. William A. "Deacon" Bross's reminiscences about the Camp Douglas conspiracy seem incredible. He incorporated them in Bross, *Biographical Sketch of the Late Brig. Gen. B. J. Sweet [and] History of Camp Douglas: A Paper Read Before the Chicago Historical Society, June 10, 1878* (Chicago, 1878).

Mayo Fesler, a journalist turned historian, gave the myths about subversive societies and treasonable plots respectability in a one-hundred-page account, "Secret Political Societies in the North During the Civil War," *Indiana Magazine of History*, XIV (1918), 183–286. He received able assistance from Curtis H. Morrow, whose doctoral dissertation was published in five installments in *Social Science*.

George Fort Milton, *Abraham Lincoln and the Fifth Column* (New York, 1942), and James D. Horan, *Confederate Agent: A Discovery in History* (New York, 1954), have perpetuated Civil War myths, doing a disservice to history.

Gilbert R. Tredway's doctoral dissertation, "Indiana Against the Administration, 1861–1865" (Indiana University, 1962) contains more on the postwar careers of the four convicted at Indianapolis than any other single source. Revised and moderated, it evolved into a book, *Democratic Opposition to the Lincoln Administration in Indiana* (Indianapolis, 1973). Clement L. Vallandigham's postwar career was treated in a lengthy chapter in my book *The Limits of Dissent: Clement L. Vallandigham and the Civil War* (Lexington, Ky., 1970). George St. Leger Grenfell's years as a prisoner on the Dry Tortugas is superbly detailed in Stephen Z. Starr, *Colonel Grenfell's Wars: The Life of a Soldier of Fortune* (Baton Rouge, 1971).

253

INDEX

Abolitionism, 4, 25, 54, 55, 58, 61, 93, 95
Abraham Lincoln and the Fifth Column, 241–42
Adams, Green, 57
Alexander, Peter, 212
American Conflict, 235–36
American Knights. *See* Order of American Knights
Among the Pines, 238
Anderson, Benjamin, 207, 208, 211, 213, 216, 233
Anderson, "Bloody Bill," 77
Andrew, Gov. John A., 46
Arbitrary arrests, 5, 16, 18, 20, 26, 82, 96, 167–68, 176, 202–205, 227–28, 231
Arnold, Isaac N., 59, 193
Athon, Dr. James A., 165
Athon, John C., 70
Atlantic Monthly, 238
Ayer, Isaiah Winslow: his shady past, 192; contacts Bross, 193; visits Yates, 193; employed by Sweet, 193; joins Democratic club, 195; calls for action, 203; wants more money, 205; testifies in Cincinnati, 207–12; authors postwar pamphlets, 238, 238n

Baker, Lafayette C.: heads spy corps, 138–39; his report for Holt, 139–40; mentioned, 143
Bancroft, George, 45
Bangs, Mark, 38
Barlow, Samuel L. M., 234
Barret, Dr. James A., 82, 85, 105
Bartley, Thomas W., 215
Bates, Edward, 58
"Battle of Pogue's Run," 99, 99n, 238
Beauregard, Gen. Pierre G. T., 160, 188, 199
Bell-Everett ticket, 42
Bellows, Rev. Henry W.: as president of U.S. Sanitary Commission, 43, 44; as Union League organizer, 43, 44–45
Bickley, Charles S., 219–20
Bickley, George: prewar career, 7–12; devises K.G.C., 8–9; involvement in poli-

tics, 12–13; and exposés of K.G.C., 13–14; in Indiana, 28, 29; in Richmond, Va., 28; in Bristol, Tenn., 28; in Bragg's army, 28; interviewed by General Johnson, 29; denies K.G.C. affiliation, 29; sent to Cincinnati, 29; arrest and imprisonment, 29–31; questioned about Lincoln's assassination, 33, 218; writes to Seward, 218; case reviewed by Holt, 219; given conditional freedom, 219; trip to England, 219; death, 219; son seeks information about him, 219, 220; mentioned, 91, 140, 244
Bingham, Joseph J.: meets with Wright, 69; joins O.A.K., 70–71; intimidated by mob, 93; sees need for mutual protection society, 95, 99, 101; attends Indianapolis meeting, 102–103; as friend of Dodd, 155; wants rights protected, 163; repudiates plot, 164–65; arrested, 176; testifies at trial in Indianapolis, 181–82; quoted, 182; testifies in Cincinnati, 212
Black, Jeremiah S., 136–37, 227
"Black Knights of Abraham," 55
Blair, Gov. Austin, 48
Blair, Francis Preston, Jr., 35
Blair, Montgomery, 53, 57, 58, 62
Blake, Thomas J., 102
Blake, William (pseudonym). *See* Blech, William
Blech, William, 242
"Blowsnakes," 5
Boatner, Mark M., 242
Boker, George H., 43, 44
Boston, 12, 14
Bowles, William A.: joins O.A.K., 70; attends council meeting, 102; as "major general," 109; ignored by Baker, 140; active in Sons of Liberty, 155; meets with Stidger, 157; decried as traitor, 161; babbles about plot, 167, 175; arrested, 174; sentenced to death, 184; awaits execution, 185, 226; takes Confederate money, 194, 200; postwar years, 224, 230; execution postponed, 226–27; sentence commuted, 227; freed

by court, 228; death, 230; mentioned, 180
Bowles, Mrs. William A., 185–86
Boyle, Gen. Jere E., 30
Bradford, Anna Marie, 91
Bragg, Gen. Braxton, 28, 200
Bragg, Edward S., 223
Bramlette, Thomas E., 86
Brant, David W., 110
Bristol (Tenn.), 28
Bross, William A.: "discovers" conspiracy, 190–91; befriends Sweet, 192; exaggerates for effect, 202; devises conspiracy story, 203; postwar speech, 238–39; plants seeds of myth, 239; mentioned, 244
Brough, John, 55, 86
Bryant, William Cullen, 44
Buchanan, James, 10, 12, 136
Buchanan administration, 12
Bucyrus *Journal*, 14, 16
Buell, Gen. Don Carlos, 191
Bullitt, Joshua F., 158–59
Burbridge, Gen. Stephen G.: releases Bullitt, 159; seconds Morton, 161; quoted, 161; criticized, 166
Burnett, Maj. Henry L.: and Indianapolis treason trials, 172–84; view of Democrats, 174–75; campaigns for Morton, 177; quoted, 177–78; interviews Sweet, 205; prepares charges for "Chicago eight," 208–10; presides at Cincinnati trial, 208–17; orders irons for prisoners, 225; as prosecutor, 236; mentioned, 3
Burnside, Gen. Ambrose E.: arrests Vallandigham, 55; violates civil rights, 67; issues "General Orders, No. 38," 96; suppresses Chicago *Times*, 97; mentioned, 29, 100
Buskirk, Samuel H., 165
Butler, Benjamin F., 227
Byington, LeGrand, 55–56

Caldwell, Col. Robert, 165
Cameron, Simon, 75, 137
Camp Chase, (Ohio), 164, 173, 189
Camp Douglas (near Chicago), 164, 173, 187–217
Camp Douglas conspiracy, 6, 187–217, 238–39
Camp Morton (Ind.), 98, 164, 167, 168, 173
Cantrell, George E., 207–11, 216
Carney, Gov. Thomas, 58
Carrington, Henry B.: reports on subversion, 21–22, 25, 26–27, 47; arrests Judge Constable, 26; and Morgan's raid, 27–28; arrested by superior, 27; condemns K.G.C.,

54; arms Union Leagues, 56, 97; issues edicts, 96; devises S.L. exposé, 131–32, 189; writes report for Holt, 140–42; exposes Dodd's conspiracy, 154–62, 167–69, 173, 186; decries Dodd's escape, 176–77; devises myths, 237, 238; mentioned, 1, 2, 94, 151, 186, 231, 244
Chandler, William E., 57
Chase, Salmon P., 53, 57, 58, 59–60, 224
Chicago conspiracy. *See* Camp Douglas conspiracy
"Chicago eight," 204–17
Chicago *Post*, 204
Chicago *Times*: opposes secret political societies, 67, 68; denies O.A.K. allegations, 89; quoted, 204; debunks Camp Douglas conspiracy, 213; mentioned, 3, 22, 109
Chicago *Tribune*: criticizes state constitutional convention, 18; publishes Forrest's K.G.C. tales, 18–20; debunks new state constitution, 19; publishes K.G.C. exposé, 20; quoted, 23, 59; prints "S.B." circulars, 49; endorses Lincoln's reelection, 59; publishes O.A.K. exposé, 87–88; publishes Holt's report, 145; publishes conspiracy story, 203; condemned by Democrats, 203–204; exposes Camp Douglas conspiracy, 238; mentioned, 34, 51, 192, 193
Christian, Dr. John M., 16
Cincinnati *Commercial*, 75, 133, 210
Cincinnati *Daily Times*, 22
Cincinnati *Enquirer*: quoted, 22, 147; denounces Holt report, 147; defends Sons of Liberty, 214; praises Vallandigham's testimony, 214; mentioned, 22
Cincinnati *Gazette*: castigates Democrats, 75; publicizes O.A.K. exposé, 88; favors rearrest of Vallandigham, 133; publishes Bickley obituary, 218; mentioned, 210, 236
Cincinnati treason trial, 6, 205–17
"Circle of Honor," 156
Civil rights: violated by mobs, 4; arrest of judge, 26; Bickley confined, 29–31; Wright's rights violated, 66–67; suppressed in Missouri, 77; Democrats intimidated, 92–101, 107; free elections threatened, 112–13, 163, 187; *Ex Parte Milligan*, 227–28. *See also* Arbitrary arrests
Civil War Dictionary, 242
Clay, Cassius M., 34
Clay, Clement L., 168
Clement, Jesse, 22, 23
Cleveland convention (May 31, 1864), 60–61

St. Joseph *Tribune*, 78
(St. Louis) *Missouri Democrat*, 87
(St. Louis) *Missouri Republican*, 88
Sanderson, Col. John P.: early career, 74–75;
as Rosecrans' provost marshal general,
76–78; decides on exposé, 77–81; orders
arrests, 82; writes O.A.K. exposé, 82–83,
84–87, 88–90; criticized by Democrats,
88–90; and Holt report, 90, 142–45;
death, 90; mentioned, 1, 64, 138, 154,
159, 178, 188, 189, 244
Schofield, Gen. John M., 58–59, 202
Scientific Artisan, 8
Scripps, John L., 51
Seddon, James A., 209
Semmes, Richard I., 204, 208, 212, 216
Seward, William H., 30, 139, 190, 218
Seymour, Horatio, 194
Shanks, John T., 197–98, 203, 210–11, 215,
216
Sheahan, James W., 204
Sherman, John, 53
Shore, Dr. John, 82
Short History of American Democracy, 242
Skinner, Col. Lewis C., 202
Slack, James R., 231
Slidell, John, 199
Society for the Diffusion of Political Knowl-
edge, 56
Society of the Illini, 195
Sons of Liberty: devised by Dodd, 102–104;
New York City conference, 104–105;
Windsor conference, 106–108; Vallan-
digham as supreme commander, 109–12,
130–35, 214; investigated by Carrington,
153, 157, 159, 162, 167–69, 173, 174,
189; and treason plot, 154–86, 193; pro-
moted by Ayer, 211; and Chicago conspir-
acy, 204, 212; defended by Judd, 215; in
postwar literature, 235–44; mentioned, 1,
2, 5, 6, 32, 73, 74, 91, 138, 139, 221,
223, 231
South Bend *Forum*, 96
Southern Bivouac, 194n
Spartan Band, 49–51, 51n, 52, 53
Speed, James, 227
Spooner, Col. Benjamin F., 174–75
(Springfield) *Illinois State Journal*, 88
(Springfield) *Illinois State Register*, 24–25,
55, 67, 68, 146
Stanbery, Henry, 227
Stanton, Edwin M.: receives reports from
Carrington, 22, 25; letter from Bickley, 30;
sends Bickley to Fort Lafayette, 31; dis-

trusts Sanderson, 82, 83, 84, 85, 87; in
cabinet, 136–37; employs Holt, 137–38;
and Holt report, 138–45, 149–50; meets
Stidger's demands, 186; and Milligan, 225,
227, 233
"States' Rights Association," 73, 105
Stevens, Dr. Richard F., 140, 145, 148
Stidger, Felix G.: writes reports, 141, 157–
59; prewar career, 156; in U.S. Army, 156;
as detective in Kentucky, 156–57; and Carrington, 157; as investigator, 158, 159,
167; on witness stand, 175, 179, 180; demands more money, 186; testifies in Cincinnati, 212; writes postwar pamphlets,
237
Stinson, William, 79
Stoddard, William O., 53–54, 58
Storey, Wilbur F., 2, 3, 68, 89, 109, 140,
204, 212
Strawn, Charles C., 212
Strong, George Templeton, 43, 44, 45
Sulgrove, Berry R.: edits Indianapolis *Journal*, 21; recites K.G.C. tales, 21, 25, 27–
28, 49; covers up for Carrington, 27; con-
dones mob action, 93, 94; as postwar author, 236, 237
Sullivan *Democrat*, 100
Sumner, Charles, 46
Sweet, Col. Benjamin J.: discredited as army
officer, 191; as commandant at Camp
Douglas, 191–205; develops conspiracy
details, 191–204, 206, 217, 238; eulogized
by Bross, 238–39; intercedes for Grenfell,
233

Talbert, John, 93
Terre Haute *Journal*, 92
Terrell, William H. H., 153, 168, 237
Thomas, Gen. George H., 75
Thompson, Jacob, 109, 154, 189, 198, 214
Tilden, Samuel J., 223, 235
Tod, Gov. David, 30, 162
Train, George Francis, 194
*Treason History of the Order of the Sons of
Liberty*, 237
Trials for Treason at Indianapolis . . . ., 236
Trimble, John, 49–50
Troutman, Jacob, 110

U.L.A. (Union League of America). *See*
Union Leagues
"Uncle Lincoln's Asses," 55
Union Leagues: founding of, 34, 37–42; and
Harlow, 37–43; Bloomington convention,